Theatre Profiles/3

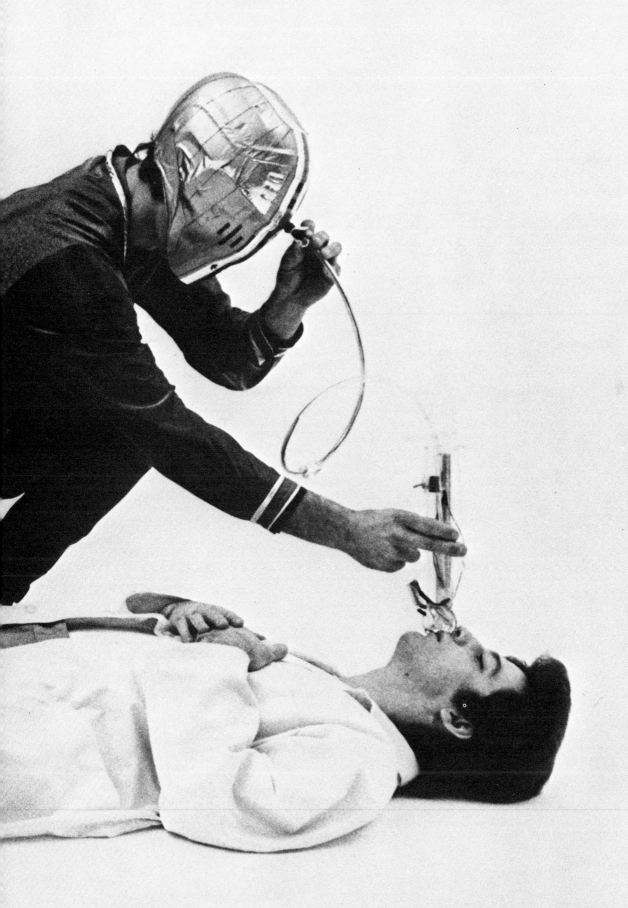

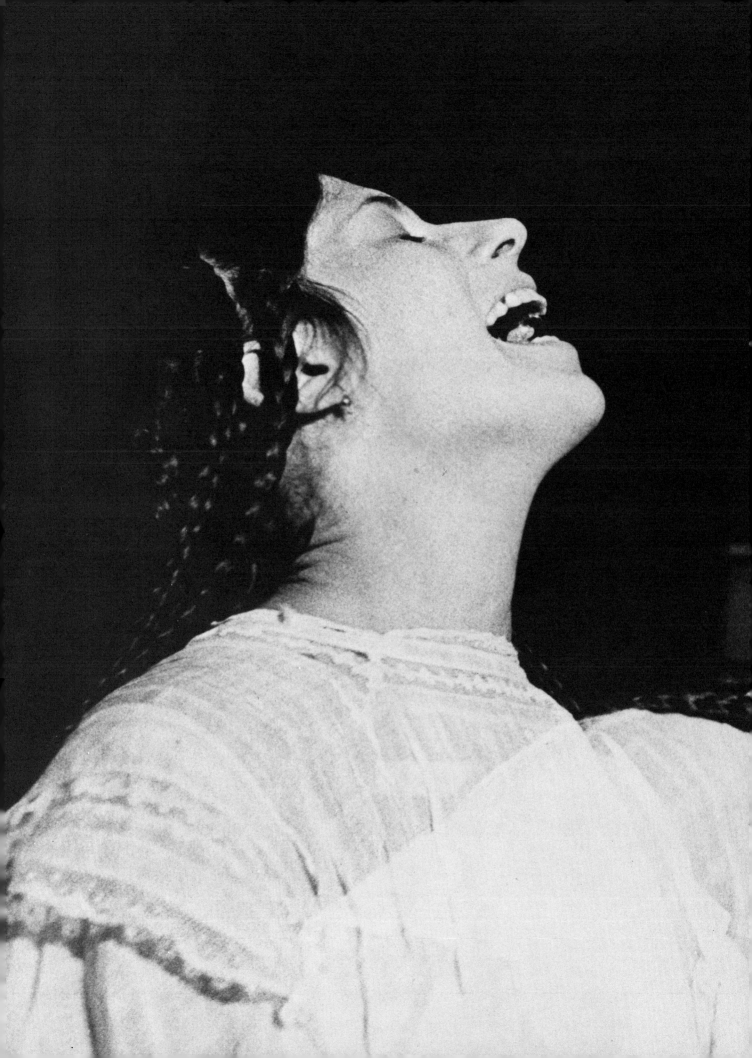

Theatre Profiles/3

A Resource Book of Nonprofit
Professional Theatres in the United States

Marsue Cumming, Editor

Arli Epton, Associate Editor

Theatre Communications Group, Inc.
New York

TCG

Theatre Communications Group is the national service organization for the nonprofit professional theatre, established in 1961 to provide a national forum and communications network for the profession and to respond to the needs of its constituents for centralized services. TCG offers a variety of artistic, administrative and informational programs and services aimed specifically at assisting noncommercial professional theatre organizations, professional theatre training institutions and individual theatre artists, administrators and technicians. Theatre Communications Group is supported by the William H. Donner Foundation, Exxon Corporation, Ford Foundation, Andrew W. Mellon Foundation, National Endowment for the Arts and New York State Council on the Arts.

Design by Everett Aison
Cover photograph by Frederic Ohringer

LC 76-641618
ISBN 0-930452-02-X

Volume 3
Price: $9.95
Copyright © 1977 by Theatre Communications Group, Inc.
355 Lexington Avenue, New York, NY 10017 (212) 697-5230.
All rights reserved including the right to reproduce this
book or portions thereof in any form.

Contents

Foreword

In the last decade the nonprofit professional theatre movement has succeeded in not only restructuring the geography of theatre in America but also in stimulating a redefinition of the role that theatre, as a humanistic and unifying force, can assume in American society. To underestimate the potential importance of theatre as a voice for individual concerns and common experience, as a true forum for contemporary thought, and as a means of illuminating our lives through the vision of playwrights, is to deny the basic needs of the diverse and multicultural population served by American theatres in the 1970s.

The complex and exciting sources within our multicultural communities influence traditional theatre and, in turn, theatre responds by assuming a role in society that goes far beyond the success of individual productions or the development of a subscription audience. The role of the theatre is just as much one of communication as it is artistic expression, just as much the examination of contemporary problems as the celebration of traditional pleasures. Our responsibilities and our obligations to the towns and cities in which our theatres are found are as great as our obligations to the craft and practitioners we follow.

What makes the work of the nonprofit theatre particularly significant is that, in the experience of theatre, we have a context in which the needs of individuals and communities can be directly and immediately addressed. Both artists and audiences bring to the theatre a desire to listen, to feel, to make their most private selves vulnerable to joy, as well as to concern. In theatre that is honest, we have an artistic phenomenon that brings people together, respects their differences as well as their intelligence and their common need for both release from and perspective on our lives and times.

So the theatre is hot in pursuit of truth, although to justify its existence it must not only tell the truth as we see it, but decide and explore where the real truths lie. Not in the heart or in the head, but in both. Theatre has to look for its subject matter in the realm of mystery. It has to question, emotionally as well as intellectually, the beliefs of man, the precepts and concepts by which he has lived since self-expression began. It has to have the courage to find the fallacies, the inadequacies, the truths and strengths of each myth, legend, symbol, by whatever means fall to hand, whether they are within the strictest bounds of theatre or not. Permanence is becoming a word reserved for the Grand Canyon, as we watch the structures, institutions and systems of order fall. We need from the theatre not diversion or reassurance. Reason and logic are unreliable. What is reliable is the combined force of the head and the heart. Whatever the subject, it must be approached in terms of universal, underlying human qualities: fears, joys, instincts and needs.

Theatre must take on the beliefs common to mankind, the myths and symbols most central to basic existence, the invisible forces which both control and elevate our lives, our deaths and our continuity. This resolution means that theatre must continually examine its own myths, beliefs and forces, and challenge their validity. Those who work in the theatre must be convinced of its potential force as a revelatory experience. If theatre is founded on basic human values, it will live through any crisis.

It is in the contact between artist and audience that one feels so strongly the profound importance which theatre as a ritual and as a humanistic and artistic force does and should have in our lives. It is the obligation of the nonprofit theatre to see that its work is central to the lives of individuals, for once in that privileged position, knowledge, tolerance and creative self-expression become a common heritage which draws on the cultural differences that characterize American society.

Gordon Davidson

Introduction

Bibliographies will describe this book as a reference work about the large and still growing national network of nonprofit professional theatres — their statistical profiles, their work and their accomplishments. But because it is the *audiences* which provide the only common denominator shared by all the theatres described in the pages that follow, I think *Theatre Profiles/3* is also about that very large and extraordinarily diverse audience which joins with these theatre companies to create theatre. Theatre is perhaps the most accessible and immediate of all the performing arts — accessible because its medium of communication is language; immediate because the audience is an active element of every performance and without whom theatre simply cannot exist.

The wide range of work addressed and confronted by these theatres has developed audiences equally diverse. These audiences both mold and are influenced by the work of "their" theatres in communities all over the United States. In other art forms, one is likely to find relatively homogeneous audiences for institutions in cities thousands of miles apart, because of the similarity of their repertoires. But both the purpose and the product of these theatres are so divergent that an "average" theatre audience just does not exist. It is this diversity of audience that gives the nonprofit professional theatre its uniqueness and its vitality. And, as the theatres increasingly respond to local needs and tastes, they become more integrally involved in the life of their communities.

The long-held assumption that the theatre is frequented only by the "carriage trade" is no longer valid. It is hard to believe that such a limited sector of the population could account for the 12 million admissions in 75 American towns and cities for these 152 theatres, filling them to more than 82 percent of seating capacity at 34,000 performances! Close to 600,000 of these theatregoers were subscribers, people committed enough to their particular theatre to purchase a ticket not just to one play, but to an entire season of plays.

A major reason these theatres have developed such large and diverse audiences is that they are not just performance facilities or pieces of real estate operated for commercial purposes; they are institutions that have devised ways of reaching out to their own special audiences by preparing and delivering an astounding number of programs and services for their communities.

Until the 1950s, what professional theatre the American public saw was that which had been deemed "successful" in London or New York. Professional theatre production was centered in New York, just as film and television is centered in California. Missouri could not see new work until it had been "proved" in New York and, even then, not until it chugged into town as a "road show" — often two years later. More important, the national perception of the theatre was determined by the taste of an audience comprising a very small percentage of the population of an extremely atypical, enormously complex, urban city in the Northeast.

Today, as much is going to New York as is coming from New York. Hundreds of new plays are being developed in theatres all across the United States. This astonishing productivity is reflected in the Index of Names and Titles. At the same time, there is a recent trend toward nonprofit theatres sharing in the development of new plays. In 1977, Christopher Durang's *A History of the American Film,* following its initial staged reading at the O'Neill Theater Center's National Playwrights Conference, was produced by Arena Stage in Washington, D.C., the Hartford Stage Company, the Mark Taper Forum in Los Angeles and the Playmakers Repertory Company in North Carolina. Similarly, Albert Innaurato's play *Gemini* "traveled" from New York City's Playwrights Horizons to the PAF Playhouse in Huntington, Long Island, then back to New York to the Circle Repertory Company. The previous season, *The Last Meeting of the Knights of the White Magnolia* by Preston Jones, a previously unknown Texan actor-turned-playwright based at the Dallas Theater Center, was produced by no fewer than eight theatres across the country. All three of these plays were also seen by Broadway audiences, but not until *after* they had been nurtured and developed in a series of nonprofit professional theatres and seen by their own special audiences.

Another component in the evolution of this network of nonprofit theatres across the country is the increasingly rapid assimilation of new techniques and ideas from the crucial laboratories provided by the "experimental" or "alternative" theatres. For example, Andrei Serban, whose company had received critical acclaim when it performed its startling interpretations of the Greek classics at La Mama E.T.C., directed innovative productions of *The Cherry Orchard* and *Agamemnon,* and Richard Foreman, known as one of New York's most avant-garde directors through the work of his own company, the Ontological-Hysteric Theater, directed *The Threepenny Opera.* All three plays were produced by the New York Shakespeare Festival. Charles Ludlam, the artistic force behind the Ridiculous Theatrical Company, crossed further barriers when he collaborated with Paul Taylor and his dance company on *Aphrodisiamania,* a commedia dell'arte dance-theatre piece. And Robert Wilson dared the impossible when he presented his five-hour "opera" *Einstein on the Beach* at the Metropolitan Opera House, to a largely "establishment" audience that included many of the Met's regular opera subscribers.

The totality of this work, and its constantly growing and expanding audience, accounts for the American theatre being the most prolific and lively theatre in the world today. In no other country does one find a comparable amount of new work being developed and produced.

It is both reassuring and gratifying that this growth in both theatre activity and the audience for it, has occurred at the very time when our society is becoming increasingly complex and depersonalized. Although inexpensive and accessible transportation tends to make us nomadic, and our urban centers seem to have become less meaningful, this country obviously still needs its marketplace, its town hall, its forum — a place in which people can act and react, celebrate and examine. The American theatre in all its various forms and in locations ranging from Catskill to Chicago, from San Juan Bautista to Louisville — and even from Anchorage to Honolulu — is providing such a forum.

Peter Zeisler

Editor's Note

First published in 1973, *Theatre Profiles* is a reference series on the nonprofit professional theatre in the United States. This expanded third edition profiles 152 theatres compared with 100 in the previous volume. *Theatre Profiles/3* represents a two-year record of each theatre, highlighting the 1975–76 and 1976–77 seasons. In addition to statistical, production and photographic information, the directors of each theatre were asked to provide an "Artistic Statement," describing their institution in their own words; this description forms the basis of the narrative section of each profile and discusses the theatre's historical background, its artistic policy and goals, and its major services and activities. New features in this edition include an appendix of directors and designers for each production listed for each theatre; founders and founding dates; and information on theatres interested in sponsoring or booking outside groups or artists.

Theatres included are constituents of TCG. Information was requested from 160 theatres, 152 of which submitted material. In 1976–77, these 152 theatres spent $79,233,584 producing 1,368 plays. Ninety-four of these institutions were founded in the last 10 years, a fact which underscores the enormous expansion of the professional noncommercial theatre in the United States in recent years.

Although Shakespeare was still the most frequently produced playwright in the last two seasons — having been produced by more than a third of the theatres in this book — a quick glance at the Index of Names and Titles shows *Vanities*, a new play by Jack Heifner, as the most produced play of the last two seasons. A close second is another new play entitled *The Last Meeting of the Knights of the White Magnolia* by Preston Jones. Alongside Shaw, Coward, Moliere, Chekhov and Ibsen, and intermingled with Williams, Miller, Pinter, Albee, Hellman and O'Neill are Athol Fugard, Ed Bullins, Tom Stoppard, Sam Shepard, Jack Gilhooley, Lanford Wilson, David Mamet and David Rabe, as some of the most frequently produced writers in the American theatre today.

The information in this book was collected over a six-month period, from July 1 through December 31, 1977. On behalf of the staff, I would like to thank each theatre, first, for their overwhelming response and desire to be included in *Theatre Profiles* — a testimonial to the book's impact and importance, both inside and outside the field — and second, for their cooperation in providing the information required.

The following explanatory notes are provided as a guide for the use of this book:

Directors
The artistic and administrative directors of each theatre are listed. This information is current, as of December 1977, and does not necessarily reflect the theatre's leadership during the 1975–76 and 1976–77 seasons.

Founding
The founding date reflects the conceptual or legal establishment of the institution or the beginning of public performances.

Season
The months listed indicate the beginning and closing dates of the theatre's season. "Year-round" indicates that the theatre company performs throughout the year without beginning or closing dates. If there is no listing, it is an indication that the theatre has no designated operating season.

Schedule
Evening and matinee performance days are included for theatres which have established regular performance schedules for the run of each production. Many theatres also present special performances (school matinees, tours, etc.) which are not reflected in the regular performance schedule.

Facilities
Seating capacities and types of stages are included only for those theatres that own, rent or regularly use a specific performing space. Theatre facility addresses are included when different from the mailing address. This information is current and may not necessarily reflect the two seasons highlighted in the book.

Budget

All financial information is based on figures submitted by the theatres for the time period indicated. Financial data appear in this book to indicate the scope of each operation, the relationship between income and operating budget and the ratio of earned to unearned income. In most cases, theatres have provided exact dollar amounts, but when audited statements were not yet available, estimated figures were submitted.

Audience

The average percent of capacity, as represented by single-ticket holders and subscribers, is provided for the most recently completed season.

Touring contact

Information is listed for theatres offering major touring and residency programs, so that potential sponsoring organizations can make direct contact regarding possible bookings.

Booked-in events

Information is listed for those theatres that regularly sponsor or rent their facilities to other performing arts groups or individual artists. A specific interest in special kinds of groups is indicated to assist companies seeking performing spaces or bookings.

Actors' Equity Association

Information on Actors' Equity Association (AEA) contracts is included for theatres operating under union jurisdiction. Please note that CORST indicates the Council of Resident Stock Theatres contract and LORT indicates the League of Resident Theatres contract, which has four categories: A, B, C, D. For specific information, contact Actors' Equity Association, 1500 Broadway, New York, New York 10036.

Programs & Services

Because of the increasing importance of theatres, not only as producing units, but as cultural resources serving their communities through a variety of outreach programs, this edition includes a listing for each theatre of activities which fall outside regular production activity.

Directors and Designers

This list, beginning on page 307 and presented alphabetically by theatre, includes the directors, and the set, costume and lighting designers for 1975- 76 and 1976-77 productions. No entry appears when design work was not attributed by the theatre to a particular person or, in a few cases, when the information was unavailable.

Regional Index

To more readily identify theatres located within a region, a geographical index begins on page 335.

Index of Names and Titles

All playwrights, play titles, artistic and administrative directors and founders appearing in this volume are listed in the index beginning on page 337. This index is designed to be useful in determining which theatres have produced a specific play or the work of a particular playwright, and the frequency of production of specific plays and playwrights.

Productions, 1976

Sizwe Bansi Is Dead, Athol Fugard, John Kani,
Winston Ntshona
The Time of Your Life, William Saroyan
Scapino, Moliere; adapted, Frank Dunlop &
Jim Dale
Desire Under the Elms, Eugene O'Neill
Relatively Speaking, Alan Ayckbourn
Boccaccio, Kenneth Cavander & Richard Peaslee
A Christmas Carol, Charles Dickens; adapted,
Gregory Falls; music, Robert MacDougall

Productions, 1977

As You Like It, William Shakespeare
Travesties, Tom Stoppard
Ladyhouse Blues, Kevin O'Morrison
Streamers, David Rabe
The Club, Eve Merriam; music, Alexandra Ivanoff
Absurd Person Singular, Alan Ayckbourn
A Christmas Carol, Charles Dickens; adapted,
Gregory Falls; music, Robert MacDougall

Tom Hill, Patricia Estrin, Christopher Duncan and
Kurt Beattie in *The Time of Your Life* by William
Saroyan, directed by Gregory Falls, sets by Jerry
Williams, costumes by Sally Richardson.

Donald Ewer and Margaret Hilton in Alan
Ayckbourn's *Relatively Speaking,* directed by Paul
Lee, sets by William Forrester, costumes by Sally
Richardson.

A Contemporary Theatre

A Contemporary Theatre (ACT) has always adapted to the times and the needs of its audience. The growing and changing Seattle theatre community, which now includes several theatres producing contemporary works, has made it possible for ACT to go beyond its original intent "to present professional productions of the important plays of our time, now, while they have particular meaning and impact." This change is evidenced by its 1977 mainstage production of Shakespeare's As You Like It, ACT's first production of a play from outside the twentieth-century repertoire. The production of contemporary plays, including musicals and new scripts, however, remains the principal focus of ACT's main stage, a policy which has resulted in the production of more than 60 playwrights including Albee, Ayckbourn, Beckett, Brecht, Ionesco, Jones, Mrozek, Pinter, Rabe, Shaffer, Stoppard, Storey and Williams.

As ACT continues to develop a discerning and sophisticated audience, the theatre hopes to produce an even greater number of new works, but at the same time keep the freedom of producing older plays as a happy alternative in its continuing adaptation to the changing theatre needs of the city. ACT next hopes to develop a smaller performance space to provide an arena for the development of new material and talent, with an emphasis on the use of music in the theatre.

During its second season in 1966, ACT began a commitment to children's theatre by introducing Brian Way's "participation plays" to America. This commitment has evolved into the Young ACT Company (YAC), a young actors ensemble. The company creates its own productions and tours throughout eight of the western states, performing primarily in schools. It works improvisationally for six months, bringing a considerable amount of physicality to its productions. While the main intent of the company's work has been to introduce children to the theatre, a portion of the material used has had sociological themes. In the past, the YAC's productions were musical revues combining story theatre, poetry, mini-operas, circus routines, dance and vaudeville. During the past two years, however, the company has moved away from revues to scripted dramatizations based on adult literature. The first of these was produced in 1976 when a Ford Foundation playwright grant helped the YAC adapt Dickens' A Christmas Carol. In 1977, ACT commissioned a play based on Homer's The Odyssey, which will tour the West in 1978.

Programs & Services: Young ACT Company, touring and residencies; internships; apprenticeships; sponsors performing arts events; student, senior citizen and group discount ticket programs; free ticket program; benefit performances; annual fund-raising drive; Backstage Club; subscriber newsletter; Playfacts, a publication of in-depth information on season; audience discussion series.

GREGORY A. FALLS
Artistic Director
ANDREW M. WITT
General Manager

709 First Avenue West
Seattle, Washington 98119
Telephone (206) 285-3220
Box Office (206) 285-5110

Founded 1965
Gregory A. Falls

Season
May – October

Schedule
Evenings
Tuesday – Sunday
Matinees
Wednesday & Saturday

Facilities
Seating capacity 431
Stage   Thrust

Budget
Jan 1, 1976 – Dec 31, 1976
Operating budget $590,030
Earned income $473,256
Unearned income $138,911

Audience
Percent of capacity 90
Number of subscribers 6,966

Touring contact
Jody Harris

Booked-in events
Regional performing arts groups

*Operates on AEA LORT (C)
and Theatre for Young
Audiences contracts.*

Productions, 1976
A Streetcar Named Desire, Tennessee
Williams
Hughie, Eugene O'Neill
Dirty Jokes, Arthur Giron
Misalliance, George Bernard Shaw

Productions, 1977
Too True to Be Good, George Bernard Shaw
The Landscape of the Body, John Guare
Tobacco Road, Erskine Caldwell; adapted,
Jack Kirkland
Old Times, Harold Pinter

Jean Marsh, Charles Kimbrough and Katharine
Houghton in *Too True To Be Good* by George
Bernard Shaw, directed by Philip Minor, sets by Fred
Kolouch, costumes by Laura Crow. Photo: Tony
Romano.

Beatrice Straight, Raul Julia and Irene Worth in *Old
Times* by Harold Pinter, directed by Marshall W.
Mason, sets by John Lee Beatty, costumes by Laura
Crow. Photo: Lisa Ebright.

4

Academy Festival Theatre

The Academy Festival Theatre completed its first decade of operation in the summer of 1977. During its initial seasons, under the direction of Marshall Migatz, AFT, then known as the Academy Playhouse, operated as a small summer stock theatre. In 1973, William Gardner assumed the position of producer and, since then, the theatre has grown. In the past four seasons, AFT has earned national recognition as an important regional theatre, and its productions have won theatre awards not only in Chicago, but in New York, Washington, Boston, Philadelphia and Los Angeles. The term "regional theatre" only approximates a description of Academy Festival Theatre. AFT has become a producing organization originating shows that have found audiences throughout America. New attention has been focused on Chicago as a city of major theatrical importance, with representatives from many other theatres visiting AFT during the summer. In the future, the theatre plans to extend its season beyond its current four-month schedule, in the hopes of furthering its contribution as a permanent institution in the Chicago area. Each year, AFT presents a season of four plays which bring together the finest artists available in America. AFT presents both classics of the stage and new plays of living playwrights.

Academy Festival first received national attention in 1973 with its production of O'Neill's *A Moon for the Misbegotten*, starring Colleen Dewhurst and Jason Robards and directed by Jose Quintero. This production later moved to Broadway, toured the United States and was taped as a special for television. Other O'Neill classics presented by AFT include *Desire Under the Elms*, with Cicely Tyson and Roscoe Lee Browne; *Ah, Wilderness!*, with Richard Kiley and Barbara Bel Geddes; and *Hughie*, starring Jason Robards. The 1975 season was highlighted by AFT's production of Tennessee Williams' *Sweet Bird of Youth*, with Irene Worth and Christopher Walken, which was later presented in the Bicentennial repertoire at Washington's John F. Kennedy Center for the Performing Arts and on Broadway.

A revival of Shaw's *Too True to Be Good* opened the 1977 season. The AFT production, featuring Jean Marsh, continued on to extended runs in Boston and Philadelphia. The 1977 season also included the world premiere of John Guare's *The Landscape of the Body*, with Shirley Knight. This play had a subsequent production at the New York Shakespeare Festival. Other Academy productions have included the world premieres of Mr. Guare's *Rich and Famous* and Arthur Giron's *Dirty Jokes*, and the Chicago premiere of David Storey's *The Farm*.

In 1977, a pilot program was initiated in association with New York's Ensemble Studio Theatre, which offered classes in acting and playwriting, as well as a second-stage production of a new play, *Reflections of a China Doll* by Susan Merson. AFT hopes to further develop this program into a professional theatre institute, with classes and an in-residence workshop series devoted to new works. The Academy Festival Theatre also offers an apprentice program for students in technical, administrative and production aspects of the professional theatre.

Programs & Services: *Apprenticeships; classes in acting and playwriting; subscriber lecture series; student, senior citizen and group ticket discounts; voucher program; benefit performances;* Subscriber Newsletter, *biannual publication.*

WILLIAM GARDNER
Producer
DANIEL CAINE
Associate Producer

700 East Westleigh Road
Lake Forest, Illinois 60045
(312) 234-6750

Founded 1967
Marshall Migatz

Season
June – October

Schedule
Evenings
Tuesday – Sunday
Matinees
Wednesday & Saturday

Facilities
Drake Theatre
Barat College
Seating capacity 628
Stage Thrust

Budget
Dec 1, 1976 – Nov 30, 1977
Operating budget $589,090
Earned income $391,184
Unearned income $108,447

Audience
Percent of capacity 85
Number of subscribers 8,000

Booked-in events
Dramatic productions

Operates on AEA Non-Resident Stock contract.

Productions, 1975–76
The Fantasticks, Tom Jones & Harvey Schmidt
The Merchant of Venice, William Shakespeare
Of Mice and Men, John Steinbeck
Sticks and Bones, David Rabe
America Hurrah, Jean-Claude van Itallie

Productions, 1976–77
America Hurrah, Jean-Claude van Itallie
As You Like It, William Shakespeare
Waiting for Godot, Samuel Beckett
The Blood Knot, Athol Fugard
Marat/Sade, Peter Weiss

John Stephens and Buck Newman, Jr. in
Shakespeare's *The Merchant of Venice,* directed by
Frank Wittow, production designed by Ezra Wittner.
Photo: Jim Karney.

Larry Larson and J. Lawrence Smith in *The Blood
Knot* by Athol Fugard, directed by Frank Wittow,
production designed by Dorset Noble. Photo: Marty
King.

Academy Theatre

The Academy Theatre of Atlanta was founded in 1956 by Frank Wittow. Its work is focused on three interlocking program areas — the mainstage season of established scripts, the developmental/new play program and the School of Performing Arts.

In each area of work, the concepts of an ensemble and creative development are central. The theatre operates year-round with the professional resident company employed for 38 to 40 weeks a year. Full-time members of the resident company plan their upcoming September-to-June season of work each May, together with Mr. Wittow, the artistic director. At that time, major roles in the next mainstage season are announced and each company member decides on additional areas of responsibility as actor, writer, teacher or director in the theatre's other programs. Decisions are based on helping each company member develop to his or her full potential. Each year, in addition to playing at the Academy, one or more of the mainstage productions tour the Southeast under the sponsorship of the Southern Federation of State Arts Agencies.

The developmental/new play program includes the Academy Children's Theatre and a new play series for adults. The Academy Children's Theatre produces three new plays each year and an Artists-in-Schools tour provides both elementary and high school performances and improvisational drama workshops throughout Georgia. Plays created for young audiences are centered on themes of evolving concern to both the audiences and artists, with primary performance values placed on the actors' skills and versatility. "Sundays at the Academy" is a series of 10 to 15 new plays for adults, produced by the Academy Second Space Company. The series presents company-developed plays as well as new scripted material. Productions range from staged readings of works-in-progress to full productions, with an emphasis on serving playwrights from the Academy's region. The work of guest companies is also presented as a part of this series. Actors from the Second Space Company often move into full-time positions with the Academy resident ensemble.

The School of Performing Arts is both a complete professional actor-training program with its own Lab Theatre and a community program providing training to nonprofessionals. It offers an Apprentice Program, averaging 30 hours a week of study, rehearsal and job assignments for adults, as well as classes for children.

In the summer of 1977, the Academy Theatre moved into a new home, a facility originally built, in 1966, for Theatre Atlanta.

Programs & Services: *Academy Theatre School of Performing Arts; apprenticeships; internships; performances and lecture-demonstrations for students; Theatre For Youth, touring; Academy Children's Theatre, resident and touring productions; Sunday at the Academy, performance program; student, senior citizen discount ticket program; free tickets to hospital groups; benefit performances; Children's Theatre Guild, support group; volunteers.*

FRANK WITTOW
Artistic Director
NANCY HAGER
General Manager

P.O. Box 11530
Atlanta, Georgia 30355
Telephone (404) 892-0355
Box Office (404) 892-0880

Founded 1956
Frank Wittow

Season
November – June

Schedule
Evenings
Thursday – Sunday
Matinees
Saturday & Sunday

Facilities
1374 West Peachtree Street, NW
Seating capacity 500
Stage ¾ Arena

Budget
Aug 1, 1976 – July 31, 1977
Operating budget $234,000
Earned income $101,500
Unearned income $133,500

Audience
Percent of capacity 81

Touring contact
Nancy Hager

Booked-in events
Experimental performing arts groups & new play productions

Productions, 1975–76
Arms and the Man, George Bernard Shaw
The Robber Bridegroom, Alfred Uhry &
Robert Waldman
The Time of Your Life, William Saroyan
She Stoops to Conquer, Oliver Goldsmith
The Way of the World, William Congreve
Diary of Adam and Eve, Sheldon Harnick &
Jerry Bock
The Three Sisters, Anton Chekhov; trans-
lated, Tyrone Guthrie & Leonard Kipnis
Edward II, Christopher Marlowe
The Taming of the Shrew, William Shakespeare

Productions, 1976–77
Camino Real, Tennessee Williams
The Way of the World, William Congreve
The Kitchen, Arnold Wesker
Love's Labour's Lost, William Shakespeare
The Duck Variations, David Mamet
Rosemary, Molly Kazan

Jeffrey Hayenga and James Harper in *The Kitchen*
by Arnold Wesker, directed by Boris Tumarin, sets
by Douglas W. Schmidt, costumes by John David
Ridge. Photo: Martha Swope.

Anderson Matthews, Mary Lou Rosato, Brooks
Baldwin and Cynthia Dickason in Congreve's *The
Way of the World,* directed by Norman Ayrton, sets
by Douglas W. Schmidt, costumes by Barbara
Matera. Photo: Martha Swope.

The Acting Company

The Acting Company is a permanent professional ensemble which tours a repertoire of classical and modern plays from coast to coast, and offers teaching demonstrations and workshops. The only permanent company in America which combines all of these features, the company in its sixth season was under the artistic direction of its founder, producer-director-actor John Houseman, and director Gerald Freedman. In 1978, Michael Kahn and Alan Schneider will join Mr. Houseman as artistic directors. The Acting Company is dedicated to the cohesive ensemble presentation of its stylistically varied repertoire. Artistic emphasis is on unified ensemble interpretation and, to that end, many members of the company have trained, worked and grown together at the Juilliard School. New members of the company are selected from Juilliard, other professional theatre training programs and regional theatres across the country, and are carefully trained to adapt to the organization's ensemble traditions. To date, the company has performed a repertoire of 27 plays in 150 cities in 39 states.

In 1972, John Houseman, then head of the drama division of the Juilliard School in New York, saw in his first graduating class a group of actors so talented that he felt they should not be disbanded. Mr. Houseman formed those young actors into a professional company, which made its debut as the dramatic arm of one of the nation's leading summer festivals, the Saratoga Performing Arts Festival in New York State. The company appeared there in residence, along with the New York City Ballet and the Philadelphia Orchestra. This group became known as the City Center Acting Company, under the auspices of New York's City Center of Music and Drama. This affiliation ceased in 1975, and the company is now known simply as The Acting Company.

In its first two seasons, the company played a successful Off Broadway engagement and an equally successful engagement on Broadway. It also played a Christmas season, for students and senior citizens, at City Center. In 1973-74, the company offered a four-week summer school, as part of its return engagement at the Saratoga Festival, and toured 37 cities in 18 states, playing to a combined audience of more than 50,000 people.

The 1974-75 season began with a month's residency at the Saratoga Festival in July and included a fall tour of the Northeast and Midwest; a month's residency at the University of Michigan, under the auspices of its Professional Theatre Program; and a spring tour of the Rocky Mountain states and the west coast. The company visited 50 cities in 21 states, with a repertoire of seven productions.

The 1975-76 season included residencies at the Saratoga Festival, the Ravinia Festival and a New York City engagement. Again at the Saratoga and Ravinia festivals at the beginning of its 1976-77 season, the company followed with a coast-to-coast tour, including teaching residencies in New York, Florida, North Carolina and California. The California residency, based in Los Angeles, lasted for three weeks, during which time a total of 18 performances were given in 21 days. While at the University of California–Los Angeles, the company also taught 25 hours of classes, workshops and demonstrations. The entire residency was videotaped as a documentary by the UCLA Media Center.

Programs & Services: *Workshops in voice, masks, makeup, theatre games and character study; internships; performances for students; touring; residencies.*

JOHN HOUSEMAN
Producing Artistic Director
MICHAEL KAHN
ALAN SCHNEIDER
Artistic Directors
MARGOT HARLEY
Executive Producer

1650 Broadway, Suite 408
New York, New York 10019
(212) 489-8548

Founded 1972
John Houseman & Margot Harley

Season
July – May

Budget
June 1, 1976 – May 31, 1977
Operating budget $1,129,818
Earned income $ 560,082
Unearned income $ 419,572

Touring contact
Anne Vaughan

*Operates on AEA LORT (C)
contract.*

Productions, 1975–76
Arms and the Man, George Bernard Shaw
The Hot l Baltimore, Lanford Wilson
Ten Little Indians, Agatha Christie
Oedipus the King, Sophocles
Scapino, Moliere; adapted, Frank Dunlop &
Jim Dale
*The Last Meeting of the Knights of the
White Magnolia*, Preston Jones
The Sunshine Boys, Neil Simon
Dear Liar, Jerome Kilty
Scott and Zelda, Paul Hunter
Measure for Measure, William Shakespeare;
adapted, Charles Marowitz
The Sea Horse, Edward J. Moore

Productions, 1976–77
The Best Man, Gore Vidal
Sexual Perversity in Chicago, David Mamet
Vanities, Jack Heifner
Reunion, David Mamet
Medal of Honor Rag, Tom Cole
Tea with Dick and Jerry, Erik A. Brogger
Much Ado About Nothing, William Shakespeare
A Christmas Carol, Charles Dickens; adapted,
Barbara Nosanow
The Resistable Rise of Arturo Ui,
Bertolt Brecht; translated, George Tabori
The Matchmaker, Thornton Wilder
Who's Afraid of Virginia Woolf?, Edward Albee
The Diary of Anne Frank, Frances Goodrich &
Albert Hackett
The Gin Game, D.L. Coburn
Indulgences in the Louisville Harem, John Orlock
Table Manners, Alan Ayckbourn
Round and Round the Garden, Alan Ayckbourn
The Rainmaker, N. Richard Nash

Andrew Davis in *The Resistible Rise of Arturo Ui* by
Bertolt Brecht, directed by Jon Jory, sets by Paul
Owen, costumes by Kurt Wilhelm. Photo: David S.
Talbott.

Adale O'Brien and John H. Fields in *Arms and the
Man* by George Bernard Shaw, directed by Jon Jory,
sets by Paul Owen, costumes by Kurt Wilhelm.
Photo: David S. Talbott.

Actors Theatre of Louisville

Actors Theatre of Louisville, founded in 1964 by Richard Block and Ewel Cornett, began in a converted loft (formerly the home of the Egyptian Tea Room) with a seating capacity of 100. One year later, sold-out houses forced Actors Theatre to move into larger quarters, this time a converted railway station.

In July 1969, Jon Jory, co-founder of New Haven's Long Wharf Theatre, became producing director. Since then, subscriptions have increased from 3,700 to the current 16,055. The musical comedy *Tricks*, which originated at ATL, opened on Broadway in 1972. *In Fashion*, another ATL world premiere, has been presented at other regional theatres and was filmed for national television as part of WNET-TV's *Theater in America* series, and was broadcast over the Public Broadcasting Service in 1974 and 1975. ATL has also participated in production exchange with the Cincinnati Playhouse in the Park.

In the Pamela Brown Auditorium, seven plays are presented each season, while a three-play "Off Broadway" series of plays with more limited audience appeal is produced in the smaller Victor Jory Theatre. A number of world and American premieres have been presented in this series, including the professional premiere, in 1977, of D.L. Coburn's *The Gin Game*. A Festival of New American Plays is scheduled for the 1977–78 season. According to Mr. Jory, the theatre's artistic policy is "to produce plays as best we can, within the scope of our talents and finances."

During its 13-year history, Actors Theatre has made contact with its community through tours to elementary schools, junior and senior high schools, and colleges; poetry programs in people's homes; assistance to local businesses by writing and performing industrial shows; a consulting service for high school and community theatres; and a speakers bureau which serves an average of 150 civic groups a year. The theatre has both male and female volunteer groups, numbering some 500 participants, and has provided active leadership in the renewal of Louisville's downtown area.

In 1972, the Actors Theatre moved into a new $1.7 million theatre complex, built in the Old Bank of Louisville building, which was erected by Gideon Shryock in 1837. Part of ATL's new home, the gracious Greek Revival–style lobby, has been designated a National Historic Landmark and attracts thousands of visitors each year.

ATL's location is in the heart of downtown Louisville, near interstate highway exits and in the midst of the waterfront development area. In addition to serving Louisville, Actors Theatre has expanded its support base beyond a statewide area and serves hundreds of subscribers from Indiana, Ohio and Tennessee. In 1974, the theatre was designated the State Theatre of Kentucky by the Kentucky state legislature.

Programs & Services: *Performances and programs for students; touring; student, senior citizen and group ticket discounts; prop auction; united arts fund-raising; Stagehands and Actors Associates, support groups; speakers bureau; restaurant and bar; newsletter; post-performance discussions.*

JON JORY
Producing Director
ALEXANDER SPEER
Administrative Director
TRISH PUGH
Associate Director

316–320 West Main Street
Louisville, Kentucky 40202
Telephone (502) 584-1265
Box Office (502) 584-1205

Founded 1964
Richard Block & Ewel Cornett

Season
October – May

Schedule
Evenings
Tuesday – Sunday
Matinees
Varies

Facilities
Pamela Brown Auditorium
Seating capacity 641
Stage Thrust
Victor Jory Theatre
Seating capacity 161
Stage ¾ Arena

Budget
June 1, 1976 – May 31, 1977
Operating budget $1,185,529
Earned income $ 966,714
Unearned income $ 289,301

Audience
Pamela Brown Auditorium
Percent of capacity 98
Number of subscribers 16,055
Victor Jory Theatre
Percent of capacity 82
Number of subscribers 1,451

Touring contact
Alexander Speer

Operates on AEA LORT (B) contract.

Productions, 1977
Scapino, Moliere; adapted, Frank Dunlop
& Jim Dale
Private Lives, Noel Coward
Clarence Darrow, Irving Stone; adapted,
David W. Rintels

Megan Cole and John Milligan in *Private Lives* by
Noel Coward, directed by Lee Salisbury, sets and
costumes by Jamie Greenleaf. Photo: Tom Keane.

Philip Pleasants as *Clarence Darrow* by David
Rintels, directed by Robert Farley, sets and
costumes by Jamie Greenleaf. Photo: Tom Keane.

12

Alaska Repertory Theatre

The Alaska Repertory Theatre was founded in 1976 to present plays of distinction chosen from classic, contemporary and original works, with special consideration given to their relevance and audience appeal. With its formation the theatre became the first professional performing arts organization in the state of Alaska. After it was determined, through a study initiated by the Alaska State Council on the Arts with help from the National Endowment for the Arts, that the people of Alaska were willing to support a professional theatre organization, Paul Brown was contracted to research its feasibility. The response by business, government and community leaders was positive, and on the advice of the Foundation for the Extension and Development of the American Professional Theatre (FEDAPT), a statewide advisory group was formed to guide the development of the project and to conduct a nationwide search for an artistic director. In July 1976, the Alaska Repertory Theatre was incorporated and plans for the first season were begun by Robert J. Farley, artistic director, and Paul Brown, producing director.

While the theatre is located in Anchorage, the state's largest city, its constituency spans a geographic landmass of four time zones in an area one–fifth the size of the 48 contiguous states. In the first season the final production of the three–play repertory, *Clarence Darrow*, played residencies in both Anchorage and Fairbanks. It is planned that *Clarence Darrow* will tour to Juneau, the capital, Ketchikan and Bethel in October 1977.

Community outreach programs, including workshops and school performances, are part of all residencies. Through technical assistance and the loan of theatrical equipment, the Alaska Repertory Theatre is a unique resource for schools and nonprofit community groups. Additionally, the theatre sponsors an Actors-in-the-Schools Program, which helps develop an awareness and appreciation for the theatre by bringing theatre artists into schools, for a two–week period, to work with students and teachers within the curriculum. In 1976–77 this program operated in eight different communities, from Arctic villages to urban schools. By carefully balancing high artistic standards, audience enjoyment and education, the Alaska Repertory Theatre, as a producing organization and artistic resource, has become an integral part of its statewide community.

Programs & Services: *Touring; technical and acting professional training programs; performances, study guides, seminars and workshops for students; actors-in-schools residencies; Theatre Library, a statewide mail service of scripts, anthologies and technical data; booked-in events; artistic and technical consultation service for performing arts organizations; student, senior citizen and group ticket discounts; free ticket program; backstage tours; speakers bureau; bar; Curtain Raisers, volunteers; post-performance discussions.*

ROBERT J. FARLEY
Artistic Director
PAUL V. BROWN
Producing Director

523 West Eighth Avenue, Suite 110
Anchorage, Alaska 99501
Telephone (907) 276-2327
Box Office (907) 264-4362

Founded 1976
Alaska State Council on the Arts

Season
January – May

Schedule
Evenings
Tuesday – Saturday
Matinees
Sunday

Facilities
Sydney Laurence Auditorium
Sixth Avenue & F Street
Seating capacity 652
Stage Proscenium

Budget
July 1, 1976 – June 30, 1977
Operating budget $301,700
Earned income $104,340
Unearned income $221,660

Audience
Percent of capacity 67
Number of subscribers 2,176

Touring contact
Paul V. Brown

Booked-in events
Regional and children's theatre, national tours, outreach programs

Operates on AEA LORT (B) contract.

Productions, 1975–76
Indians, Arthur Kopit
The Front Page, Ben Hecht &
Charles MacArthur
*The Last Meeting of the Knights
of the White Magnolia*, Preston Jones
Juno and the Paycock, Sean O'Casey
The Show-Off, George Kelly
The Cocktail Party, T.S. Eliot
Tiny Alice, Edward Albee
A Christmas Carol, Charles Dickens;
adapted, William Trotman
Scenes from American Life, A.R. Gurney
Purgatory, William Butler Yeats
The Harmful Effects of Tobacco, Anton
Chekhov

Productions, 1976–77
The Sty of the Blind Pig, Phillip
Hayes Dean
You Never Can Tell, George Bernard Shaw
The Corn Is Green, Emlyn Williams
The Runner Stumbles, Milan Stitt
How the Other Half Loves, Alan Ayckbourn
The Collection, Harold Pinter
The Dock Brief, John Mortimer
Loot, Joe Orton
Endgame, Samuel Beckett

Robert Symonds in *Purgatory* by William Butler
Yeats, directed by Mr. Symonds, designed by the
Lunchtime Theatre production staff. Photo: Allen
Currie.

Michael Ball and Brian Tree in Pinter's *The
Collection*, directed by Nina Vance, sets by John
Kenny, costumes by Julie Jackson. Photo: Allen
Currie.

Alley Theatre

The Alley Theatre, among the early leaders in the decentralization of the arts, has never deviated from the artistic philosophy on which it was founded in 1947: to maintain a resident acting company and to produce a balanced, but unrestricted, repertoire from the full panoply of dramatic literature — serious and comedic, classic and contemporary, challenging original works, notable revivals and plays by outstanding international authors.

The sprawling, vibrant, dynamic metropolis of Houston, celebrated for its growth, is young as cities go, but its pioneering accomplishments are staggering to the imagination. The Alley Theatre began its surge forward along with the city of Houston three decades ago, and during this time, both have grown immensely in size and stature.

It is impossible to separate the history and growth of the Alley Theatre and native Texan Nina Vance, the theatre's founding director. The Alley began with 214 penny postcards, the amount of change Ms. Vance had in her purse. The postcards brought 100 enthusiasts to a meeting in June 1947, and when the meeting ended, a new theatre had been born. The names of Nina Vance and Alley Theatre have been interchangeable ever since, giving the Alley the very rare advantage of continuity in artistic leadership throughout its history.

The Alley opened its first production in 1947 in an 87-seat dance studio. The theatre's name was inspired by its location, which was reached by walking down a narrow alleyway. The theatre's second home, a converted fan factory seating 231, opened with Lillian Hellman's *The Children's Hour*, a daring choice for 1949. This quaint building was to be the Alley's home for the next 19 years. The design for the permanent facility, which opened in 1968, was conceived, by architect Ulrich Franzen and Ms. Vance, to respond to the functional and artistic needs of the Alley. The result of this endeavor was the creation of a building which provided two completely different types of stages under one roof. Constructed at a cost of more than $5.5 million, the building was funded by major foundations and more than 15,000 individual contributors, and the Houston Endowment donated a square block in downtown Houston. Recipient of the Honor Award from the American Institute of Architects, Alley Theatre's building has been graphically described as being "at once southwestern and medieval — capturing the pioneering quality of the Alley." As further evidence of its role as pioneer, in 1976–77, the Alley Theatre hosted the first public debate in history between candidates for Vice-President of the United States. Certainly, this was an honor for the Alley, but it was also one which focused nationwide attention on all American resident professional theatres.

The 1976–77 season presented a repertoire which conformed to the Alley's artistic philosophy. The range of plays selected for the Large Stage Series was very broad, from the powerful contemporary questions addressed by the authors of *The Sty of the Blind Pig* and *The Runner Stumbles*, to works of Emlyn Williams and George Bernard Shaw, to a sampling of the comedic expertise of Alan Ayckbourn. The Arena Series continued programming that included plays that are esoteric in nature, selected for a small, but knowledgeable and dedicated, audience for contemporary, rarely produced works. The Alley Theatre operates year-round, with the subscription series on the two stages comprising a minimum of 30 weeks. During this period, the 300-student theatre school for young people between the fourth and twelfth grades, is also in session full-time. Immediately following the close of the theatre season, the annual summer Cinemafest of classic films opens and plays a full weekly schedule, until the company returns for the next season.

Programs & Services: *Alley Merry-Go-Round, classes for young people; workshop productions; internships; adult workshops; Cinemafest, summer film festival; lunchtime theatre; Sunday Afternoon Jazz; student, senior citizen and group discounts; Alley Gala, fund-raising; united arts fund-raising; Alley Theatre Guild, volunteers; speakers bureau; Alley Theatre Cookbook; post-performance discussions; Tuesday Supper Series, free to subscribers.*

NINA VANCE
Producing Director
IRIS SIFF
Managing Director

615 Texas Avenue
Houston, Texas 77002
Telephone (713) 228-9341
Box Office (713) 228-8421

Founded 1947
Nina Vance

Season
October – May

Schedule
Evenings
Tuesday – Sunday
Matinees
Saturday & Sunday

Facilities
Large Stage
Seating capacity 798
Stage   Thrust
Arena Stage
Seating capacity 296
Stage   Arena

Budget
Oct 1, 1976 – Sept 30, 1977
Operating budget $1,473,360
Earned income $ 975,642
Unearned income $ 455,306

Audience
Large Stage
Percent of capacity 77
Number of subscribers 18,647
Arena Stage
Percent of capacity 76
Number of subscribers 2,031

Operates on AEA LORT (B) contract.

Productions, 1975-76
*The Last Meeting of the Knights of the
White Magnolia,* Preston Jones
The Miracle Worker, William Gibson
To Be Young, Gifted and Black,
Lorraine Hansberry; adapted, Robert
Nemiroff
The Skin of Our Teeth, Thornton Wilder
The Member of the Wedding, Carson
McCullers
The Tempest, William Shakespeare

Productions, 1976-77
Scapino, Moliere; adapted, Frank Dunlop &
Jim Dale
Hedda Gabler, Henrik Ibsen
*Come Back to the 5 and Dime, Jimmy Dean,
Jimmy Dean,* Ed Graczyk
Misalliance, George Bernard Shaw
All the Way Home, Tad Mosel
Henry IV, Part I, William Shakespeare
Who's Afraid of Virginia Woolf?,
Edward Albee

Travis L. Fine and Philip Kraus in *All the Way Home*
by Tad Mosel, directed by Fred Chappell, designed
by Michael Stauffer. Photo: Charles Rafshoon.

Patricia Miller, Jane Dentinger and Bette Glenn in
Vanities by Jack Heifner, directed by Fred Chappell,
sets by Erik Magnuson, costumes by Pat McMahon.
A special Studio Theatre production, 1977. Photo:
Charles Rafshoon.

Alliance Theatre Company

The Alliance Theatre Company makes its home in the Atlanta Memorial Arts Center. This multimillion-dollar complex also houses the Atlanta Symphony Orchestra, the High Museum of Art, the Atlanta College of Art and the Atlanta Children's Theatre. The Alliance Theatre Company was founded in 1969 by the Atlanta Arts Alliance.

The Alliance Theatre Company is committed to the presentation of high-quality theatre to its community and region. Plays are selected to offer a diversified season of classic and contemporary works by major playwrights. Actors are engaged on a per-production basis, but many remain for several productions during a season, a policy which helps provide the continuity and harmony of an acting ensemble. In 1976–77, seven productions were presented on the main stage, each running three weeks.

In the belief that new works by American playwrights should be fostered, the theatre presents at least one new script each season. During the 1976–77 season, Atlanta audiences saw the premiere of Ed Graczyk's *Come Back to the 5 and Dime, Jimmy Dean, Jimmy Dean.* Plans are currently underway to present staged readings of new works in Alliance's 200-seat Studio Theatre.

The Alliance Theatre Company is also committed to educating young audiences in the live theatre experience. Through the Shakespeare Student Audience Program, more than 9,000 high school students saw the theatre's production of *Henry IV, Part I.* In the fall of 1976, Alliance Theatre toured to more than 25 high schools for five weeks, with a Shakespearean collage entitled *The Lover and the Poet.* In 1977–78, the theatre will sponsor a festival in its Studio Theatre for area college students.

The theatre works with Hospital Audiences, Inc., in distributing approximately 4,000 free tickets each year for special previews, to people who would otherwise be unable to attend performances.

In addition to the theatre's mainstage productions, special programs are presented. In 1976–77, audiences enjoyed a production of Jack Heifner's *Vanities,* which played to capacity houses for more than three months. In 1977–78, the theatre will sponsor performances by the National Theatre of the Deaf.

In August of 1977, a merger was effected between the Alliance Theatre Company and the Atlanta Children's Theatre, a professional company which presents in-school performances to some 130,000 children each year. The Atlanta Children's Theatre also offers an educational workshop program to area schools and tours productions throughout the state. The merger of these two theatres results in one company with the capacity to provide a full range of theatre activities for both adult and youth audiences.

Programs & Services: *Apprenticeships; performances for students; touring; student, senior citizen and group ticket discounts; free ticket program; united arts fund-raising; Alliance Theatre Guild, volunteers; Sunday matinee post-performance discussions; booked-in events.*

FRED CHAPPELL
Artistic Director
BERNARD HAVARD
Managing Director

1280 Peachtree Street, NE
Atlanta, Georgia 30309
Telephone (404) 892-2797
Box Office (404) 892-2414

Founded 1969
Atlanta Arts Alliance

Season
November – April

Schedule
Evenings
Tuesday – Saturday
Matinees
Sunday

Facilities
Alliance Theatre
Seating capacity 868
Stage   Proscenium
Studio Theatre
Seating capacity 200
Stage   Flexible

Budget
Aug 1, 1976 – July 31, 1977
Operating budget $271,441
Earned income $261,877
Unearned income $ 45,382

Audience
Alliance Theatre
Percent of capacity 54
Number of subscribers 3,500
Studio Theatre
Percent of capacity 97

Touring contact
Bernard Havard

Operates on AEA LORT (B) contract.

Productions, 1975–76
The Ragtime Blues, Mitch Douglas
The Big Knife, Clifford Odets
Godsong, J.W. Johnson; adapted, Tad Truesdale

Productions, 1976–77
Bojangles!, Norman Mitgang
The Mikado AMAS, W.S. Gilbert & Arthur Sullivan;
adapted, Rosetta LeNoire & Irving Vincent
Save the Seeds Darling, Helen Powers
Come Laugh & Cry with Langston Hughes,
Langston Hughes; adapted, Rosetta LeNoire &
Clyde Williams; music, Clyde Williams

Ramona Brooks and Vernon Spencer in *Come
Laugh and Cry with Langston Hughes* by Rosetta
LeNoire and Clyde Williams, directed by Ms.
LeNoire, sets by Michael Meadows. Photo: Ambur
Hiken.

Anthony Lawrence in *Save the Seeds Darling* by
Helen Powers, directed by Arthur Whitelaw, sets by
Michael Meadows. Photo: Ambur Hiken.

AMAS Repertory Theatre

AMAS Repertory was incorporated by Rosetta LeNoire in 1969. The company's work is based on the belief that theatre is a powerful instrument for the unification of all people. Celebration — not separation — is the key factor in all of the company's productions. From its inception, AMAS has had a completely integrated theatre company where people from all races and creeds work together to further the joy of learning, and where quality of product overrides all other interests. Furthermore, AMAS, totally committed to the development of nonprofessionals as well as professionals, brings together artists from both worlds to explore and develop new work.

The theatre, which began as a workshop in the Bronx basement of Ms. LeNoire's home, has, in eight years, become an active Off-Off Broadway showcase theatre. The prestige enjoyed by the company today is a direct result of the arduous labor and determination of its artistic director, Rosetta LeNoire, along with its artistic, technical and administrative staff. *Bubbling Brown Sugar*, currently on Broadway, was conceived by Ms. LeNoire and received its premiere at the AMAS Theatre during the 1974 season. The commercial interest and success generated by *Bubbling Brown Sugar* has been an instrumental factor in the development of the company's reputation. Productions like *The Ragtime Blues* and *Bojangles!*, both slated for Broadway runs, were originally showcased at AMAS. Directors and performers like Charles Nelson Reilly, Ira Cirker, Lucia Victor, Avon Long, Helen Powers, Bernard Johnson and Arthur Whitehall are all active participants in the theatre and have aided in fulfilling AMAS' commitment to develop new work through the unified effort of both nonprofessionals and professionals alike.

Though theatrical productions are the main impulse of its programming, AMAS does not exclusively limit itself to the presentation of plays. Other integral programs include workshops for adults and children which provide interested participants with voice theory, dance and acting training for a minimal fee. Classes are held weekly on a year-round basis, and are conducted by an experienced group of artists. Students, nine years and older, are introduced to theatre arts as vocational training that is not intended to replace academic instruction, but rather to enhance each individual's self-understanding, as well as that of human nature. The training workshops culminate with two public performances at the end of the term, at which time participants are evaluated by a panel that gives suggestions and encourages those with talent to continue their training or careers.

The 1977-78 AMAS season includes two musical premieres, *Helen* by Lucia Victor and Johnny Brandon, and *Beowulf* by Bettie Jane Wylie and Victor Davies. Both productions are additional evidence of AMAS' continued commitment to the development of new work.

Programs & Services: *Workshops for children and adults; internships in various theatre disciplines; summer touring program sponsored by NYC Department of Cultural Affairs; dance training for adults and senior citizens; student and senior citizen discount ticket programs; annual Eubie Blake Children's Theatre Fund benefit for children's theatre workshop.*

ROSETTA LeNOIRE
Artistic Director

1 East 104th Street
New York, New York 10029
(212) 369-8000

Founded 1969
Rosetta LeNoire, Gerta Grunen,
Mara Kim

Season
October – May

Schedule
Evenings
Thursday – Saturday
Matinees
Sunday

Facilities
Seating capacity 94
Stage   Proscenium

Budget
May 1, 1976 – Apr 30, 1977
Operating budget $126,661
Earned income $ 82,438
Unearned income $ 84,180

Audience
Percent of capacity 75

Touring contact
Rosetta LeNoire

Operates under AEA Showcase Code.

Productions, 1975-76

Tiny Alice, Edward Albee
The Matchmaker, Thornton Wilder
Desire Under the Elms, Eugene O'Neill
General Gorgeous, Michael McClure
The Merry Wives of Windsor, William Shakespeare
This Is (an Entertainment), Tennessee Williams
Equus, Peter Shaffer
Peer Gynt, Henrik Ibsen; translated,
Allen Fletcher
The Taming of the Shrew, William Shakespeare
Cyrano de Bergerac, Edmond Rostand; translated,
Brian Hooker; adapted, Dennis Powers

Productions, 1976-77

Othello, William Shakespeare
Man and Superman, George Bernard Shaw
Equus, Peter Shaffer
A Christmas Carol, Charles Dickens; adapted,
Dennis Powers & Laird Williamson
Knock Knock, Jules Feiffer
The Bourgeois Gentleman, Moliere; translated,
Charles Hallahan & Dennis Powers
Valentin and Valentina, Mihail Roschin;
translated, Irene Arn Vacchina &
Edward Hastings
Travesties, Tom Stoppard
Peer Gynt, Henrik Ibsen; translated,
Allen Fletcher

Joy Carlin and Daniel Davis in Ibsen's *Peer Gynt*, directed by Allen Fletcher, sets by Ralph Funicello, costumes by Robert Blackman. Photo: William Ganslen.

Members of the company of *The Bourgeois Gentleman* by Moliere, directed by William Ball, sets by Richard Seger, costumes by Robert Fletcher. Photo: William Ganslen.

American Conservatory Theatre

The American Conservatory Theatre is one of the largest and most active of the nation's resident professional companies and is unique among them. One of a handful playing in true repertory, ACT is the only company whose annual seasons of public performances are concurrent with, and inseparable from, a continuing program of theatre training for professional actors as well as students.

The company employs more than 200 people annually, including actors, directors, teachers, designers, administrators, craftsmen and technicians. Every year it presents a 33-week season at the Geary Theatre, offering some 280 performances of nine plays in repertory, to an audience exceeding 300,000. ACT also sponsors engagements of non-repertory productions at the smaller Marines' Memorial Theatre and at the Geary when the company itself is not performing there. Since settling in San Francisco in 1967, ACT has presented more than 150 productions, seen by more than four million playgoers, in its two theatres. ACT draws its repertoire from the classics of dramatic literature, outstanding works of the modern theatre and new plays. Since plays are presented in the rotating repertory style, audience members may choose, in a given week, from three or four widely differing works. At the same time, ACT actors and directors are able to expand their artistry and implement their training as they meet the challenges of a constantly changing variety of dramatic forms, styles and periods. Concurrent with the repertory season is the Plays in Progress series, presenting previously unproduced works by new American writers.

From its inception, the company has maintained its dual objectives as a producing organization and a full-time professional conservatory. William Ball, an actor and director whose work in theatres across the country had given him firsthand knowledge about the state of the art, saw the need for a place—an environment—a theatre that would support and encourage the theatre artist in his search for fulfillment. He founded ACT as an alternative to the producer-oriented commercial theatre where the needs of the artist become secondary to the box office, and where creative growth is limited. The two halves of the ACT whole, training and performance, nourish each other in many ways. Not only do actors apply what they learn to their work onstage, they also often teach their fellow company members, as well as students, in the conservatory programs. Actors teach, teachers act, directors act and actors direct, while students learn professional technique and discipline through close association with experienced theatre artists. A primary goal of the company is to bring each actor and student even closer to the fulfillment of his own potential and, by extension, to help raise the standards of American acting as a whole. The directors and teachers at ACT believe that actors in this country are often inhibited in their development by the lack of a real tradition from which they can draw. Therefore, ACT emphasizes the responsibility of the mature artist not only to continue his growth, through study and training, but to bequeath what he has learned to younger members of the profession; to *conserve* theatre in the literal meaning of the word — "to keep from being damaged, lost or wasted."

ACT's productions of *Cyrano de Bergerac* and *The Taming of the Shrew* were both broadcast over the Public Broadcasting Service. Over the years, ACT has toured extensively, including visits to Los Angeles and New York, and to Hawaii, where the company has annually presented performances and training residencies since 1973. In 1976, ACT celebrated the nation's Bicentennial with a State Department–sponsored tour of the Soviet Union.

Programs & Services: *Training programs for young people, students and professionals; Asian-American and black theatre workshops; performances for students; speakers bureau; touring and residencies; Plays in Progress, new play productions and publication; booked-in events; student, senior citizen and group discount programs; free ticket program; benefits; lecture series; Friends of ACT, volunteers; California Association for ACT, fund-raising group; newsletter.*

WILLIAM BALL
General Director
JAMES B. McKENZIE
Executive Producer

450 Geary Street
San Francisco, California 94102
Telephone (415) 771-3880
Box Office (415) 673-6440

Founded 1965
William Ball

Season
October – May

Schedule
Evenings
Monday – Saturday
Matinees
Wednesday & Saturday

Facilities
415 Geary Street
Seating capacity 1,354
Stage Proscenium

Budget
June 1, 1976 – May 31, 1977
Operating budget $4,256,488
Earned income $3,178,826
Unearned income $ 894,740

Audience
Percent of capacity 74
Number of subscribers 21,300

Touring contact
James B. McKenzie

Booked-in events
Commercial theatrical productions and dance companies

Operates on AEA LORT (A) contract.

Productions, 1975–76
Gorky, Steve Tesich
Every Night When the Sun Goes Down,
Phillip Hayes Dean
The Old Glory, Robert Lowell

Productions, 1976–77
Jack Gelber's New Play: Rehearsal,
Jack Gelber
Domino Courts and *Comanche Cafe,*
William Hauptman
Isadora Duncan Sleeps with the Russian Navy,
Jeff Wanshel
Cold Storage, Ronald Ribman

Marian Seldes and David Rasche in *Isadora Duncan
Sleeps with the Russian Navy* by Jeff Wanshel,
directed by Tom Haas, costumes by Bobbi Owen.
Photo: Martha Holmes.

Martin Balsam and Michael Lipton in *Cold Storage*
by Ronald Ribman, directed by Joel Zwick, sets by
Kert Lundell, costumes by Ruth Morley. Photo:
Martha Holmes.

American Place Theatre

The American Place Theatre was founded as a theatre for living American writers by Wynn Handman, Sidney Lanier, Myrna Loy and Michael Tolan at St. Clement's Church in 1964. With its move to a new building in 1971, the theatre has continued its purpose to provide a place, program and stage for American writers who wish to write for the theatre. The selection of writers and their plays is eclectic, covering a broad spectrum of styles, points of view and ethnic origins. This diversity of programming is reflected in the more than 50 plays which have been given full productions in the theatre's 13-year history including William Alfred's *Hogan's Goat*, Robert Lowell's *The Old Glory*, plays by Sam Shepard and Ronald Tavel, the first plays of Ronald Ribman and Steve Tesich. Works by black playwrights Ed Bullins, Ronald Milner, Charlie Russell and Phillip Hayes Dean, Asian-American Frank Chin and by distinguished writers from other media such as Robert Coover, Anne Sexton, Joyce Carol Oates and Bruce Jay Friedman have also been presented at the theatre.

A total program, in a creative environment free of commercial pressure, is sustained, providing each writer with optimum conditions for the growth and realization of his or her work. In addition to each season's four full productions, there are numerous works in progress — from rehearsed readings to fully staged productions without scenery — each specifically designed to serve the particular needs of the writer and the play. The Basement Space Series, begun in 1975, presents plays, generally by young writers experimenting with theatre language and form, that will work well in an informal space. The American Humorist Series, initiated in 1974 with *Jean Shepherd and the America of George Ade*, has subsequently covered the works of Robert Benchley, Donald Barthelme and, most recently, Jules Feiffer. This series presents, as cabaret entertainment in the theatre's Sub-Plot cafe, works adapted from the literary pieces of important American humorists.

In recent years the American Place has expanded its efforts to draw audiences from various sectors of the community. A particular effort has been made to attract college students, who will hopefully be among the audiences of the future. To aid in this effort, the 13-year "membership only" policy of the American Place was modified in the spring of 1977 to include single-ticket sales. Other elements demonstrating the theatre's outreach to a wider audience include a ticket subsidy program, post-play discussions, study guides and a college press night. It is hoped that a concerned and knowledgeable audience, reflective of the theatre's diverse community, will participate in the whole process of contemporary theatre to the mutual benefit of both artist and audience member alike.

Programs & Services: *Training apprenticeships; performances for students; children's theatre; staged readings; booked-in events; student, senior citizen and group discount ticket programs; free ticket distribution; benefit performances; APT Sponsor Club; bar; post-performance discussions; workshop productions of in-progress pieces.*

WYNN HANDMAN
Director
JULIA MILES
Associate Director

111 West 46th Street
New York, New York 10036
Telephone (212) 246-3730
Box Office (212) 247-0393

Founded 1964
Wynn Handman, Michael Tolan,
Sidney Lanier, Myrna Loy

Season
September - June

Schedule
Evenings
Tuesday - Sunday
Matinees
Wednesday & Saturday

Facilities
Seating capacity 299
Stage Flexible

Budget
July 1, 1976 - June 30, 1977
Operating budget $663,856
Earned income $295,787
Unearned income $231,779

Audience
Percent of capacity 75
Number of subscribers 6,330

Touring contact
Julia Miles

Booked-in events
Children's theatre, foreign theatre productions

Operates on AEA special contract.

Productions, 1975-76

Long Day's Journey Into Night, Eugene O'Neill
An Enemy of the People, Henrik Ibsen;
translated, John Patrick Vincent;
adapted, Zelda Fichandler
Once in a Lifetime, Moss Hart &
George S. Kaufman
The Tot Family, Istvan Orkeny; music,
Robert Dennis
Heartbreak House, George Bernard Shaw
Waiting for Godot, Samuel Beckett
Dandelion Wine, Ray Bradbury; adapted,
Peter John Bailey; music, Vance Sorrells
Death of a Salesman, Arthur Miller
The Front Page, Ben Hecht & Charles
MacArthur
Our Town, Thornton Wilder

Productions, 1976-77

Saint Joan, George Bernard Shaw
Saturday Sunday Monday, Eduardo de Filippo;
translated, Keith Waterhouse & Willis Hall
Streamers, David Rabe
The Autumn Garden, Lillian Hellman
Catsplay, Istvan Orkeny; adapted,
Clara Gyorgyey; music, Robert Dennis
The Lower Depths, Maxim Gorky;
translated, Kitty Hunter-Blair &
Jeremy Brooks
A History of the American Film,
Christopher Durang; music, Mel Marvin
Forever Yours, Marie-Lou, Michel Tremblay;
translated, John Van Burek & Bill Glassco
Play and *That Time* and *Footfalls,* Samuel
Beckett

Max Wright and Howard Witt in Beckett's *Waiting for Godot,* directed by Gene Lesser, sets by Ming Cho Lee, costumes by Marjorie Slaiman. Photo: Alton Miller.

The cast of *A History of the American Film* by Christopher Durang, directed by David Chambers, sets by Tony Straiges, costumes by Marjorie Slaiman. Photo: Joe B. Mann.

Arena Stage

The story of Arena Stage's growth since its inception in 1950 parallels the story of America's regional cultural awakening, as nonprofit professional theatres were created by the people of one city after another across the United States and Canada. Arena is one of a very few American theatre institutions that has enjoyed continuity of leadership. The artistic and philosophic point of view of the theatre has been molded since the beginning by its co-founder and producing director, Zelda Fichandler, a pioneer in the development of regional theatre.

New American plays, premieres of important European plays, plays from the past re-embodied in vivid modern interpretations, recent plays that proved financially unsuccessful in the commercial theatre but can be given new life are presented in Arena's three modern, intimate playhouses which, in different forms, were designed to give fresh imagination to the theatrical experience. A nucleus acting company is supplemented by actors from around the country who come for one or more plays each season. Ms. Fichandler directs one or more productions each season and directors such as Alan Schneider, Edwin Sherin, Edward Payson Call, Gene Lesser, Mel Shapiro, David Chambers, Martin Fried and Romania's Liviu Ciulei have served as Arena resident or guest directors.

The Arena began in the Hippodrome, an old movie house, where 55 productions were presented in the first five years. During this period, Arena Stage learned much about the rediscovered arena form, which proved economically and artistically suited to twentieth-century American theatre. Directors, designers, actors and audiences were attracted to this "modern" theatre shape, with its simplicity, immediacy and audience involvement, which offered a major departure from the footlights and elevated distance of commercial proscenium stages.

Soon the potential income from a 247-seat house proved too small to support production costs, and a new home was found at an old brewery, which became known as the Old Vat. The theatre had 500 seats and 40 productions were presented there from 1955 through 1960. When the Old Vat was slated for demolition, architect Harry Weese was selected to work with Zelda Fichandler on designing a new theatre based on the direct experience of an existing theatre company. It is the only dramatic playhouse in the country to be built as a total arena. All facilities were designed from the pooled knowledge of people who had pioneered in the development of the arena form. The new 827-seat theatre opened in 1961, and a second stage, the Kreeger Theater, also designed by Mr. Weese, opened in 1971. Its flexible endstage and 514-seat, fan-shaped house is a striking contrast to the Arena. In 1976, an intimate 160-seat cabaret theatre, dubbed the Old Vat Room after Arena's previous home, was opened in the Kreeger basement for the production of experimental works and musicals.

In 1973, Arena Stage was the first American theatre to represent the United States in the Soviet Union, where it presented productions of *Our Town* and *Inherit the Wind*. Arena's production of *The Madness of God* was seen on PBS-TV's *Theater in America* series in 1975. In 1976, Arena became the first theatre outside New York to receive a special Tony Award for theatrical excellence, an award that reflects the commercial theatre world's increasing respect for and dependence on regional theatre. During the same year, Arena launched a new playwrights series called "In The Process," to allow young writers to develop their craft in a creative environment free of commercial pressure. Since 1965 Arena has also housed and supported the Living Stage, an improvisational community outreach company.

Programs & Services: *Internships; student performances; Living Stage, performances and workshops; In The Process, new play series; student, senior citizen and group discounts; auction; benefits; playwright-in-residence; volunteers; subscriber newsletter; Arena Stage Associates, support group; post-performance discussions.*

ZELDA FICHANDLER
Producing Director
THOMAS C. FICHANDLER
Executive Director
DAVID CHAMBERS
Associate Producing Director

6th and Maine Avenue, SW
Washington, DC 20024
Telephone (202) 554-9066
Box Office (202) 554-7890

Founded 1950
Zelda Fichandler, Edward Mangum,
Thomas C. Fichandler

Season
October – June

Schedule
Evenings
Tuesday – Sunday
Matinees
Saturday

Facilities
Arena Stage
Seating capacity 827
Stage Arena
Kreeger Theater
Seating capacity 514
Stage Endstage
Old Vat Room
Seating capacity 160
Stage Cabaret

Budget
July 1, 1976 – June 30, 1977
Operating budget $2,052,443
Earned income $1,113,069
Unearned income $ 859,804

Audience
Percent of capacity 92
Number of subscribers 16,800

Touring contact
Robert Alexander, Director
Living Stage

Operates on AEA LORT (B) contract.

Productions, 1975–76

The Dybbuk, S. Ansky; adapted, John Hirsch
The Sunshine Boys, Neil Simon
Rashomon, Ryunosuke Akutagawa; adapted,
Fay & Michael Kanin
Diamond Studs, Jim Wann & Bland Simpson
The Sea Horse, Edward J. Moore
The Devil's Disciple, George Bernard Shaw

Productions, 1976–77

In Fashion, Jon Jory; music,
Jerry Blatt; lyrics, Lonnie Burstein
Sizwe Bansi Is Dead, Athol Fugard, John Kani,
Winston Ntshona
Ah, Wilderness!, Eugene O'Neill
Hamlet, William Shakespeare
Vanities, Jack Heifner
*Jacques Brel Is Alive and Well and Living in
Paris,* Jacques Brel, Eric Blau, Mort Shuman

Lowell Harris, Nancy Booth and Virginia Lee in *In
Fashion* by Jon Jory, Jerry Blatt and Lonnie
Burstein, directed by David Pursley, sets by Reagan
Cook, costumes by Sandra Mourey. Photo: Tim
Fuller.

Robert Delegall and Zakes Mokae in *Sizwe Bansi Is
Dead* by Athol Fugard, John Kani and Winston
Ntshona, directed by Dean Irby, sets by John
Walker & Cynthia Beeman, costumes by Sandra
Mourey. Photo: Tim Fuller.

Arizona Civic Theatre

The Arizona Civic Theatre was founded in 1966 by Sandy Rosenthal, with a 10-year goal of establishing a fully professional resident theatre in the Southwest. Over this 10-year period, ACT developed from a community theatre, to a middle stage as a semiprofessional organization using actors on Equity Guest Artist contracts and, finally, to a fully professional company of actors, designers, directors and administrators. In 1973, ACT moved its base of operation to a 526-seat theatre in the Tucson Community Center. The 1976-77 season, celebrating a decade of production and the achievement of the theatre's original goal, brought forth new plans to strengthen the institutional base of the organization in its second decade.

The artistic goals of the next 10 years will concentrate on the development of a resident acting company; the increased production of plays by Shakespeare, Shaw and other classical authors; and the showcasing of work by new American playwrights, particularly those from the Southwest. A growing number of actors, directors and designers who have worked at the theatre in the past will provide a foundation for the formation of an ensemble company. Based on a number of successful experiments in the past five years, the ensemble will aid in the further development of plans for in-school workshops and a second performing space. These programs will serve to broaden ACT's audience and help to establish ACT's identity as integral to the cultural life of the community.

The 1976-77 season included productions of *Hamlet* and *Sizwe Bansi Is Dead* which, in a sense, reflected the dual artistic direction of the future — a respect for the literature of the past and an awareness of contemporary writing. The enthusiastic response of the community, and especially of the student audiences, to this new direction has led to the development of the Encompass program, which provides training in theatre arts for all ages, as well as trips by the theatre's actors, designers and directors to various community centers. In 1977, ACT began a limited summer season operating a small dinner theatre at the Doubletree Inn in Tucson. The success of this program, which presented *Vanities*, has enabled ACT to plan on a full summer season in future years.

In 1977-78, ACT will be in residence at the Scottsdale Center in the nearby city of Phoenix, a first step toward its goal of becoming Arizona's "state theatre."

Programs & Services: *Performances and workshops for students; special workshops on specific aspects of production; student, senior citizen and group discounts; free ticket program; Arizona Civic Theatre Guild, volunteers; ACT Newsletter; seminar series.*

SANDY ROSENTHAL
Producing Director
DAVID HAWKANSON
Managing Director

120 West Broadway
Tucson, Arizona 85701
Telephone (602) 884-8210
Box Office (602) 622-2823

Founded 1966
Sandy Rosenthal

Season
November – April

Schedule
Evenings
Tuesday – Sunday
Matinees
Varies

Facilities
Seating capacity 526
Stage Proscenium

Budget
July 1, 1976 – June 30, 1977
Operating budget $392,655
Earned income $200,602
Unearned income $198,535

Audience
Percent of capacity 60
Number of subscribers 2,635

Operates on AEA LORT (C) contract.

Productions, 1975–76

The New York Idea, Langdon Mitchell
Hogan's Goat, William Alfred
Going Ape, Nick Hall
Boy Meets Girl, Bella & Samuel Spewack
A Streetcar Named Desire, Tennessee Williams
The Quibbletown Recruits, Eberle Thomas
The Music Man, Meredith Willson
Look Homeward, Angel, Thomas Wolfe;
adapted, Ketti Frings
Win With Wheeler, Lee Kalcheim

Productions, 1976–77

The Ruling Class, Peter Barnes
Mummer's End, Jack Gilhooley
Cat on a Hot Tin Roof, Tennessee Williams
The Waltz of the Toreadors, Jean Anouilh;
translated, Lucienne Hill
Desire Under the Elms, Eugene O'Neill
My Love to Your Wife, Brian McFadden;
music, John Franceschina
Cyrano de Bergerac, Edmond Rostand;
translated, Brian Hooker
Saturday Sunday Monday, Eduardo de Filippo;
translated, Keith Waterhouse & Willis Hall
Cromwell, David Storey
Knock Knock, Jules Feiffer
The Sea Horse, Edward J. Moore
Oh Coward!, Noel Coward; devised,
Roderick Cook
Two for the Seesaw, William Gibson
Serenading Louie, Lanford Wilson

Isa Thomas and Stephen Van Benschoten in *Look Homeward, Angel* by Ketti Frings, directed by Richard G. Fallon, sets by Robert C. Barnes, costumes by Catherine King. Photo: Gary Sweetman.

Members of the cast of *Cromwell* by David Storey, directed by Richard G. Fallon, sets by Robert C. Barnes, costumes by Catherine King. Photo: Gary Sweetman.

Asolo State Theater

The Asolo State Theater is one of a very few theatres in this country to operate on a true British repertory system. Since its founding 17 years ago, Asolo has been committed, by choice as well as demographic necessity, to a full season of rotating repertory with a resident company whose members are engaged for an entire season. The full acting company assembles for the commencement of rehearsals in mid-January and remains intact throughout the more than 220 performances of Asolo's nine-play resident season which closes Labor Day eve, more than seven-and-a-half months later. Directors, designers, choreographers and musicians are frequently brought in for individual productions, but actors each play in six of the nine shows. Casting exigencies in this kind of operation assume more than usual prominence in the choice of repertoire. Economics and the productive and efficient utilization of actors are of prime importance.

Demands at Asolo on the performers' versatility are extraordinary, where in a single season, actors confront a range of stylistic challenges. If the actor in meeting these challenges is expected to give uncommonly of himself, he can expect to flourish uncommonly in return. Working in an increasingly well-tuned and stable ensemble, fueled by the best texts available and by an unusual variety of directorial techniques and points of view, the actor at Asolo is able to concentrate on work and personal growth to a degree which is unusual in the American theatre experience. At its best, Asolo, like its "British rep" equivalents, prides itself not only on the entertainment and enrichment value of its productions, but equally on its capacity to develop talent. This development extends beyond its professional company to the students enrolled in the Asolo/Florida State University Conservatory of Acting, which offers an intensive two-year training program leading to a Master of Fine Arts degree. After two or three seasons — even one, in fact — of continuous repertory, the actor begins to find the bottom of his breath, both as an artist and as a human being.

Asolo selects the plays which make up its repertoire with a mind to the broadest eclecticism, and with the conviction that shows that are the most challenging to actors, and offer them the greatest potential for growth and development, prove to be shows that are preeminently charged with excitement, dense in experience and generative of meaningful perceptions.

Programs & Services: *FSU/Asolo Conservatory in Professional Actor Training; MFA programs in technical theatre, directing and management; Theater for Young People, by conservatory students; student discounts; Asolo Theater Festival Associates, support group; Glad Tidings, bimonthly newsletter.*

RICHARD G. FALLON
Executive Director
ROBERT STRANE
Artistic Director
HOWARD J. MILLMAN
Managing Director

P.O. Drawer E
Sarasota, Florida 33578
Telephone (813) 355-7115
Box Office (813) 355-2771

Founded 1960
Arthur Dorlag, Richard G. Fallon,
L. Eberle Thomas, Robert Strane

Season
February – September

Schedule
Evenings
Tuesday – Sunday
Matinees
Tuesday, Wednesday, Saturday

Facilities
Asolo Theater
Ringling Museums
5401 Bayshore Road
Seating capacity 320
Stage Proscenium
Asolo Stage Two
1247 First Street
Seating capacity 185
Stage ¾ Arena

Budget
Oct 1, 1976 – Sept 30, 1977
Operating budget $929,301
Earned income $531,273
Unearned income $347,865

Audience
Percent of capacity 97
Number of subscribers 3,500

Operates on AEA LORT (C) contract.

Productions, 1975-76
A Raisin in the Sun, Lorraine Hansberry
Payments, Martin Duberman
Doomed Love, Bruce Serlen
The Taking of Miss Janie, Ed Bullins

Productions, 1976-77
Woyzeck, Georg Buchner; translated,
Kim Peter Kovac & Henrietta Schatz
Design for Living, Noel Coward
Small Craft Warnings, Tennessee Williams
Short Eyes, Miguel Pinero
Gandhiji, Rose L. Goldemberg
The Sun Always Shines for the Cool, Miguel Pinero

James Knight as Gandhi in *Gandhiji* by Rose Leiman
Goldemberg, directed by Kim Peter Kovac, sets by
Mr. Kovac, costumes by Pat Presley. Photo: Diem
M. Jones.

Cast of *Short Eyes* by Miguel Pinero, directed by
Fredric Lee, sets by Ted Ciganik. Photo: Diem M.
Jones.

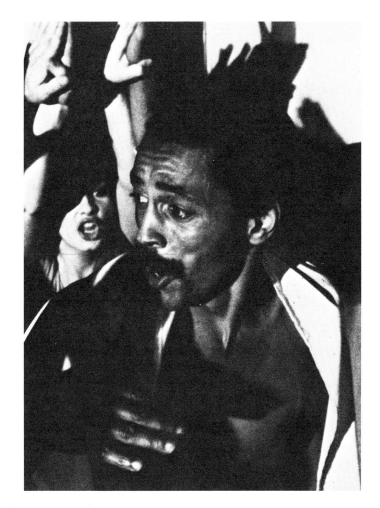

Back Alley Theatre

The Back Alley Theatre, Inc., was founded by Naomi Eftis in 1967, in the back alley of her home in Washington, D.C. Since 1967 it has served the interests of a variety of minority and ethnic performing artists and groups in the Washington area. The objective of Back Alley, now as in the past, is to encourage the development of an art program, based upon artistic standards of excellence, that derives its inspiration from the culture of its community's ethnic groups.

Since its inception, the Back Alley has sponsored programs in theatre arts for community residents seeking career training. These programs are designed to give directors, actors, playwrights, technicians and other theatre artists an opportunity to work together to develop their individual talents. Some of the existing programs include ACTTEEN, a performing company of teenagers; SAGE (Society for the Artistic Growth of the Elderly), a cross-generation performance group; Works-In-Progress, a program for new playwrights; master and beginning acting classes.

One of Back Alley's principal goals is to make quality theatre available to those community members who might otherwise never be exposed to it. Through the years grant support has come from the Strong, Stern, Meyer and Cafritz foundations, the Ford Foundation, the National Endowment for the Arts, the D.C. Commission on the Arts and Humanities, the D.C. Department of Manpower and other agencies on the local and federal level.

The theatre has had a long history of "firsts." In 1972, Back Alley was the recipient of three local Emmy Awards for the premier performance of Bill Gunn's *Johnnas*, a play produced for WRC-TV (NBC). Back Alley was the first Washington theatre to present continuous runs of plays based on the black experience and to cast traditional plays multiracially. Back Alley pioneered tours for children and adults through the National Park Service's Summer In The Parks program and created the Teatro Doble Spanish-English Theatre for children, to respond to the needs of the growing Spanish-speaking population in the Washington area. Back Alley also initiated the Focus Series, a group of productions combining dramatic presentations of social issues with audience discussions. In addition, Back Alley has emphasized Washington-area and world premieres of contemporary plays by minority playwrights.

Due to the diversity of its programs, Back Alley has been able to provide its artists with a freedom of expression which has helped contribute to the theatre's growth and development. Through this freedom Back Alley has created a viable outlet for new playwrights, directors, actors and other theatre artists. In spite of its growing pains, Back Alley has survived and its multifaceted program has emerged as a thriving and unique concept which serves the needs of aspiring theatre artists as well as its community.

Programs & Services: *ACTTEEN, teenage performing company; SAGE, cross-generation acting company; master classes; technical theatre training; playwriting internships; drama criticism workshops; karate courses; Works-In-Progress; playwright residencies; free performances for students; informal lunchtime discussions; student, senior citizen and group discount ticket programs; free ticket program; booked-in events; benefit performances; member of United Black Fund, fund-raising for minority organizations; Another Voice, alternative drama criticism; post-performance discussions with playwrights.*

NAOMI EFTIS
Producing Director

617 F Street, NW
Washington, DC 20001
Telephone (202) 638-2181
Box Office (202) 723-2040

Founded 1967
Naomi Eftis

Season
October – July

Schedule
Evenings
Thursday – Sunday

Facilities
Studio
Seating capacity 60–70
Stage Flexible
Playhouse
1365 Kennedy Street, NW
Seating capacity 94
Stage Thrust

Budget
Oct 1, 1976 – Sept 30, 1977
Operating budget $125,821
Earned income $ 20,725
Unearned income $102,748

Audience
Studio
Percent of capacity 52
Playhouse
Percent of capacity 71

Touring contact
Naomi Eftis

Booked-in events
Mime, experimental theatre and dance companies

Productions, 1976

The New York Idea, Langdon Mitchell
The Three Sisters, Anton Chekhov;
translated, Stark Young

Rene Auberjonois and Blythe Danner in *The New York Idea* by Langdon Mitchell, directed by Frank Dunlop, sets by William Ritman, costumes by Nancy Potts. Photo: Martha Swope.

Rosemary Harris, Tovah Feldshuh and Ellen Burstyn in *The Three Sisters* by Chekhov, directed by Frank Dunlop, sets by William Ritman, costumes by Nancy Potts. Photo: Martha Swope.

BAM Theatre Company

When England's Young Vic Company's productions of *Scapino* and *The Taming of the Shrew* were playing at the Brooklyn Academy of Music (BAM), Frank Dunlop, founder of the Young Vic, explored with BAM's executive director, Harvey Lichtenstein, the possibility of founding a repertory company which would have its headquarters and play at BAM.

The result of their combined efforts was the formation of the BAM Theatre Company in the fall of 1976. The company has one basic goal: the formation of an ensemble of the best American actors doing the best plays. The selections for the first season were *The New York Idea* and *The Three Sisters*, one a rarely seen American play and one a great classic. Many of the members of the initial company, which included Rene Auberjonois, Ellen Burstyn, Stephen Collins, Blythe Danner, Denholm Elliott, Tovah Feldshuh, Margaret Hamilton, Rosemary Harris, Barnard Hughes, Austin Pendleton and Rex Robbins, appeared in both of the theatre's premier productions. The small administrative and production staff included veterans from some of the major American repertory theatres.

In its second season, the company will increase both the number of plays it produces and the length of its performing season, with the goal of a year-round season of plays, presented at BAM and at other theatrical centers both in the United States and abroad. In that way, a company can grow, and actors will have the opportunity to work together doing good plays, both new and old.

Programs & Services: *Student, senior citizen and group discount ticket programs.*

FRANK DUNLOP
Director
BERENICE WEILER
Administrative Director
HARVEY LICHTENSTEIN
Executive Director, BAM

Brooklyn Academy of Music
30 Lafayette Avenue
Brooklyn, New York 11217
Telephone (212) 636-4156
Box Office (212) 636-4100

Founded 1976
Frank Dunlop &
Harvey Lichtenstein

Season
February – June

Schedule
Evenings
Tuesday – Sunday
Matinees
Saturday & Sunday

Facilities
Helen Carey Playhouse
Seating capacity 1,078
Stage Proscenium

Budget
July 1, 1976 – June 30, 1977
Operating budget $498,944
Earned income $242,697
Unearned income $256,247

Audience
Percent of capacity 80
Number of subscribers 8,763

*Operates on AEA Production
contract.*

Productions, 1976
You Can't Take It with You, George S. Kaufman
& Moss Hart
The Diary of Anne Frank, Frances Goodrich &
Albert Hackett
Ten Nights in a Barroom, William W. Pratt;
adapted, Fred Carmichael
Biography, S.N. Behrman
The Glass Menagerie, Tennessee Williams
The Threepenny Opera, Bertolt Brecht
& Kurt Weill
Democracy, Romulus Linney
The Matchmaker, Thornton Wilder
Relatively Speaking, Alan Ayckbourn
Sweet Mistress, Ira Wallach; music,
David Spangler; lyrics, Susan Dias
Beyond the Fringe, Allen Bennett,
Peter Cook, Jonathan Miller, Dudley
Moore; arranged, Dorothy Marie

Productions, 1977
The Matchmaker, Thornton Wilder
The Taming of the Shrew, William Shakespeare
Relatively Speaking, Alan Ayckbourn
All My Sons, Arthur Miller
Hay Fever, Noel Coward
The Playboy of the Western World,
John Millington Synge
Man with a Load of Mischief, John Clifton
& Ben Tarver
Bubba, Sam Havens
The Mousetrap, Agatha Christie
Never Too Late, Sumner Arthur Long

Dorothy Marie and Robert Rutland in *The
Threepenny Opera* by Brecht and Weill, directed by
John Going, sets by Bennet Averyt, costumes by
Sigrid Insull. Photo: Larry White.

Members of the company of *The Matchmaker* by
Thornton Wilder, directed by Rex Partington, sets
by Bennet Averyt, costumes by Sigrid Insull. Photo:
Larry White.

Barter Theatre

The Barter Theatre is recognized as Virginia's state theatre and its many activities, including production, touring, training and community service, operate on the ideal of providing quality theatre in an exciting cultural environment. Located in a town of fewer than 5,000 inhabitants, the Barter was founded at the height of the Great Depression by Robert Porterfield, an enterprising young actor. Faced with the darkened marquees of Broadway, he conceived of the unique idea that became the Barter Theatre. Mr. Porterfield, joined by 22 other actors, arrived in Abingdon in the spring of 1933 and advertised that their plays could be seen "for 30¢ or the equivalent in produce." This plan of allowing people to barter produce for tickets was an innovative success and resulted in a unique theatre operation which was a forerunner in the decentralization of the arts in this country. In 1972, following the death of Robert Porterfield, Rex Partington was selected as the artistic director/producer of the Barter. Placing a primary emphasis on quality, he guides Barter's growth as an ensemble repertory company in producing drama of merit from a wide range of theatrical styles and periods.

Barter is a true regional theatre, serving the five-state area of Virginia, Tennessee, North Carolina, West Virginia and Kentucky. In addition to producing plays the Barter provides its community with many other services: the summer children's theatre in Barter's small Playhouse; production clinics for public school drama teachers and community theatre personnel; workshops on a variety of topics; a speakers bureau; and the free Theatre Lore series, a discussion program between Barter's resident theatre professionals and the public.

With a resident company augmented by guest performers, directors and designers, Barter performs in Abingdon from April through October, producing eight or nine plays on the main stage and several works in progress at the Playhouse. At least one new play or musical is included in the mainstage repertoire, while the Works-In-Progress program gives new playwrights an opportunity to see and revise their work in rehearsal, then watch the piece grow during the production period.

Touring has always been an important part of Barter's program. In 1949 the Barter production of *Hamlet* was chosen to represent the United States at Kronborg Castle in Elsinore, Denmark. Touring remains an integral part of Barter's overall operation with one or two mainstage productions touring regionally, and if feasible, nationally, each spring. The Artists-In-Schools residency/tour provides plays and workshops in educational environments, and short-term residencies of up to 13 weeks are also arranged for the company.

Barter offers two-year internships in professional theatre to bridge the gap between academic theatre and the professional theatre world. Ten interns are selected, through the audition process, and receive room, board, as well as training and the opportunity to perform in Playhouse productions. Barter also maintains a summer apprenticeship program for students 18 years and older. Admission to the Barter Playhouse, located across the street from the main theatre, is still by donation of cash or produce, thus keeping alive the barter tradition.

Programs & Services: *Barter Apprentice Ensemble, productions for young audiences; touring; production clinics for drama teachers; two-year internships; performances for students; artists-in-schools residencies; consultants and speakers bureau; New American Plays and Works-In-Progress programs; Theatre Lore Series, public discussions with artists in residence; student and group discount ticket programs; Friends of Barter, support organization; playwright residencies; post-performance symposia.*

REX PARTINGTON
Artistic Director/Producer

P.O. Box 867
Abingdon, Virginia 24210
Telephone (703) 628-2281
Box Office (703) 628-3991

Founded 1933
Robert Porterfield

Season
April – October

Schedule
Evenings
Tuesday – Sunday
Matinees
Wednesday & Saturday

Facilities
Theatre
Seating capacity 380
Stage   Proscenium
Playhouse
Seating capacity 100
Stage ¾ Arena

Budget
Nov 1, 1975 – Oct 31, 1976
Operating budget $510,719
Earned income $282,645
Unearned income $103,822

Audience
Theatre
Percent of capacity 61
Number of subscribers 5,317

Touring contact
Pearl Hayter

Booked-in events
*Virginia Highlands
Arts and Crafts Festival*

*Operates on AEA LORT (C)
contract.*

Productions, 1975–76
Seven Keys to Baldpate, George M. Cohan
The Iceman Cometh, Eugene O'Neill
Arsenic and Old Lace, Joseph Kesselring
Cat on a Hot Tin Roof, Tennessee Williams
Of Mice and Men, John Steinbeck
Yankee Doodle, Douglas Johnson; music,
John Aschenbrenner
Rope, Patrick Hamilton
The Importance of Being Earnest, Oscar Wilde

Productions, 1976–77
Candida, George Bernard Shaw
Bus Stop, William Inge
Twelfth Night, William Shakespeare
The Philanthropist, Christopher Hampton
Mann Ist Mann, Bertolt Brecht; translated,
Roderic Prindle; adapted, Michael Leibert
The Country Wife, William Wycherley
Private Lives, Noel Coward
Our Town, Thornton Wilder

Linda Lee Johnson and Douglas Johnson in Noel
Coward's *Private Lives*, directed by George Kovach,
sets by Ron Pratt and Gene Angell, costumes by
Marie Anne Chiment. Photo: David Baer.

Steve Knox, Roderic Prindle and Robert Hirschfeld
in Brecht's *Mann Ist Mann*, directed by Michael
Leibert, sets by Andrew DeShong, costumes by
Diana Smith. Photo: David Baer.

Berkeley Repertory Theatre

The Berkeley Repertory Theatre was founded in 1968 with the hopes of bridging the gap between university, community and professional theatre. The founding theatre members joined both university theatre artists and experienced professional performers, to utilize the expertise and talent of both worlds. With the goal of growing together as artists, came the need to keep the company together a number of years with an emphasis on creating productions as an ensemble. The Berkeley Rep never aspired to be a theatre "school," nor just a mode of employment, but rather, in the best sense of the word, a partnership among actor, director, designer, technician and playwright. This partnership, along with the energy generated between actor and audience, supported by the theatre's intimate performing space, has helped to create a viable artistic venture, successfully fulfilling its goal of 10 years ago.

No longer drawing solely on classical material, the theatre's second decade will see a strong commitment to new works and ideas. Two world premier plays, both written by local playwrights specifically for the company, will mark the tenth season. Newly acquired funding will enable the theatre to bring in guest directors and designers for special productions. The theatre's summer apprentice program, which had modest beginnings, has developed into a major contributor to the theatre's growth. A new and larger board of directors has begun charting goals for seasons ahead. The second decade also brings a move into a new theatre plant. This will provide for more programs, which include touring, a second stage and a year-round apprentice/intern program to train high school and college graduates, through a practical and intensive work experience in professional theatre. It is hoped that the new larger theatre facility will accommodate as well as nourish this active company and continue to attract new and talented members to its ensemble.

Programs & Services: *Summer apprentice program; lecture series; programs in schools; student, senior citizen and group discount ticket programs; free ticket distribution to senior centers and rehabilitation groups; benefit performances; Backstagers, volunteer support organization; Subscriber News, a biannual publication; Tenth Anniversary Book; post-performance discussions.*

MICHAEL W. LEIBERT
Producing Director
MITZI K. SALES
General Manager

2980 College Avenue
Berkeley, California 94705
Telephone (415) 841-6108
Box Office (415) 845-4700

Founded 1968
Michael W. Leibert

Season
September – May

Schedule
Evenings
Tuesday – Sunday
Matinees
Sunday

Facilities
Seating capacity 153
Stage ¾ Arena

Budget
Jan 1, 1976 – Dec 31, 1976
Operating budget $173,321
Earned income $147,187
Unearned income $ 20,635

Audience
Percent of capacity 83
Number of subscribers 4,469

Operates on AEA Bay Area Theatre contract.

Productions, 1976
Smack, Drury Pifer
Beclch, Rochelle Owens
High on Pilet's Bluff, Richard Garlinghouse
Coyote, John O'Keefe
Pontifex, Theodore Roszak; adapted,
Angela Paton; music, Steve Mencher
Kaspar, Peter Handke
Winterspace, Drury Pifer

Productions, 1977
Feedlot, Patrick Meyers
Womansong; adapted, Angela Paton
The Sea, Edward Bond
The IX John Paul, Rick Foster
Three Sons, Richard Lortz
The Caucasian Chalk Circle, Bertolt Brecht;
translated, Eric Bentley; music, Morton Subotnik
Safe House, Nicholas Kazan
Earthworms, Albert Innaurato

Scene from *The Caucasian Chalk Circle* by Bertolt
Brecht, directed by Tony Arn, sets by Mr. Arn,
costumes by Beverly Schor. Photo: Jerry Morse.

Deni Deutsch and Kathryn Howell in *Womansong,*
adapted and directed by Angela Paton. Photo: Jerry
Morse.

Berkeley Stage Company

Berkeley Stage Company, whose primary mission is the production of new plays, was founded in 1974 by Angela Paton, Robert Goldsby and Drury Pifer. Thus far 42 original scripts have been presented, the majority with playwrights in residence, at Berkeley Stage's home, a converted garage named Waystation 99. This space has been used with actors surrounding the audience; with the audience encircling the actors; with the audience on three sides, two sides, the conventional one side; or with no audience/actor separation at all. At present all creative work in the theatre is done for love rather than money — adding strength to Berkeley Stage's ambition to develop a second, larger space where artists can be adequately paid for their labor — hence the name, Waystation. The choice of plays is influenced by the company's interest in the process of the individual writer and his interpreters, rather than a predetermined aesthetic or ideology. All forms have been presented, from naturalism to "image-ism," from nonverbal experiments to plays centered in the complexities of language, from the remembrances of Old West wagon trains to visions of eastern phantasmagoria. As touchstones of excellence Berkeley Stage has also produced each year one or two major works by the finest writers of the contemporary theatre, including plays by Beckett, Bond, Brecht, Handke and Rabe. The company's first anniversary was celebrated on two continents with Berkeley Stage actors performing in Italy at the Venice Biennale in David Rabe's *Sticks and Bones*, while Brecht's *Good Woman of Setzuan* was being presented in Berkeley.

Illustrating the growth of this company as a theatre devoted to new writers and the continued exposure of their work, a new production of *The People vs. Inez Garcia*, by Rena Down, went from Berkeley Stage's 99 seats to thousands of nationwide TV viewers through the Public Broadcasting System; Patrick Meyers' *Feedlot*, discovered in Berkeley Stage's Playwrights Workshop and later performed as a major production, will go to New York audiences through the Circle Repertory Company's 1977-78 production; and creating an invigorating crosscurrent, Berkeley Stage will present in 1977-78, Albert Innaurato's *Earthworms*, coproduced with the New York Shakespeare Festival.

Other activities fostering new work include a Wednesday night series of one-acts presented to the public for 99 cents. These are chosen by actors and directors who have earned a place in the company by working on mainstage productions. Whenever possible throughout the year, plays still in draft form are given readings in the Playwrights Workshop. The major outreach program of Berkeley Stage Company is Poetry Playhouse, a creation of Angela Paton and Barbara Wolfinger. This program employs eight actors who take several theatrical performances of poetry into every Berkeley elementary classroom. Like the theatre, this federally supported program is entering its fourth year.

Programs & Services: *Wednesday One-Acts; performances and post-performance discussions for students; Playwrights Workshop, workshop productions and staged readings; Poetry Playhouse, poetry dramatizations for children; booked-in events; student, senior citizen and special group discount ticket programs; free ticket program; playwright residencies; Berkeley Stage Notes, subscriber newsletter.*

ROBERT GOLDSBY
ANGELA PATON
Artistic Directors
ROSSI SNIPPER
General Manager

P.O. Box 2327
Berkeley, California 94702
(415) 548-4728

Founded 1974
Robert Goldsby, Angela Paton,
Drury Pifer

Season
January – December

Schedule
Evenings
Wednesday – Sunday

Facilities
1111 Addison Street
Seating capacity 99
Stage   Flexible

Budget
Jan 1, 1976 – Dec 31, 1976
Operating budget $138,401
Earned income $ 20,380
Unearned income $132,327

Audience
Percent of capacity 50
Number of subscribers 585

*Operates under AEA
99–Seat Waiver.*

Productions, 1975-76
Alice in Wonderland, Lewis Carroll;
adapted, A.J. Russell, Joseph
Raposo, Sheldon Harnick
Winnie the Pooh, A.A. Milne; adapted,
A.J. Russell; music, Jack Brooks

Productions, 1976-77
Davy Jones' Locker, Arthur Birnkrant
& Waldo Salt; music, Mary Rodgers

The Duchess from *Alice in Wonderland* by Lewis
Carroll, adapted by A.J. Russell, Joseph Raposo and
Sheldon Harnick, directed by Paul Leaf, sets by
Howard Mandel. Photo: John Hart.

The Mad Hatter's tea party from *Alice in
Wonderland.* Photo: Nat Messik.

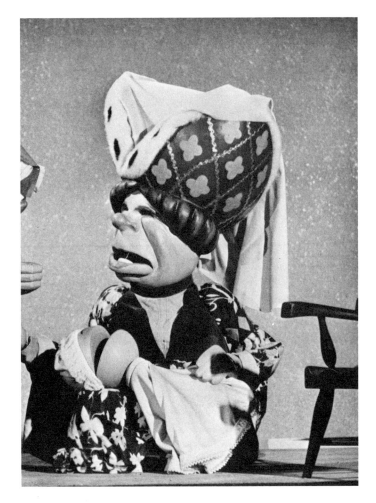

Bil Baird Theater

Since the theatre opened on Christmas Day in 1966, the puppetry of Bil Baird, in collaboration with such accomplished theatre artists as Sheldon Harnick, Burt Shevelove, E.Y. Harburg and Mary Rodgers, has created a unique children's theatre that is enjoyed by adults and children alike. To date the audience has numbered over a quarter-million, and for many children, Mr. Baird's productions are their first experience with theatre.

Created to preserve the special genius of puppet theatre, the company is housed in a unique facility on Barrow Street, in New York's Greenwich Village. On the ground floor is a special 194-seat theatre with a marionette bridge, a pit for rod and hand puppets and three playing areas. Upstairs are studios, storage space and three separate workshops for building puppets.

During its annual New York season, the company plays eight performances each week — four performances for school groups during the week and four shows for the general public on weekends. Prices for tickets are low to moderate on weekends and always low for school groups during the week. Groups from disadvantaged neighborhoods, or groups from schools for children with learning disabilities, often pay nothing at all. In this way the shows are kept accessible to children in all economic groups.

As a result of this policy, ticket income is never sufficient to cover costs, even when supplemented by concession sales and touring fees. The American Puppet Arts Council sponsors the productions at the Bil Baird Theater and raises the funds for expenses not met by earned income. In past years, the American Puppet Arts Council has received contributions and grants from federal and state governments, private foundations, corporations and individuals.

Each season the company presents up to three productions. In past seasons the company has performed its own adaptations of *Pinocchio, Peter and the Wolf, Alice in Wonderland, Ali Baba, Winnie the Pooh,* and *The Wizard of Oz,* in addition to original scripts for children. Although the Bil Baird company will not tour during the 1977–78 season, it has toured extensively in the past. Under the auspices of the New York State Medallion Tour, the company presented three productions and workshop-seminars, which reached more than 20,000 children and adults. The company has also participated in the annual Mid-America Arts Alliance tour, performing throughout Nebraska, Kansas, Oklahoma and Missouri.

Programs & Services: *Internships; performances for students; group ticket discounts; touring.*

BIL BAIRD
Artistic Director
SUSANNA BAIRD
Executive Director

59 Barrow Street
New York, New York 10014
Telephone (212) 989-9840
Box Office (212) 989-7060

Founded 1966
Bil Baird

Season
December – March

Schedule
Matinees
Tuesday – Sunday

Facilities
Seating capacity 194
Stage Proscenium

Budget
July 1, 1976 – June 30, 1977
Operating budget $93,017
Earned income $49,652
Unearned income $48,635

Audience
Percent of capacity 55

Touring contact
Walter Gould
Century Artists Bureau
866 Third Avenue
New York, New York 10022
(212) 752-3920

*Operates on AEA LORT (D)
contract.*

Productions, 1975-76

Philosophers in Skirts, Moliere; translated
& adapted, Kirk Denmark
Orpheus Descending, Tennessee Williams
As I Lay Dying, William Faulkner
Heritage, Thane Gower & Dream Theater
company
Your Own Thing, Tom Driver; music,
Hal Hester & Danny Apolinar

Productions, 1976-77

The Real Inspector Hound and *After
Magritte,* Tom Stoppard
Who's Happy Now, Oliver Hailey
Knock Knock, Jules Feiffer
Johnnie Will, Victor Power

Jack Wallace and Elizabeth Forsyth in *Who's Happy
Now* by Oliver Hailey, directed by Joseph Slowik.
Photo: Bruce R. Schulman.

Steve Marmer, Suzanne Quinlan and Harry Stopek
in *Knock Knock* by Jules Feiffer, directed by
Anthony Petito. Photo: Mark Doyel.

The Body Politic

In 1969, the Community Arts Foundation (CAF) purchased a building on Chicago's famous Lincoln Avenue in order to expand its "community and arts" program by establishing a multi-theatre, multimedia visual arts center. The CAF hoped to provide a space where a relationship could be established between artists and their work and the community. The facility, called the Body Politic, is a complex including three performing spaces, as well as rehearsal and workshop areas. With a major emphasis on theatre as the most immediate way of implementing its program, the Body Politic has housed through the years numerous companies, including William Russo's Free Theater, Paul Sills' Story Theater and James Shiflett's Dream Theater. In its eight-year history, the Body Politic has played an important role in the emergence of a vast, diverse and energetic alternative theatre community in Chicago. Some of its alumni have become internationally known, and its wide range of activity has influenced the plans and careers of a large number of performers, directors and playwrights. As a place "where the arts are," the Body Politic also shelters, supports, advises and sustains artists in other fields, including distinguished muralists, dancers, poets and teachers.

In 1976, the Body Politic began a transition from a "complex," acting primarily as a facilitator in the growth and development of a wide range of theatre companies, to a "theatre laboratory." While continuing to house the experimental, explorative and ensemble work of the Dream Theater, the Body Politic created the Body Politic Theatre Laboratory (BPTL). Public performance is the Body Politic Theatre Laboratory's principal focus, but as a *laboratory* it is committed to the development of resident theatre artists by providing a place for training and experience, as well as audience exposure. In its role as an organization dedicated to its community, BPTL provides an opportunity for community members to participate in the laboratory's public classes, workshops and programs, as well as presenting to its audience a wide variety of theatrical experiences.

As part of a vital neighborhood with a remarkably high percentage of people involved in all phases of education, communication and culture, the Body Politic and its personnel are active in festivals, meetings, benefits and a myriad of other affairs consistent with its equal commitment to the community and the arts.

Programs & Services: *Internships; classes in acting, directing, movement, mime and Alexander Technique; Bible Theatre, dramatizations by Dream Theater; Yellow Press Poets, weekly readings; booked-in events; student, senior citizen and group discounts; benefit performances; residencies by theatres at the Body Politic; Friends of the Body Politic, contributors; volunteers.*

JAMES A. SHIFLETT
Executive Director
DALE McFADDEN
Artistic Coordinator

2261 North Lincoln Avenue
Chicago, Illinois 60614
Telephone (312) 525-1052
Box Office (312) 871-3000

Founded 1969
James A. Shiflett

Season
September – August

Schedule
Evenings
Wednesday – Sunday
Matinees
Sunday

Facilities
The Upstairs Theatre
Seating capacity 200
Stage Flexible
The Center Theatre
Seating capacity 150
Stage Thrust
The Little Theatre
Seating capacity 70
Stage Proscenium

Budget
Jan 1, 1976 – Dec 31, 1976
Operating budget $210,000
Earned income $100,000
Unearned income $100,000

Audience
Percent of capacity 51

Booked-in events
Mime, puppet, experimental & children's theatre, dance companies, mixed media events

Productions, 1975-76

Our Town, Thornton Wilder
Ernest in Love, Oscar Wilde; adapted,
Anne Croswell; music, Lee Pockriss
The Imaginary Invalid, Moliere;
translated, John Reich
The Three Sisters, Anton Chekhov
Enrico IV, Luigi Pirandello;
translated, John Reich
What Price Glory?, Laurence Stallings
& Maxwell Anderson
A Very Gentle Person, Hans Steinkellner
A Midsummer Night's Dream, William
Shakespeare

Productions, 1976-77

Hamlet, William Shakespeare
Blithe Spirit, Noel Coward
The Good Woman of Setzuan, Bertolt
Brecht
The Odd Couple, Neil Simon
The Rainmaker, N. Richard Nash
The Innocents, Henry James;
adapted, William Archibald
Rashomon, Ryunosuke Akutagawa;
adapted, Fay & Michael Kanin
Bierce Takes on the Railroad,
Philip A. Bosakowski

Dakin Matthews in Pirandello's *Enrico IV*, directed
by John Reich, sets by Steven Howell, costumes by
Marcia Frederick and Gini Vogel.

Terry Wills and Dakin Matthews in *The Odd Couple*
by Neil Simon, directed by G.W. Bailey, sets by
Ronald Krempetz, costumes by Sarah Godbois.

California Actors Theatre

The California Actors Theatre is a nonprofit professional repertory theatre founded in 1974 by Sheldon Kleinman. The choice of Los Gatos as a location was opportune and logical, yet fraught with potential hazard. The theatre site needed to be in a pleasant, easily reached area, with ample parking and proximity to restaurants. It needed to be an area far enough removed from San Francisco's theatres so that competition was not an issue.

At first glance, the Old Town Theatre in Los Gatos seemed to be a likely prospect, with its quaint Old World atmosphere, charming shops and plentiful restaurants. Lying hazardously beneath the surface, however, was the fact that the previous tenant had been unable to make a financial success of a theatre in that location, with an apathetic community atmosphere as a result. Still, the other factors seemed right and, though the theatre's seating capacity was small, the decision was made to press forward. The theatre felt that, under the circumstances, fund-raising would be difficult and it would have to succeed initially on box office revenue alone, until such time as the stability of the organization was proved. A careful, methodical campaign was launched to sell the community on the idea of the theatre, rather than on individual productions. By opening night in 1974, 4,000 persons had subscribed to the theatre, a figure which was doubled in the subsequent two seasons. In 1977-78, it seems likely that subscribers will reach 9,500 to 10,000 persons, or a virtually sold-out status. When combined with its separate summer audience of nearly 4,000 persons, the theatre's total attendance forms one of the largest performing arts audiences in the Bay Area.

The California Actors Theatre "labors in love" to make this regional company a strong artistic force in its community. Mr. Kleinman, along with artistic director James Dunn, feels that the company is bound together by a single passion — "our love for, faith in and dedication to living theatre. If, in our proselytizing we sound a bit fanatical at times, it's because the making of plays is for us more — much more — than a rather uncertain, surely underpaid career. As Norman Mailer writes in the introduction to his play *The Deer Park*: 'Good plays . . . attempt to find a piece of that most mysterious and magical communion some call ceremony, some church, and some theatre. They are plays which attempt to reach a moment sufficiently magical to live in the deepest nerves and most buried caves of the memory of the people who have seen them; these plays speak of the fire at the edge of the wood and hair rising on the back of the neck when the wind becomes too intimate in its sound.' This is what we intend to do."

Programs & Services: *Performances and workshops for students; OPCAT, staged readings of new plays; student and senior citizen ticket discounts; free ticket program; united arts fund-raising; CAT Lovers, auxiliary; CAT CHAT, quarterly newsletter; What's Happening, public series of lectures, forums and demonstrations.*

SHELDON KLEINMAN
Executive Director
JAMES DUNN
Artistic Director

P.O. Box 1355
Los Gatos, California 95030
Telephone (408) 354-3939
Box Office (408) 354-6057

Founded 1974
Sheldon Kleinman

Season
July – May

Schedule
Evenings
Tuesday – Sunday
Matinees
Varies

Facilities
Old Town Theatre
50 University Avenue
Seating capacity 429
Stage Proscenium

Budget
July 1, 1976 – June 30, 1977
Operating budget $517,040
Earned income $498,578
Unearned income $ 12,931

Audience
Percent of capacity 92
Number of subscribers 8,100

Operates on AEA LORT (C) contract.

Productions, 1975–76
Deathwatch, Jean Genet
Gulliver's Travels, Cambridge Ensemble;
adapted, Joann Green
Judgement, Barry Collins
Best of Chelm, Cambridge Ensemble;
adapted, Joann Green

Productions, 1976–77
Oresteia, Aeschylus; translated,
Robert Fagles; adapted, Joann
Green
The Scarlet Letter, Nathaniel Hawthorne;
adapted, Joann Green
Br'er Rabbit and His Friends, Cambridge
Ensemble; adapted, Joann Green

Gayle Youngman and Tim McDonough in *Oresteia*
by Aeschylus, directed and designed by Joann
Green. Photo: Eric Levenson.

Tsai Chin, David Neill and Tim McDonough in *Br'er
Rabbit and His Friends,* adapted from Uncle Remus
stories, directed and designed by Joann Green.
Photo: Eric Levenson.

The Cambridge Ensemble

The Cambridge Ensemble is a professional resident theatre, dedicated to introducing new playwrights, creating original works and performing adaptations. Founded by Joann Green and Barbara Bregstein in 1973, the theatre was built in the back of a sanctuary in the Old Cambridge Baptist Church at Harvard Square. The theatre seats 120, and the playing space is flexible, thus enabling it to be changed for each production.

In its four-year history, the Cambridge Ensemble has produced 16 plays, among them 6 American premieres and 4 original adaptations of literary works including *Gulliver's Travels* and *The Scarlet Letter*. The two original children's shows, *Tales of Chelm* and *Br'er Rabbit and His Friends*, have been performed free of charge in hospitals and in various school systems. The Ensemble's adaptation of Aeschylus' *Oresteia* was performed in prisons after its successful run at the theatre. In September 1975, the Cambridge Ensemble brought Genet's *Deathwatch* to the Wonderhorse Theatre in New York City, and sold out its six-week engagement there.

In addition to performances, the Ensemble's Acting Workshop Program operates weekly from September to June, and daily for three weeks during the summer months. Director Green and veteran actor Tim McDonough focus the workshops on structured improvisation, physical and vocal training, and character and scene study.

The Ensemble's Touring Program began in 1974 with a limited engagement at La Poudriere Theatre International de Montreal. Since then the company has toured as far west as Denver, and to Toronto, with such productions as *I Came into the World* (originally entitled *Self Accusation*), *Calling for Help* by Peter Handke, *Judgement* by Barry Collins and the original *Gulliver's Travels*. Residencies, which include performances, workshops and discussions with the cast and director, are also offered.

Two guest directors have been invited to work at the theatre: Maxine Klein, who directed her original *Tania*, about the life of Tamara Bunke, the revolutionary; and Peter Sanders, who wrote and directed *Kafka: The World of Parable*. Joann Green has directed and adapted all other Cambridge Ensemble productions. Ms. Green uses improvisation, imagery and modern ensemble explorations to develop concept, script and set. Actors create their own characters and sometimes write their own dialogue. The size of the cast varies from two to seven, and often includes a musician who has composed music for the play.

Programs & Services: *Acting workshops; performances for students; lecture-demonstration series; Educational Theatre Program, children's theatre productions; touring program; free tickets to charitable and social service groups; group discounts and voucher program; membership and patron contribution campaign; post-performance discussions as requested by groups.*

JOANN GREEN
Artistic Director
BARBARA BREGSTEIN
General Manager

1151 Massachusetts Avenue
Cambridge, Massachusetts 02138
Telephone (617) 876-2545
Box Office (617) 876-2544

Founded 1973
Joann Green & Barbara Bregstein

Season
September – June

Schedule
Evenings
Thursday – Saturday

Facilities
Seating capacity 120
Stage   Flexible

Budget
Sept 1, 1976 – Aug 31, 1977
Operating budget $56,035
Earned income $31,090
Unearned income $30,865

Audience
Percent of capacity 85
Number of subscribers 121

Touring contact
John Adams, Daedalus Productions
Box G, West Newton, MA 02165

Productions, 1975–76
Illustrated Sports; adapted, William M. Hardy
& John W. Morrow, Jr.
Appalachia Sounding, Romulus Linney; music,
Jan Davidson & Scotty Collier
The Great American Fourth of July Parade,
Archibald MacLeish

Productions, 1976–77
Appalachia Sounding, Romulus Linney; music,
Jan Davidson & Scotty Collier

Barbara Lea, David Adamson and Gina McMather in
Appalachia Sounding by Romulus Linney, directed
by John W. Morrow, Jr., sets by Mr. Morrow,
costumes by Judy Adamson. Photo: Fred Lloyd.

Company members of *Illustrated Sports* by William
M. Hardy and John W. Morrow, Jr., direction and
sets by Mr. Morrow, costumes by Judy Adamson.
Photo: David Adamson.

Carolina Regional Theatre

The Carolina Regional Theatre, a touring theatre based in Chapel Hill, North Carolina, was founded in 1972, as the Carolina Readers Theatre. The stated purpose of the organization at that time was "to make professional theatre available to *all* communities in North Carolina at an affordable price." The growth CRT exhibited in its first four years led to an expansion of its purpose and, to reflect more accurately CRT's services as a regional touring theatre, its name was changed in 1976 to the Carolina Regional Theatre.

CRT's interest in touring came about because North Carolina is basically a rural state with few population centers. Therefore, in order to attract people to the theatre, it seemed necessary to take the theatre to them. By allowing people to see professional productions in their own communities, the theatre hoped that a theatregoing audience could be developed, thus improving the climate for all performing arts groups in the region.

During its first three years, CRT produced 11 tours which reached 150 public schools and more than 100 adult audiences. In its fourth year, CRT expanded its services to include not only public school and adult performances, but also intensive in-school professional training workshops. The theatre's first regional tour presented performances across the Southeast from Georgia to West Virginia. In 1977, CRT once again expanded its touring boundaries, covering an 11-state region from Mississippi to Pennsylvania. CRT has played for schools, churches, hospitals, arts councils, community theatres, libraries, art museums, state dinners, Governor's awards banquets and several special performances for the North Carolina legislature. In addition, three of CRT's productions have been videotaped and broadcast by the state educational television network, and a fourth production will be broadcast to an 11-state region and possibly nationwide.

As a touring theatre trying to develop audiences, CRT has always attempted to gear its various productions to corresponding target groups, while maintaining widespread appeal. This effort has given emphasis to the production of new works, many of which have been commissioned by CRT. The early "readers-theatre" productions gave rise to the development of new scripts which could be focused for a particular audience, as well as produced for efficient touring. As CRT's budget grew, so did the scope and complexities of its productions. Although the readers-theatre format is no longer characteristic of all of CRT's productions, the emphasis on new works is still a significant element of the theatre's artistic thrust. Of the 15 productions CRT has toured, 12 have been new scripts.

CRT's biggest project to date has been the development and touring of *Appalachia Sounding*, a dramatic tribute to a unique culture. A research project, as well as an artistic one, this production's chief goal was to be as authentic as possible in representing Appalachian history, folkways, music and tradition. Almost a year was spent gathering materials and information. A colloquium of experts on Appalachian history and culture was held to provide for an exchange of ideas and suggestions for the concept of the play. Using this material, Romulus Linney wrote the script for the production which has toured for two seasons. *Appalachia Sounding* was videotaped on location in northern Georgia in June 1977, and is scheduled for a regional broadcast.

Programs & Services: *Touring; student, senior citizen and group ticket discounts; free ticket program;* The CRT Traveller, *quarterly newsletter.*

MARTHA NELL HARDY
Executive Director
JOHN W. MORROW, JR.
Artistic Director
WILLIAM BATES
General Manager

P.O. Drawer 1169
Chapel Hill, North Carolina 27514
(919) 933–5854

Founded 1972
Martha Nell Hardy

Season
October – May

Budget
Oct 1, 1976 – Sept 30, 1977
Operating budget $185,000
Earned income $ 90,000
Unearned income $ 95,000

Touring contact
William Bates

*Operates on AEA LORT (C)
contract.*

Productions, 1975–76
Tartuffe, Moliere; translated, Richard
Wilbur
Busy Bee Good Food All Night Delicious
and *Borders,* Charles Eastman
Dream on Monkey Mountain, Derek Walcott
Old Times, Harold Pinter
The Cherry Orchard, Anton Chekhov
The Real Inspector Hound, Tom Stoppard
Black Comedy, Peter Shaffer

Productions, 1976–77
She Stoops to Conquer, Oliver Goldsmith
When You Comin' Back, Red Ryder?,
Mark Medoff
Misalliance, George Bernard Shaw
Toys in the Attic, Lillian Hellman
The First Breeze of Summer, Leslie Lee
Knock Knock, Jules Feiffer
A Sorrow beyond Dreams, Peter Handke

Bess Armstrong as Joan of Arc in *Knock Knock* by
Jules Feiffer, directed by John Henry Davis, sets by
Charles Cosler, costumes by Elizabeth P. Palmer.
Photo: Richard Anderson.

Deborah Offner and Beeson Carroll in Lillian
Hellman's *Toys in the Attic,* directed by Stanley
Wojewodski, Jr., sets by Peter Harvey, costumes by
Elizabeth P. Palmer. Photo: Richard Anderson.

Center Stage

Center Stage is a theatre which considers quality of production its hallmark; recognizes the need to bring to its audiences well-balanced seasons, including classic, contemporary and innovative theatre productions, as well as programs off the mainstage which provide theatre exposure to audiences who might otherwise be excluded; and provides opportunities, through intern programs and creative workshops, for the development of new talent.

Center Stage was founded in 1963 by a group of Baltimore citizens interested in establishing a permanent, professional theatre in their community. First located in a converted gymnasium in downtown Baltimore, the company moved in 1965 to a renovated cafeteria, where it remained until fire destroyed the facility in 1974. The autumn of 1977 marked the opening of Center Stage's third season in its new location, the Loyola College and Prep School complex in downtown Baltimore. A gift to the theatre from the Jesuit province of Maryland, the facility was renovated at a cost of $1.7 million.

The mainstage season of six plays is structured by artistic director Stanley Wojewodski, Jr., to include classics — both period pieces and modern masterworks — and second productions of works by outstanding contemporary writers. Easy access to New York City makes it possible to supplement a small resident group of actors with those specifically suited to individual productions. Principal Center Stage designers include Peter Harvey and Charles Cosler (sets), Ian Calderon (lighting), and Elizabeth Palmer and Robert Wojewodski (costumes). Close association with such designers stimulates full and varied utilization of existing facilities and insures continuity in the theatre's plans for additional working and performance spaces.

Long conscious of its role in the community beyond its mainstage subscription series, Center Stage's Young People's Theater tours annually, bringing to more than 100,000 students throughout Maryland's 23 counties and in Baltimore City specially developed theatre pieces and classroom performances by individual company members. The internship program for secondary school students, recently developed by Mr. Wojewodski in association with the Maryland Alliance for Arts Education, highlights the unique accessibility of a community-based arts resource to the secondary school curriculum. Performance workshops at the theatre for students and an accredited directing seminar for teachers round out the Young People's Theater activities. During the 1977–78 season, an additional company of five members will join forces with the Young People's Theater to develop original pieces for performance in hospitals, detention homes, prisons, and centers for disabled and older citizens.

The 1977–78 season will mark the beginning of an extensive developmental program for diversified new work, which will eventually be housed in a second flexible theatre space and an outdoor courtyard cabaret. The initial phase will include staged readings and workshop productions, as well as an internship program for local playwrights. Also, during the 1977–78 season, the Public Broadcasting Service will air two teleplays produced by Center Stage in conjunction with the Maryland Center for Public Broadcasting: Herman Melville's *Bartleby the Scrivener*, adapted for television by Israel Horovitz and directed by Mr. Wojewodski, and Diane Johnson's *An Apple, An Orange*, which stars Kathleen Freeman and Beulah Quo and was directed by Jeff Bleckner. Other planned projects include a summer film festival, a dance concert series, and a summer season of three plays in repertory. These programs are moving Center Stage toward its goal of a year-round performance schedule for its Maryland audiences and diverse production challenges for its artists, craftspeople and administrators.

Programs & Services: *Administrative, technical and design interns; Young People's Theater, tours and workshops in schools; summer film series; booked-in events; student and group ticket discounts; free ticket program; benefit performances; cafe and bar; Center Stage Hands, support group; restaurant; Sunday Curtain Call, post-performance discussions.*

STANLEY WOJEWODSKI, JR.
Artistic Director
PETER W. CULMAN
Managing Director

700 North Calvert Street
Baltimore, Maryland 21202
Telephone (301) 685-3200
Box Office (301) 332-0033

Founded 1963
Community arts committee

Season
October – May

Schedule
Evenings
Tuesday – Sunday
Matinees
Wednesday & Sunday

Facilities
Seating capacity 500
Stage   Modified Thrust

Budget
July 1, 1976 – June 30, 1977
Operating budget $820,327
Earned income $495,836
Unearned income $298,117

Audience
Percent of capacity 82
Number of subscribers 9,544

Touring contact
Peter B. England

Operates on AEA LORT (B) contract.

Productions, 1975–76

Dummies and *F-Yoo-Hoo* and *Dragons in the Wall*, Teresa Marffie-Evangelista
Cracks, Martin Sherman
Alferd Packer: A Colorado Ritual, Bob Breuler
Freebies, Neil Yarema
Coupling, Alfred Brooks & Charley George
Webs, Mark Friedman, Ralph Palasek, Stephen Weld; music, Ron Metzger
Music for Crumhorn & Sackbutt and *George & Franz: Taking Sides in the Boer War*, Don Katzman
Requiem...1/1, Pat Rule
The Longest Way Home, Bob Breuler

Productions, 1976–77

Cowgirl Ecstasy, Michael Smith
The Quannapowitt Quartet, Israel Horovitz
The Gift of a Doll, Joseph Baldwin
The Begonia and the Bygones, David E. Lang
Hey, Rube, Janet McReynolds
Stitches, Bo Slocomb, David E. Lang, Jerry Fine, Kathleen Bradley; lyrics, Alan Deans & John Simcox; music, Alfred Brooks & Alan Deans

Ingrid Hagelberg, Stephen Weld, E. Michael Miller and Melanie Kern in Michael Smith's *Cowgirl Ecstasy*, direction and costume design by Mr. Smith, sets by Charles Parson. Photo: Wesley Wada.

Debra Jones and David E. Lang in *The Quannapowitt Quartet: Stage Directions* by Israel Horovitz, directed by Richard Lore, sets by Charles Parson, costumes by Rebecca Hill. Photo: Zorba.

The Changing Scene

During the nine years since its founding in 1968, the Changing Scene has premiered 533 creative works spanning a wide range of artistic disciplines including drama, dance, film, poetry and music as well as productions combining elements from each of these. Presenting an average of 20 programs each season, the theatre has become a center for all of the arts. With each new program, the theatre's lobby is transformed into a gallery presenting one-man shows by local artists. Founded by Maxine Munt and Alfred Brooks, two New York dancers who heeded the call for decentralization, the Changing Scene is the realization of their dream of a theatre unlike any they had known. In the belief that theatre is the natural meeting place for all the arts, they envisioned an environment where sculptors, painters, filmmakers, composers and poets would be as much at home as playwrights, actors, directors, choreographers and designers.

Within the process of providing for the development of work by regional artists, a policy of bringing artists to Denver for residencies continues. Playwrights who have developed and directed their plays in Denver include Michael Smith, Neil Yarema, Walter Hadler and Robert Heide. Dancers, choreographers, poets and filmmakers are also brought to the theatre to share with and help in the development of local artists.

In 1977-78, Alfred Brooks and Maxine Munt will conduct weekly sessions, with invited professionals forming a core group, focusing on physical and vocal warm-ups, improvisations, the reading of new scripts, the exchanging of ideas and the development of new works. In the spring of 1977 three of the Changing Scene's premier works were given New York productions: *Hagar's Children* by Ernest Joselovitz at the Public Theater, Michael Smith's *Cowgirl Ecstasy* by the New York Theater Strategy, and *Cracks* by Martin Sherman at Playwrights Horizons.

Programs & Services: *Developmental theatre workshop; dance training in schools; film, poetry, music, mime and dance programs; free staged readings; group discounts; Friends of The Changing Scene, open forum discussions; playwright residencies; monthly newsletter.*

ALFRED BROOKS
President

1527½ Champa Street
Denver, Colorado 80202
(303) 893-5775

Founded 1968
Alfred Brooks & Maxine Munt

Season
October – September

Schedule
Evenings
Thursday – Sunday

Facilities
Seating capacity 78
Stage   Flexible

Budget
Jan 1, 1976 – Dec 31, 1976
Operating budget $105,477
Earned income $ 16,242
Unearned income $ 90,415

Audience
Percent of capacity 37

Touring contact
Alfred Brooks

Booked-in events
Mime, experimental theatre,
dance, poetry, film

Productions, 1975-76

By Bernstein, Betty Comden &
Adolph Green; music, Leonard
Bernstein; lyrics, Leonard Bernstein,
Betty Comden, Adolph Green, John Latouche,
Jerry Leiber, Stephen Sondheim
The Family, Lodewijk de Boer; translated,
Albert Maurits
Ice Age, Tankred Dorst with Ursula
Ehler; translated, Peter Sander
The Boss, Edward Sheldon
Vanities, Jack Heifner

Productions, 1976-77

The Prince of Homburg, Heinrich von Kleist;
translated, James Kirkup
Lincoln, Saul Levitt
The Crazy Locomotive, Stanislaw Ignacy
Witkiewicz; translated, Daniel C. Gerould
& C.S. Durer
Happy End, Dorothy Lane; lyrics, Bertolt
Brecht; music, Kurt Weill; adapted, Michael
Feingold
Vanities, Jack Heifner

Frank Langella and other cast members of *The
Prince of Homburg* by Heinrich von Kleist, directed
by Robert Kalfin, sets by Christopher Thomas,
costumes by Ruth Morley. Photo: Martha Swope.

Benjamin Rayson, John A. Coe, Raymond Barry,
Christopher Lloyd and Robert Weil in *Happy End* by
Dorothy Lane, Bertolt Brecht and Kurt Weill,
directed by Michael Posnick, sets by Robert U.
Taylor, costumes by Carrie F. Robbins. Photo:
Martha Swope.

Chelsea Theater Center

The Chelsea Theater Center is a *creative* producing organization. It is dedicated to providing an environment in which artists can be at their most vulnerable while taking risks in producing work that either is, or will be, of lasting value — work which ideally can be measured against and counted as a contribution to international dramatic literature. The theatre's staff works with directors in conceiving and evolving physical concepts for productions that will amplify and explode the text. Chelsea often brings together various individuals with the specific aim of stretching their artistic gifts through interaction toward a common artistic goal. Each play itself determines the theatre's approach, affecting everything from rehearsal methods to the redefining of the physical relationship of the audience to the material at hand. The Chelsea Theater Center can be considered chameleonlike in its attempt to function as a living organism whose adaptations are driven by the energy, thrust and goals of the plays it produces.

As a nonprofit institution, the Chelsea's role is that of a service organization relating to its immediate theatrical community as well as to theatres throughout the nation and the world. In order to keep the American theatre abreast of what is theatrically possible elsewhere, the Chelsea feels an obligation to offer work in New York which is neglected by others, and which can have an impact on the American theatre as well as individual theatre artists. The Chelsea has chosen to offer theatrical experiences which are not, and very often cannot be, presented by existing commercial producers and other nonprofit theatre institutions. Play selection is influenced primarily by the aim of achieving artistic fulfillment in the realization of a play's potential, rather than any consideration of material success. The joy is in the work itself, and the fulfillment of the theatre's purpose lies in the struggle to achieve "perfection" in the artistic goals that are set. This desire for perfection includes an idealistic goal — to produce "classics." Toward this goal, the theatre seeks out works of universal lasting value, works that may be remembered long after they've been seen — works which may even influence the thoughts and the souls of men.

Chelsea looks for plays which have the possibility of becoming classics because of their intrinsic value as contributions to world dramatic literature. The Chelsea is interested in theatre as part of the humanities as well as of the arts — theatre that is concerned with time, space, history and the exploration and evolution of the human soul in all its universal potentials. Toward that end Chelsea particularly seeks out works which deal with large issues and philosophical statements on a universal scale.

The boundaries of Chelsea's self-chosen mandate allow it to concentrate on works which are selected and developed from new plays by American playwrights; new theatre works created from other sources including novels, poems, film and television scripts as well as adaptations of existing dramatic works; foreign works by major contemporary playwrights; and major works of international dramatic literature previously unknown, or rarely performed for American audiences.

Programs & Services: *Internships for college credit; student, senior citizen and group discount ticket programs; Fund for Chelsea Theater Center, support group; Westside Theater bar.*

ROBERT KALFIN
Artistic Director
MICHAEL DAVID
Executive Director

30 Lafayette Avenue
Brooklyn, New York 11217
Telephone (212) 783-5110
Box Office (212) 636-4100

Westside Theater
407 West 43rd Street
New York, New York 10036
Telephone (212) 541-8616
Box Office (212) 541-8394

Founded 1965
Robert Kalfin

Season
October – March

Schedule
Evenings
Tuesday – Saturday
Matinees
Wednesday & Sunday

Facilities
Chelsea Theater
Brooklyn Academy of Music
Seating capacity 275
Stage Flexible
Westside Theater
Seating capacity 284
Stage Flexible
Westside Theater Downstairs
Seating capacity 196
Stage Flexible

Budget
July 1, 1976 – June 30, 1977
Operating budget $1,529,189
Earned income $ 837,202
Unearned income $ 624,480

Audience
Chelsea Theater
Percent of capacity 61
Number of subscribers 2,325
Westside Theater
Percent of capacity 71
Number of subscribers 2,283

Booked-in events
Experimental theatre companies

Operates on AEA Off-Broadway contract.

Productions, 1975-76

Treasure Island, Robert Louis Stevenson; adapted, Timothy Mason; music, Hiram Titus
The Little Match Girl, Hans Christian Andersen; adapted, John Clark Donahue
Mother Goose; adapted, Myron Johnson; music, Steven Rydberg
The Snow Queen, Hans Christian Andersen; translated & adapted, Michael Dennis Browne; music, Steven Rydberg
The Seagull, Anton Chekhov; music, Steven Rydberg
Twelfth Night, William Shakespeare
A Room in Paradise; adapted, Timothy Mason; music, Hiram Titus

Productions, 1976-77

Goldilocks and the Three Bears and *Little Red Riding Hood;* translated & adapted, George Muschamp; music, Roberta Carlson
The Adventures of Tom Sawyer, Mark Twain; adapted, Timothy Mason
Cinderella, Charles Perrault; adapted, John Davidson; music, John Gessner & Diane Cina Sherman
The Dream Fisher, John Clark Donahue; music, Steven Rydberg
Oliver!, Lionel Bart
The Importance of Being Earnest, Oscar Wilde; music, Steven Rydberg
Romeo and Juliet, William Shakespeare
Variations on a Similar Theme (An Homage to Rene Magritte), John Clark Donahue

Brendan McNellis and Bain Boehlke in *The Dream Fisher,* written and directed by John Clark Donahue, sets by Don Pohlman, costumes by Gene Davis Buck. Photo: Paul Hager.

Sean McNellis and Sara Duffy in *The Adventures of Tom Sawyer,* adapted by Timothy Mason, directed by John Clark Donahue, design by Dahl Delu. Photo: Paul Hager.

The Children's Theatre Company

The founding, in 1961, of the first full-time children's theatre company in Minnesota — the Moppet Players — provided the initial stimulus for what was to become one of the most ambitious undertakings in the area of theatre for young people in the United States. Operating out of the back room of an Italian restaurant, the Moppets produced eight plays that first season and later began offering classes in creative dramatics, dance and play-production. In 1964 John Clark Donahue became artistic director of the company. The following year the Minneapolis Institute of Arts opened its old auditorium and office facilities to the group, and in 1965 they produced their first season as the Children's Theatre Company of the Minneapolis Institute of Arts (CTC). The company has grown from a paid staff of 4 and an audience of 28,000 to a professional staff of 60 and a yearly attendance, drawn from the region, of more than 140,000.

In 1969 the company's educational programs achieved accreditation with the founding of the Children's Theatre School. Operating in cooperation with the Minneapolis public schools, the theatre school offers to some 90 junior and senior high school students intensive training in performing and technical disciplines, including dance, music, movement, improvisation, pantomime, set construction, lighting, sound and stage management.

The year 1974 marked the opening of the CTC's new $4.5 million theatre-classroom building, designed by Architect Kenzo Tange in association with Parker-Klein Associates of Minneapolis — the largest, most comprehensive facility in the United States devoted primarily to theatre for young people and families. Late in 1975 the CTC, which had been operating as a division of the Minneapolis Society of Fine Arts, became an independent organization.

The Children's Theatre Company and School today maintains its original artistic philosophy. In John Clark Donahue's words: "It seems to me that, if we think children's theatre is a good thing for our children, and indeed for us, it is because we think it will have something to do with those sensations, perceptions and feelings of our collective childhoods. If we have done anything to bring children's theatre closer to the center of theatrical energy and creation, it is because adults as well as children have been moved and impressed with the total effect of certain works that they have seen. But adults must be there with the children, so that together we create a chemistry and a communion that make the event meaningful and as deep as the subject matter."

Under Mr. Donahue's direction, the CTC has evolved a unique ensemble approach to production, where script, music, acting and design develop simultaneously throughout the production period. Original scripts, including those in foreign languages and in different cultural styles, are used for all children's plays. The CTC has produced nine of Director Donahue's own works for children and adults. With the addition of several productions each season designed for adult audiences, the CTC has become a full-fledged repertory company with the ability to create and share works of theatre for all ages. Eight CTC scripts have been published by the University of Minnesota Press, and in 1972 Filmmaker D.A. Pennebaker completed a color documentary entitled *A Children's Theatre.*

Programs & Services: *Theatre design program; internships; Children's Theatre School; performances, lectures, demonstrations for students; in-school residencies; Contemporary Chamber Chorale and Madrigal Singers; touring; dance classes and company residencies; workshop productions; student, senior citizen and group discounts; free ticket program; voucher program; slide presentations; restaurant; bar; Association of the Children's Theatre and School, support group; newsletter; post-performance demonstrations.*

JOHN CLARK DONAHUE
Artistic Director

2400 Third Avenue South
Minneapolis, Minnesota 55404
Telephone (612) 874-0500
Box Office (612) 874-0400

Founded 1961
Beth Linnerson

Season
September – July

Schedule
Evenings
Thursday – Saturday
Matinees
Wednesday – Sunday

Facilities
Seating capacity 736
Stage Proscenium

Budget
July 1, 1976 – June 30, 1977
Operating budget $1,015,853
Earned income $ 396,113
Unearned income $ 625,864

Audience
Percent of capacity 63

Touring contact
Jeff Thomas

Productions, 1975–76
Death of a Salesman, Arthur Miller
Relatively Speaking, Alan Ayckbourn
The Little Foxes, Lillian Hellman
What the Butler Saw, Joe Orton
The Contrast, Royall Tyler
Where's Charley?, George Abbott &
Frank Loesser

Productions, 1976–77
Cat on a Hot Tin Roof, Tennessee
Williams
Oliver!, Lionel Bart
A Month in the Country, Ivan
Turgenev
*When You Comin' Back, Red
Ryder?*, Mark Medoff
Heartbreak House, George Bernard
Shaw
The Hostage, Brendan Behan
Vanities, Jack Heifner

Ellen Barber as Maggie in *Cat on a Hot Tin Roof* by
Tennessee Williams, directed by Michael Murray,
sets by Paul Shortt, costumes by Annie Peacock
Warner. Photo: Sandy Underwood.

Company members of *The Contrast* by Royall Tyler,
directed by Michael Murray, sets by John Lee
Beatty, costumes by Mark Kruger. Photo: Sandy
Underwood.

Cincinnati Playhouse in the Park

Situated in a park on a high hill near the center of the city, the Cincinnati Playhouse in the Park is the principal professional theatre for Cincinnati and surrounding regions in Ohio and Kentucky. Under the leadership, since 1975, of Michael Murray, producing director, and Robert W. Tolan, managing director, the Playhouse has attempted to respond to the special character of this region and, as its major professional theatre, to offer its audience a wide range of theatre experiences. The program of six productions per season on the main stage, each running four weeks, is designed for variety and challenge. A special effort is made to include neglected but significant works from the past, important contemporary plays and works from the standard repertoire which are believed to have a continuing vibrancy for modern audiences. Cincinnati has a tradition of concern for the arts and the Playhouse is encouraged to make the professional theatre a lively and influential presence in its community.

Simply stated, the primary artistic concern is for quality and the full realization of each play. Productions are cast separately, although many actors, directors and designers return frequently to help form a floating company. Although it is not specifically involved in training, the Playhouse hopes to provide a base and an atmosphere for artists drawn from the Midwest as well as both coasts, to perform, expand and experiment within the contexts of vital drama and an interested community.

Mainstage productions are performed in the Robert S. Marx Theatre, an innovative structure designed by Hugh Hardy and built in 1968 when Brooks Jones was producing director. The building features a large asymmetrical thrust stage and a steeply raked 627-seat auditorium. The Shelterhouse, a 229-seat theatre located nearby, was the original home of the Cincinnati Playhouse and is now being used for smaller productions, experimental work and occasional workshops.

A week of student previews is offered for most productions, with frequently scheduled discussion sessions between actors, designers, technicians and the young audience. In addition the Playhouse attempts to collaborate with other arts organizations in the community. Recent productions have been mounted with the assistance of the School for Creative and Performing Arts, the Cincinnati Opera and the Cincinnati Chamber Orchestra among others. Since its founding in 1960 the Playhouse in the Park has presented 150 productions in both theatres, including 10 world premieres and 4 American premieres.

Programs & Services: *Internships; student performance series, supplementary material and in-class speakers; chamber orchestra concerts; Peggy Lyman Dance Workshop, training and recitals; student, senior citizen and group discount ticket programs; benefit performances; membership organization; concession stand; "Prompters" and Women's Committee, support groups; The Subscriber, newsletter; Sunday seminar series.*

MICHAEL MURRAY
Producing Director
ROBERT W. TOLAN
Managing Director

P.O. Box 6537
Cincinnati, Ohio 45206
Telephone (513) 559-9500
Box Office (513) 421-3888

Founded 1960
Community members

Season
October – June

Schedule
Evenings
Tuesday – Sunday
Matinees
Sunday

Facilities
962 Mt. Adams Circle
Robert S. Marx Theatre
Seating capacity 627
Stage Thrust
Shelterhouse
Seating capacity 229
Stage ¾ Arena

Budget
Jan 1, 1976 – Dec 31, 1976
Operating budget $930,765
Earned income $580,656
Unearned income $331,216

Audience
Robert S. Marx Theatre
Percent of capacity 77
Number of subscribers 11,404
Shelterhouse
Percent of capacity 85

Booked-in events
Experimental and children's theatre companies

Operates on AEA LORT (B) contract.

Productions, 1975-76
Ah, Wilderness!, Eugene O'Neill
The Glass Menagerie, Tennessee Williams
The Lady from the Sea, Henrik Ibsen;
translated, Michael Meyer
Pal Joey, Richard Rodgers, Lorenz Hart,
John O'Hara

Productions, 1976-77
Days in the Trees, Marguerite Duras;
translated, Sonia Orwell
The Night of the Iguana, Tennessee
Williams
Romeo and Juliet, William Shakespeare
The Importance of Being Earnest, Oscar
Wilde
The Club, Eve Merriam

Kathleen Widdoes and Patricia Conolly in Oscar
Wilde's *The Importance of Being Earnest*, directed
by Stephen Porter, sets by Zack Brown, costumes
by Ann Roth. Photo: Martha Swope.

Vanessa Redgrave in *The Lady from the Sea* by
Ibsen, directed by Tony Richardson, designed by
Rouben Ter-Arutunian. Photo: Inge Morath.

Circle in the Square

Theodore Mann and Paul Libin, as the directors of Circle in the Square, have pursued a policy of presenting great plays with great actors. Circle presents four plays a year with each production running for three months. This limited-run policy not only affords such actors as George C. Scott, Vanessa Redgrave and Richard Chamberlain, who are unable to commit themselves to an extended run, a chance to work in the theatre, but also gives New York audiences the opportunity to watch some of the world's finest actors performing on the stage.

In the fall of 1972, after 21 years Off Broadway, Circle in the Square moved into a new theatre complex at Broadway and 50th Street, the first new theatre to open in the Broadway district in 44 years. The former Circle in the Square theatre in Greenwich Village, now called Circle in the Square Downtown, continues to be operated as an Off Broadway theatre.

Circle in the Square celebrated its twenty-fifth year of continuous production during the 1975-76 season. In the past two decades, Circle has presented more than 100 productions and has provided a home for the important works of such noted playwrights as Eugene O'Neill, Tennessee Williams, Truman Capote, Dylan Thomas, Saul Bellow, Thornton Wilder, John Steinbeck, Jules Feiffer and Arthur Miller. In addition to its interest in presenting the work of distinguished writers, Circle in the Square explores new material and playwrights in workshop productions. *Walking Papers*, a new musical adapted by Sandra Hochman from her novel of the same name, was directed by actress Phyllis Newman in the fall of 1976. It was presented in open rehearsals, which gave the actors and playwright the chance to learn from the audience's reaction before expanding it into a complete production. In its downtown theatre, Circle presented a workshop production of *Hamlet*, with Rip Torn, Madelaine Thornton-Sherwood and David Margulies, directed by Jack Gelber. This workshop allowed the actors to explore the play without the pressure of a full production and gave audiences a chance to experience the complete Shakespearean text.

Circle has also recently started a program for playwrights in which new plays are given readings in its uptown theatre. These readings benefit playwrights by giving life to their written words and by providing the opportunity for audience discussion in seminars immediately following each reading.

In conjunction with its mainstage productions, Circle in the Square, believing that audiences should have the opportunity to actively participate in the theatre, offers colloquies, which allow audience members and actors to discuss material being presented — the actual production and the theatre in general. Actors have attributed such colloquies with greatly contributing to their play interpretations and performances.

The Circle in the Square Theatre School and Workshop, founded in 1961, offers a training program with a teaching staff of professional actors and directors. This affiliation with a professional theatre enables students to experience productions as a learning laboratory. Another program, affiliated with New York University, provides students with theatre training classes at Circle, in conjunction with academic classes at NYU.

Programs & Services: *Circle in the Square Theatre School, professional training; Acting-Directing Workshops; internships; play readings and workshop productions; student, senior citizen and group discounts; free ticket program; fund-raising galas; bar; volunteers; Subscriber's Newsletter, biannual; post-performance discussions.*

THEODORE MANN
Artistic Director
PAUL LIBIN
Managing Director

1633 Broadway
New York, New York 10019
Telephone (212) 581-3270
Box Office (212) 581-0720

Founded 1951
Emily Stevens, Jason Wingreen,
Aileen Cramer, Edward Mann,
Jose Quintero, Theodore Mann

Season
September – August

Schedule
Evenings
Tuesday – Saturday
Matinees
Wednesday, Saturday, Sunday

Facilities
Seating capacity 650
Stage ¾ Arena
Circle in the Square Downtown
159 Bleecker Street
Seating capacity 299
Stage ¾ Arena

Budget
July 1, 1976 – June 30, 1977
Operating budget $2,998,965
Earned income $2,099,095
Unearned income $ 329,154

Audience
Percent of capacity 73
Number of subscribers 17,590

*Operates on AEA Production
& Off-Broadway contracts.*

Productions, 1975–76
The Elephant in the House, Berrilla Kerr
Dancing for the Kaiser, Andrew Colmar
Knock Knock, Jules Feiffer
Who Killed Richard Cory?, A.R. Gurney
Serenading Louie, Lanford Wilson
Mrs. Murray's Farm, Roy London

Productions, 1976–77
The Farm, David Storey
A Tribute to Lili Lamont, Arthur Whitney;
music, Norman Berman
My Life, Corinne Jacker
Gemini, Albert Innaurato
Exiles, James Joyce
Unsung Cole, Cole Porter; conceived,
Norman Berman

Nancy Snyder and William Hurt in *My Life* by
Corinne Jacker, directed by Marshall W. Mason,
sets by David Potts, costumes by Kenneth M. Yount.
Photo: Ken Howard.

Danny Aiello, Jessica James and Robert Picardo in
Albert Innaurato's *Gemini,* directed by Peter Mark
Schifter, sets by Christopher Nowak, costumes by
Ernest Allen Smith. Photo: Joan James.

Circle Repertory Company

For nine years Circle Repertory Company has been dedicated to creating distinguished new American drama for the contemporary theatre. Founded in 1969 by artistic director Marshall Mason, playwright Lanford Wilson, director Robert Thirkield and actress Tanya Berezin, Circle Repertory is composed of a resident company of 15 actors, 3 designers, 3 directors, 7 resident playwrights, 5 graduate interns and a full-time support staff of 15.

After five years in a loft at 83rd Street and Broadway in Manhattan, Circle Repertory moved to Greenwich Village's famous Sheridan Square Playhouse. The acting company meets for physical, vocal and ensemble training for 15 hours each week and works closely with the theatre's resident writers. This kind of interaction works to reinforce the company's basic concept that the action of the play should become the experience of the audience. Many of the plays are written expressly for the members of the company to perform. Classics are used to develop and sharpen actors' skills. In addition to its six major productions each year, Circle Repertory presents "The Late Show," a series of six new one-act plays. The company is planning to expand its operation of developing new plays to a new theatre in Los Angeles — Circle Repertory West — which will be under the artistic direction of company member Neil Flanagan.

In its nine years of operation, the Circle Repertory Company has presented 62 world premieres, including Lanford Wilson's *The Hot l Baltimore* and *The Mound Builders*, Mark Medoff's *When You Comin' Back, Red Ryder?*, Edward J. Moore's *The Sea Horse*, Jules Feiffer's *Knock Knock*, Megan Terry's *Hothouse*, Howard Ashman's *The Confirmation*, and Corinne Jacker's *Harry Outside*. Among the 16 new plays given their New York premieres at Circle Repertory are Sam Shepard's *Suicide in B*^{b}, Dylan Thomas' *The Doctor and the Devils*, David Storey's *The Farm*, Lanford Wilson's *Serenading Louie*, and Tennessee Williams' *Battle of Angels*. Twenty-eight revivals have included Chekhov's *The Three Sisters*, Ibsen's *When We Dead Awaken*, e.e. cummings' *him*, Wedekind's *Spring's Awakening*, Strindberg's *Ghost Sonata*, James Joyce's *Exiles*, and Cole Porter's *Unsung Cole*.

The work of Circle Repertory was seen on national television when Mr. Wilson's *The Mound Builders* was broadcast on the WNET-TV *Theater in America* series. The company has also transferred productions to theatres both on and Off Broadway. Mr. Wilson's *The Hot l Baltimore* ran for 1,200 performances Off Broadway, and Mr. Feiffer's *Knock Knock* and Albert Innaurato's *Gemini* were produced on Broadway.

Programs & Services: *Internships; young audience production; Late Show, adaptations and one-acts; play readings; student, senior citizen and group ticket discounts; Friends of Circle, support group; bimonthly subscriber newsletter; director, designer and playwright residencies; volunteers.*

MARSHALL W. MASON
Artistic Director
JERRY ARROW
Executive Director

186 West Fourth Street
New York, New York 10014
Telephone (212) 691-3210
Box Office (212) 924-7100

Founded 1969
Marshall W. Mason, Robert Thirkield,
Lanford Wilson, Tanya Berezin

Season
October – July

Schedule
Evenings
Tuesday – Saturday
Matinees
Sunday

Facilities
Seating capacity 150
Stage Flexible

Budget
Oct 1, 1976 – Sept 30, 1977
Operating budget $315,800
Earned income $119,000
Unearned income $194,037

Audience
Percent of capacity 64

Operates on AEA Off-Broadway contract.

Productions, 1975–76

In Celebration, David Storey
First Monday in October, Robert E. Lee
& Jerome Lawrence
The Prague Spring, Lee Kalcheim;
music, Joseph Raposo
Bingo, Edward Bond
Caesar and Cleopatra, George Bernard
Shaw
Abigail Adams, Edith Owen
Relatively Speaking, Alan Ayckbourn
Dr. Jekyll and Mr. Hyde, Robert Lewis
Stevenson; adapted, Paul Lee
The Dark at the Top of the Stairs,
William Inge
Get-Rich-Quick Wallingford, George M. Cohan
*The Last Meeting of the Knights of the
White Magnolia*, Preston Jones
Of Mice and Men, John Steinbeck
Scapino, Moliere; adapted, Frank Dunlop
& Jim Dale
The World of Carl Sandburg, Norman Corwin

Productions, 1976–77

The Sunshine Boys, Neil Simon
The Cat and the Fiddle, Jerome Kern &
Otto Harbach
Are You Now or Have You Ever Been,
Eric Bentley
A Moon for the Misbegotten, Eugene O'Neill
The Yellow Jacket, George C. Hazelton
& J.H. Benrimo
Man and Superman, George Bernard Shaw
Ladyhouse Blues, Kevin O'Morrison
Macbeth, William Shakespeare
Table Manners, Alan Ayckbourn

Yolande Bavan and Clayton Corzatte in *Caesar and
Cleopatra* by George Bernard Shaw, directed by
Paul Lee, sets by Robert Steinberg. Photo: James
Fry.

Melvyn Douglas in *First Monday in October* by
Robert E. Lee and Jerome Lawrence, directed by
Mr. Lawrence, sets by Richard Gould, costumes by
Estelle Painter. Photo: James Fry.

Cleveland Play House

The Cleveland Play House, America's first resident professional theatre, is in the business of nourishing art and artists. Its principal aims are to produce a full variety of theatre for the community of Cleveland and northeastern Ohio and to provide a challenging repertoire for a resident artistic company.

The 1977–78 season marks the Play House's sixty-second year. Begun in 1915 with just three full time staff members and a handful of spectators, the Play House now employs nearly 100 full-time staff members and plays to more than 148,000 audience members each year. The Play House operated in private homes, barns and attics until its 1917 move to a renovated church. In 1929, because of growing staff and audience, the Play House moved into a new building with two theatres, which has been designated a National Historic Place in United States theatre architecture. The land was donated by Mr. and Mrs. Francis Drury, and the larger of the two theatres was named in their honor. The Play House has since expanded its physical domain to include a remodeled church, the 560-seat Euclid-77th Street Theatre. This building also houses the Play House Club and an art gallery.

The Play House season runs from October to April with the range of 12 or more productions per season varying from classics to premieres of contemporary plays. Thus, audiences are offered varied exposure to theatre, and the staff benefits from a wide range of theatrical experiences. Among the more than 70 world and American premieres that have been staged at the Play House since 1915 are Tennessee Williams and Donald Windham's *You Touched Me*, Donald Freed's *The United States vs. Julius and Ethel Rosenberg*, Paul Zindel's *The Effect of Gamma Rays on Man-in-the-Moon Marigolds*, and Lawrence and Lee's *First Monday in October*.

The Play House contributes to the Cleveland community by providing area students with a multitude of educational services. "Play House Comes to School," launched during the 1971–72 season, is a troupe of young actors who offer drama workshops to junior and senior high school students in preparation for attendance at theatre performances. In affiliation with nearby Case Western Reserve University, the Play House provides practical experience to students working toward Master of Fine Arts degrees. Other long-standing Play House outreach services include the apprentice and fellowship programs, which offer on-the-job training with professionals to young theatre aspirants; the student matinee series, which provides morning performances at the Play House and enables students to see productions at discount rates; and the Youtheatre program, begun in 1933, which offers instruction in puppetry, voice, movement, improvisation, acting, theatre appreciation, stage combat and makeup, to students 8 to 18 years of age.

In 1929, the Play House established a summer theatre, staffed by Play House personnel, at the world-renowned Chautauqua Institution in Chautauqua, New York. The season is an eight-week series comprised of the most successful productions from the previous Cleveland season. Play House personnel provide a six-week, college-accredited, theatre training school for students.

Richard Oberlin, director of the Play House since 1972, has been on the staff since 1954. During that time he has acted in, or directed more than 200 productions. Upon his appointment as director, Mr. Oberlin gained the opportunity to further his progressive philosophy for America's first resident theatre. Under his guidance, the Play House has committed itself to reviving neglected plays, providing continued life for worthy scripts and presenting premier productions of scripts that are deemed exciting and valuable.

Programs & Services: *Youtheatre classes; apprenticeships; MFA Exchange Program; performances, workshops and post-performance discussions for students; booked-in events; student, senior citizen and group ticket discounts; auction; benefit performances; speakers bureau; bar and restaurant; support groups;* Play House Curtain Times, *subscriber newsletter.*

RICHARD OBERLIN
Director
NELSON ISEKEIT
Business Manager

P.O. Box 1989
Cleveland, Ohio 44106
(216) 795-7000

Founded 1915
Raymond O'Neil

Season
October – April

Schedule
Evenings
Wednesday – Saturday
Matinees
Thursday & Sunday

Facilities
2040 East 86th Street
Drury Theatre
Seating capacity 515
Stage Proscenium
Brooks Theatre
Seating capacity 160
Stage Proscenium
Euclid-77th Street Theatre
Seating capacity 560
Stage Thrust

Budget
July 1, 1976 – June 30, 1977
Operating budget $1,028,753
Earned income $ 553,414
Unearned income $ 477,167

Audience
Number of subscribers 9,221
Drury Theatre
Percent of capacity 69
Euclid-77th Street Theatre
Percent of capacity 56

Operates on AEA LORT (C) contract.

Productions, 1975–76

The Cast Aways, Mordecai Noah; adapted,
Anthony Stimac; music, Don Pippin; lyrics,
Steve Brown
Abie's Irish Rose, Anne Nichols
The Subject Was Roses, Frank D. Gilroy
Arsenic and Old Lace, Joseph Kesselring
Of Mice and Men, John Steinbeck

Productions, 1976–77

Life with Father, Howard Lindsay &
Russel Crouse
Babes in Arms, Richard Rodgers &
Lorenz Hart
Blithe Spirit, Noel Coward
Death of a Salesman, Arthur Miller
The Importance of Being Earnest,
Oscar Wilde

Erika Peterson and Mike Mazurki in Steinbeck's *Of
Mice and Men,* directed by David Kitchen, sets by
Greg Dunn, costumes by Dean Reiter. Photo: Paul
Bouchey.

Dorothy Blackburn, James Selby, Jill O'Hara and
Barbara Berge in *The Importance of Being Earnest*
by Oscar Wilde, directed by Robert Mandel, sets by
Michael Anania, costumes by Bob Wojewodski.
Photo: Paul Bouchey.

Cohoes Music Hall

Cohoes Music Hall, one of the oldest restored theatre buildings in the United States, was slated for demolition when, in 1969, the tenant and landlord, a local bank, sold the building for one dollar to the city of Cohoes so that it might be preserved. In 1970 a four-year project of restoration began and on November 23, 1974, a production in the newly revived theatre marked the centennial of the first performance in the Music Hall. All of this was due to the united efforts and beliefs of the local citizenry.

From its inception the Cohoes Music Hall has endeavored to involve its community, the Capitol District Region of New York State, in its total operation. Believing that every theatre has a responsibility to its community as one of its two primary objectives, Cohoes is committed to the cultural and artistic growth of the area residents. The Cohoes Music Hall's audience is one whose theatrical experience is limited. Geographic and economic barriers have prevented many from being exposed to professional theatre, so that for them a visit to the Music Hall is an introduction to a new art form. In the first few seasons the selection of plays emphasized entertainment, but through a slow process of introducing more sophisticated material, the Music Hall is now able to present a varied repertoire. These plays have enjoyed an enthusiastic reception, allowing for even more adventurous play selection in an attempt to further enhance the audience's theatre experience. There is a need and desire expressed by the theatre's audience to become more involved. As a result Cohoes sponsors a Thursday evening seminar series wherein the audience has the opportunity to talk with the actors. This series has been so successful that it will be repeated during the 1977-78 season. It is through the consistent involvement of its audience that a theatre lives up to its responsibility to the community that supports it.

The second objective of the Cohoes Music Hall is the creation of the best environment possible for its staff. The communication between director, actor, designer and technician must take place in an atmosphere where the creative process can be developed and achieved. The theatre, striving for artistic quality and expression, believes in giving its artists the freedom to explore and experiment, the premise on which regional theatre was born. Through sufficient rehearsal time, a pleasant environment, and mutual consideration and respect among the entire staff, this goal can be accomplished.

The relationship of the community to artistic growth enables the theatre to explore all avenues of development — to enlighten the imagination of its audience, provide an environment for each artist to create and to preserve theatre as an art form. When the complete interrelationship between artist and audience is accomplished, the Music Hall will be able to provide its artists with the best environment for the creative process.

Programs & Services: *Community acting workshops; student performances and seminars; artist-in-classroom program; film series; script readings; student, senior citizen and group discount ticket programs; benefit performances; bar; Theatre Guild and Booster Club, support groups; post-performance seminar series.*

LOUIS J. AMBROSIO
Executive Director

58 Remsen Street
Cohoes, New York 12047
Telephone (518) 237-7700
Box Office (518) 237-7045

Founded 1974
James D. O'Reilly, Louis J. Ambrosio, City of Cohoes

Season
October – April

Schedule
Evenings
Wednesday – Sunday
Matinees
Saturday & Sunday

Facilities
Seating capacity 500
Stage Proscenium

Budget
July 1, 1976 – June 30, 1977
Operating budget $272,000
Earned income $176,000
Unearned income $ 50,000

Audience
Percent of capacity 62
Number of subscribers 4,700

Booked-in events
Opera and community theatre productions

Operates on AEA LORT (C) contract.

Productions, 1975-76

Second Wind, David Morgan; music,
Joseph Blunt
A Month in the Country, Ivan Turgenev;
adapted, David Morgan
Reflections, Oscar Wilde; adapted,
David Morgan; music, Miriam Moses
Cinema Soldier, Paavo Tammi; music,
Alexandra O'Karma & Miriam Moses

Productions, 1976-77

Warbeck, Louis Phillips
Reflections, Oscar Wilde; adapted,
David Morgan; music, Miriam Moses
A Flea in Her Ear, Georges Feydeau;
translated, David Morgan
A Servant of Two Masters, Carlo Goldoni;
adapted, A.G. Brooks; music, Susan J. Peters

Bill E. Noone in *Warbeck* by Louis Phillips, directed
by Michael Lessac, sets by Robert U. Taylor,
costumes by Kenneth M. Yount. Photo: Gerald M.
Kline.

Peter Kingsley and Bill E. Noone in Feydeau's *A Flea
in Her Ear,* directed by Krikor Satamian, sets by
Robert U. Taylor, costumes by John Helgerson.
Photo: Gerald M. Kline.

Colonnades Theatre Lab

The Colonnades Theatre Lab was founded in 1973 to provide a permanent home for a resident acting company, where the actors could develop a flexibility of style through training, to meet the demands of a traditional theatre repertoire, as well as the best of new theatre experimentation. The company performs the works of both new American playwrights and established classical authors, in rotating repertory. In addition, an annual developmental season places new works in a laboratory framework, in preparation for a second full production, mounted subsequently in the regular season. From the beginning, the Colonnades Theatre was also conceived as an interdisciplinary laboratory, where the unexplored relationships between theatre and science — particularly the sciences of human development and behavior — could be developed. With such broad and diverse aims, there is the danger of a dispersion of energy and dilution of art, but it is the theatre's belief that ultimately its goals will provide the swiftest route to creating a growing, lasting and complete theatre. All of these things, although time consuming and expensive, are enriching and efficient when done concurrently. Considered with the right spirit, they become mutually lifegiving.

A theatre's essence is always in its work and its people. Over the last few years, it has been helpful to talk about the Colonnades by answering some of the questions that were raised when it first started. They are good and natural questions, especially for what is basically a regional theatre trying to survive in the middle of New York City. Why rotating repertory in a laboratory theatre committed to the development of new plays and new playwrights? The theatre craft demands it, as repertory defines the craft. It demands and builds better actors, and ultimately good actors will make it easier for new literate playwrights to emerge with consistency. . . . Why rotating repertory in a city where a different kind of show can be seen every night of the week? It offers audiences the opportunity to see actors constantly in movement, living different characters within a single week. It provides excitement and a most real communication between actor, playwright and audience. . . . Why a permanent company in New York, where it is easier and so much less expensive to cast for each production? Repertory does not make sense without a core company, and only a core resident company can maintain the institutional energy to make a commitment to long-term growth. . . . Why devote energy to research and human ecology and not just concentrate on producing plays? So much of training is a recapturing of things lost. For most people the balance between the logical and the intuitive is a rare and precious thing, but for the actor, it is a necessity.

The Colonnades can be appreciated on two levels. First, for the sake of artistic survival, it must be a theatre built with a continuing sense of humor, fed with the courage to fail, and possessing an almost primitive love for mystique. At the same time, it can be a theatre capable of expanding upon this mystique, courage and humor, with a continually growing understanding of the human mind, body and emotions.

Theatre is a superstitious craft, which implies magic, and theatre artists work to create this magic. But to train, to perform with consistency and growth, and to maintain uniqueness, artists need to know that under all magic lies basic awareness. In so doing, human potential itself is explored, and artists become important — no longer a luxury, no longer expendable, but a necessity. Theatre artists can enthusiastically give back something more than the surface result of the craft and can perhaps prevent the stultifying self-indulgence that so often affects an isolated art. And in this way a viable alternative financial foundation can perhaps be developed for survival. Nothing is compromised. A theatre's value as a resource can only come out of its greatness as a theatre — they feed each other.

Programs & Services: *Actor training; internships; First Draft Theatre, new plays lab; performances for students; artists-in-residence at schools; student, senior citizen and group ticket discounts; free ticket program; voucher program; benefit performances; Guild, support group.*

MICHAEL LESSAC
Artistic Director
STEPHEN SIMON
Administrative Director

428 Lafayette Street
New York, New York 10003
Telephone (212) 228-6640
Box Office (212) 673-2222

Founded 1973
Michael Lessac

Season
October – March

Schedule
Evenings
Wednesday – Sunday
Matinees
Sunday

Facilities
Seating capacity 55–75
Stage   Flexible

Budget
July 1, 1976 – June 30, 1977
Operating budget $151,453
Earned income $ 25,758
Unearned income $123,605

Audience
Percent of capacity 70

Operates on AEA Off-Broadway contract.

Productions, 1975-76
The Journey of the Fifth Horse,
Ronald Ribman
6 Rms Riv Vu, Bob Randall
Snow White Goes West; adapted, Jim Eiler;
music, Jim Eiler & Jean Bargy
When You Comin' Back, Red Ryder?, Mark Medoff
It Strikes a Man, Patrick Ferris Bennett;
music, Patrick Ferris Bennett & Robert Scott
The Sea Horse, Edward J. Moore
The Martian Chronicles, Ray Bradbury

Productions, 1976-77
Artichoke, Joanna Glass
Subject to Fits, Robert Montgomery
The Mound Builders, Lanford Wilson
And Where She Stops Nobody Knows,
Oliver Hailey
*The Last Meeting of the Knights of the
White Magnolia,* Preston Jones
A Tribute to Lili Lamont, Arthur Whitney;
music, Norman Berman
Who's Afraid of Virginia Woolf?,
Edward Albee

Clive Rosengren, David Willis, William Halliday and
William Schoppert in *The Last Meeting of the
Knights of the White Magnolia* by Preston Jones,
directed by Lou Salerni, sets by Dick Leerhoff,
costumes by Christopher Beesley. Photo: Connie
Britzius.

Cast members of Mark Medoff's *When You Comin'
Back, Red Ryder?,* directed by Arif Hasnain, sets by
Dick Leerhoff, costumes by Patty Facius. Photo:
Paul Hager.

The Cricket Theatre

The Cricket Theatre is dedicated to the production of plays by living American playwrights. Entering its seventh season in 1977–78, the Cricket will produce seven contemporary American plays. In addition, the theatre is inaugurating a works-in-progress series which will stage another 14 new American plays in workshop productions, with playwrights in residence. The Cricket Theatre's artistic vision is projected to include an ever-increasing number of world-premier productions, with many of those generated by its playwright commission program, begun in 1976.

In its effort to generate professional productions of new American writers, the Cricket Theatre joins the company of a growing number of professional theatres principally dedicated to the American writer. Devoted to the establishment of a productive intercourse between developing American theatre personnel and, in order to establish a broader base for such an artistic exchange of views, the Cricket Theatre has recently established a working alliance with two other theatres with a strong interest in new plays — the Circle Repertory Company in New York and the Magic Theatre in San Francisco. This alliance is intended to result in the exchange of artistic directors, actors, plays and playwrights, in the conviction that such relationships between theatres will aid in the lessening of artistic isolation and the threat of provincialism engendered by the decentralization of theatre in the past two decades.

The theatre's goal, in the simplest possible terms, is to be known as a playwright-actor theatre. In the seasons ahead, the theatre aims to expand and refine its support of new and established writers in order to build and retain a small coterie of innovative and talented authors supported by the Cricket Theatre to write specifically for the Cricket Theatre. The Cricket envisions a program of small stipends and workshop-production grants in the future to encourage the development of promising writers and is aiming toward the establishment of a company of actors assembled according to the needs of the plays presented in rotating repertory.

With the scheduled move into a new and more centrally located production facility in 1978, the Cricket Theatre will not alter its basic artistic direction. Unlike American industry, which seems to function on the assumption that "bigger is better," the progress and future of the Cricket Theatre is predicated on the belief that, as it moves forward, "better is better."

Programs & Services: *Internships; performances for students; playwrights commissions; works-in-progress series, 14 new plays; student, senior citizen and group discounts; free ticket program; Cricket Members; Preview, subscriber newsletter.*

LOU SALERNI
Artistic Director
WILLIAM H. SEMANS
Producing Director

345 13th Avenue, NE
Minneapolis, Minnesota 55413
(612) 379-1411

Founded 1970
William H. Semans

Season
October – June

Schedule
Evenings
Wednesday – Sunday
Matinees
Saturday

Facilities
Seating capacity 304
Stage Thrust

Budget
July 1, 1976 – June 30, 1977
Operating budget $294,498
Earned income $ 94,566
Unearned income $171,615

Audience
Percent of capacity 46
Number of subscribers 860

Operates on AEA LORT (D) contract.

Productions, 1975–76
The Homecoming, Harold Pinter
Hedda Gabler, Henrik Ibsen;
translated, Christopher Martin
Antigone, Jean Anouilh;
translated, Alex Szogyi
A Country Scandal, Anton Chekhov;
translated, Alex Szogyi
School for Buffoons and *Escurial,*
Michel de Ghelderode; translated,
Kenneth A. White & George Hauger
Measure for Measure, William Shakespeare
Hound of the Baskervilles, Arthur
Conan Doyle; adapted, Christopher Martin
La Celestina, Fernando de Rojas;
translated, Rene Buch
Tartuffe, Moliere; translated,
Christopher Martin

Productions, 1976–77
Heartbreak House, George Bernard Shaw
Tartuffe, Moliere; translated,
Christopher Martin
Bingo, Edward Bond
The Homecoming, Harold Pinter
The Balcony, Jean Genet; translated,
Terry Hands & Barbara Wright

John Fitzgibbon and Christopher Martin in *School
for Buffoons* by Michel de Ghelderode, direction and
set design by Mr. Martin, costumes by Evelyn
Thompson. Photo: Goodstein.

Noble Shropshire and Ara Watson in Moliere's
Tartuffe, directed by Christopher Martin, sets by
Clay Coyle and Mr. Martin, costumes by Donna
Meyer. Photo: Goodstein.

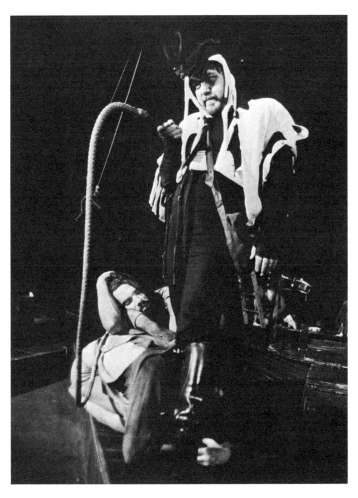

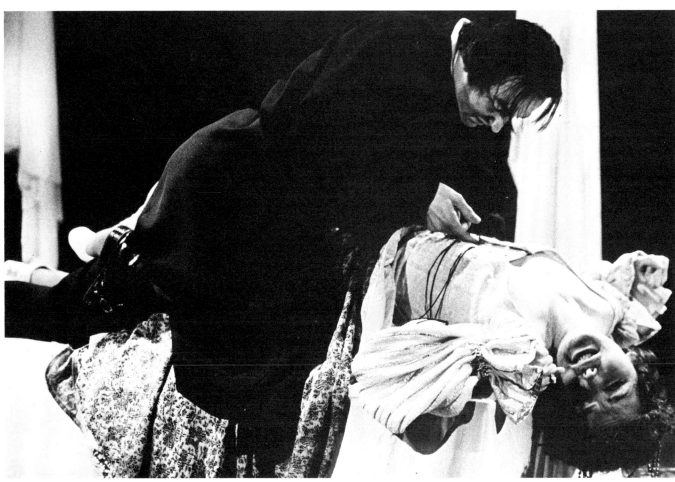

CSC Repertory

Classics in the present tense, an artistic imperative articulated by Christopher Martin, CSC Repertory's founder and artistic director, demands that each play produced must be examined as a new work to be interpreted by the resident company. The task at hand is the discovery of a "bridge" between the world of the playwright and contemporary society. The work must be translated into a production that is true to the author's intent and, moreover, has an effect on its contemporary audience comparable to that of its original impact. This goal necessitates a careful selection of repertoire, and, in some cases, new translations commissioned by CSC.

Three major forces govern the final production: the author and his words, the company and its technique, the audience and its imagination. The CSC company, therefore, is selected from highly trained young actors, many of whom have trained in Europe. Workshops in mime, fencing, speech and verbal interpretation, are an integral part of the company activity, with special sessions incorporated into rehearsals of productions demanding a specific technique. Long and rigorous auditions are held each season for additional company members.

After 10 years of growth and audience development, CSC Repertory has grown from an Off-Off Broadway showcase theatre to a professional resident theatre on an Equity Off-Broadway contract. Over the past 10 seasons the theatre has mounted more than 75 productions, maintaining many of them for several seasons in rotating repertory.

As CSC moves into the 1977-78 season, emphasis will be placed on presenting the more rarely produced works of the classic canon and new plays by major foreign authors. The season includes new plays by Jean Anouilh, Friedrich Durrenmatt and Latin American authors Egon Wolff and Isaac Chocron. CSC will also present the premiere of a new commissioned work, by company actress Karen Sunde, set against the winter of 1777 during the American Revolution, and a new translation of Ibsen's *Rosmersholm* by Mr. Martin. The company will also be working together experimentally in preparation for future productions of Yeats' *Cuchulain Cycle* and Seneca's *Phaedra*, now planned for the 1978-79 season.

Programs & Services: *Internships in administration and production; workshop productions of new plays; student, senior citizen and group discounts; free ticket program; volunteers; Director's Forum, post-performance discussions.*

CHRISTOPHER MARTIN
Artistic Director
DENNIS TURNER
Executive Director

136 East 13th Street
New York, New York 10003
Telephone (212) 477-5808
Box Office (212) 677-4210

Founded 1967
Christopher Martin

Season
November – May

Schedule
Evenings
Tuesday – Saturday
Matinees
Sunday

Facilities
Seating capacity 255
Stage ¾ Arena

Budget
July 1, 1976 – June 30, 1977
Operating budget $121,010
Earned income $ 61,309
Unearned income $ 63,914

Audience
Percent of capacity 45
Number of subscribers 1,700

Operates on AEA Off-Broadway contract.

Productions, 1975–76
Croon, Andrea Balis, Elizabeth Levy,
Cutting Edge company

Productions, 1976–77
Croon, Andrea Balis, Elizabeth Levy,
Cutting Edge company
Untitled work, Andrea Balis & Elizabeth Levy

Sara Christiansen and Abigail Costello in *Croon,*
company developed, directed by Andrea Balis.
Photo: Lear Levin.

Sara Christiansen and Abigail Costello in *Croon.*
Photo: Lear Levin.

The Cutting Edge

The Cutting Edge is a permanent ensemble company comprised of women actors, designers, writers and directors. They create their own pieces which are comedies evolved from discussions, interviews and improvisations. Over the last six years the members of the Cutting Edge have refined and developed improvisational skills which enable them to use as source material songs, stories, newspaper articles, conversations and other matter not usually considered theatrical text. The ensemble creates pieces based on their lives in America in the 1970s. They do not consider themselves feminists in the didactic sense, but rather women, aware of and supportive of the feminist movement, working and producing art together. Many of their feelings about feminism and the position of women in society today help to form the core of their work. It is not intended that their pieces be seen or appreciated only by women. The ensemble is most interested in creating technically precise comedy, stemming from a woman's appreciation and shared perception of humor — a perception which has not often been expressed. It is the company's belief that how a group is viewed and views itself is reflected in its humor.

The ensemble's artistic roots are in improvisational skills which have formed the basis of a 20-year tradition of comedy and social satire. They are using those skills to make pieces, as women, "for our jokes, our humor, our perceptions and our dreams." If women do not create heroines, legends, literature and roles for themselves, they will be forced to continue relying on man's perception of women.

The company teaches workshops in improvisation, piece composition, movement and mask construction. The members of the Cutting Edge have taught at American University, the American Academy of Dramatic Art, New York University, Connecticut College and State University of New York at New Paltz, as well as having given lectures and demonstrations at many other colleges and universities.

Programs & Services: *Directing, acting and improvisation workshops; lectures and seminars in schools; student, senior citizen and group ticket discounts; benefit performances; residencies.*

ANDREA BALIS
Artistic Director
CATHERINE SMITH
Administrative Director

New Arts Management
47 West 9th Street
New York, New York 10011
(212) 691-5434

Founded 1975
Andrea Balis

Season
October – March

Budget
July 1, 1976 – June 30, 1977
Operating budget $30,000
Earned income $10,000
Unearned income $21,000

Touring contact
A Bunch of Experimental Theaters
105 Hudson Street
New York, New York 10013
(212) 966-0400

Productions, 1975-76
Saturday Sunday Monday, Eduardo de Filippo
Manny, Randolph Tallman, Steven Mackenroth,
Glenn Allen Smith
A Place on the Magdalena Flats, Preston Jones
Much Ado About Nothing, William Shakespeare
Stillsong, Sallie Baker Laurie
*Sherlock Holmes and the Curse of the
Sign of Four*, Arthur Conan Doyle;
adapted, Dennis Rosa
Sam, Sally Netzel

Productions, 1976-77
Once in a Lifetime, Moss Hart &
George S. Kaufman
Scapino, Moliere; adapted, Frank Dunlop &
Jim Dale
The Three Sisters, Anton Chekhov; translated,
Robert Corrigan
Something's Afoot, James McDonald, David
Vos, Robert Gerlach
Santa Fe Sunshine, Preston Jones
Equus, Peter Shaffer
Absurd Person Singular, Alan Ayckbourn

Synthia Rogers and Drexel H. Riley in *A Place on the
Magdalena Flats* by Preston Jones, directed by Ken
Latimer, sets by Yoichi Aoki, costumes by Susan A.
Haynie. Photo: Linda Blase.

Company members in *Manny* by Randolph Tallman,
Steven Mackenroth and Glenn Allen Smith, directed
by Dolores Ferraro, sets by Sam Nance, costumes
by Gina Taulane. Photo: Linda Blase.

Dallas Theater Center

The Dallas Theater Center was constructed in 1959 as a nonprofit civic institution for the development and presentation of theatre arts. The theatre's building is the only public theatre facility designed by Frank Lloyd Wright. The artistic policy of the Center, as set forth by director Paul Baker, is to develop a theatre that is a source of creative energy. The Center aspires to achieve such a theatre through a wide range of activities.

The theatre aims to develop audience excitement and enthusiasm for a very broad selection of plays directed, designed and performed by a resident company. DTC is also committed to the development of playwrights and the production of new plays. The past two seasons have seen the world premieres of 15 new scripts, including *A Place on the Magdalena Flats* and *Santa Fe Sunshine* by Preston Jones; *Manny* by Randolph Tallman, Steven Mackenroth and Glenn Allen Smith; *Stillsong* by Sallie Laurie; *Standoff at Beaver and Pine* and *Sam* by Sally Netzel; *Canzada and the Boys* by Sam Havens; *Get Happy!* by John Henson, John Logan, Randolph Tallman and Steven Mackenroth; *War Zone* by Paul R. Bassett; and *Hermit's Homage* by Lewis Cleckler. In May 1976, DTC sponsored a "Play Market," where several of these plays were presented for an invited group of critics, agents, producers, writers and directors. The next Play Market is planned for the spring of 1979, which will be the twentieth anniversary season of the DTC.

The theatre also operates a graduate theatre program, in conjunction with Trinity University in San Antonio, for the training of theatre artists, and a children's theatre school, devoted to an in-depth approach to helping children discover their talent. Performing and teaching in schools through an artist-in-the-school program, DTC artists, in short-term residencies, conduct classes for students in such subjects as Shakespeare, techniques of play production and mime.

DTC tours many of its productions. In 1976, under a grant from the National Endowment for the Arts and the Texas Commission on the Arts and Humanities, *Mirror under the Eagle* by Philip C. Lewis and Lawrence and Lee's *The Night Thoreau Spent in Jail* were taken to several communities in Texas. The tour included a residency at a school in each community, where members of the casts also held seminars. In 1977, the DTC made an eight-state tour of mid-America with its productions of *Hamlet ESP* and *Get Happy!* This same series will continue in 1978 with *Scapino* and *The Oldest Living Graduate*. DTC also regularly takes its productions to Trinity University.

Another community service is the presentation of free performances in Dallas parks. In the summers of 1976 and 1977, DTC, in association with the Dallas Park Board, presented 55 performances to an estimated 35,000 people. Free performances in children's hospitals and special plays and symposia devoted to human problems are also presented on tour throughout Texas. In 1976–77, a series entitled *Close to Home*, written by Charles Beachley III, dealt with the problems of the aged, neighborhood crime and child abuse. In 1977–78, a scheduled series entitled *The Cause of This Effect*, also by Mr. Beachley, will deal with the rural Texas family, divorce, the Texas penal system and the industrialization of rural Texas.

The Theater Center, located on a wooded site four miles from downtown Dallas, serves the Dallas–Fort Worth "metroplex" of three million people. In 1973, the Theater Center board of directors presented the theatre complex, debt-free, as a gift to the city of Dallas, which now maintains the property as a major civic asset.

Programs & Services: *Professional theatre training in conjunction with Trinity University; children's theatre and workshops; performances, seminars and workshops for students; touring performances and symposia; Theater in the Parks, free performances; free ticket program; group ticket discounts; auction; DTC Women's Committee; Off Stage, subscriber newsletter; post-performance discussions.*

PAUL BAKER
Managing Director

3636 Turtle Creek Boulevard
Dallas, Texas 75219
Telephone (214) 526-0107
Box Office (214) 526-8857

Founded 1959
Robert D. Stecker, Sr., Beatrice Handel,
Paul Baker, Dallas citizens

Season
October – July

Schedule
Evenings
Tuesday – Saturday
Matinees
Wednesday & Saturday

Facilities
Kalita Humphreys Theater
Seating capacity 416
Stage   Thrust
Down Center Stage
Seating capacity 56
Stage   Proscenium

Budget
Sept 1, 1976 – Aug 31, 1977
Operating budget $1,041,119
Earned income $ 634,725
Unearned income $ 412,042

Audience
Kalita Humphreys Theater
Percent of capacity 75
Number of subscribers 10,238
Down Center Stage
Percent of capacity 80
Number of subscribers 311

Touring contact
Bill Feagan
Ozark Attractions
P.O. Box 7
Mountain View, Arkansas 72560
(501) 269-8040

Productions, 1976
As You Like It, William Shakespeare
The Contrast, Royall Tyler
Girl Crazy, Guy Bolton & Jack McGowan;
music, George Gershwin; lyrics,
Ira Gershwin
Tom Sawyer, Mark Twain; adapted,
Frank Luther

Productions, 1977
Babes in Arms, Richard Rodgers &
Lorenz Hart; adapted, George
Oppenheimer
The Dell'Arte Clown Circus;
adapted, Dell'Arte company
The Loon's Rage, Joan Holden, Steve Most,
Jael Weisman

Victoria Thatcher and Jon' Paul Cook in *The Loon's Rage* by Steve Most, Jael Weisman and Joan Holden, directed by Jael Weisman, sets & masks by Alain Schons, costumes by Nancy Malsie. Photo: Frank Condon.

Joan Schirle and Daniel Smith in Shakespeare's *As You Like It*, directed by Jael Weisman, sets by Alan Choy, costumes by Jill Peterson. Photo: Richard Duning.

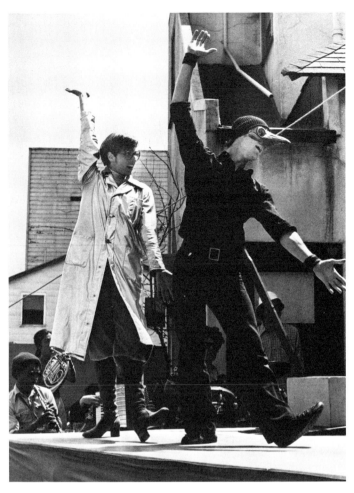

Dell'Arte

The Dell'Arte company is a multifaceted organization with service as its main objective. It serves theatre arts students through training; its local community through a professional repertory company; the community-at-large through a professional touring company and outreach programs; and theatre arts in general through the preservation of classical forms, the development of new forms and a respect for theatre as a reflection of the human condition.

The Dell'Arte School of Mime and Comedy is an intensive two-year training program in which theatre philosophy and techniques are taught to young performers, with an emphasis on physical skills and the commedia style. The curriculum, under the instruction of performer-teachers from all over the world, includes mime, acrobatics, juggling, clowning, acting, dance, commedia and related skills.

The Grand Comedy Festival (GCF) at Qual-a-wa-loo, a summer festival repertory company, has presented more than 23 classic, contemporary and experimental plays in the past six years. The GCF has been in residence at the College of the Redlands in Eureka but is seeking its own permanent home.

Dell'Arte also includes a professional touring company which presents original works during state, regional and national tours. *The Loon's Rage*, an original musical satire, is performed in the commedia style and is based on native American mythological characters. This production tours throughout the state of California, with funding from the California Arts Council's theatre touring program. Dell'Arte also makes live theatre available to the sick, aged, incarcerated and the socially or economically deprived, through its outreach programs. Student projects, developed at the School of Mime and Comedy, are taken into the community and performed at schools, senior citizen centers, hospitals, rural health centers and Indian reservations. In the spring of 1977, Dell'Arte students developed the Clown Circus, and the last two weeks of their training were devoted to daily performances at area schools.

Programs & Services: *Dell'Arte School of Mime and Comedy, two-year professional training; performances and teacher workshops in elementary schools; touring; film series; Environmental Education Program, workshops for children.*

CARLO MAZZONE-CLEMENTI
Artistic Director
JOAN SCHIRLE
Administrative Director

P.O. Box 816
Blue Lake, California 95525
(707) 668-5411

Founded 1971
Carlo & Jane Mazzone-Clementi

Season
July – August
Touring
October – December

Schedule
Evenings
Tuesday – Saturday
Matinees
Saturday & Sunday

Budget
Oct 1, 1976 – Sept 30, 1977
Operating budget $55,000
Earned income $34,700
Unearned income $20,300

Touring contact
Joan Schirle

Productions, 1975–76
Goosebumps; compiled, Dinglefest
Theatre Company
Vacuum Pact; compiled, Dinglefest
Theatre Company
Chautauqua, Patti McKenny

Productions, 1976–77
Cap Streeter, Robert Fiddler; music,
Tony Flacco & Gary Konigsfeld
Fresh or Frozen; compiled, Dinglefest
Theatre Company
Split the Differents, Colin Stinton,
Gareth Mann, Frank Fetters
Young Bucks, John Kunik

Dean Matthews, Don Humbertson and Chuck Bailey
in *Cap Streeter* by Robert Fiddler, Tony Flacco &
Gary Konigsfeld, directed by Byron Schaffer, sets by
Thomas Herman, costumes by Teri Brown. Photo:
B. Schaffer.

Doris Salisbury, Robert Fiddler and Alice Molter in
Vacuum Pact by Dinglefest Theatre Company,
directed by Byron Schaffer, sets by David Jewell,
costumes by Doris Salisbury. Photo: B. Schaffer.

Dinglefest Theatre Company

The Dinglefest Theatre Company was founded in 1969 with three basic purposes: an artistic goal of applying contemporary performance theory and practice to socially significant comedy theatre, and to create original comedic scripts based on the American experience; a professional goal to strengthen and refine the performance abilities of the company, while providing experience and training in arts management skills; and a community service goal to share the work of the company with the community through performance, with students through workshops and discussions, and with fellow professionals through the exchange of information, equipment and facilities.

The Luther Burbank Dingleberry Festival (shortened to the Dinglefest) began out of a seminar on contemporary rehearsal technique, to explore the relationship of communal development techniques and the production of comedy. The results of these continued explorations have ranged from the production of an audience-participation piece entitled *Vegetable Night* to "happenings" and guerilla theatre. The single most important component of each of these techniques has been the maintaining of an atmosphere conducive to the spontaneous development of work through the ensemble process. The Dinglefest has developed what the company calls the "verbatim technique," or the word-for-word usage of excerpts from popular literature, including cereal boxes, essays and magazine articles, in the improvised development of a theme for full-length productions. Five choreographed satirical comedies have been created by the company using this technique, including *Verbatim, Guessworks* and, perhaps the most successful, *Tom Swift.*

From its inception, the company has maintained a strong touring program. In January 1976, the theatre was able to support a touring company, as well as a company in residence. That year the resident company presented the theatre's first scripted play, *Chautauqua* by Patti McKenny.

In November 1976, the company began renovations on the Theatre Building, a permanent multi-performance space facility, which they now share with the Travel Light Theatre and Chrysalis, a children's theatre company. The new facility opened in March 1977, with the company's play, *Cap Streeter.*

The Dinglefest is very concerned about encouraging the involvement of the Lake View community in the Theatre Building. To that end, the company sponsored a Building Festival to acquaint, through free performances and other activities, community members with the work of its resident companies and artists.

Programs & Services: *Arts management and performance internships; touring; performances for students; student and senior citizen ticket discounts; free ticket and voucher programs; "verbatim technique" workshops;* Dinglefest Newsberry, *newsletter;* Let's Dingle, *tour brochure.*

BYRON SCHAFFER, JR.
Artistic Director/Producer
RUTH E. HIGGINS
Producer

1225 West Belmont Avenue
Chicago, Illinois 60657
Telephone (312) 929-7367
Box Office (312) 327-5252

Founded 1969
Byron Schaffer, Jr.

Season
August – July

Schedule
Evenings
Wednesday – Sunday
Matinees
Sunday

Facilities
North Theatre
Seating capacity 150
Stage Flexible

Budget
Jan 1, 1976 – Dec 31, 1976
Operating budget $130,393
Earned income $ 62,841
Unearned income $ 72,571

Audience
Percent of capacity 63

Touring contact
Thomas Doman

Booked-in events
Performing arts groups

Productions, 1975–76
The Chickencoop Chinaman, Frank Chin
*Nobody on My Side of the Family
Looks Like That*, Dom Magwili
The Three Sisters, Anton Chekhov
The Asian American Hearings; compiled,
East West Players

Productions, 1976–77
*That's The Way The Fortune
Cookie Crumbles*, Ed Sakamoto
And the Soul Shall Dance, Wakako
Yamauchi
Gee Pop, Frank Chin

Ralph Brannen in Dom Magwili's *Nobody on My Side
of the Family Looks Like That*, directed by Alberto
Isaac, sets by Rae Creevey, costumes by R.A.G.'s.
Photo: Rae Creevey.

Acting ensemble of *The Asian American Hearings*,
company compiled and directed, sets by Rae
Creevey and David Hirokane, costumes by Denice
Kumagai. Photo: Rae Creevey.

East West Players

The East West Players is a nonprofit Asian-American theatre and workshop dedicated to a continuing and growing program of community involvement through the performing arts. Founded in 1965 in a church basement, for the purpose of developing a cultural understanding between the East and West, the East West Players is the only Asian-American repertory company in the United States. It now occupies three buildings including a 95-seat theatre, a media center for experimental television work, classrooms, rehearsal areas and offices. The East West Players' season includes original works and revivals ranging from Chinese opera to classical Asian and European drama. The emphasis, however, is on original work and in the past 10 years over 35 plays have received their initial presentation at the theatre.

The Players' company has channeled their collective talents toward the development of an Asian-American theatre with a literature of its own. It is hoped that this will be accomplished through the sharing of past experiences as well as the newer understanding of history which has been developed from the Asian-American point of view. For the past 100 years the desire to assimilate has markedly influenced the Asian-American cultural development. Now the present must be considered — the current problems of stereotyping, racial discrimination leading to economic discrimination and a Caucasian-dominated business world. The point must be reached where Asian-American actors are considered American actors. These are the seeds the East West Players is planting. The harvest will be an Asian-American theatre with a new language and literature based on Asian-American "lingo," a new sound heard through Asian-American music and, finally, a new movement based on the contemporary as well as the traditional expression of the Asian-American experience.

Currently the East West Players offers three full productions in repertory, three experimental productions, two touring productions, one theatre-for-youth production which tours, and two children's workshops. As part of a developmental program for playwrights, a writer-in-residence has been commissioned to work with the company to develop a full-length play. The company also sponsors an annual, national playwriting contest. The company's Total Theatre Ensemble performs annually in a city-wide tour of children's plays. These programs are supplemented by an intensive training program for instructors and students in both Eastern and Western theatre forms. This workshop in theatre arts offers training in acting, directing, movement, dance, writing, stage managing, design and special children's classes in drama and dance.

Programs & Services: *Acting workshops; directing seminar; technical and administrative internships; Total Theatre Ensemble, children's theatre workshop and performance group; demonstration workshops in schools; touring; slide and lecture series; student, senior citizen and group discount ticket programs; free ticket program; Friends of East West Players; newsletter to company; East West Journal, a biannual publication.*

MAKO IWAMATSU
Artistic Director
RAE CREEVEY
Executive Producer
NORMAN COHEN
Administrator

4424 Santa Monica Boulevard
Los Angeles, California 90029
(213) 660-0366

Founded 1965
Beulah Quo, Mako, Pat Li, Guy Lee,
Jimmy Hong, June Kim

Season
October – April

Schedule
Evenings
Thursday – Sunday

Facilities
Seating capacity 95
Stage Flexiscenium

Budget
July 1, 1976 – June 30, 1977
Operating budget $123,703
Earned income $ 73,024
Unearned income $ 51,027

Audience
Percent of capacity 60
Number of subscribers 225

Touring contact
Norman Cohen

*Operates on AEA Hollywood Area
and Theatre for Youth contracts.*

Productions, 1975–76
El Fin del Mundo (El Huracan), El
Teatro Campesino company
La Virgin del Tepeyac; adapted, El
Teatro Campesino company
Pastorela; adapted, El Teatro Campesino
company

Productions, 1976–77
El Fin del Mundo II, El Teatro
Campesino company
Rose of the Rancho, David Belasco,
Richard Walton Tully; adapted, Cesar
Flores
Pastorela; adapted, El Teatro Campesino
company
La Virgen del Tepeyac; adapted, El
Teatro Campesino company
La Carpa de los Rasquachis, El Teatro
Campesino company

Rosa and "Smiley" in *El Corrido*, a satirical look at
the stereotyping of Chicanos in the United States,
shown by KCET-TV as part of the *Visions* series. *El
Corrido* was adapted from El Teatro's stage
production, *La Carpa de los Rasquachis.*

Company members in *El Fin del Mundo* by the El
Teatro Campesino company.

El Teatro Campesino

Born out of the social struggle of the United Farm Workers in California, the work of El Teatro Campesino is part of an international movement of cultural activists struggling to recapture the power of self-determination and to establish anew the humanity and dignity of Chicano reality, through the popular arts. If Chicanos remain a mystery to the rest of America, it is a mystery whose story can only be accurately expressed in Chicano words.

The artistic aims of El Teatro have basically remained the same: to replace the lingering negative stereotype of the Mexican in the United States with a new positive image created through Chicano art, and to continue to dramatize the social despair of Chicanos living in an Anglo-dominated society. As a theatre company and cultural organization, El Teatro is a group of people striving to express Chicano reality to other Americans who are, perhaps, unfamiliar with what Chicanos represent as a people or a cause. El Teatro's cultural responsibility commits it to the inspiration and development of actors, actresses, directors and playwrights, giving them the opportunity to work locally, nationally and internationally in television, motion pictures and professional theatre. El Teatro is presently involved in the development of a training program able to accommodate more visiting artists interested in working with the company, as well as other theatre and media experts seeking professional exchange. In short, El Teatro is committed to the involvement of Chicano *teatro* in the mainstream of American theatrical arts.

El Teatro Campesino has produced theatre, films, records, radio and television programs, books and puppet shows. It also produces folk theatre pieces for its local community in San Juan Bautista, a small mission town of 1,200 people. The folk theatre productions reflect an effort to revive and maintain popular cultural traditions which are slowly being forgotten in this media age.

The root of El Teatro Campesino is at the very heart of this popular theatre, and the Campesino troupe has searched for a new expression drawing from historical sources. These roots are apparent in the traditional *Pastorelas* or Shepherds' plays of Mexico, brought from Europe by the Spanish Franciscan missionaries in the sixteenth century. Town by town, the tradition has been forgotten, extinguished, one by one, like so many candles. El Teatro now lights a candle to the colorful *Pastorela* each Christmas season in the streets of San Juan Bautista. El Teatro's intent is to present a simple, direct and yet charming, up-to-date version of this ancient and wonderful traditional celebration. Since 1971, also during the Christmas season, El Teatro has offered its adaptation of the play *La Virgen del Tepeyac* from the original eighteenth-century version. The heart of the play is the living story of Juan Diego and his *Senora*, the Virgin of Guadalupe. This miracle play is part of the spiritual, cultural and historical heritage of El Teatro's region and symbolically achieves its deepest significance when staged inside the old mission of San Juan Bautista, the "cathedral of California missions."

Each year on June 24, in its community, El Teatro presents *El Baile de los Gigantes* (*The Dance of the Giants*), a recreation of a thousand-year-old ceremony of the Chorti Indians of the Yucatan. Presented at the summer solstice, when the sun is at its zenith, it is based on the mythology of a Mayan sacred book, which dramatizes the creation of the world. The performance ties the entire human race to the universe and maintains the continuity of a religious tradition that implies a cultural unity across the centuries. In drawing from the character of San Juan Bautista, El Teatro also presents new portrayals of early California history through adaptations of traditional plays, as well as original works based on historical characters or events.

Programs & Services: *Pensamiento Serpentino, workshops on the method and working techniques of El Teatro; lectures about El Teatro with films and music; children's productions; touring; film festival;* El Teatro Campesino Newsletter, *monthly.*

LUIS VALDEZ
Director
PHIL ESPARZA
Administrative Director

P.O. Box 1278
San Juan Bautista, California 95045
(408) 623–4505

Founded 1965
Luis Valdez

Season
Year-round

Budget
Jan 1, 1976 – Dec 31, 1976
Operating budget $151,366
Earned income $109,407
Unearned income $ 24,812

Touring contact
Phil Esparza

Productions, 1975-76
Ronnie Bwana, Jungle Guide, Phil Shallat
& John Engerman
Vampire, Snoo Wilson
Gertrude, Wilford Leach
Dandy Dick, Arthur Wing Pinero
Bullshot Crummond, Ron House, Diz White,
Alan Shearman, John Neville-Andrews,
Derek Cunningham
The Sea, Edward Bond
Molly Bloom, James Joyce; adapted,
Randi Douglas
Pilk's Madhouse, Ken Campbell & Henry Pilk
Yanks 3 Detroit 0 Top of the Seventh,
Jonathan Reynolds
Gammer Gurton's Needle, anonymous

Productions, 1976-77
American Buffalo, David Mamet
Knuckle, David Hare
Heat, William Hauptman
School for Clowns, Ken Campbell
Butley, Simon Gray
Sexual Perversity in Chicago and
Squirrels, David Mamet
Jesse and the Bandit Queen, David Freeman
Klondike!, Phil Shallat & Martin La Platney
Born to Maximize, Phil Shallat & John
Engerman
The Amazing Faz, or Too Good To Be Twoo,
Ken Campbell

Diane Schenker in *Gammer Gurton's Needle,*
anonymous, directed by Lori Larson, sets by Karen
Gjelsteen. Photo: Bob Peterson.

Steve Tomkins and Glenn Mazenn in David Mamet's
American Buffalo, directed by M. Burke Walker,
sets by Karen Gjelsteen, costumes by Celeste
Cleveland. Photo: Don Wallen.

The Empty Space Theater

The Empty Space is a script-oriented company that serves as a crucible for young theatre professionals. Actors, playwrights, directors, designers and production staff work in close collaboration with each other, utilizing a flexible theatre space that converts to any type of stage, from proscenium to arena, to present a busy schedule of contemporary scripts and carefully chosen period plays.

Begun as a summer project in 1970 by Burke Walker, the Empty Space was formally incorporated in 1971. Working in a 65-seat borrowed space, the company presented in its first two seasons 18 productions, which ranged from *The Tempest* and *Happy Days* to the first Seattle productions of the works of writers Peter Handke and Sam Shepard. Following a season on the road, September 1973 saw the Empty Space relocated in the light industry and warehouse section of Seattle's Capitol Hill district.

The pattern for the theatre's repertoire was established early on: new plays by contemporary authors and offbeat choices from the classical and modern repertoire—plays which bounce off and illuminate each other, with a strong emphasis on what the Empty Space calls Low Comedy. The company's approach is very physical, but never to the detriment of text; the approach is textual, but never at the sacrifice of vitality. Low Comedy productions grow out of burlesque, commedia, vaudeville, Delsarte, parody, Lecoq mask and clown techniques, nightclub revues, and popular American culture from Classic Comics to American Bandstand. While fostering a healthy disregard for traditional theatrical conventions, these productions help preserve company sanity and have become vital actor-training tools for the development of precision timing, spontaneity, daring, and a crucial sense of economy, all of which have created a maniacally articulate and presentational performance signature.

To augment the regular season schedule, the theatre's work has branched out to include an evening of seventeenth-century theatre and music with the Seattle Symphony Orchestra; Midnight Theater on Fridays and Saturdays; a core resident company; the loan of personnel to the city for the coordination of Seattle's Alternative Theater Festival; winter programs of workshops for gifted high school students from all over the state; a statewide touring program under federal and state sponsorship; and annual agency-sponsored free theatre in Seattle's Volunteer Park during the summer.

By choice, the emphasis in the 1975–76 mainstage season shifted even further to new plays, and, in 1976–77, the entire mainstage season focused on premieres by playwrights who had never been produced in Seattle. Together, those two seasons included premier Seattle productions for 10 major contemporary playwrights, including Edward Bond, Snoo Wilson (who was in residence with the Space to adapt *Vampire* for American audiences), William Hauptman, Simon Gray and David Mamet.

The theatre has begun commissioning new works from area playwrights such as Phil Shallat, John Engerman and Kurt Beattie, and is planning future residencies for authors from outside the Northwest. After seven seasons and 59 productions of 63 plays, 43 of which were area premieres, the heavy emphasis on new scripts is expected to continue, although not to the complete neglect of earlier plays. The Empty Space is continuing to expand its subscription audience and, by 1979–80, hopes to move to a larger facility.

Programs & Services: *Acting workshops; internships; performances and seminars for students; touring; free theatre in park series; In Progress Series, workshops and readings; student, senior citizen and group discounts; free ticket program; benefit performances.*

M. BURKE WALKER
Artistic Director
KATHY ROSMAN
Business Manager

919 East Pike Street
Seattle, Washington 98122
Telephone (206) 325-4443
Box Office (206) 325-4444

Founded 1971
M. Burke Walker, Julian Schembri,
Charles Younger, James Royce

Season
October – September

Schedule
Evenings
Wednesday – Sunday

Facilities
Seating capacity 99
Stage   Flexible

Budget
Oct 1, 1976 – Sept 30, 1977
Operating budget $144,978
Earned income $ 99,611
Unearned income $ 47,168

Audience
Percent of capacity 73

Touring contact
Joan Klynn

Booked-in events
*Small American & international
experimental or alternative
theatre companies*

Productions, 1975–76
The Shortchanged Review, Michael Dorn Moody
Getting Through The Night, John Ford Noonan
Possession, Lyle Kessler
Adam's Rib, Adam Keefe
Money, Arthur Giron

Productions, 1976–77
The Contest, Shirley Mezvinsky Lauro
Good-By And Keep Cold, John Ford Noonan
How Do You Do It?, Barbara Tarbuck
Reflections of a China Doll, Susan Merson
The Soft Touch, Neil Cuthbert
Relationships, Phillip Hayes Dean

Jack Gilpin and Beverly Barbieri in *Good-By And Keep Cold* by John Ford Noonan, directed by James Hammerstein. Photo: Ohringer.

Loren Brown, Estelle Omens and Mordecai Lawner in *The Contest* by Shirley Mezvinsky Lauro, directed by Paul Austin.

Ensemble Studio Theatre

The Ensemble Studio Theatre was founded in 1971 as a nonprofit organization for professional playwrights, actors, directors, designers and technicians. Its performance space is a fully equipped 100-seat theatre located in a city-owned warehouse in New York City, which also houses offices, dressing rooms, a shop and two floors of rehearsal space.

EST resulted from a need which arose within the professional theatre to create a unique nonprofit working environment. Its major objective is to preserve and develop the resources of the professional theatre by supporting, artistically and financially, the individual theatre artist, and by developing and presenting new works for the stage.

EST works toward accomplishing these goals by providing a physical home base for 26 playwrights in residence and a permanent company of more than 130 professional actors, directors, designers and technicians, as well as through its regular programs. EST's ongoing activities consist of a major production series of five new American plays each season; a workshop series wherein approximately 60 experimental projects — including improvisations, works in progress, readings and evaluation sessions — are conducted each year; a writers' support program, wherein playwrights receive financial aid to participate in productions and workshops and to complete works in progress; a directors' unit, recently formed to aid in the development of professionals in this much neglected area; an actors' workshop conducted by the actor-members, providing an opportunity for training in a creative, supportive atmosphere; and an internship program, which provides fully accredited training and work experience for college students and recent graduates.

EST's major production series of new American plays has led to the publication and production of new works both in the United States and abroad. EST has also conducted summer programs at Johnson State College in Johnson, Vermont; Rutgers University in New Brunswick, New Jersey, and at the Academy Festival Theatre in Lake Forest, Illinois. During these residencies, company members teach courses, develop new plays and present readings and workshops.

Programs & Services: *Directing and acting workshops; internships; new music series; workshop productions; staged readings; grants and aids to individual artists; voucher program.*

CURT DEMPSTER
Artistic Director
MARIAN GODFREY
Associate Director

549 West 52nd Street
New York, New York 10019
(212) 247-4982

Founded 1971
Curt Dempster

Season
October – June

Schedule
Evenings
Thursday – Sunday

Facilities
Seating capacity 100
Stage   Flexible

Budget
Oct 1, 1976 – Sept 30, 1977
Operating budget $86,490
Earned income $10,530
Unearned income $72,675

Audience
Percent of capacity 55

Operates under AEA Showcase Code.

Productions, 1975–76
The Duck Variations, David Mamet
Jumpers, Tom Stoppard
The Au Pair Man, Hugh Leonard
Nourish the Beast, Steve Tesich

Productions, 1976–77
Candida, George Bernard Shaw
A Day in the Death of Joe Egg, Peter Nichols
The Birthday Party, Harold Pinter
Seascape, Edward Albee
The Little Hut, Andre Roussin; adapted, Nancy Mitford

Nancy Kawalek and Mike Murphy in *Dreams* by Tom Sharkey, directed by Dennis Zacek, sets by Maher Ahmad, costumes by Marsha Kowal. Photo: Maher Ahmad.

Barry Cullison, Linda Kimbrough and Patricia Fraser in Edward Albee's *Seascape*, directed by George Keathley, sets by David Emmons, costumes by Jessica Hahn. Photo: Maher Ahmad.

The Evanston Theatre Company

The Evanston Theatre Company was founded in 1974 by Gregory Kandel, its current producing director, with the dual purpose of presenting theatrical productions and providing community service programs.

In the course of its brief history, the company has produced 13 productions, highlighted by the Midwest premieres of 2 major works of the 1970s, Tom Stoppard's *Jumpers* and *Seascape* by Edward Albee. Evanston is committed to the production of plays which contribute new ideas to Chicago theatregoers. The theatre's season, with productions of major contemporary works and revivals of well-known plays of the past, reflects a definite contemporary thrust in play selection. A goal of the theatre continues to be the formation of a permanent company, drawn from the rich resources of Chicago area talent. When the theatre moves to a larger space, it will begin to present plays in a rotating repertory schedule, which will make the company's operation unique in Chicago.

Community service projects have ranged from a 10-week program in creative dramatics for the elderly to a children's theatre company which tours to Chicago area parks. In 1977–78, the theatre is undertaking a major effort to secure funding for the development of a children's theatre program to include classes, in-school programs, professional productions and touring. The theatre's rehearsal-in-progress program, where the public is invited to watch directors and actors at work, has been particularly popular with the theatre's audience. In its first season of operation, the theatre instituted a second stage program which presents two works in progress with the playwrights in residence.

Due to the depth of its community roots, the Evanston Theatre Company has already received the financial support of over 60 companies and foundations, as well as the municipality of Evanston. The Theatre Company's offices, shops and rehearsal facilities are located at the Evanston Cultural Arts Center, a city center for both visual and performing artists and organizations.

Programs & Services: *Adult and children's acting workshops; management internships; performances and demonstrations for students; Rehearsal in Progress program, exploration of actor-director relationships with public in attendance; lecture-discussions with local critics; seminars in theatre production; student, senior citizen and group ticket discounts; free ticket program; speakers bureau; Advisory Council; Regional Relations Council, women's auxiliary;* Subscriber Newsletter; *post-performance discussions.*

GREGORY KANDEL
Producing Director

927 Noyes Street
Evanston, Illinois 60201
Telephone (312) 869-7732
Box Office (312) 869-7278

Founded 1974
Gregory Kandel

Season
September – January

Schedule
Evenings
Tuesday – Sunday
Matinees
Sunday

Facilities
Kingsley School Theatre
2300 Greenbay Road
Seating capacity 292
Stage Proscenium

Budget
July 1, 1976 – June 30, 1977
Operating budget $146,686
Earned income $ 97,734
Unearned income $ 50,438

Audience
Percent of capacity 57
Number of subscribers 2,360

Touring contact
Gregory Kandel

Operates on AEA LORT (D) contract.

Productions, 1975-76
A Whinny and A Whistle, Cheryl Scammon &
Mary Steenburgen; music, Matthew Kaplowitz
Alice Through the Looking Glass; adapted,
Susan Dias & Meridee Stein; lyrics,
Susan Dias; music, Philip Namanworth
Guess Again, Benjamin Goldstein; music,
Philip Namanworth
Who's Next?, David Damstra &
Matthew Kaplowitz
Adventures of Pinocchio; adapted, Meridee
Stein; music, Susan Dias & Matthew
Kaplowitz

Productions, 1976-77
A Whinny and A Whistle, Cheryl Scammon &
Mary Steenburgen; music, Matthew Kaplowitz
Alice Through the Looking Glass; adapted,
Susan Dias & Meridee Stein; lyrics,
Susan Dias; music, Philip Namanworth
Guess Again, Benjamin Goldstein; music,
Philip Namanworth
Three Tales at a Time, Candace Crisman,
Meridee Stein, Matthew Kaplowitz; lyrics,
Denny Douglas, Judie Thomas,
Susan Dias; music, Judie Thomas &
Jalalu'ddin Kalvert Nelson
Dorothy & the Wizard of Oz; adapted, Meridee Stein;
music, Matthew Kaplowitz & Philip Namanworth

Teen Company members in *A Whinny and a Whistle*
by Cheryl Scammon, Mary Steenburgen and
Matthew Kaplowitz, directed by Cheryl Scammon,
Meridee Stein and Paul Kreppel, designed by Ken
Holaman. Photo: Irvin Schwartz.

The Meri Mini Players in *The Clown Who Lost His
Smile* by Susan Dias and Norman Curtis, directed by
Meridee Stein, sets by Anthony Stein, Kathy Kunkel
and Denise Weber, costumes by Patricia Kraft.
Photo: ABC Television.

The First All Children's Theatre Company

In 1969, a unique concept in children's theatre was initiated when the Meri Mini Players, a repertory company of 6- to 13-year-olds, began presenting musical theatre productions by and for children. These works with original scores and books were, for the most part, created especially for the company. In the first three years the audience range expanded, the productions became more professional and the company members grew up. In 1972, to allow those older "Minis" to continue their training and performing, the Teen Company was formed. In 1976, a producing company now known as the First All Children's Theatre Company (First ACT) was incorporated as the nonprofit umbrella organization to oversee the programs of the two performing troupes.

Over the past eight years, the two companies have produced 13 original musical works. The organization, dedicated to training and developing young performers, teaches them to use their awakened interests and talents in every aspect of their lives; serves as a catalyst for writers, composers and lyricists in the development of quality works for young people; and inspires and cultivates a youthful audience to be aware of live theatre's ability to excite, reveal and challenge. The past two seasons have seen tremendous growth, with company enrollment doubling and audience size representing 95 percent of capacity. At the same time, the new works created for the company have become more and more sophisticated.

In the spring of 1975, both troupes performed a six-week residency at the New York Shakespeare Festival's Public Theater. The company also created an original musical, *The Clown Who Lost His Smile*, aired by WABC-TV, first as a Christmas special and later rebroadcast. First ACT has also appeared at the O'Neill Theater Center, on the NBC-TV *Today Show* and on the WNEW-TV special *Making It in New York*.

A special accomplishment of the company was the completion and production of a new musical, *Three Tales at a Time: A Trilogy of Shapes*. This piece, which includes a space fantasy, an African folk tale done in mime and a sea legend with chanties, took more than two years and a team of eight creative artists to develop.

In April of 1977, First ACT took a major step in its development as a performing arts center for children, when it acquired a new home across from Lincoln Center. Plans for this 10,000-square foot space call for two flexible theatres, scene and costume shops, and administrative offices. The new facility will allow for the incorporation of several new programs. The company's arts-in-education program will be expanded in coordination with the Fordham University Learning Center and offered to public schools in the New York City area. Plans for a school of the arts are now underway and will utilize the talents of First ACT's resident creative artists, technicians and administrators.

Each summer the Teen Company tours one or two productions throughout upstate New York and New England to camps and performing arts centers. In addition to their performances, the Teens offer workshops emphasizing theatre techniques, acting and mime skills, vocal training, and performance preparation and exercises.

Programs & Services: *Internships; performances, discussions and workshops for students; arts-in-education program in conjunction with Fordham University; touring; group discounts; free ticket program; benefit performances; quarterly newsletter.*

MERIDEE STEIN
Producer/Artistic Director
JACQUELINE BURNHAM
General Manager

37 West 65th Street
New York, New York 10023
(212) 873-6400

Founded 1969
Meridee Stein

Season
October – May

Schedule
Matinees
Saturday & Sunday

Facilities
Seating capacity 150
Stage ¾ Arena

Budget
May 1, 1976 – Apr 30, 1977
Operating budget $67,360
Earned income $ 8,611
Unearned income $72,777

Audience
Percent of capacity 75

Touring contact
Jacqueline Burnham

Productions, 1975-76
Caspar Hauser, Peter Handke; adapted, FST company
Mime, Etc., FST company
The Judicial Woes of Peter Bowes; adapted, Richard Hopkins
Endgame, Samuel Beckett
Florida: Feast of Flowers, FST company

Productions, 1976-77
Insight Out, Jerry Brown & Terri Mastrobuono
Florida: Feast of Flowers, FST company
Extremities, FST company

Karen Grant and Finnean Jones in *Extremities,* ensemble created, directed by Jon Spelman. Photo: George Goethe.

Mady Schutzman, Jerry Brown, Preston Boyd and Terri Mastrobuono Brown in *Florida: Feast of Flowers,* ensemble created. Photo: George Goethe.

Florida Studio Theatre

The Florida Studio Theatre (FST) was founded in 1973 by Jon Spelman, its artistic director. FST is engaged in the long-range exploration of what is central to the act of theatre. The company's work focuses on answering such questions as: what is acting; what causes a theatre piece to "work"; how can plays best be made; what forms can be evolved which speak both widely and deeply to a variety of audiences; how do nontraditional theatre audiences respond to a theatrical event; what kinds of training, process, organizational structure and conditions best prepare the theatre worker for meetings with those audiences; what makes theatre different from film and television and how can those differences be enhanced; what theatrical "rules" and "conventions" seem essential to performance; how are these kinds of questions and explorations both useful and possible in the current context of the American theatre and society?

FST has worked with new plays and published scripts by Handke and Beckett; experimented with plays adapted from the medieval era; collaborated on mime and street theatre pieces with historians and scientists; and developed a number of works through the group process. How the group and collaborative process is best served is one of the company's chief concerns. In the future FST plans further exploration of this process and more collaborative efforts with playwrights in residence. The company also plans to develop work with a resident literary manager, explore the different theatrical uses of narrative and other nondramatic material, present bilingual productions, and perform Shakespearean plays in both studio and large outdoor productions. Most FST productions use simple scenery and lights with the prime focus being each actor's presence, versatility, intensity and immediacy.

FST is a touring theatre. The major part of its performing year is used for touring productions, usually two or three in a traveling repertoire, to many locations throughout Florida. The company has also toured throughout the Southeast and to Washington, D.C., and Baltimore, where it performed at the New Theatre Festival. Performances are given at colleges and theatres, but most touring shows are staged in traditionally nontheatrical spaces for audiences who do not normally attend the theatre. Regularly scheduled performance sites include prisons, community centers, churches, recreation centers and housing complexes. In order to attract as many different kinds of people as possible, most FST performances are offered without an admission charge. In addition to single touring performances, the company offers workshops, community residency programs, lecture-demonstrations and post-performance discussions.

After a long search for an appropriate space, Florida Studio Theatre is now headquartered in an historic building in downtown Sarasota, built in 1913. The building contains administrative offices, meeting space, a small technical workshop, and a 75-seat theatre where the company rehearses and performs 20 to 30 times a year for the general public. In its new space, the company plans to expand its local programs and to host other touring groups and conferences aimed at sharing ideas, methods and programs with other theatres. In December 1976, the company hosted a "Sharing Conference" for 12 southeastern alternative theatre groups. In September 1977, the company was represented at an international colloquium, organized by UNESCO and the International Theatre Institute, in Bergamo, Italy.

Programs & Services: *College credit work-experience program; performances in schools with demonstrations, workshops and discussions; touring to non-theatregoing audiences; free and benefit performances; member of Sarasota Professional Arts Alliance, fund-raising organization; FST Association, contributing members; prison residencies; volunteers; newsletter; performance-centered discussions.*

JON SPELMAN
Artistic Director
MARTY ARDREN
Managing Director

4619 Bay Shore Road
Sarasota, Florida 33580
(813) 355-4096

Founded 1973
Jon Spelman

Season
October – June

Facilities
1241 North Palm Avenue
Seating capacity 75
Stage Flexible

Budget
Jan 1, 1976 - Dec 31, 1976
Operating budget $80,761
Earned income $25,089
Unearned income $58,868

Audience
Percent of capacity 78

Touring contact
Marty Ardren

Booked-in events
Experimental & children's theatre, mime, dance & music groups

Productions, 1975–76
The Collected Works of Billy the Kid,
Michael Ondaatje; music, Desmond McAnuff
The Comedy of Errors, William Shakespeare
Medal of Honor Rag, Tom Cole
Henry V, William Shakespeare
All's Well That Ends Well, William Shakespeare

Productions, 1976–77
The Fool: Scenes of Bread and Love,
Edward Bond
Much Ado About Nothing, William Shakespeare
Mummer's End, Jack Gilhooley
Black Elk Speaks, John G. Neihardt;
adapted, Christopher Sergel
A Midsummer Night's Dream, William Shakespeare

John LaGioia in *Mummer's End* by Jack Gilhooley,
directed by Louis W. Scheeder, sets by David
Chapman, costumes by Bob Wojewodski. Photo:
Joe B. Mann.

Etain O'Malley and Steven Gilborn in *Much Ado
About Nothing* by William Shakespeare, directed by
Jonathan Alper, sets by Raymond C. Recht,
costumes by Jennifer Von Mayrhauser. Photo: Joe
B. Mann.

Folger Theatre Group

The Folger Theatre Group is a division of the internationally recognized Folger Shakespeare Library. In 1969 newly appointed Library Director O.B. Hardison set out to break down the barriers between the community and the library's resources of Elizabethan, Renaissance and eighteenth-century materials. In this effort to make the library accessible to both scholars and the general public in new and vibrant ways, the Folger Theatre Group was founded. Since its modest first season of four productions and 84 performances, the Folger Theatre Group has become the library's most successful and visible public program, and has matured into a nationally recognized professional theatre.

The Theatre Group is a working member of several distinct communities. It contributes to the programs of the Folger Shakespeare Library by bringing life to the works of the playwright which the library enshrines. Located two blocks from the United States Congress, the theatre provides a unique forum for plays dealing with social issues. And as a part of the regional theatre movement, it contributes to the development of the theatre with the premieres of challenging new works by American, Canadian and British playwrights.

Capitalizing on its facility, a replica of an Elizabethan stage, and the scholastic wealth of the library, the Folger Theatre Group has embraced Shakespeare as its "playwright in residence." After seven seasons of producing nearly one-third of his works, the Theatre Group has developed an American approach to Shakespeare's classics. Relying heavily on the text itself — its lyricism, inherent sensibility and almost symphonic qualities — the Folger's regularly returning actors, directors and designers continually "go back to the words," by avoiding the arbitrary imposition of artifice upon Shakespeare's works.

From the beginning, the premieres of new plays have been an integral part of the Folger's identity. The parallel production of classic and contemporary plays has caused a cross-fertilization and constructive friction of style and approach.

Since Louis W. Sheeder became Folger's producer in 1973, the theatre has increased its number of subscribers from 638 to 5,853, its yearly attendance from 15,694 to 55,772 and its weeks of performance to 36. The 1976–77 season played to 105 percent attendance, and for the first time earned income broke the quarter-million dollar mark. Entering its eighth season, the Folger Theatre Group continues to expand its activity. It will resume its lecture-demonstration program with both students and teachers next season in cooperation with the D.C. school system and the D.C. Commission on the Arts. Its accessibility will be broadened by special performances for the deaf community of Washington with sign language interpreters on stage. Two Folger productions have been staged Off Broadway in New York: Tom Cole's *Medal of Honor Rag* in 1976, and the 1973 production of David Freeman's *Creeps*. The production of new plays and Shakespearean works by the Folger, many directed by Mr. Scheeder and Literary Consultant Jonathan Alper, has contributed greatly to the emergence of Washington as a major cultural center in the United States.

Programs & Services: *Internships; performances for students; Actors In The Schools program; performances for the deaf; student, senior citizen and group discounts; benefit performances; volunteers; Asides, subscriber and contributor newsletter; Midday Musings, informal discussion series.*

LOUIS W. SCHEEDER
Producer
MICHAEL SHEEHAN
General Manager

201 East Capitol Street, SE
Washington, DC 20003
Telephone (202) 547-3230
Box Office (202) 546-4000

Founded 1970
O.B. Hardison &
Richmond Crinkley

Season
October – July

Schedule
Evenings
Tuesday – Sunday
Matinees
Saturday & Sunday

Facilities
Seating capacity 214
Stage   Thrust

Budget
July 1, 1976 – June 30, 1977
Operating budget $530,224
Earned income $331,453
Unearned income $170,479

Audience
Percent of capacity 99.8
Number of subscribers 5,818

*Operates on AEA LORT (D)
contract.*

Productions, 1975–77
Frank Silvera Writers' Workshop presented more than 150 laboratory readings in the two-year period from 1975 through 1977.

Lloyd Richards at a critique session after the reading of *The Two Bit Garden* by Ruby Dee, 1975. Photo: Adger Cowans.

A reading of *Transcendental Blues* by Aishah Rahman. Photo: Adger Cowans.

Frank Silvera Writers' Workshop

The Frank Silvera Writers' Workshop (FSWW) was founded in 1973 by Garland Lee Thompson and since that time has developed a writers' laboratory that is now presenting over 90 new playwrights' work each year. The Workshop remains a living memorial to Frank Silvera who, prior to his death, was active in the production of black plays and the nurturing of black dramatic artists. His Theatre of Being, based in Los Angeles, provided a model for the Writers' Workshop. It is the purpose of FSWW to encourage the growth of black and third-world playwrights and to assist them in the development of their craft. The Monday and Saturday series of laboratory readings are geared to the needs of each playwright and also provide an opportunity for other writers to benefit from comments and suggestions made during the critique session immediately following each reading. In addition to the playwrights' workshops, FSWW's program includes a writers'-directors' unit, which in 1976–77 presented five staged readings of new works in progress, focusing on the development of the writer-director relationship. One of these staged readings, Richard Wesley's *The Last Street Play*, has since been showcased at the Manhattan Theatre Club and is scheduled for a Broadway production in 1977–78. Also in 1976–77, a new Artistic Technical Assistance Collective (ATAC) was formed to serve as a technicians pool for the Workshop, as well as other companies across the nation. More than 50 lighting and set designers, stage managers and production assistants are presently on file. It is the hope and aspiration of the ATAC program to create an important new school of communication specialists. The FSWW staged readings, through its writers'-directors' unit, provide the ATAC apprentices with actual theatrical situations in which to work and practice their skills. Monthly seminars, conducted by experts, are held on various aspects of stage productions.

As a result of a successful Playwriting Seminar Series sponsored by FSWW in the spring of 1977, four more playwriting seminars are planned for 1977–78. These seminars, to be conducted by Adrienne Kennedy, Richard Wesley, Owen Dodson and Alice Childress, are designed to help playwrights gain new perspectives on their craft and help experienced writers refine their work.

Programs & Services: *ATAC program, technical theatre training; writers'-directors' projects, staged readings; internships; Playwriting Seminar Series; ATAC workshop productions; theatre symposia; auction; New Audience and Grants Committee, support group.*

GARLAND LEE THOMPSON
Director
KAREN A. BAXTER
Administrative Coordinator

317 West 125th Street
New York, New York 10027
(212) 662-8463

Founded 1973
Garland Lee Thompson

Season
September – June

Schedule
Evenings
Monday
Matinees
Saturday

Facilities
Seating capacity 125
Stage   Flexible

Budget
July 1, 1976 – June 30, 1977
Operating budget $49,238
Earned income $16,908
Unearned income $32,750

Productions, 1975–76
Sonata, Bill Duke
The Secret Place, Garrett Morris

Productions, 1976–77
NOT, Daniel Owens
Emily T., Daniel Owens
Transcendental Blues, Aishah Rahman

Yvonne Warden and Richard Gant in
Transcendental Blues by Aishah Rahman, directed
by Kimako Baraka, sets by Carole Byard, costumes
by Linda Lee. Photo: Lynda Welch.

Naydne C. Spratt and Elizabeth Van Dyke in *Emily
T.* by Daniel Owens, directed by Kimako Baraka,
sets by Carole Byard, costumes by Linda Lee.
Photo: Lynda Welch.

Frederick Douglass Creative Arts Center

The Frederick Douglass Creative Arts Center (FDCAC) opened its doors in October 1971, as an outgrowth of the highly acclaimed Watts Writer's Workshop, begun in Los Angeles in 1965 by author Budd Schulberg. Open to any interested person, the Center, under the direction of playwright and screenwriter Fred Hudson, offers professional training in all forms of creative writing. In addition, a theatre performing ensemble, an actors' training program, and other writer-related projects are integral to the Center's program.

The primary goals of FDCAC are to bring completed, professional theatre experiences *to* the community *from* the community; develop black writers; encourage the creation of black artists' products and give both the artists and products exposure; place artists in a position of economic viability; and generate income in the community.

The Center's programs are product-oriented and offer professional training at both the beginner and advanced levels. Apprentices and participants in the training process reflect a unique mixture of the poor and affluent, coming together as a diverse group of emerging writers in an environment shared by working professionals. Since its inception, the Center has consistently fed developed talent and commercial products into the theatrical mainstream, based on the philosophy that FDCAC should not turn inward, but rather prepare its students for active participation in existing economic institutions.

The Center has evolved, from a single creative-writing class of eight students and an instructor, to a program of 17 free workshops — ranging from playwriting to poetry — and 15 instructors. The growth of FDCAC is reflected in the caliber of playwriting that now comes out of these workshops. For some, the experience at the Center has helped construct a real first chance for a productive life and, for others, it has offered a unique space for generating new and contemporary statements for the literature and performing arenas of theatre, television and film.

The Center's theatre program has defined for itself a special place in the black theatre world. It is writer oriented and committed to producing works that explore the deeper relationships and forces comprising the black experience today. With the writer as focus, the Center provides an intimate and supportive environment where the writer is encouraged and aided in shaping new insights and statements about the black ethos and the post-1960s era.

Complementing the training program for new playwrights, the Center's theatre program also consists of a performing ensemble of professional actors. The acting ensemble functions in a way that is organic to the writing process. In each case, plays have either a prepared reading or extensive work in the Center's playwriting unit, prior to public presentation. In the past, the Center has found its theatrical showcase program to be the most effective way of bringing the young writer and his work to public attention. Consequently, as a result of showcase productions, the works of writers developed at the Center have been produced by the New York Shakespeare Festival, KCET-TV's *Visions* series, La Mama E.T.C., the Negro Ensemble Company, the American Place Theatre, Theatre Genesis, and the New Heritage Theatre. In 1976–77, *Transcendental Blues* by Aishah Rahman and *Emily T.* by Daniel Owens were given showcase productions at the Manhattan Theatre Club.

Through its prepared reading series and the careful selection of scripts, FDCAC will continue to provide the support and direction essential for the growth and development of playwrights.

Programs & Services: *Acting workshops; Black Roots Festival, poetry readings; playwriting workshops and productions; student, senior citizen and group discounts; Friends of FDCAC, contributors; residencies; Advisory Council, fund-raising and audience development.*

FRED HUDSON
President/Artistic Director
CAROLYN TUCKER COUCH
Administrative Assistant

1 East 104th Street
New York, New York 10029
(212) 831–6113

Founded 1971
Budd Schulberg & Fred Hudson

Season
November – June

Schedule
Evenings
Friday – Sunday
Matinees
Sunday

Budget
July 1, 1976 – June 30, 1977
Operating budget $112,224
Earned income $ 5,919
Unearned income $ 92,822

Operates under AEA Showcase Code.

Productions, 1975-76
Workaday
A Crowd of People
Tomorrow, Etc.
Can the Human Race Survive Itself
Lexicon
Safari
FST Story

Productions, 1976-77
To Life
Declaration '76
Two Minutes Each
The Third Duckling
A Crowd of People
Workaday
Can the Human Race Survive Itself

All productions are created by Patrick Henry and the FST company.

Actress Frankie Hill and an audience member in a Free Street Theater warm-up session prior to a performance. Photo: Joany Carlin.

David Bush, Anne Binion and Hilda McLean from Free Street Too in *To Life*, adapted by Patrick Henry from discussions with the Free Street Too company.

Free Street Theater

The goal of the Free Street Theater is to stimulate a more creative society by bringing the arts into a responsible and meaningful relationship with daily life through programs which are free to the participating public. The original Free Street program, founded in 1969, is a mobile public theatre which presents free outdoor performances in parks, plazas, shopping malls — wherever people congregate. Based in Chicago, the company also tours original musical theatre productions to cities, towns and rural areas in 23 other states. In addition to performance activities, the company offers a variety of workshops and seminars designed to give direction, inspiration and encouragement to community-based arts organizations, and to provide a model for creative outreach programs which celebrate community spirit.

"Free Street Too" is a performing ensemble of older Americans, aged 67 and older, whose purpose is to focus public attention on the positive contributions older Americans can and still do make to society. This group instigates cross-generational communication and understanding through performance and workshop activities.

The Free Street Theater at the Chicago Public Library is the first free professional theatre season in the Chicago downtown area. The combined Free Street Theater performing companies present a variety of 14 productions at the library's Cultural Center. The schedule includes six plays for adults, six programs for children and two special events. The performance program focuses on literary heritage by bringing to life new scripts and adaptations of both classic and contemporary material. Many of the productions tour to branch library facilities as well.

The "Stucher Project" is Free Street's educational program which places performing artists in elementary school classrooms where they function as full-time student/teachers for a one-month period. The Stucher (part student and part teacher) program provides a catalyst by which students and teachers together develop alternative ways of understanding and applying standard classroom curriculum through the introduction of performing skills and methods.

Free Street's Arts and the Handicapped Program utilizes performance techniques to augment the rehabilitation processes of handicapped persons. Both performance and workshop components, focusing on the *whole* person, take place in hospitals and involve patients and therapeutic staff in new, stimulating relationships.

In addition to the above programs, Free Street Theater is frequently called upon to consult with representatives of municipal governments, social service organizations and urban renewal agencies. For these groups Free Street Theater is a resource for developing broadly based community arts activities. Free Street Theater is committed to engaging the 90 percent of the American population that has remained uninvolved in the arts. Nine years of experience has shown that their lack of involvement is not a result of disinterest, but rather of disconnection. Free Street Theater provides the conduit through which creative energy can begin to flow in order to generate a more positive and productive community environment.

Programs & Services: *Journeyman program in performance, technical and administrative areas; Stucher Program, in-school workshops; benefit performances; community residencies; touring; The Free Streeter, quarterly publication.*

PATRICK HENRY
Artistic Director/Producer

59 West Hubbard Street
Chicago, Illinois 60610
(312) 822-0460

Founded 1969
Patrick Henry & Perry Baer

Season
June – May

Schedule
Evenings
Varies (summer)
Wednesday &
Thursday (Oct – May)
Matinees
Wednesday &
Thursday (summer)
Friday &
Saturday (Oct – May)

Budget
Apr 1, 1976 – Mar 31,1977
Operating budget $298,231
Earned income $ 96,685
Unearned income $214,246

Touring contact
Roger Turpin

Operates on AEA Actor/Teacher contract.

Productions, 1975–76
Luv, Murray Schisgal
Fortune and Men's Eyes, John Herbert
Till Eulenspiegel's Merry Pranks;
adapted, George Street Playhouse company
Count Dracula, Ted Tiller
The Glass Menagerie, Tennessee Williams
The Threepenny Opera, Bertolt Brecht &
Kurt Weill

Productions, 1976–77
That Championship Season, Jason Miller
Brothers, Eric Krebs
Oh Coward!, Noel Coward; devised,
Roderick Cook
A Midsummer Night's Dream, William Shakespeare
The Mousetrap, Agatha Christie
The Memoirs of Charlie Pops, Joseph Hart
Waiting for Godot, Samuel Beckett

Samuel Maupin and John Vennema in *Waiting for
Godot* by Samuel Beckett, directed by Peter
Bennett. Photo: Suzanne Karp Krebs.

Bronwyn Rucker and Mark Blum in *Brothers* by Eric
Krebs, directed by Dino Narizzano. Photo: Suzanne
Karp Krebs.

George Street Playhouse

Born in a former supermarket which was renovated by an army of volunteers, and funded by 300 small donations totaling $10,000, the George Street Playhouse opened in September 1974, with George Bernard Shaw's *Arms and the Man*. Founded by Eric Krebs and John Herochik, the Playhouse presents a mixture of new American plays, classics and light entertainment; and for the 1977–78 season will play to an audience of more than 2,000 subscribers.

During its four years of operation, the Playhouse has grown in both its operating budget and number of subscribers. With a full Actors' Equity company, the Playhouse presents seven major productions each season, drawing heavily on the actor and director pool of New York City, which is located less than one hour away.

The Playhouse will tour a children's company through central New Jersey during the 1977–78 season, with more than 150 scheduled performances. The theatre has also maintained a program which sends one person from the Playhouse staff to area high schools to offer an introduction to theatre. Funds for these two programs have been made available through the Comprehensive Employment and Training Act (CETA).

Long-range goals of the theatre include the renovation of the existing building from its current 230 seats to 450, and the creation of a second space for experimental work. The Playhouse has continually emphasized developmental work on projects suggested by directors, which often lead to full productions.

Programs & Services: *Internships; performances for students; Reflections, one-man performance in schools; children's theatre productions and workshops; creative dramatics workshops for adults; booked-in performances; student, senior citizen and group ticket discounts; free ticket program; George Street Playhouse Guild, contributors; speakers bureau; cafe; Playhouse News, monthly newsletter; Sunday Discussions, post-performance.*

ERIC KREBS
Producer
JOHN HEROCHIK
Managing Director
BOB HALL
Artistic Director

414 George Street
New Brunswick, New Jersey 08901
Telephone (201) 246-3530
Box Office (201) 246-7717

Founded 1974
John Herochik & Eric Krebs

Season
October – May

Schedule
Evenings
Thursday – Sunday
Matinees
Wednesday & Sunday

Facilities
Seating capacity 230
Stage   ¾ Arena

Budget
July 1, 1976 – June 30, 1977
Operating budget $211,500
Earned income $119,000
Unearned income $ 85,000

Audience
Percent of capacity 77
Number of subscribers 1,300

Booked-in events
One-man shows

Productions, 1975–76
Arms and the Man, George Bernard Shaw
A Thurber Carnival, James Thurber
Play Strindberg, Friedrich Durrenmatt
Who Dunnit?, Paul Portner
The Contrast, Royall Tyler

Productions, 1976–77
Private Lives, Noel Coward
Sleuth, Anthony Shaffer
Much Ado About Nothing, William Shakespeare
Tartuffe, Moliere; translated,
Richard Wilbur
The Birthday Party, Harold Pinter
Relatively Speaking, Alan Ayckbourn
I Do! I Do!, Tom Jones & Harvey Schmidt

Cyril Mallett and Thora Nelson in *Relatively Speaking* by Alan Ayckbourn, directed by Gideon Y. Schein, sets by David Herwitz, costumes by Danica Eskind. Photo: Peter Blakely.

Timothy D. Landfield, Roger Forbes and Josh Burton in *The Birthday Party* by Harold Pinter, directed by Gideon Y. Schein, sets by David Herwitz, costumes by Danica Eskind. Photo: Pat Thornton.

GeVa Theatre

Founded in 1972 as the Genesee Valley Arts Foundation, GeVa is Rochester's only not-for-profit professional resident theatre. GeVa is located in the heart of downtown Rochester, providing a central location for all the outlying communities it serves, while contributing to the revitalization of the city.

GeVa was originally created with a resident repertory company of actors, and the selection of plays was dictated by the resources of the acting company. A change in the artistic and administrative leadership of the theatre in 1976–77 led to a change in the production philosophy, which now emphasizes the selection of the plays themselves, with the choice of actors based on the requirements of each play. While encouraging the frequent return of its theatre artists to maintain a sense of continuity for both the theatre and its audience, the theatre now emphasizes the play in production. Thus the choice of actor, director and designer now thoroughly reflects the needs of each individual production, which assures the flexibility in environment and technique required by each play.

Although its artistic philosophy has changed, GeVa's community programs remain. As the only professional resident theatre serving the greater Rochester area, GeVa maintains a large diversity of projects. At the core of GeVa's programs is its evening mainstage subscription series of six plays drawn from past and present literature of the American and international repertoire. Although the current emphasis is on a dynamic study of extant plays, GeVa hopes in the near future to serve the new playwright as well. In addition to its evening series, GeVa offers a series of six lunchtime productions for its downtown working public. In the 1977–78 season, these plays will also tour to schools, civic and social centers throughout the city. Finally, as in the past, GeVa maintains an active theatre-in-education program. In 1976–77, a National Endowment for the Humanities grant resulted in a touring company project to explore the uses of theatre techniques as teaching instruments. In 1977–78, a grant, under the Comprehensive Employment and Training Act (CETA), will aid in the production and tour of two children's shows aimed at two age groups. The grant will also help to continue the Saturday morning acting workshops at the theatre, and to expand a touring workshop program that will continue to develop future audiences.

Programs & Services: *Internships; performances and lectures for students; touring to schools; Saturday Morning Children's Workshop, theatre games and creative dramatics; plays for young audiences; touring; Lunchtime Theatre, series of one-acts; student, senior citizen and group discounts; speakers bureau; GeVa Stagehands, volunteers; subscriber newsletter.*

GIDEON Y. SCHEIN
Artistic Director
JESSICA L. ANDREWS
Managing Director

168 Clinton Avenue, South
Rochester, New York 14604
Telephone (716) 232–1366
Box Office (716) 232–1363

Founded 1972
William & Cynthia Selden

Season
October – April

Schedule
Evenings
Tuesday – Sunday
Matinees
Saturday & Sunday

Facilities
Seating capacity   185–230
Stage   Flexible

Budget
June 1, 1976 – May 31, 1977
Operating budget $300,272
Earned income $ 68,201
Unearned income $120,898

Audience
Percent of capacity   47
Number of subscribers   698

Touring contact
Bruce Rodgers

Operates on AEA LORT (D) contract.

Productions, 1975–76

Our Town, Thornton Wilder
Benito Cereno, Robert Lowell
Mourning Becomes Electra, Eugene O'Neill
The Last Meeting of the Knights of the White Magnolia, Preston Jones
Our Father's Failing, Israel Horovitz
The Devil's Disciple, George Bernard Shaw
American Buffalo, David Mamet
Three Plays of the Yuan Dynasty;
translated, Liu Jung-en
Chicago, Sam Shepard
The Local Stigmatic, Heathcote Williams
Dandelion Wine, Ray Bradbury; adapted,
Peter John Bailey
Statues and *The Bridge at Belharbour*,
Janet L. Neipris

Productions, 1976–77

Design for Living, Noel Coward
Long Day's Journey Into Night,
Eugene O'Neill
The Show–Off, George Kelly
Richard III, William Shakespeare
Streamers, David Rabe
Don Juan, Moliere; translated,
Christopher Hampton
Sizwe Bansi Is Dead, Athol Fugard,
John Kani, Winston Ntshona
The Sport of My Mad Mother, Ann Jellicoe
A Life in the Theatre, David Mamet
Kaspar, Peter Handke
George Jean Nathan in Revue; adapted,
Sidney Eden

W.H. Macy and Robert Christian in *Streamers* by
David Rabe, directed by Gregory Mosher, sets by
Joseph Nieminski, costumes by Marsha Kowal.

David Dukes, Carrie Nye, Aviva Crane and Brian
Murray in Noel Coward's *Design for Living*, directed
by William Woodman, sets by Joseph Nieminski,
costumes by James Edmund Brady.

Goodman Theatre

The Goodman Theatre, now in its fifty-second season, has a history spanning the 1920s when an acting company was in residence; the 1930s when a school of drama was formed under Dr. Maurice Gnesin and David Itkin; the 1940s when graduates included Geraldine Page, Karl Malden, Sam Wanamaker and Jose Quintero; the 1950s when John Reich reorganized the school and instituted a subscription series presenting professional guest artists performing with students on the main stage; and the burgeoning regional theatre movement in the 1960s when the Goodman, still under Mr. Reich, once again became a fully professional resident theatre.

The mainstage subscription series of six plays has been under the artistic direction of William Woodman since 1973. Mr. Woodman, directing two productions a year himself, brings in guest directors such as Michael Kahn, George Keathley and Gene Lesser, as well as performers from around the country to work with the Goodman's core of Chicago-based actors. Highlights from recent Goodman seasons include the U.S. premieres of Brian Friel's *Freedom of the City* and Edward Bond's *The Sea*; the world premiere of Israel Horovitz's *Our Father's Failing*; the Chicago premier presentations of Sam Shepard's *Tooth of Crime*, Christopher Hampton's *The Philanthropist* and Bertolt Brecht's *Arturo Ui*.

In 1974 Mr. Woodman initiated Goodman's Stage 2, under the direction of Gregory Mosher, which has since grown into one of the country's most active second-stage series. Utilizing a variety of spaces both in and around the Goodman complex, Stage 2 has offered the world premieres of David Mamet's *American Buffalo* and *A Life in the Theatre*; Chicago premieres of Peter Handke's *Kaspar* and Ann Jellicoe's *The Sport of My Mad Mother*; and productions of Ray Bradbury's *Dandelion Wine* and *Sizwe Bansi Is Dead* by Athol Fugard, John Kani and Winston Ntshona, which toured extensively in Illinois under the auspices of the State Arts Council.

During the 1970s the theatre has become a prime resource center for Chicago's young Off Loop theatres, with many Goodman staff members providing leadership, advice and information for these rapidly developing institutions.

The Goodman is located next to the Art Institute of Chicago, and maintains its own shops for set, prop and costume construction. The auditorium has wood-paneled walls and crystal chandeliers, while the proscenium stage is equipped with a plaster dome cyclorama and an Izenour electronic pre-set lighting system.

In July of 1977 the Chicago Theatre Group, Inc., was formed as the new producing unit and fund-raising arm for the Goodman Theatre. Most of Goodman's 35 staff members have joined the new group, and the recently formed board of directors includes a majority of the people who served on the Committee on the Goodman Theatre and School of Drama of the Art Institute. Over the next three years the Art Institute's financial responsibility will decrease, while the Chicago Theatre Group takes on the full task of maintaining one of Chicago's major cultural assets.

Programs & Services: *Internships; performances and seminars for students; student, senior citizen and group discount ticket programs; post-performance discussions; backstage tours for subscribers and students.*

WILLIAM WOODMAN
Artistic Director
JANET WADE
Managing Director

200 South Columbus Drive
Chicago, Illinois 60603
Telephone (312) 443-3811
Box Office (312) 443-3800

Founded 1925
The Art Institute of Chicago

Season
September – June

Schedule
Evenings
Tuesday – Sunday
Matinees
Thursday & Sunday

Facilities
Seating capacity 683
Stage Proscenium

Budget
July 1, 1976 – June 30, 1977
Operating budget $1,308,627
Earned income $ 728,930
Unearned income $ 579,697

Audience
Percent of capacity 68
Number of subscribers 15,320

Operates on AEA LORT (B) and (D) contracts.

Productions, 1976
Going Up, Otto Harbach & Louis A. Hirsch
Dearest Enemy, Herbert Fields, Lorenz Hart,
Richard Rodgers
Annie, Martin Charnin, Thomas Meehan,
Charles Strouse

Productions, 1977
Sweet Adeline, Oscar Hammerstein II &
Jerome Kern
Hit the Deck, Herbert Fields, Vincent Youmans,
Leo Robin, Clifford Grey, Irving Caesar,
Oscar Hammerstein II
The Red Blue-Grass Western Flyer Show,
Conn Fleming & Clint Ballard, Jr.

Sandy Goodspeed and Andrea McArdle in *Annie* by
Thomas Meehan, Martin Charnin and Charles
Strouse, directed by Mr. Charnin, sets by Edward
Haynes, costumes by David Toser. Photo: Wilson
Brownell.

Brad Blaisdell and Kimberly Farr in *Going Up* by
Otto Harbach and Louis A. Hirsch, directed by Bill
Gile, sets by Edward Haynes, costumes by David
Toser. Photo: Wilson Brownell.

Goodspeed Opera House

The Goodspeed Opera House, located in a restored antique playhouse on the banks of the Connecticut River, is the only theatre in America dedicated to the preservation of the American musical and to the development of new musical works. As such it has gained the attention of the theatre world with its annual production of two revivals of significant plays from America's musical heritage, and of a new musical theatre piece. Under the direction of Michael P. Price since 1968, Goodspeed's commitment is to be the home of the American musical theatre. As the musical is one of the few indigenous performing arts in America, the Goodspeed's creation of a theatre devoted exclusively to preserving and carrying forth that tradition is a unique service to both the public and the theatre community. The Opera House, seeking worthwhile vintage pieces to perform and thereby keep alive, follows four criteria when choosing revivals: the inherent worth of the script; the script's contribution to the American musical theatre tradition; its entertainment value; and the infrequency of its production. As authenticity is a hallmark of Goodspeed revivals, the Opera House employs the skills of musical theatre historians and musicologists in the preparation of productions.

Much the same criteria are applied to new works. For the authors of a new show, Goodspeed provides a well-equipped theatrical laboratory where their product can be tested in a congenial atmosphere. Now well regarded as a birthplace for the production of new musicals and revivals, it has been possible for the Goodspeed to transfer productions to theatres in New York, throughout the country and to London's West End. Seven Goodspeed productions have been produced on Broadway including *Man of La Mancha, Shenandoah, Something's Afoot, Going Up, Very Good Eddie* and *Annie*.

The Opera House itself is a model of Victorian architecture. Towering six stories over the Connecticut River, it was built by steamboat entrepreneur and theatre buff William Goodspeed in 1876. At that time East Haddam, Connecticut, was a thriving resort between Hartford and New York. The Opera House went into steady decline after Mr. Goodspeed's death in 1882 and ceased to function in 1920. In 1959 it was saved from the wrecker's ball by the Goodspeed Opera House Foundation, a nonprofit organization that undertook the costly and delicate task of restoration which lasted four years.

The Opera House Foundation has continued to preserve the Goodspeed as both a historic landmark and a living theatre. Members of the foundation now number over 4,000, thus insuring a broad base of audience and financial support through dues and contributions. Another important function of the foundation is its auxiliary arm, the Goodspeed Guild. The Guild extends hospitality to actors during their stay in East Haddam, gives tours of the facility, provides Saturday night suppers between shows for the cast and generally serves to provide a congenial and warm atmosphere for everyone involved.

The Goodspeed's audience is a major factor in its development as the home of the American musical. They have come to identify with the institution and through their support have enabled the theatre to expand from a 9-week summer operation to a 22-week season which runs from early spring through late fall.

Programs & Services: *Technical apprenticeships; Goodspeed Opera House Foundation, support group; London theatre tour and travelogue film series for Foundation members; bar; Goodspeed Guild, service group;* Goodspeed Opera House News, *quarterly publication for Foundation members.*

MICHAEL P. PRICE
Executive Director

Goodspeed Landing
East Haddam, Connecticut 06423
Telephone (203) 873-8664
Box Office (203) 873-8668

Founded 1963
Goodspeed Opera House
Foundation

Season
April – October

Schedule
Evenings
Tuesday – Saturday
Matinees
Wednesday, Saturday, Sunday

Facilities
Seating capacity 375
Stage   Proscenium

Budget
Jan 1, 1976 – Dec 31, 1976
Operating budget $776,490
Earned income $722,975
Unearned income $127,487

Audience
Percent of capacity 100

Operates on AEA special contract.

Productions, 1975–76
The Tempest, William Shakespeare
Dear Liar, Jerome Kilty
Ah, Wilderness!, Eugene O'Neill
The Devil's Disciple, George Bernard Shaw
Romeo and Juliet, William Shakespeare

Productions, 1976–77
Hamlet, William Shakespeare
Peg o' My Heart, J. Hartley Manners
In a Fine Frenzy; devised, Frederik N. Smith
The Glass Menagerie, Tennessee Williams
The Importance of Being Oscar,
Michael MacLiammoir
The Taming of the Shrew, William
Shakespeare

Sara Woods and Dennis Lipscomb in *The Taming of
the Shrew* by William Shakespeare, directed by
Daniel Sullivan, sets by John Ezell, costumes by
Algesa O'Sickey. Photo: Karabinus and Associates.

Bairbre Dowling as Laura in *The Glass Menagerie* by
Tennessee Williams, directed by Vincent Dowling,
sets by John Ezell, costumes by Michael Olich.
Photo: Karabinus and Associates.

Great Lakes Shakespeare Festival

In 1962, the Great Lakes Shakespeare Festival (GLSF) was chartered by its board of trustees as a professional nonprofit theatre with a mandate to produce classical drama. Since that time, the theatre has produced more than 80 different plays by some of the world's great dramatists, with an emphasis on the works of Shakespeare.

In its 16-year history, GLSF has reached considerably more than three-quarters of a million people. In its ongoing search for a larger and more knowledgeable audience, the theatre concentrates on developing a special relationship with young people. Consequently, in addition to the 80 regular evening performances during each summer season, special student matinees are scheduled each fall to introduce more than 16,000 young people annually to the excitement of classical theatre.

The Festival's single-ticket and subscription sales generate 63 percent of the theatre's total income. Additional funds are raised from federal and state arts agencies, local foundations, business and industry and loyal supporters from the greater Cleveland area.

Vincent Dowling, GLSF artistic director, defines the theatre's style in terms of the "pressure" of material. The Festival is developing as a theatre where artists, in an ensemble, can create clear, emotionally true, and intellectually stimulating dramatic work out of the raw materials of their own experience, imagination and talent, through the poetry of writers of enduring quality. These are primary pressures. The GLSF audience, consisting largely of people with roots in the state of Ohio, represents yet another pressure in the development of a coherent style for the theatre.

The 1976 and 1977 seasons were marked by significant growth in all areas. In 1976, Mr. Dowling, who had won recognition as an actor-director at Dublin's Abbey Theatre, was named the Festival's first resident artistic director. In 1977, an intern program was initiated to utilize and train outstanding university talent from all over the country; a major reorganization of administrative personnel brought with it the new full-time positions of general manager and director of development; the theatre produced its first world premiere; and the Festival visited 14 Ohio cities during its first major tour. The 1976 and 1977 seasons also resulted in a 13 percent increase in attendance for regular performances in Lakewood and a 33 percent increase in overall audience for both resident and touring productions.

Programs & Services: *Internships; performances for students; actor-in-the-classroom program; touring; student, senior citizen and group ticket discounts; free ticket program; Curtain Call, benefit performance; slide presentation; Women's Committee, volunteers.*

VINCENT DOWLING
Artistic Director
WILLIAM H. WITTE
General Manager

Lakewood Civic Auditorium
Lakewood, Ohio 44107
Telephone (216) 228-1225
Box Office (216) 521-0090

Founded 1962
Community members

Season
July – September
Touring
October

Schedule
Evenings
Tuesday – Sunday
Matinees
Sunday

Facilities
Franklin Boulevard at
Bunts Road
Seating capacity 989
Stage Proscenium

Budget
Nov 1, 1976 – Oct 31, 1977
Operating budget $389,070
Earned income $281,155
Unearned income $153,513

Audience
Percent of capacity 53
Number of subscribers 1,765

Touring contact
William H. Witte

Operates on AEA LORT (B) contract.

Productions, 1975-76
Arsenic and Old Lace, Joseph Kesselring
The Caretaker, Harold Pinter
A Streetcar Named Desire, Tennessee Williams
Loot, Joe Orton
Private Lives, Noel Coward
Under Milk Wood, Dylan Thomas
Mother Courage and Her Children, Bertolt
Brecht; translated, Robert Hellman
A Christmas Carol, Charles Dickens;
adapted, Barbara Field
Measure for Measure, William Shakespeare

Productions, 1976-77
The Matchmaker, Thornton Wilder
Cat on a Hot Tin Roof, Tennessee Williams
Doctor Faustus, Christopher Marlowe
An Enemy of the People, Henrik Ibsen;
translated, John Patrick Vincent
Rosencrantz & Guildenstern Are Dead,
Tom Stoppard
The Winter's Tale, William Shakespeare
A Christmas Carol, Charles Dickens;
adapted, Barbara Field
The National Health, Peter Nichols

Karen Landry, Peter Michael Goetz, Helen Carey
and John Pielmeier in Thornton Wilder's *The
Matchmaker,* directed by Michael Langham,
designed by Desmond Heeley.

Patricia Conolly and Peter Michael Goetz in *A
Streetcar Named Desire* by Tennessee Williams,
directed by Ken Ruta, sets by Jack Barkla, costumes
by Lewis Brown. Photo: Act Two Photography.

The Guthrie Theater

Now in its fifteenth year, the Guthrie Theater has become the largest resident theatre in the vast center of the United States. Its geographic isolation has played a part, albeit an ironic one, in the theatre's success, for it has been permitted to grow on its own terms, far away from the pressures and hazards of the coastal centers of American culture. It has thus had a rare leisure in which to explore its identity and its place in the community. This community, the Twin Cities metropolitan area and the five upper midwestern states which surround it, has accepted the Guthrie as an institution reflective of and sensitive to its special needs. And, in turn, Guthrie artists have discovered a faithful, partisan and well-educated audience, open to a wide variety of theatrical experiences.

The Guthrie Theater's main stage contains a vast 200-degree arc of seats which partly surround an asymmetrical thrust stage. This thrust provides an atmosphere of immediacy and excitement, as well as a sense of intimacy surprising in an auditorium with 1,441 seats. The actors are part of a permanent repertory company and the directors and designers are both resident and guest artists. The supporting technical facilities are among the most complete in the world. The plays of the Guthrie season are performed in rotating repertory, offering a theatregoer three or four choices in a given week.

The theatre's second stage, Guthrie 2, provides a balance to the primarily classical orientation of the main stage. Since its opening in 1976, it has produced works of new playwrights, as well as fresh, innovative examinations of classic plays. Guthrie 2 has also served the community by providing a space for experimental productions by other groups.

The Guthrie's Outreach Program responds to a variety of community needs. In addition to touring its five-state region with mainstage productions, a number of smaller programs have also toured. Outreach has also pursued an imaginative course in educational programming with community classes in all aspects of theatre scheduled year-round; workshops conducted in state prisons; and an innovative hospital-tour show taking a troupe of exuberant young entertainers into hospital wards, senior citizen centers and nursing homes.

Student matinees have become an accepted part of the Twin Cities' educational planning with the Guthrie providing printed study materials, as well as staff-led discussions, upon request. Interested high school students are able to pursue a work-study program at the theatre in conjunction with the Minneapolis schools' Urban Arts program. The Bush Fellowships have provided an opportunity for gifted young actors, playwrights, designers and directors to attend the University of Minnesota's Department of Theatre Arts and to spend the following season as journeymen at the Guthrie. There are additional internships in every department of the theatre. A unique humanities program, supported in part by the Minnesota Humanities Commission, has brought a number of scholars and experts together with audiences. These post-performance discussions, free and open to the public, have concentrated on the broader social and humanitarian implication of the dramas. Special student and senior citizen ticket discounts have provided these and other groups with greater opportunities to attend productions. In this way, the Guthrie has drawn its audience from an increasingly wide sector of the Twin Cities community.

Programs & Services: *Internships; Bush Fellow Program; student performances & seminars; community workshops; touring; informal play readings & discussions; Noon at the Guthrie, free weekly program; booked-in events; humanities symposia; student, senior citizen, family & group discounts; voucher program; auction; residencies; speakers bureau; restaurant; bar; volunteers; Guthrie News, newsletter for subscribers & donors; post-performance discussions & demonstrations.*

ALVIN EPSTEIN
Artistic Director
DONALD SCHOENBAUM
Managing Director

725 Vineland Place
Minneapolis, Minnesota 55403
Telephone (612) 377-2824
Box Office (612) 377-2224

Founded 1963
Tyrone Guthrie, Oliver Rea,
Peter Zeisler

Season
June – February

Schedule
Evenings
Monday – Saturday
Matinees
Wednesday & Saturday

Facilities
Seating capacity 1,441
Stage Thrust
Guthrie 2
Seating capacity 180
Stage Flexible

Budget
Jan 1, 1976 – Dec 31, 1976
Operating budget $3,043,147
Earned income $2,592,560
Unearned income $ 724,780

Audience
Percent of capacity 90
Number of subscribers 16,400
Guthrie 2
Percent of capacity 44

Touring contact
Carolyn Bye

Booked-in events
Performing arts companies

Operates on AEA LORT (A)
contract.

Productions, 1975–76
Awake and Sing, Clifford Odets
All Over, Edward Albee
Oh Coward!, Noel Coward; devised,
Roderick Cook
The Estate, Ray Aranha
Dream on Monkey Mountain, Derek Walcott
Born Yesterday, Garson Kanin

Productions, 1976–77
The Glass Menagerie, Tennessee Williams
The Blood Knot, Athol Fugard
The Waltz of the Toreadors, Jean Anouilh;
translated, Lucienne Hill
Counting the Ways and *Listening,* Edward
Albee
A History of the American Film, Christopher
Durang
Candida, George Bernard Shaw

William Prince, Angela Lansbury and Maureen
Anderman in *Listening* by Edward Albee, directed by
Edward Albee, sets by David Jenkins, costumes by
Robert Mackintosh. Photo: Goodstein.

Margaret Phillips and John Newton in *The Waltz of
the Toreadors* by Jean Anouilh, directed by Paul
Weidner, sets by John Conklin, costumes by Caley
Summers.

Hartford Stage Company

Founded in 1964 by Jacques Cartier in a renovated warehouse, the Hartford Stage Company has now offered 14 seasons of varied theatre to north-central Connecticut and opened its 1977–78 season in a new, fully equipped 469-seat theatre in downtown Hartford.

In its early years, the Stage Company built its audience by slowly and steadily increasing its subscription base. The season of productions was eclectic, with a majority of productions chosen from the standard and classical repertoire, but it always included controversial, challenging plays. Since 1968, when Paul Weidner became producing director, the Stage Company's offerings have come to favor the work of contemporary and American playwrights, and a premier production has been an important part of each season. Ray Aranha, author of the Stage Company's 1973 production of *My Sister, My Sister*, completed the 1976 premiere, *The Estate*, under a Rockefeller playwright grant. Two one-acts written and directed by Edward Albee, opened in Hartford in 1977, and Christopher Durang's *A History of the American Film* received triple premier productions by the Stage Company, the Mark Taper Forum in Los Angeles and Washington's Arena Stage during the spring of that year.

The Margo Jones Award went to the Stage Company in 1975 for its significant contribution to American theatre, and in the following year, the company's production of Edward Albee's *All Over* was presented in the *Theater in America* television series sponsored by the Exxon Corporation.

The Hartford acting company is a fluid group of performers engaged almost entirely on a per-production basis. Actors return frequently, however, and a sense of ensemble has developed among them over the years, with new members joining the group each season.

Associate director Irene Lewis has directed not only mainstage productions but, since 1971, has headed Hartford's Touring Theatre, a small Equity company offering original documentary theatre. The company has toured schools throughout Connecticut, but in 1977 became part of the broader New England Touring Program. Ms. Lewis is also the artistic director of the Stage Company's Kinsley Street Theatre, which emphasizes new plays, classes and workshops, and a variety of community-related activities. Special student matinees with discussions following the performances are offered by the theatre, as well as reduced ticket prices for students. Accompanying each of the six mainstage productions is a subscriber magazine, *On the Scene*, and subscribers are invited to a panel analysis at the end of every production's run. A series of classes has been offered to area high school students since 1971.

William Stewart joined the Stage Company in 1969 as managing director, and since then the theatre's financing has cleared away a burdensome accumulated deficit, provided a stable fiscal base for growth and development, and enabled the company to embark on its capital program. The new $2.5 million theatre, designed by Robert Venturi with theatrical consultation by Abe Feder, recreates but enlarges the company's original three-quarter arena stage, more than doubles the seating capacity and provides adequate backstage space, as well as set and costume shops, dressing rooms, green room and offices. Support for the building by Hartford's Downtown Council, an association of city-based corporations, in the amount of $1 million, attests to the Stage Company's significant role in the dynamic revitalization of Hartford's central city. Private donations amounting to another million dollars, along with government and foundation contributions, completed the funding.

Programs & Services: *Internships; performances and classes for students; artists-in-schools program; study guides; Touring Theatre; student and group discounts; speakers bureau; bar; Hartford Stagehands, volunteers; On the Scene, subscriber newsletter; Sunday discussion series.*

PAUL WEIDNER
Producing Director
WILLIAM STEWART
Managing Director
IRENE LEWIS
Associate Director

50 Church Street
Hartford, Connecticut 06103
Telephone (203) 525-5601
Box Office (203) 527-5151

Founded 1964
Jacques Cartier

Season
October – June

Schedule
Evenings
Tuesday – Sunday
Matinees
Wednesday & Sunday

Facilities
John W. Huntington Theatre
Seating capacity 469
Stage ¾ Arena
Kinsley Street Theatre
65 Kinsley Street
Seating capacity 225
Stage ¾ Arena

Budget
July 1, 1976 – June 30, 1977
Operating budget $684,184
Earned income $426,284
Unearned income $246,313

Audience
Kinsley Street Theatre
Percent of capacity 97
Number of subscribers 8,322

Touring contact
Jeffrey W. Gordon

Booked-in events
Experimental, ethnic & children's theatre groups

Operates on AEA LORT (C) contract.

Productions, 1975-76
The Government Inspector, Nikolai Gogol
The Hostage, Brendan Behan
The Runner Stumbles, Milan Stitt
Tom Jones, Henry Fielding; adapted,
Larry Arrick; music, Barbara Damashek
Joan of Lorraine, Maxwell Anderson
Portrait of a Madonna and *27 Wagons
Full of Cotton* and *I Rise in Flame,
Cried the Phoenix,* Tennessee Williams
Catch 22, Joseph Heller

Productions, 1976-77
The Reason We Eat, Israel Horovitz
Arsenic and Old Lace, Joseph Kesselring
Tartuffe, Moliere; translated, Richard Wilbur
As to the Meaning of Words, Mark Eichman
Death of a Salesman, Arthur Miller
He Who Gets Slapped, Leonid Andreyev;
adapted, Larry Arrick; music,
Barbara Damashek

Paul Collins, Alfred Hinckley and Earle Hyman in *As
to the Meaning of Words* by Mark Eichman, directed
by John Dillon, sets by Akira Yoshimura, costumes
by Gerda Proctor. Photo: Goodstein.

Ed Waterstreet, Jr., Richard Kavanaugh, James
Brick and A. Linda Bove in Leonid Andreyev's *He
Who Gets Slapped,* adapted and directed by Larry
Arrick, sets by Akira Yoshimura, costumes by David
Murin. Photo: Goodstein.

Hartman Theatre Company

Coinciding with the Bicentennial celebration, the Hartman Theatre Company opened in revitalized downtown Stamford, Connecticut, with its 1975–76 season. The brainchild of Margot and Del Tenney, the theatre is located in a 50-year-old vaudeville house, the Palace Theatre, which was easily converted into a flexible theatre, with a seating capacity ranging from 500 to 1,500, to accommodate the work of the new regional resident company. Only 45 minutes from Broadway, HTC has the opportunity to tap New York City's abundant theatrical resources.

The Hartman Theatre Company strives to present a balanced mixture of classics, revivals and new plays. From its inception, however, the company has been dedicated to the development of new American plays, and has presented six new plays, four of which were world-premier productions, in its first two years of existence. In its first year, the Hartman Theatre Company presented seven mainstage productions and one staged reading, playing to over 70 percent capacity, with 5,100 subscribers making up a large part of the audience. In 1976–77, HTC mounted six mainstage productions, presented to an even larger audience, including 8,100 subscribers, which represents an increase of nearly 60 percent over the first season.

From the beginning, the Tenneys believed that a performing arts training program was an essential element of any working professional theatre. The Hartman Theatre Conservatory, an intensive two-year training program designed to prepare actors, directors and playwrights for work in the professional theatre field, opened with the mainstage theatre in 1975 and is headed by Larry Arrick. The teaching faculty is comprised of individuals who are working professional artists in all areas of the performing arts. Interaction between the professional mainstage company and the conservatory students is a primary goal of the training program. The Company Store, the performance wing of the Hartman Theatre Conservatory, operates out of the new Landmark Square Playhouse, across Atlantic Street from the mainstage theatre. The Company Store has been performing since the summer of 1976, and has five productions planned for the 1977–78 season. In addition, the community's younger population will be served, beginning in the fall of 1977, by the Candy Store, a new conservatory performance group, which will present theatre events for children.

One of the theatre's outreach programs, Project Interact, is designed to provide students who attend the theatre's productions with a greater understanding of live theatre through pre-performance workshops and demonstrations by the conservatory, as well as written study material which they receive prior to attendance at a matinee.

The Hartman Theatre League, a volunteer organization, serves the theatre through its fund-raising efforts, which have included a special gifts campaign in the spring of 1977, a Rudolph Valentino evening, and the publication of an HTC cookbook. The League also assists the theatre by organizing opening night dinners and after-theatre receptions and by assisting with general administrative work in Hartman's office.

Programs & Services: *Hartman Theatre Conservatory, training program for actors, directors and playwrights; internships; performances for students; Project Interact, lecture-demonstrations for students; booked-in events; student, senior citizen and group ticket discounts; Curtain Raisers, contributors; Hartman Theatre League, volunteers; benefit performances; speakers bureau; bar; Callboard, newsletter; Sunday Evening Discussion Series.*

DEL TENNEY
MARGOT TENNEY
Producing Directors
ROGER MEEKER
Managing Director

61 Atlantic Street
Stamford, Connecticut 06901
Telephone (203) 324–6781
Box Office (203) 323–2131

Founded 1974
Del & Margot Tenney

Season
October – April

Schedule
Evenings
Tuesday – Sunday
Matinees
Wednesday, Saturday, Sunday

Facilities
Hartman Theatre
Seating capacity 550
Stage   Thrust
Landmark Square Playhouse
Seating capacity 110
Stage   Flexible

Budget
July 1, 1976 – June 30, 1977
Operating budget $1,040,078
Earned income $ 401,911
Unearned income $ 735,325

Audience
Hartman Theatre
Percent of capacity 77
Number of subscribers 8,145
Landmark Square Playhouse
Percent of capacity 86
Number of subscribers 1,001

Booked-in events
Dance, mime, experimental theatre, music groups, individual artists

Operates on AEA LORT (B) contract.

119

Productions, 1975–76

Scuba Duba, Bruce Jay Friedman
Line, Israel Horovitz
Ravenswood, Terrence McNally
A Midsummer Night's Dream, William Shakespeare
Catch 22, Joseph Heller
Frankenstein, Living Theatre Collective;
adapted, Kerry McKenney
Evening of one-act plays, Maria Irene Fornes,
Edna St. Vincent Millay, Harold Pinter,
Megan Terry, Tennessee Williams
The Ruling Class, Peter Barnes
Tom Jones, Henry Fielding; adapted,
Mary Hausch, Gregory Hausch, John Osborne,
David Rogers

Productions, 1976–77

The Real Inspector Hound, Tom Stoppard
Two Gentlemen of Verona, William Shakespeare;
adapted, Hippodrome Theatre Workshop
Feiffer's People, Jules Feiffer; adapted,
Hippodrome Theatre Workshop
In the Boom Boom Room, David Rabe
Rubbers, Jonathan Reynolds
The Duck Variations, David Mamet
Vanities, Jack Heifner
Butley, Simon Gray
Steambath, Bruce Jay Friedman

Marshall New, Bruce Cornwell and Michael Doyle in
Butley by Simon Grey, directed by Kerry McKenney,
designed by the Hippodrome Theatre company.
Photo: Gary Wolfson.

Company members in *A Midsummer Night's Dream*
by Shakespeare, directed by Kerry McKenney and
Bruce Cornwell, sets by Ms. McKenney, costumes
by Fernando Fonseca. Photo: Mark Landsberg.

Hippodrome Theatre Workshop

The Hippodrome Theatre Workshop was founded in 1973 as an experimental environmental theatre, to create daring and exciting theatrical experiences. The theatre is primarily dedicated to the production of new plays, though its repertoire also includes classical work with a contemporary viewpoint. Hippodrome Theatre's leadership in all areas of production and management evolves from the constant interaction and inspiration of the five core members. The Hippodrome has also been fortunate to attract invaluable talent from the community. The five artistic directors encourage artistic freedom through improvisational techniques which are combined with professional skill and discipline. Seven mainstage productions a year are designed to discover and explore the unexpected and dynamic interactions between the audience and performer. The performing space is transformed with each production to heighten audience involvement and visual imagination.

Originally located in a plumbing warehouse, Hippodrome later moved to a larger space in 1975 as a result of artistic growth and audience recognition. Subsequently full-capacity audiences prompted the conversion of the theatre from a three-quarter to a full arena with an increased seating capacity of 375. The Hippodrome Theatre Workshop tours both mainstage and smaller-scale productions throughout the state. During the summer of 1977, Shakespeare's *Two Gentlemen of Verona* and David Mamet's *Duck Variations* were presented outdoors in the Gainesville Community Plaza free of charge, to crowds of over 5,000 every night. Hippodrome's production of *Feiffer People* represented the Florida Fine Arts Council and the National Endowment for the Arts at the Kennedy Space Center during the Bicentennial's "Third Century America Exposition." Also during the summer of 1977, *Vanities* by Jack Heifner extended its enormously successful run by moving to Ft. Lauderdale for two months. Hippodrome Theatre has also toured locally to the University of Florida, junior colleges, schools, prisons and other institutions.

The Hippodrome Children's Theatre Workshop offers workshop classes in acting, improvisation, movement, makeup and costuming. Productions created and adapted by workshop students and directors are performed at the theatre and tour locally. Special workshops are also commissioned by schools, prisons and other organizations in the community. The Hippodrome Visiting Artist Program sponsors major theatrical touring companies as well as various dance companies and musical performers. The Hippodrome Visual Arts Program has received a grant from the National Endowment for the Arts to create its 1977-78 play posters. Internationally and nationally known artists including Doug Prince, Todd Walker, Richard Ross, Jerry Uelsmann, Ken Kerslake and Robert Skelly have been commissioned to design the posters.

Programs & Services: *Acting and technical training; apprenticeships; Hippodrome and Santa Fe Junior College Children's Theatre; workshops for young people; Artists in the Schools; children's theatre workshop; touring; booked-in events; visual arts program; student, senior citizen and group discounts; auction; residencies in prisons and hospitals; bar; Hippodrome Angels, support group; preview night discussions.*

Collective Leadership
Contact: Kerry McKenney

1540 NW 53rd Avenue
Gainesville, Florida 32601
Telephone (904) 373-5968
Box Office (904) 375-4477

Founded 1973
Bruce Cornwell, Gregory Hausch, Mary Hausch, Kerry McKenney, Marshall New

Season
July – June

Schedule
Evenings
Wednesday – Saturday

Facilities
Seating capacity 370
Stage Flexible

Budget
July 1, 1976 – June 30, 1977
Operating budget $96,867
Earned income $77,302
Unearned income $29,908

Audience
Percent of capacity 84
Number of subscribers 200

Touring contact
Kerry McKenney

Booked-in events
Performing arts companies

Productions, 1975-76

The Hobbit, J.R.R. Tolkien;
adapted, Patricia Gray
Maui the Trickster; created,
Wallace Chappell
A Christmas Carol, Charles Dickens;
adapted, Wallace Chappell
Tanuki, Clive Rickabaugh; adapted,
Jim Nakamoto
*The Cotton Blossom Floating Palace
Theatre*, Augustin Daly; adapted,
HTY company
Hamlet, William Shakespeare
The Mirrorman, Brian Way

Productions, 1976-77

Marco Polo, Jonathan Levy
*The Tragical History of Dr.
Faustus*, Christopher Marlowe
*The Lion, the Witch and the
Wardrobe*, C.S. Lewis
Tales of the Pacific, Wallace
Chappell
The Magic Circle, Wallace
Chappell and HTY company

Ron Nakahara in *The Mirrorman* by Brian Way,
directed by Wallace Chappell, sets by Charles
Walsh, costumes by Linda Letta. Photo: Nelson Ho.

Rap Reiplinger and Earll Kingston in *Maui the
Trickster* by Wallace Chappell, directed by Mr.
Chappell, sets by Charles Walsh, costumes by Linda
Letta. Photo: Stan Rivera.

Honolulu Theatre for Youth

The Honolulu Theatre for Youth (HTY), under the artistic direction of Wallace Chappell since 1975, has sought to "celebrate the community in which it exists." Its community is the state of Hawaii and HTY's "celebration" has been the exploring and developing for the stage the legends and folktales of the many lands whose cultures blend in the island state. This work has made HTY a cultural force in Hawaii and a theatre with a total audience since 1955 of 1,300,000 people. Emerging from Mr. Chappell's direction is a Hawaiian theatre form with roots in Paul Sills' "story theater," in the music, mime and movement of Asian drama and in the "talk story" (storytelling) tradition of Polynesia. Two original productions, *Maui the Trickster* and *Tales of the Pacific,* have resulted from the blending of these various styles. In celebrating its Hawaii community of varied cultural backgrounds, HTY has presented the Manhattan Project's adaptation of *Alice in Wonderland,* Fred Gaines' *The Legend of Sleepy Hollow,* the Japanese legend of *Tanuki,* Dickens' *A Christmas Carol,* Tolkien's *The Hobbit,* Marlowe's *Faustus* and plays by Brian Way. The celebration theme is ever present, as is the emphasis on the unique gift of theatre as a live and vital exchange of energy between actors and audience.

As HTY has developed, there has been an inevitable broadening of audience to include families and adults as well as young people. The program that began as theatre for youth has become theatre for everyone. The Honolulu Theatre for Youth was founded in 1955 by Nancy Corbett, then director of dramatic activities for the Honolulu Parks Department, as an extension of their program for children in drama and creative dramatics. In 1959 HTY was incorporated as a nonprofit cultural organization with a community board of trustees. Ms. Corbett placed strong emphasis on professional administration and artistic direction and, through the efforts of a core staff in the 1960s, the HTY has developed toward fully professional status. In 1959 the HTY inaugurated a program with the state school system that today brings nearly 100,000 Hawaii schoolchildren to Youth Theatre productions each year. All HTY presentations play both to school groups and public audiences with at least one production a season touring to neighbor islands. The HTY receives annual funding from the state to underwrite touring costs. In 1976 the state made possible a production of *Hamlet* with Randall Duk Kim in the title role. HTY is funded by the National Endowment for the Arts and in 1976–77 was awarded a Ford Foundation grant under the New American Plays Program.

HTY has never had its own theatre facility and, while it continues to seek funding for its own space, uses various auditorium and theatre facilities in Honolulu, where it is based. Seating capacities range from 400 to 1,250, and playing areas include proscenium, modified thrust and arena stages.

Programs & Services: *HTY Conservatory for children and young adults; internships; workshops in conjunction with rehearsals; in-school performances, lectures and workshops; Neighbor Island Tour; student, senior citizen and group discounts; free ticket program; benefit performances; Stagehands, membership organization; HTY Women's Association.*

WALLACE CHAPPELL
Artistic Director
JANE CAMPBELL
Managing Director

P.O. Box 3257
Honolulu, Hawaii 96801
(808) 533-3472 & 537-6763

Founded 1955
Nancy Corbett

Season
July – May

Budget
June 1, 1976 – May 31, 1977
Operating budget $159,047
Earned income $ 58,843
Unearned income $ 79,993

Audience
Percent of capacity 74

Touring contact
Jane Campbell

Productions, 1975–76
Ceremonies in Dark Old Men, Lonne Elder III
Who's Happy Now?, Oliver Hailey
The Disintegration of James Cherry,
Jeff Wanshel
Where's My Little Gloria?, Hector Troy

Productions, 1976–77
The Diary of Anne Frank, Frances Goodrich &
Albert Hackett
The Admirable Crichton, J.M. Barrie
Creditors and *Miss Julie* and
The Stronger, August Strindberg
Savages, Christopher Hampton
Dance on a Country Grave, Kelly Hamilton

Sam Freed and Kate Kelly in *Dance on a Country Grave* by Kelly Hamilton, directed by Robert Brewer, sets by Tom Warren, costumes by Donna Meyer. Photo: Charles Marinaro.

Catherine Schreiber, Stan Lachow, Dorothy Lancaster and Mark Winkworth in *The Diary of Anne Frank* by Frances Goodrich and Albert Hackett, directed by Craig Anderson, sets by Tom Warren, costumes by Michele Suzanne Reisch. Photo: Simon Robert Newey.

The Hudson Guild Theatre

In 1901, Dr. John Lovejoy Elliot, founder of the Hudson Guild, a neighborhood center, began a Shakespeare Club for New York City's Chelsea area residents. In 1922, the Cellar Players was formed and semiprofessional productions attracted theatregoers to the center. During the 1930s a WPA theatre group was in residence and performed there until 1943. Numerous theatre companies used the space until the mid-1950s, when a closed-circuit television system was installed and all theatre events were telecast to area residents. In 1968, the Hudson Guild Players and the Fulton Theatre Company took up residence at the Guild, operating under the Actors' Equity Showcase Code. These two groups performed until 1975, when there was a change in artistic leadership. Since then, the Hudson Guild Theatre (HGT) has operated as a professional theatre, dedicated to the presentation of a wide variety of plays — from classics to world premieres. Hudson Guild's 1976–77 repertoire of three plays by August Strindberg, with Geraldine Page and Rip Torn, moved to the New York Shakespeare Festival's Public Theater, where it played for an additional three months.

For the 1977–78 season, HGT is committed to producing all New York City premieres. Three out of the season's five plays will be new American plays, with the theatre increasingly focusing on new plays and writers. Special events, such as one-woman or one-man shows, performances by dance and mime troupes, concerts, and productions by other theatre companies, are also offered throughout each season. Every Christmas, HGT presents Handel's *Messiah* with a full orchestra and chorus, and soloists from the Metropolitan and New York City Opera companies.

The HGT Playwrights Program offers readings, many of which are open to the public, of new scripts and works in progress. The theatre hopes to expand this program by adding a second performing space for workshop productions of original plays and experimental works. Current programming also includes children's dance and theatre workshops, and adult community workshops, with a combined enrollment of more than 300 participants.

Programs & Services: *Children's theatre and dance workshops; adult theatre workshops; Playwrights Program, readings; Guest Artist Series, performers in concert; children's workshop productions; Helping Hands, benefactors.*

CRAIG ANDERSON
Producing Director
JUDSON BARTEAUX
Administrative Director

441 West 26th Street
New York, New York 10001
Telephone (212) 760–9810
Box Office (212) 760–9847

Founded 1968
Phillip Barry

Season
October – May

Schedule
Evenings
Wednesday – Sunday
Matinees
Sunday

Facilities
Seating capacity 124
Stage Proscenium

Budget
Oct 1, 1976 – Sept 30, 1977
Operating budget $85,777
Earned income $27,505
Unearned income $58,381

Audience
Percent of capacity 87

Booked-in events
Mime, music groups, dance & theatre companies

Productions, 1975-76

The American Stickball League,
Howard Kuperberg
Rondelay, Peter Swet
The Hairy Ape, Eugene O'Neill
Ivanov, Anton Chekhov; translated,
Robert Corrigan
Caesar, William Shakespeare;
adapted, George Ferencz

Productions, 1976-77

Please Hang Up and Dial Again,
Michael Zettler
The Dark at the Top of the Stairs,
William Inge
Dynamo, Eugene O'Neill
Macbeth, William Shakespeare
The Dybbuk, S. Ansky
Jungle of Cities, Bertolt Brecht;
translated, Anselm Hollo
Stage Door, George S. Kaufman &
Edna Ferber
The Refrigerators, Mario Fratti; lyrics,
Ed Kleban; music, William Goldstein

Sara Chodoff and Harold G. Meyer in *Ivanov* by
Chekhov, directed by Ted Story, sets by Ron Daley,
costumes by Margo La Zaro. Photo: Michael Zettler.

John Cunningham in Shakespeare's *Macbeth,*
directed by Ted Story, sets by Ron Daley, costumes
by J. Brent Porter. Photo: Michael Zettler.

Impossible Ragtime Theatre

The Impossible Ragtime Theatre was founded in 1974 by Ted Story, George Ferencz, Pam Mitchell and Cynthia Crane. It started as a theatre of directorial diversity based on the work of Messrs. Story and Ferencz. The theatre is located in an old public-school-turned-printing-plant, in the flower district of Manhattan's west side. The founders built a "face-to-face" theatre space, because it presented an interesting spatial challenge to the directors. In 1975, a second theatre was built in a church on the east side of Manhattan to provide additional space to allow for the work of other directors. In 1976, Stage II was created, across the hall from the original theatre, to take the place of the performing space in the church. Stage II is a three-quarter arena, with the audience seated in only two rows — one above the other. Once again, an interest in creating directorial challenges dictated the design of the theatre's performance space.

With IRT's commitment to the director came the formation of its Directors' Laboratory, which now supports the work of the 10 directors who frequently work at the theatre. As an outgrowth of the theatre's exploration into the work of the director, came an involvement with the entire theatrical process. Because theatre is an art form which uses the knowledge and discoveries of all other arts, IRT's directors are seeking to expand their views to encompass the entire range of artistic expression in all its forms. Toward this end, the Laboratory invites participation by anyone who might contribute to this broader view of theatre, including writers, musicians, actors and designers. The actual work of the Laboratory is vast and varied, touching on the literary, the conceptual, the physical, the theoretical, the visual and the aural. The IRT and its Directors' Laboratory provide a place, an environment and the flexibility conducive to free-form experimentation and exploration.

The original diversity of the theatre's work has grown with the addition of each new director and the theatre now presents a range of work from realism to expressionism and surrealism. Through its ongoing program of experimental work and round-table discussions, the Laboratory directors subject their ideas to the criticism of IRT's entire staff of professionals. This electric atmosphere is conducive to the co-mingling of directorial philosophies. IRT's goal is to produce a new breed of American director, influenced by many schools of thought, with the capability of translating ideas to the stage. The theatre is also attempting to forge a new director-playwright relationship which takes into account dramatic structure and directorial vision. In the past 18 months, IRT staff members have read more than 100 new scripts. Of these, five have been produced, including *The American Stickball League* by Howard Kuperberg, *Rondelay* (based on *La Ronde*) by Peter Swet, *Please Hang Up and Dial Again* by Michael Zettler, *The Gypsys* by Bob Jewett, and *Prairie Passion* by Bob Jewett and Stephen Zuckerman.

The Impossible Ragtime Theatre has become known for its interesting treatments of lesser-known works by major dramatists, such as Eugene O'Neill's *The Hairy Ape* and Chekhov's *Ivanov*, as well as its innovative productions of new plays. Since its founding, the IRT has produced 46 plays along with numerous play readings, musical events and directorial projects.

Programs & Services: *Directors' Laboratory, directors' and playwrights' workshops, workshop productions and staged readings; internships; children's theatre series; booked-in events; student, senior citizen and group discounts; voucher program; benefit performances.*

TED STORY
Artistic Director
GEORGE FERENCZ
Associate Director
PAM MITCHELL
CYNTHIA CRANE
Co-Producers

120 West 28th Street
New York, New York 10001
(212) 243-7494

Founded 1974
Ted Story, George Ferencz,
Cynthia Crane, Pam Mitchell

Season
October – June

Schedule
Evenings
Thursday – Saturday,
Monday
Matinees
Sunday

Facilities
Stage One
Seating capacity 90
Stage   Flexible
Stage II
Seating capacity 70
Stage   ¾ Arena

Budget
Aug 1, 1976 – July 31, 1977
Operating budget $55,565
Earned income $19,124
Unearned income $25,660

Audience
Stage One
Percent of capacity 66
Stage II
Percent of capacity 71

Booked-in events
*Mime, dance companies,
music & experimental
theatre groups*

*Operates under AEA Showcase
Code.*

Productions, 1975–76
Song Stories, Conrad Bishop
The Money Show, Conrad Bishop
Sunshine Blues, Conrad Bishop
Dessie, Conrad & Linda Bishop

Productions, 1976–77
Dreambelly, Conrad Bishop
Song Stories, Conrad Bishop
Sunshine Blues, Conrad Bishop
Dessie, Conrad & Linda Bishop

Conrad Bishop in *Sunshine Blues* by Mr. Bishop.
Photo: Torry Bruno.

Linda and Conrad Bishop in *Song Stories* by Mr.
Bishop. Photo: Torry Bruno.

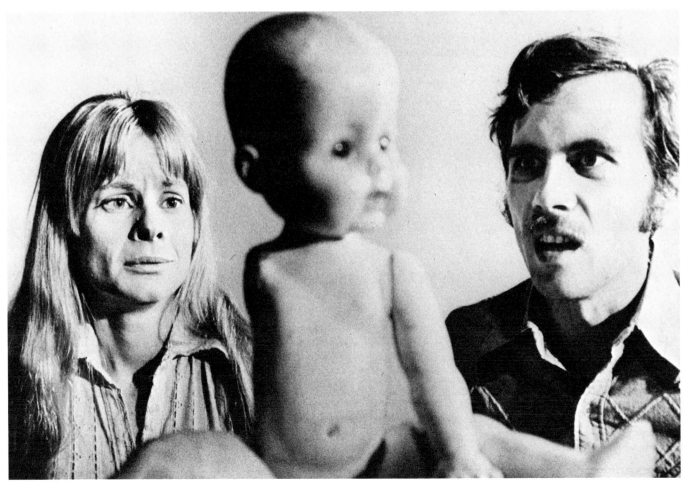

The Independent Eye

The Independent Eye is a professional touring theatre which creates drama using popular entertainment to reflect deeply felt and commonly shared experience. Founded in 1974 by Conrad and Linda Bishop, the company decided to tour full-time and has subsequently reached a widely varied audience. In three seasons it has presented over 500 performances and 150 workshops in 24 states, for colleges, alternative theatres and festivals, churches, conferences, high schools, social agencies and community groups of all kinds. Locations have ranged from major metropolitan areas to tiny towns, with the same material being presented to sophisticated audiences and non-theatregoers alike. The company's earned income and total audience have doubled each year, with a minimal reliance on subsidy.

The Independent Eye presents comic theatre in the broad sense, looking closely at basic human incongruities and depending on a combination of accuracy and humor to elicit audience identification with life situations. Topics are not necessarily funny, and consequently a broad range of styles is used to fuse communication with entertainment. While innovation is not an end in itself, the company's repertoire has embraced Gothic horror melodrama in *Goners,* contemporary vaudeville in *Sunshine Blues, Song Stories* and *The Money Show,* dream fantasy in *Dreambelly,* and fragmentary naturalism in *Dessie.* In each production the plot and the audience's personal stake in the story are primary.

At the heart of the work is a close tie between the aesthetic and the functional. Most performances are for people who are not regular theatregoers, and the strategy is to meet them "on their own ground" literally and figuratively. Productions are designed to fit nearly any circumstance, relying on the author–actor–viewer relationships rather than on technical or design support. This flexibility allows for presentation in formats and locations already familiar to any given group, be they college students or prison inmates. While the company is not oriented to specific social issues, it is sensitive to the questions raised by the stories it tells and seeks audiences responsive to those questions. For instance, *Dessie,* a play about a woman involved in child abuse, was originally developed as a dramatic character portrait and premiered in a circuit of alternative theatre spaces. The nature of the finished piece demanded a context beyond the theatrical, however, and the production was integrated with a discussion forum and showcased to family service professionals. It now functions as a vehicle for community-education projects and professional sensitivity-raising workshops.

The Independent Eye also places strong emphasis on workshops and residencies, many in conjunction with groups that are not theatre-oriented but can potentially use theatre for their own purposes. In 1976-77 the National Endowment's Expansion Arts program funded 15 midwestern residencies, with workshops in very simple, character-oriented improvisational techniques designed to tap the participants' ability to create and *use* theatre for sharing.

In 1977 the Independent Eye moved its base of operations to Lancaster, Pennsylvania, with plans to expand its ensemble and establish a permanent theatre location to supplement touring work.

Programs & Services: *Workshops in improvisational techniques; performances, workshops and discussions for students; touring; post-performance discussions; residencies; quarterly newsletter.*

CONRAD BISHOP
Artistic Director
LINDA BISHOP
Business Manager

409 Fairway Drive
Lancaster, Pennsylvania 17603
(717) 393-9088

Founded 1974
Conrad & Linda Bishop

Season
August – June

Budget
July 1, 1976 – June 30, 1977
Operating budget $30,323
Earned income $22,830
Unearned income $11,250

Touring contact
Linda Bishop

Productions, 1975-76

That Championship Season, Jason Miller
Arms and the Man, George Bernard Shaw
Long Day's Journey Into Night,
Eugene O'Neill
The Envoi Messages, Louis Phillips
The Real Inspector Hound, Tom Stoppard
Black Comedy, Peter Shaffer
The Tavern, George M. Cohan
The Sea Horse, Edward J. Moore
The Caretaker, Harold Pinter
The Old Jew, Murray Schisgal
The Harmfulness of Tobacco,
Anton Chekhov; translated, Eric Bentley
*The Man with the Flower in His
Mouth*, Luigi Pirandello; translated,
William Murray

Productions, 1976-77

*The Last Meeting of the Knights of
the White Magnolia*, Preston Jones
When You Comin' Back, Red Ryder?,
Mark Medoff
The Threepenny Opera, Bertolt Brecht; music,
Kurt Weill; translated, Marc Blitzstein
The Tempest, William Shakespeare
Private Lives, Noel Coward
Sleuth, Anthony Shaffer
Who's Afraid of Virginia Woolf?, Edward Albee
The Brixton Recovery, Jack Gilhooley
Miss Julie, August Strindberg

Randall Duk Kim in *The Tempest* by Shakespeare,
directed by Leland Moss, sets by Christopher
Hacker, costumes by Susan Denison. Photo:
McGuire Studio.

Nicholas Hormann and Sara Woods in Noel
Coward's *Private Lives*, directed by Edward Stern,
sets by Eric Head, costumes by Carol H. Beule.
Photo: McGuire Studio.

Indiana Repertory Theatre

Founded in 1972, the Indiana Repertory Theatre is based in Indianapolis and housed in the Athenaeum, an historic landmark built in 1897. Begun by Edward Stern, Benjamin Mordecai and Gregory Poggi, the IRT operates a 396-seat proscenium theatre, as well as a flexible studio space seating approximately 100.

During its first three seasons the IRT produced a varied combination of classics, "standards," and contemporary plays of proven success. Since 1975, play selection has expanded to include original works, such as Jack Gilhooley's *The Brixton Recovery* and Louis Phillips' *The Envoi Messages,* as well as worthwhile shows which did not fare well within the commercial sector. The IRT presently runs a six-play mainstage season plus approximately three studio productions between October and April.

The acting company has changed from primarily a resident acting company to actors employed on a per-production basis. Numerous actors, however, do return each year, thereby creating a fluid company with the feeling of an ensemble.

The IRT is chartered to "provide and promote educational and charitable theatrics, both resident and touring, to the general public of Indiana." This statement reflects IRT's strong belief in reaching all segments of Indiana's population. A director of community services is responsible for coordinating the theatre's numerous student matinees, as well as arranging for small-cast productions, readings, and workshops presented in churches, hospitals, prisons and senior citizen centers throughout central Indiana. An extensive ticket distribution program makes the IRT's regular performances available to the disadvantaged. In 1976, to insure the continuance of these varied civic programs, the Indianapolis city government allocated funds to the theatre.

As Indiana's only professional resident theatre, the IRT is committed to an extensive statewide school program of performances, workshops and lectures. In the past, actual mainstage productions, such as *The Servant of Two Masters,* toured high schools. As costs mounted in bringing such elaborate productions into the schools, the IRT began to mount smaller-scale shows specifically designed for touring, such as *Musical Mirage Express,* an original children's show, and *Lift Ev'ry Voice,* an original play for high school students dealing with the black experience. Each season these performances are seen by more than 25,000 students, the majority of whom have rarely, if ever, been exposed to professional theatre.

Other elements of the IRT's activities include an intern program whereby recent college graduates can work in a specific theatrical area while receiving a stipend; a newsletter for subscribers which examines each play as well as the artists responsible for mounting the show; an adult education class, entitled "An Evening with the Indiana Repertory Theatre," held in conjunction with a local university; and the hosting of other performing arts events.

Programs & Services: *Acting, design and management classes; internships; performances for students; touring; speakers bureau; student, senior citizen and group discounts; free ticket program; Beggar's Bash, annual fund-raising event; Workers Involved in Theatre, support group; Marquee, subscriber newsletter; post-performance discussions.*

EDWARD STERN
Artistic Director
BENJAMIN MORDECAI
Producing Director

411 East Michigan Street
Indianapolis, Indiana 46204
Telephone (317) 635-5277
Box Office (317) 635-5252

Founded 1972
Gregory Poggi, Benjamin Mordecai,
Edward Stern

Season
October – April

Schedule
Evenings
Tuesday – Saturday
Matinees
Saturday & Sunday

Facilities
Athenaeum Theatre
Seating capacity 396
Stage Proscenium
Second Stage
Seating capacity 100
Stage Flexible

Budget
July 1, 1976 – June 30, 1977
Operating budget $596,245
Earned income $264,136
Unearned income $368,636

Audience
Athenaeum Theatre
Percent of capacity 86
Number of subscribers 6,250
Second Stage
Percent of capacity 55
Number of subscribers 713

Touring contact
Benjamin Mordecai

*Operates on AEA LORT (C)
contract.*

Productions, 1975–76
La Dama Boba, Lope de Vega
Cap-a-Pie II, Maria Irene Fornes;
music, Jose Raul Bernardo
La Herencia Puertorriquena;
adapted, Marianne Loner
Yoruba, Antonio Alvarez & Doris Castellanos
La Cencicienta; translated, Ilka Tania Payan;
adapted, Manuel Martinez
Greta Garbo de la calle 42, Fernando Melo;
translated, Aide Saran; adapted,
Max Ferra, Mateo Gomez, Manuel Martinez

Productions, 1976–77
Greta Garbo de la calle 42, Fernando Melo;
translated, Aide Saran; adapted,
Max Ferra, Mateo Gomez, Manuel Martinez
Nuestro New York!, Estrella Artau
The House of Bernarda Alba, Federico
Garcia Lorca
Lolita en el Jardin, Maria Irene Fornes;
music, Richard Weinstock

Caroline Thomas, Tamara Daniel and Peg Osborne
in *The House of Bernarda Alba* by Federico Garcia
Lorca, directed by Max Ferra, sets by Sally Locke,
costumes by Betty Chlystek. Photo: Rafael Llerena.

Manuel Martinez and Mateo Gomez in *Greta Garbo
de la calle 42* by Fernando Melo, directed by Max
Ferra, sets by Ken Holamon. Photo: Edy Sanchez.

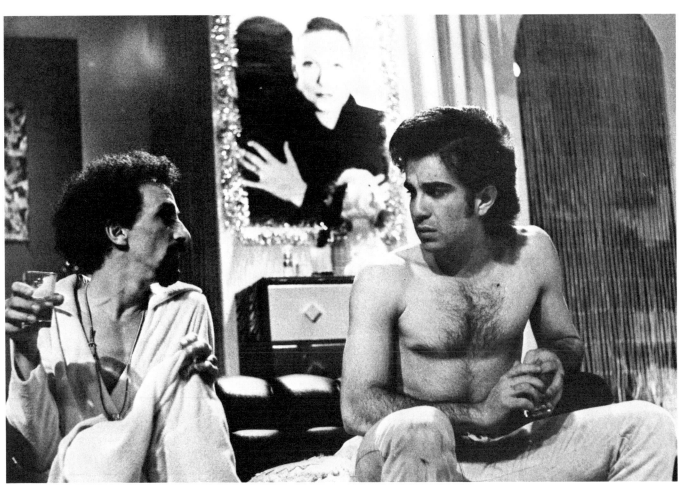

INTAR
International Arts Relations

INTAR, International Arts Relations, Inc., believes that the future of Hispanic theatre in the United States depends upon the development of local playwrights and of new plays which reflect the variety and complexity of the Hispanic experience in this country. This "new" Hispanic theatre, as it speaks to the needs and experiences of Spanish-American communities, is a necessary element for massive audience development. It is also through the development of this new repertoire that Hispanic theatre, as other immigrant and ethnic theatres before it, will have an impact upon the American theatre at large.

The commitment to the development of a new Hispanic theatre is exemplified by INTAR's frequent production in recent seasons of new works; by the resources the theatre has allocated to its Playwright Unit; by the funding INTAR has received for the commissioning, development and production of new plays; and by the reorganization of INTAR's Children's Theatre Program as a professional unit devoted to the development of new scripts. Although INTAR's priority is to produce new, original works, an attempt is also made to provide a bridge between the Hispanic community and the community at large, by the bilingual production of works from the classical, modern Spanish and Spanish-American repertoires.

INTAR's Workshop Program, which has been functioning continuously since 1968, complements the theatre's performing company by providing professional training for aspiring actors, many of whom join INTAR's performing troupe or other Hispanic theatre groups throughout the country. The workshop presents one production a year, consisting of short plays and improvisations performed by the students.

The Children's Theatre Unit is a professional group of actors and writers who travel to schools and community centers to present lecture-demonstrations and conduct discussion sessions with children. From these discussions they develop new plays which reflect the children's views and concerns. The Children's Theatre Unit develops one major script and presents one major production a year.

The Touring Program offers mainstage productions for school groups and travels to community centers, schools, parks, hospitals and prisons throughout the state. It is one of INTAR's major efforts in audience development and community outreach. Performances are offered either free of charge or, when presented at the theatre, for a small fee.

The Playwright Unit brings together playwrights, both beginning and experienced, to develop new scripts and improve writing skills through group discussion and criticism. Each season the Playwright Unit stages one of the plays which it has developed.

INTAR's move in January 1978, to the new Theatre Row on 42nd Street, sponsored by the 42nd Street Redevelopment Corporation, will strengthen its programs as it provides a better location for its main stage. The theatre's new location will also improve communication with other Off-Off Broadway theatres; and supply additional space for the further development of workshops,and for the theatre's gallery, which provides an exhibition area for Hispanic artists.

Programs & Services: *Acting and technical workshops; performances for students; children's theatre workshop; Playwright Unit; lectures, recitals and poetry readings; student, senior citizen and group discounts; benefit performances; Carnival, fund-raising event.*

MAX FERRÁ
Artistic Director
LOURDES CASAL
Executive Director

P.O. Box 788
Times Square Station
New York, New York 10036
(212) 247-6776/6777

Founded 1966
Max Ferrá, Elsa Robles,
Frank Robles, Leonor

Season
September – June

Schedule
Evenings
Thursday – Sunday
Matinees
Saturday & Sunday

Facilities
508 West 53rd Street
Seating capacity 110
Stage Proscenium
420 West 42nd Street
Stage Proscenium

Budget
July 1, 1976 – June 30, 1977
Operating budget $78,745
Earned income $ 7,158
Unearned income $69,544

Audience
Percent of capacity 63
Number of subscribers 300

Touring contact
Teresa Yenque

133

Productions, 1975-76
The First of April, Nina Voronel; translated,
Phillipe Lewis; music, Bill Perlman
Matushka-Barynya, Nina Voronel; translated,
Martin Horowitz; music, Bill Perlman
Video Toys, Wendy Clarke
Acrobatics, Joyce Aaron & Luna Tarlo

Productions, 1976-77
Crab Quadrille, Myrna Lamb; music,
Nicholas Meyers
Still Life, Susan Yankowitz
The Expelled, Samuel Beckett;
adapted, Lenore Stein
New Roots; adapted, Kay Carney;
music, Marianne de Pury
Cross Country, Susan Miller;
music, Ron Striano
Quarry, Meredith Monk

Virginia Stevens and Jerry Jarrett in *Still Life* by
Susan Yankowitz, directed by Rhea Gaisner, sets by
Christina Weppner, costumes by Susan Tsu. Photo:
Sheila O'Hara.

Emily Nash, Brian Gordon and Rebecca Stanley in
Cross Country by Susan Miller, directed by Elinor
Renfield, sets by Christina Weppner, costumes by
Margo La Zaro. Photo: Rosalie Winard.

Interart Theatre

To understand the intent and direction of the Interart Theatre, one must view it within the context of its parent organization, the Women's Interart Center, Inc. The Center is a nonprofit membership organization of women artists from varying arts disciplines, who joined together in 1969 because of the need to inform and educate the public as to the breadth and quality of work by contemporary women artists.

The founding members were themselves amazed to realize how many women were involved in producing high-quality art. Emerging from isolation, they collectively formed an institution which would serve two primary purposes. Through multi-art programming not limited to members, the Center aims to bring to the attention of the general public the work of as many talented women artists as funds permit. At the same time, the Center provides space and facilities for artists to explore different media, through training and workshops, including film, photography, video, silkscreen, ceramics, sculpture, painting, writing and theatre. The concept of "interart" — the interactive process that occurs by working in proximity to other art forms and sharing and exchanging ideas and responses — is intrinsic to the total organization. The dedication to interart as a way of approaching the creative process, of growing and expanding one's talent and vision, becomes a sharing experience with an audience as well.

The Interart Theatre evolved organically within the context of the Center, coming into being more than two years after the Center itself had been formed. The first production, in a newly constructed space, opened in 1973. Since then, the theatre has presented 31 productions, of which 20 were new works. Most of the pieces have involved a variety of art forms including film, music, video and dance. Many have been nontraditional productions displaying a wide span of dramatic styles and very different theatrical techniques. All have been professional productions of plays which demand as much from the audience as from the performers. The core of the Interart Theatre is a group of approximately 100 professional men and women, including playwrights, designers, directors, actors and technicians, who are dedicated to the theatre and to developing their work within it. In 1976–77, as further evidence of Interart's belief in cooperation and interrelationship within the arts, the theatre coproduced *Quarry* by Meredith Monk/The House, thus enabling this production to have a continued life before an audience.

Since the theatre is committed to bringing the interactive nature of the theatrical experience clearly to the audience, the setting, lights and other media components are emphasized within the total concept of each production, and all design elements are realized as completely as possible.

In defining the Interart Theatre, it must be understood that it does not think of itself as a "feminist" theatre. Artists tend to work from their own lives and bring their personal views to the creative process. Historically, since the majority of established artists have been male, a predominantly male sensibility has been communicated. Part of what the Interart Theatre accomplishes, by bringing the work of women to the public, is to open up a new perspective which draws from the life experiences of its creators and enables audiences to share in the discovery of a female sensibility.

Programs & Services: *Internships; playwriting workshop; Scarsdale-Theatre Training and Production, workshops leading to production of new script; children's theatre production; booked-in events; student discounts; free ticket program; TDF voucher program; post-performance discussions; Women's Interart Center memberships.*

MARGOT LEWITIN
Artistic Director/Coordinator

549 West 52nd Street
New York, New York 10019
Telephone (212) 246-6570
Box Office (212) 246-6569

Founded 1970
Marjorie De Fazio, Margot Lewitin,
Alice Rubinstein, Jane Chambers

Season
October – June

Schedule
Evenings
Thursday – Sunday
Matinees
Varies

Facilities
Seating capacity 40–90
Stage   Flexible

Budget
July 1, 1976 – June 30, 1977
Operating budget $82,539
Earned income $26,609
Unearned income $47,934

Audience
Percent of capacity 55

Booked-in events
Experimental theatre companies

Operates under AEA Showcase Code.

Productions, 1976
Arms and the Man, George Bernard Shaw
Electra, Sophocles; translated, David Grene
Anatol, Arthur Schnitzler
Bus Stop, William Inge
The Northwest Show, Barry Pritchard;
music, Peter S. Lewis

Productions, 1977
Toys in the Attic, Lillian Hellman
The Importance of Being Earnest, Oscar Wilde
Ghosts, Henrik Ibsen; translated,
Margaret Booker
The Playboy of the Western World,
John Millington Synge
A Moon for the Misbegotten, Eugene O'Neill

Cast members of *Toys in the Attic* by Lillian
Hellman, directed by Margaret Booker, sets by
Robert A. Dahlstrom, costumes by Nanrose
Buchman. Photo: Chris Bennion.

John Gilbert and Megan Cole in *Anatol* by Arthur
Schnitzler, sets by Charles Kading, costumes by
Donna Eskew. Photo: Chris Bennion.

Intiman Theatre Company

Intiman, which is named after August Strindberg's small theatre in Stockholm, is dedicated to producing classics and modern masterpieces in a space small enough for the audience to feel in intimate contact with the actors. Cast size is limited and the emphasis is on a fine-tuned ensemble, well-defined style and faithfulness to the playwright's original intentions. Although Intiman's main season, strongly influenced by the artistic director's interest in Scandinavian drama, is in the summer, the company has successfully anchored its repertoire on serious plays by writers such as Sophocles, Ibsen, Chekhov, Strindberg and O'Neill.

With employment continuity for Northwest residents being of prime consideration, Intiman is dedicated to a resident company. Only in special circumstances are actors engaged for fewer than two plays in a season or brought in from outside the region. Guest directors and designers, however, are brought in frequently throughout the season, in order to keep the company vital through the introduction of diverse artistic viewpoints. Technicians are hired for the entire season.

Intiman is visible evidence of a tremendous growth of interest in professional theatre by the Seattle community. Founded in 1972 by its current artistic director, Margaret Booker, Intiman initially performed in a 62-seat theatre adjacent to a pottery studio in Kirkland, a small suburb of Seattle. The theatre's first production, Ibsen's *Rosmersholm*, opened inauspiciously in the year's worst snowstorm to an audience huddled together to keep warm, because of a malfunctioning heater. The stage and scenery had to be washed every day to remove the pottery dust. The intent of creating a fully professional theatre existed from the beginning, however, and after a year and a half, the company moved to a larger theatre at the Cornish Institute of Allied Arts in Seattle, where three productions were mounted with a salaried company. In 1975, the Seattle Repertory Theatre opened its 2nd Stage Theatre and Intiman, having completed its evolution to an Actors' Equity operation, moved there in the Rep's off-season. Intiman thus became one of the few professional theatres in the United States presenting a summer season of classical theatre not based on Shakespeare. Throughout the theatre's expansion, attendance has grown rapidly from 600 in 1972 to more than 30,000 in 1977. Audience support, outside of ticket sales, has also blossomed, with nearly 20 percent of the company's income coming from small audience donations in 1976. This evolution has all occurred in a city of 500,000 that supports several other professional theatre companies, an opera and a symphony. The strong demand for tickets this year, which resulted in near-capacity attendance, virtually guarantees expansion in 1978, from a three- to a four-week run for each production.

Other company activities in 1977 included a two-actor show, which toured 40 high schools located primarily in rural sections of Washington; a Dark-Night Theatre Series presenting small actor-produced shows; a touring Christmas production which had about 30 benefit performances in nontraditional theatre spaces such as homes, libraries and churches; and an ongoing apprentice program for actors, technicians and designers.

Programs & Services: *Internships; touring; Dark-Night Theatre Series, lecture-demonstrations, actor-produced works; student, senior citizen and group ticket discounts; free ticket program; benefit performances; united arts fund-raising; Intiman Friends, contributors; Standby, volunteers;* Intiman Newsletter; *post-performance discussions.*

MARGARET BOOKER
Artistic Director
SIMON SIEGL
General Manager

P.O. Box 4246
Seattle, Washington 98104
Telephone (206) 624-4541
Box Office (206) 447-4651

Founded 1972
Margaret Booker

Season
July – October

Schedule
Evenings
Tuesday – Saturday
Matinees
Saturday

Facilities
2nd Stage Theatre
1419 Eighth Avenue
Seating capacity 342
Stage ¾ Arena

Budget
Jan 1, 1976 – Dec 31, 1976
Operating budget $124,878
Earned income $ 85,661
Unearned income $ 32,589

Audience
Percent of capacity 96
Number of subscribers 3,250

Touring contact
Simon Siegl

Operates on AEA LORT (D) contract.

Productions, 1975–76
Dauntless, Bob Campbell & Tim A. Janes
Noises, Rebecca C. Peters
Echoes, R.L. Cherry
Vienna Play, Scott Carter
Let Us Now Praise the Good Old Days,
Harry S. Robins; music, Merl Reagle

Productions, 1976–77
Sideshow; adapted, Molly McKasson &
Invisible Theatre Ensemble
Weeds, Molly McKasson
A Midsummer Night's Dream, William
Shakespeare

John Brownlee, Susan Holtschlag and Keith Dick in
Let Us Now Praise the Good Old Days by Merl
Reagle and Harry Robins, directed by Greg
McCaslin and Susan Claassen, sets by Keith Dick,
costumes by Peter Conway. Photo: Tim Fuller.

Susan Claassen, Becca Stuart and Scott Donavan in
Shakespeare's *A Midsummer Night's Dream,*
directed by Page Burkholder, sets by Reagan Cook,
costumes by Jan Olson. Photo: Tim Fuller.

The Invisible Theatre

The Invisible Theatre of Tucson has produced 43 original productions, including dramas, comedies, full-scale musicals, improvisational satire and children's theatre. Founded in 1971, the Invisible Theatre takes its name, an anagram for "I believe in th' arts," from the invisible energy that must flow between performer and audience in creating the magic of theatre. Starting as an alternative to already existing theatre companies in Tucson, the Invisible Theatre has evolved into a full-time staff of artists who not only create original theatre but also produce it. Each member of the permanent staff performs in an artistic capacity as well as an administrative one. As a collective of artists, the Invisible Theatre has been, and will continue to be, a forum for new playwrights and new ideas developed through the collaborative process. The Invisible Theatre's approach to production is as varied and unique as the plays themselves. The ensemble adapts and incorporates many approaches in relation to the demands of the play.

In the fall of 1976, the Invisible Theatre, with some help from its friends, renovated an old laundry building which is its new permanent home, housing the administrative offices, workshop space and performance facility. The performance space seats 80 and allows for the flexible staging which is essential to the company's approach to theatre.

The theatre has toured throughout Arizona in a residency program under National Endowment for the Arts sponsorship, offering full-scale productions, workshops, lectures and children's theatre. In 1975-76 the Invisible Theatre toured Minnesota and Colorado. Touring is an important aspect of the company's philosophy of bringing theatre to all people. The residency program allows performers to reach out to communities that are not often afforded the opportunity to view live professional theatre.

The Children's Theatre Workshop was founded in 1974. This program has received funding to offer productions and workshops in schools and to work with teachers in helping them understand the values of incorporating theatre techniques into their classroom curriculum.

As a professional regional theatre committed to the production of new works, the company feels a responsibility to its community. As the Invisible Theatre grows, its audience is afforded the opportunity of watching artists develop their craft individually and as a company. The Invisible Theatre works as an ensemble, with actors, directors, designers, writers and technicians working together to bring life to the stage and the stage to life.

Programs & Services: *Acting workshops; performances, workshops and lectures for students; children's theatre workshop; student, senior citizen and group discounts; free ticket program; benefit performances; residencies; volunteers.*

Collective Leadership
Contact: Susan Claassen

1400 North First Avenue
Tucson, Arizona 85719
(602) 882-9721

Founded 1971
Dennis Hackin

Season
October – July

Schedule
Evenings
Thursday – Sunday

Facilities
Seating capacity 80
Stage Flexible

Budget
July 1, 1976 – June 30, 1977
Operating budget $42,532
Earned income $26,366
Unearned income $16,255

Audience
Percent of capacity 74

Touring contact
Susan Claassen

*Operates on AEA Guest
Artist contract.*

Productions, 1975–76
The Naming
Dancer without Arms
Moby Dick
Sweetbird
Judas-Pax

Productions, 1976–77
Passage

All productions are created by the company.

Derek Neal in *Passage*, developed and designed by
Iowa Theater Lab ensemble, directed by Ric Zank.
Photo: Ric Zank.

Christopher Amato and Scott Duncan in *Sweetbird*,
developed and designed by Iowa Theater Lab
ensemble, directed by Ric Zank. Photo: Ric Zank.

Iowa Theater Lab

The Iowa Theater Lab was founded by Ric Zank in 1970. For six years the Lab was a resident theatre ensemble, first at the University of Iowa's Center for New Performing Arts and then, in 1975-76, at the Theatre Project in Baltimore. In the fall of 1976, the company left Maryland and settled in its present home outside the village of Catskill, New York.

The Lab's move to a home of its own in the country marked a turning point in the company's work — a change that began with the development of *Judas-Pax* in the spring of 1976. From *The Naming* in 1972 to *Sweetbird* in 1975-76, the Lab's work had focused intensely on the actor's inner life and personal relationships. These pieces aimed to strip away the protective outer structures of narrative, history, social behavior and verbal communication in order to permit the inner, private compulsions and fantasies that underlie them to become the action for the piece. Each spectator had a one-to-one relationship with the self-contained and self-propelling world of the work. He could enter it only by allowing his own fantasies, dreams and impulses to surface and become identified with those of the piece. By encouraging him to release these inner sources of energy the Lab sought both to activate the spectator and to intensify his perceptions of his everyday experience.

To energize and intensify, to stimulate action and release feeling, remain the goals of the Lab's work. At the same time the company is moving away from a theatre which creates a number of intense — but separately experienced — worlds within the same space. Instead the Lab envisions a new form of work that seeks to make the deepest possible connections between the participants (no longer simply actors and spectators) by focusing on their shared consciousness of the world around them.

In this new work social contexts which were deliberately destroyed in the earlier works have become significant again. Shared associations, shared symbols, the shared environment of home, workspace and community, as well as the elements of earth, water, fire and air, natural rhythms and changing seasons, all become the object of the actor's explorations. His inner life is still a source of richness and energy in his work, but rather than expressing his personal emotions directly, his intention is to stimulate the creation of a communal field of energy and feeling with which the company and guests, whether audience, students or fellow artists, can connect as equals.

In Catskill the distinction between private work-process and public performance has begun to seem less meaningful. The company's special training work with emotionally disturbed and retarded students, the resident actor workshops held in Catskill, and the Catskill House Project, which opens up the Lab's home to visiting artists, are all part of the same impulse: to break out of the closed artistic world of the "old" work and to share a place, a way of life and a set of values, rather than an isolated theatre experience.

Programs & Services: *Actor-training workshops; special education workshops for emotionally disturbed and mentally retarded children and young adults; Catskill House Project, facilities for visiting artists for private creative work and public performances.*

RIC ZANK
Director
GILLIAN RICHARDS
Administrative Director

Box 37, RD 1
Catskill, New York 12414
(518) 943-2949

Founded 1970
Ric Zank

Season
Varies

Facilities
37 Cauterskill Creek Road
Seating capacity 45
Stage Flexible

Budget
July 1, 1976 - June 30, 1977
Operating budget $33,069
Earned income $15,175
Unearned income $17,983

Touring contact
Gillian Richards

Booked-in events
*Artists' private work
and public performances*

Productions, 1975–76
Twelfth Night, William Shakespeare
Brecht on Brecht, George Tabori
Desire Under the Elms, Eugene O'Neill
The Importance of Being Earnest, Oscar Wilde
Endgame, Samuel Beckett
The Count of Monte Cristo, Marshall Borden
Vera, Oscar Wilde
Winterset, Maxwell Anderson
The Lesson, Eugene Ionesco

Productions, 1976–77
The Lesson, Eugene Ionesco
Macbeth, William Shakespeare
Rhinoceros, Eugene Ionesco
Androcles and the Lion, George Bernard Shaw
The Caretaker, Harold Pinter
The Cenci, Percy Bysshe Shelley
She Stoops to Conquer, Oliver Goldsmith
Salome, Oscar Wilde
The Brass Butterfly, William Golding

Donna Rowe as Beatrice Cenci in Percy Bysshe Shelley's *The Cenci*, directed by Eve Adamson.

James S. Payne in Shakespeare's *Twelfth Night*, directed by Eve Adamson. Photo: Gerry Goodstein.

Jean Cocteau Repertory

Jean Cocteau Repertory, one of the few rotating repertory companies in America, presents unusual classics, both old and new, or plays seen more often in the pages of anthologies than on the stage. Whether the work is a masterpiece, once frequently revived but not recently produced in this country, such as Philip Massinger's *A New Way To Pay Old Debts*; a "closet" drama by a writer famous in another field, as in the case of *The Cenci* by Percy Bysshe Shelley; or a forgotten work by a well-known playwright, like *Vera* by Oscar Wilde, the Cocteau focuses on making the audience's experience strong and immediate. Physical production values are purposely minimal, with the emphasis placed on the relationships among the play, the actors and the audience.

All of the plays in the repertoire are performed by a resident acting company, some of whom have been with the Cocteau since its inception. It is the Cocteau's goal to create an American acting ensemble as highly trained, sensitized and flexible as some of the great European companies. Toward this end, the resident acting ensemble, in addition to its rigorous rehearsal and performance schedule, participates in weekly workshops in acting, dance, speech, mime and stage dueling. The Cocteau also has an active apprenticeship program, whereby serious and dedicated theatre students may participate with the resident ensemble in workshops and productions.

In addition to its regular repertory schedule, the Cocteau presents a special matinee series of innovative productions of better-known classics for school groups. These performances take place at the theatre during school hours and are followed by discussions among teachers, students, cast and director.

Founded in 1971 by Eve Adamson in a storefront on Manhattan's lower east side, the Cocteau has occupied the historic Bouwerie Lane Theatre for the past three seasons. The company is strongly involved in the promotion of New York's Bowery area as a revitalized arts community.

Programs & Services: *Company workshops in voice, dance, acting, speech and dueling; performances and seminars for students; student, senior citizen and group ticket discounts; free ticket program; voucher program; Friends of Jean Cocteau Repertory, volunteers.*

EVE ADAMSON
Artistic Director
CORAL S. POTTER
Administrator

330 Bowery
New York, New York 10012
(212) 677-0060

Founded 1971
Eve Adamson

Season
August – June

Schedule
Evenings
Friday – Sunday
Matinees
Sunday

Facilities
Bouwerie Lane Theatre
Seating capacity 140
Stage Proscenium

Budget
July 1, 1976 – June 30, 1977
Operating budget $47,000
Earned income $32,900
Unearned income $23,800

Audience
Percent of capacity 34
Number of subscribers 372

Productions, 1975–76

Rip Van Winkle, Dion Boucicault
Thunder Rock, Robert Ardrey
April Fish, Ted Pezzulo
The Wooing of Lady Sunday, Ted Pezzulo
Memory of a Large Christmas, Lillian Smith
Morning's at Seven, Paul Osborn
John, Philip Barry
Jack Fallon Fare Thee Well, Joseph Caldwell

Productions, 1976–77

Rip Van Winkle, Dion Boucicault
U.S.A., John Dos Passos & Paul Shyre
The Well; adapted, Seymour Reiter; music,
Mitsuo Kitamura
Johnny Belinda, Elmer Harris
Skaters, Ted Pezzulo
The Second Man, S.N. Behrman

June Stein in *Johnny Belinda* by Elmer Harris,
directed by William Koch, sets by Gerald Weinstein.
Photo: Michael Uffer.

Richard Zavaglia and Jennifer Dawson in *Skaters* by
Ted Pezzulo, directed by Bill Herndon, sets by Bill
Groom. Photo: Michael Uffer.

Joseph Jefferson Theatre Company

In 1870, when the famous American actor Joseph Jefferson attempted to make funeral arrangements for his friend George Holland at a church on Manhattan's Madison Avenue, he found himself rebuffed because Mr. Holland had been an actor. When told by the minister to "go to the little church around the corner, for they do that sort of thing there," Mr. Jefferson responded with the heartfelt words, "If that be so, then God bless the little church around the corner." For the past century the theatre profession has been blessed by the presence of the Little Church, formerly known as the Church of the Transfiguration. Recently proclaimed a National Landmark, the church is a charming, gardenlike enclave amid the frenetic activity of mid-Manhattan. When the present company formed at the Little Church in 1972, there was unanimous agreement that they would call themselves the Joseph Jefferson Theatre Company.

The Joseph Jefferson Theatre Company is a nonprofit organization dedicated to the production of American plays with the aim of celebrating the past, present and future of the American theatre. Productions feature professional actors, actresses, directors and designers who work freely between JJTC and the commercial theatre. JJTC's major season of five productions combines revivals of plays by writers such as Odets, van Druten and Dos Passos, with new works by young playwrights from the company's own Playwrights Workshop. Revivals are chosen to reflect the tremendous scope and variation of twentieth-century American theatre, and are frequently accompanied by informal discussions headed by prominent theatre personalities who were associated with the play's original Broadway production. Among the theatre luminaries who have spoken at JJTC are Harold Clurman, Brendan Gill, Peggy Wood and the late Kermit Bloomgarden.

In addition to the Playwrights Workshop, where carefully selected playwrights work with resident actors and directors in developing new material, JJTC has organized a unique theatre program known as Theatre for Older People (TOP). Initiated during the 1976-77 season, TOP is a community service program and consists of an afternoon performance-lecture series which deals with the problems of aging. TOP productions, which feature professional actors of all ages, originate at JJTC's home base at the Little Church and have proven so successful, to audiences of all ages, that the shows are scheduled to tour colleges, nursing homes and senior citizen centers throughout the tri-state area of New York, Connecticut and New Jersey.

During the summers of 1973 through 1976, the company performed Dion Boucicault's nineteenth-century comedy-drama *Rip Van Winkle*, in which Joseph Jefferson starred during the last century, on the grounds of Sunnyside, Washington Irving's restored home in Tarrytown, New York.

Programs & Services: *Internships; Theatre for Older People, performance-discussion series; staged readings; senior citizen ticket discounts;* Subscriber Newsletter; *Conversation Series, post-performance discussions.*

CATHY ROSKAM
Executive Director
MARSHALL PURDY
General Manager

1 East 29th Street
New York, New York 10016
(212) 679-7174

Founded 1972
Cathy Roskam

Season
October – June

Schedule
Evenings
Wednesday – Saturday

Facilities
*Little Church Around
the Corner*
11 East 29th Street
Seating capacity 100
Stage Proscenium

Budget
July 1, 1976 – June 30, 1977
Operating budget $56,947
Earned income $43,115
Unearned income $15,882

Audience
Percent of capacity 45

Touring contact
Davidson Garrett

*Operates under AEA Showcase
Code.*

Productions, 1975–76

Home Free, Lanford Wilson
Margaret, Goodbye, Robert Morse
The CIA Makes a Hit, Edward Weingold
A Very Gentle Person, Hans Steinkellner
Documents from Hell, Enrique Buenaventura;
translated, Maruja Cid
The Mound, George Crowe
Rumpelstiltskin and the Magic Eye; compiled,
Julian company; music, Donald Santina
Ralph Who Must Run and *The Temptations of
Sister Aimee Semple McPherson*, Edward Weingold
The Maids, Jean Genet
Hamlet, William Shakespeare

Productions, 1976–77

The Architect and the Emperor of Assyria,
Fernando Arrabal; translated, Everard
d'Harnoncourt & Adele Shank
Along the Garlic Route, Barbara Graham
The Inheritance, Daniel Langton
Daddies, Douglas Gower
The Long Voyage Home and *The Rope* and
Where the Cross Is Made and *Ile*, Eugene O'Neill
Awake and Sing, Clifford Odets

Kevin Gardner and Dana Kelly in *Daddies* by
Douglas Gower, directed by Alma Becker, sets by
Roh Madonia. Photo: Allan Nomura.

Lewis Brown and Alma Becker in *The Mound* by
George Crowe, directed by Edward Weingold, sets
by Bill Wolf. Photo: Allan Nomura.

146

Julian Theatre

The Julian Theatre considers itself fortunate to have survived 12 years in San Francisco, where the mortality rate of theatre companies has been high. Established in 1965, the Julian has remained faithful to its original purpose — to be a neighborhood-based theatre, interacting with community groups, students, teachers, other artists and interested individuals.

The resident theatre company of the Potrero Hill Neighborhood House — a 55-year-old, Julia Morgan-designed landmark building overlooking the San Francisco Bay — the Julian presents a full season of new and published plays in its home space and tours, with free or low-cost performances, to Bay Area libraries, schools, parks, community centers and hospitals, and sometimes throughout California and the West.

Emphasizing new plays dealing with social issues, and older plays which can be re-interpreted to relate to issues of this decade, the company sees the serious theatre professional as an extremely important being in modern urban society. Its desire is to create a true collective of writers, directors, designers, performers and audience, all being of equal importance and all with the maximum opportunity of contributing to the ideas explored by the theatre. Toward this end the company holds open readings of all plays being considered for production, conducts post-performance discussions and critiques, and solicits ideas from its regular audience.

New plays are accepted and considered on all topics, and from writers of any background. Though especially interested in California or other west coast writers, the Julian accepts and reads scripts from anywhere. In addition to a fall-winter and winter-spring subscription series, the Julian also offers a matinee series of new and experimental works.

New works which have gone on to other theatres include Hans Steinkellner's *A Very Gentle Person* and Douglas Gower's *Daddies*, which was one of the plays presented during Actors Theatre of Louisville's New Play Festival in 1977. The company also commissioned and produced the first English-language production of Enrique Buenaventura's *Documents from Hell*.

The Julian does not have a full-time salaried acting company, but pays shares of income to all actors and technicians, and professional fees to designers, playwrights, dramaturgs and directors for each production. Julian company members and directors are actively involved in political activity to increase support for the theatre. These activities involve assistance in the setting up of costume- and equipment-sharing banks through the Alliance of Theatres of San Francisco, helping in the organization of a ticket voucher project for the Bay Area, and the encouragement of public funding for new and rehabilitated theatre spaces in San Francisco.

Programs & Services: *Julian Training Program, workshops in theatre arts; workshops, performances and lectures for students; children's theatre production; touring; new play and staged readings; lecture, poetry, music and dance programs; NExT Series, workshop productions of new plays; student, senior citizen and group discounts; free ticket program; voucher program; benefit performances; Artist in Community program; speakers bureau; New Plays, a publication of new scripts; post-performance discussions.*

RICHARD REINECCIUS
General Director
BRENDA BERLIN REINECCIUS
Administrative Director

953 De Haro Street
San Francisco, California 94107
Telephone (415) 647-5525
Box Office (415) 647-8098

Founded 1965
Douglas Giebel,
Richard Reineccius, Brenda
Berlin Reineccius

Season
September – June

Schedule
Evenings
Thursday – Sunday
Matinees
Saturday & Sunday

Facilities
Potrero Hill Neighborhood House
Seating capacity 99
Stage Flexible

Budget
Sept 1, 1976 – Aug 31, 1977
Operating budget $51,597
Earned income $12,348
Unearned income $39,242

Audience
Percent of capacity 62

Touring contact
Barbara Graham

Booked-in events
*Experimental, ethnic &
children's productions*

Productions, 1975–77

All performances are improvisations created by the Living Stage company.

An improvised scene with Living Stage company and audience members at a workshop-performance with a youth arts organization in Washington, D.C. Photo: Fletcher Drake.

A physical-vocal ritual with Living Stage company members and the audience, composed of students from Ballou High School in Washington, D.C. Photo: Nick Mann.

Living Stage

Living Stage was conceived in 1965 when director Robert Alexander, after 19 years of working in conventional theatre forms, decided to go directly to the feelings and concerns of his audience for the material of his theatre. The result was a small, multiracial company of improvisational actors and musicians committed to a concept of theatre which inevitably made the audience members both participants and artistic collaborators in the performance process.

When housed at Arena Stage in 1966, the company first took its "living stage" to the minority children and teenagers of Washington, D.C.'s inner city, performing and giving workshops free of charge in a variety of settings. The original artistic concept and social focus of Living Stage have not changed. The nature of Living Stage's work is an artistic dialogue between the actor-artist-human being and the participant-artist-human being. Living Stage takes its audiences very seriously as creators, and asks them, for the three hours that they are together, to take themselves very seriously as artists. In all Living Stage performances, actors and audiences together explore and discover organically, through a workshop structure, the shape and meaning of experiences and events common to all people, such as racism, love, war and dreams, in an attempt to "live" answers to the problems posed.

Over the past five years, the form of Living Stage's work has evolved and its audiences have expanded. In 1972 the company began to develop "rituals," sequences of nonutilitarian movement and sound, to reveal the deeper feelings and levels of behavior of improvised characters. At about the same time, the company's search for an artistic form that could express a greater range of human emotion led to the creation of a "language" made up of nonverbal sounds. Each of these sounds is a statement of a particular emotion. In combination they form a rich chorus that both physically and vocally is meant to reveal the human predicament. Both "language" and "rituals" have become an integral part of the company's form of improvisational theatre.

The company has also begun to develop theatre pieces having fixed themes and characters, which allow improvisational exploration to continue into performance. *Faces of Fascism*, based on months of improvisation on the themes of *Weeping in the Playtime of Others*, Ken Wooden's documentary of the brutalities suffered by the victims of the United States juvenile justice system, is such a piece. Living Stage gave public performances of *Faces of Fascism* in the Washington, D.C., area during the 1976–77 season and also performed the piece at the 1977 New Theatre Festival in Baltimore.

The company continues to spend a major portion of each season working in outreach and educational programs for a variety of groups. In 1977–78 the company will give a series of intensive, seven-hour workshops for inmates at Lorton Reformatory in Lorton, Virginia. The improvisational actors, who have worked with handicapped children for the past five years, will also conduct a program of workshops and teacher-training sessions for physically handicapped children and staff in Fairfax, Virginia. And in 1978, past and present members of Living Stage will conduct the company's thirteenth series of summer workshops at Arena Stage for 200 children, teenagers, women and men.

Living Stage has toured regularly to colleges, universities, libraries, museums and school systems for the past nine years and, in 1977–78, plans to tour the East and Midwest from January through May. Living Stage, a venture of Arena Stage, receives administrative support from the Arena but is budgeted separately from the Arena operation.

Programs & Services: *Improvisational workshops for all ages; performances, lectures and seminars for students; prison workshops and performances; touring; auction; benefit performances; Lovers of Living Stage, support group; newsletter.*

ROBERT ALEXANDER
Artistic Director
THOMAS C. FICHANDLER
Executive Director
Arena Stage

Sixth and Maine Avenue, SW
Washington, DC 20024
(202) 554-9066

Founded 1966
Robert Alexander

Season
July – June

Budget
July 1, 1976 – June 30, 1977
Operating budget $137,000
Earned income $ 35,000
Unearned income $ 80,000

Touring contact
Elizabeth Brunazzi

Operates on AEA LORT (B) contract.

Productions, 1975-76
Artichoke, Joanna Glass
The Show-Off, George Kelly
What Every Woman Knows, J.M. Barrie
Streamers, David Rabe
On the Outside, Thomas Murphy &
Noel O'Donoghue
On the Inside, Thomas Murphy
The House of Mirth, Edith Wharton;
adapted, John Tillinger; music,
Terrence Sherman
Daarlin' Juno, Joseph Stein &
Marc Blitzstein; adapted, Richard
Maltby, Jr. & Geraldine Fitzgerald

Productions, 1976-77
Alphabetical Order, Michael Frayn
The Autumn Garden, Lillian Hellman
Home, David Storey
The Shadow Box, Michael Cristofer
Saint Joan, George Bernard Shaw
Absent Friends, Alan Ayckbourn
The Rose Tattoo, Tennessee Williams
The Gin Game, D.L. Coburn

Colleen Dewhurst and Brian Murray in *Artichoke* by
Joanna Glass, directed by Arvin Brown, sets by
David Jenkins, costumes by Bill Walker. Photo:
William Smith.

Peter Evans, John Heard and Herbert Jefferson, Jr.
in David Rabe's *Streamers,* directed by Mike
Nichols, sets by Tony Walton, costumes by Bill
Walker. Photo: Martha Swope.

Long Wharf Theatre

Long Wharf Theatre is now in its thirteenth season, having been founded in 1965 by producer Harlan Kleiman and director Jon Jory. The theatre facility, which was enlarged in 1974 to provide additional seating, office and lobby space, is located in the New Haven Food Terminal complex off New Haven Harbor. The year 1977 witnessed a further Long Wharf expansion with the construction of a permanent rehearsal hall and a flexible theatrical space for the development of new work.

Under the artistic direction of Arvin Brown and the administrative leadership of M. Edgar Rosenblum, the emphasis of the Long Wharf Theatre for the past 10 years has been on plays of character — works both old and new that explore human relationships and provide the opportunities for the finest available actors to explore their art. Long Wharf is, in this sense, an actors' theatre. Its intimacy suggests an intense involvement between actor and audience and that connection is its greatest strength.

Long Wharf has presented the premieres of major new works by many of the world's most important playwrights, including Robert Anderson, Alan Ayckbourn, Michael Cristofer, Marguerite Duras, Michael Frayn, Athol Fugard, Thomas Murphy, Peter Nichols, Edna O'Brien, David Rabe, David Rudkin and David Storey. Long Wharf Theatre has also devoted its energies to revivals of little-known classics. It has led the way in the re-examination of Gorky as a dramatist, with its productions of *Country People* and *Yegor Bulichov*; it created renewed interest in D.H. Lawrence as a playwright with its production of *The Widowing of Mrs. Holroyd*; and it introduced Edith Wharton as a playwright with the first professional production, since 1906, of her play, *The House of Mirth*.

The challenges of the theatre's repertoire have been met by the talents of some of the world's finest theatrical craftsmen. Long Wharf's fortunate location, with its proximity to New York, yet its total independence in the thriving, sophisticated yet relaxed environment of New Haven, has allowed accessibility to leading theatre artists. It also provides an opportunity for national and international recognition due to New York's position as the theatrical and press center of the country.

Long Wharf is a theatre deeply ingrained in its own community, serving its local audience not only with a wide variety of mainstage productions, but with the best in children's and young people's theatre as well, provided by a talented and energetic second company. Yet Long Wharf has also provided New York City with some of its most interesting theatre events, when Long Wharf productions have had their lives extended through transferring to Broadway and Off Broadway after their New Haven runs. These productions have included *The Changing Room, The Shadow Box, Sizwe Bansi Is Dead* and *The Island, The National Health, Solitaire/Double Solitaire, Whistle in the Dark, A Place Without Doors* and the 1975 revival of O'Neill's *Ah, Wilderness!* Long Wharf has reached a national audience by creating, for television's *Theater in America* series, three productions: *The Widowing of Mrs. Holroyd, Forget-Me-Not Lane* by Peter Nichols, and *Ah, Wilderness!*, as well as two children's theatre productions for Connecticut Public Television: *Doors of Mystery* and *Kaleidoscope*.

Programs & Services: *Young People's Theatre, touring; Monday Night Series, new play readings; booked-in events; student, senior citizen and group ticket discounts; speakers bureau; bar; Long Wharf Associates, volunteers; Loading Dock, subscriber newsletter; Long Wharf Cooks, cookbook; post-performance seminars.*

ARVIN BROWN
Artistic Director
M. EDGAR ROSENBLUM
Executive Director

222 Sargent Drive
New Haven, Connecticut 06511
Telephone (203) 787 4284
Box Office (203) 787-4282

Founded 1965
Jon Jory & Harlan Kleiman

Season
October – June

Schedule
Evenings
Tuesday – Sunday
Matinees
Wednesday, Saturday, Sunday

Facilities
Seating capacity 484
Stage ¾ Arena

Budget
July 1, 1976 – June 30, 1977
Operating budget $1,134,162
Earned income $ 741,090
Unearned income $ 364,725

Audience
Percent of capacity 95
Number of subscribers 14,747

Booked-in events
Small-cast dramatic & music productions

Operates on AEA LORT (C) contract.

Productions, 1975–76
Tjupak; adapted, John Emigh
How That Incredible Rhode Island Jonnycake
Baked by That Inestimable Narragansett
County Cook Phillis Was the True Inspiration
for the Burning of His Majesty's Hated and
Piratical Schooner Gaspee and the Indirect
Cause of the American Revolution,
Greer Sucke; music, Arthur Custer

Productions, 1976–77
Earthwatch, Jack Carroll; music,
George Goneconto
Alice in the American Wonderland,
James Schevill; music, Shep Shapiro

Valerie Mehlig, Rob Anderson and Divinna
MacKenzie in *Alice in the American Wonderland* by
James Schevill, directed by Bernice Bronson, sets by
Robert Soule, costumes by Betsey Sherman. Photo:
Johanne Killeen.

Stephen Martin in *Tjupak,* adapted by John Emigh,
directed by Bernice Bronson, sets and costumes
from Bali. Photo: Johanne Killeen.

Looking Glass Theatre

A theatre that excites children and inspires them, that they can feel a part of — a theatre that gives form to children's imaginings and importance to their strivings — these were the goals set forth for the Looking Glass Theatre by a group of Rhode Island actors, artists, writers, dancers, sociologists, parents and children.

For five years the group held workshops continually and produced experimental plays periodically. Their efforts led them to an approach to theatre for children that has affected all subsequent work. This approach includes the belief that the depth of involvement for children at a play is directly proportional to their proximity to the performance and the opportunity afforded them to invest themselves physically, verbally and empathetically in the dramatic action. The theatre also believes that to reach children, you must go where they are. Looking Glass, therefore, became a touring theatre of six actors performing audience-participation plays in elementary school cafeterias, with children seated on carpets around the performance area.

To meet the challenge of this kind of performance situation — an unlit, distracting space with up to 200 children all hoping to participate spontaneously, joyously, seriously and fully in the production — the "Looking Glass technique" evolved. Actors work in a strongly physical style and are adept at creating imaginary environments through the participation of the audience. They are sensitive and artful in their interaction with the children. The prelude to each performance is a classroom workshop where an actor prepares the children for their particular roles in the performance.

Since there were initially few appropriate plays for this kind of theatre, the artistic director and company developed their own through improvisation. In the process, they discovered great freedom in selecting scenarios and plays with a broad range of content, from literature, myths, fantasy and folklore to science, social ideas and politics. As an example, *Tjupak*, produced in 1975, is a synthesis of a Balinese village piece — exotic, earthy, colorful, open — using the Looking Glass audience-participation style. Director John Emigh used authentic Balinese masks, musical instruments and costumes to stage his American adaptation. *How That Incredible R.I. Jonnycake...* was a Bicentennial musical, conceived by Greer Sucke with music by Arthur Custer. It told, in fantastical manner, of the burning of the H.M.S. Gaspee by Rhode Islanders, the first of the overt acts of rebellion by the 13 colonies. Having looked backward with mirth, the theatre then looked forward with awe. *Earthwatch* by Jack Carroll, the group's first science fiction piece, focused on today's increasing environmental and social crises. A completely different view of our world was James Schevill's *Alice in the American Wonderland*, Looking Glass' first scripted play and Mr. Schevill's first play for children. Looking Glass' street theatre has also produced original material including *The Ringmaster's Tale*, a free-wheeling movement piece about evolution and the concept of extinction.

The last several years have seen a re-emergence of workshops in the overall program. Most important of these is *Let's Put Our Heads Together*, classroom workshops fusing drama and curriculum. In the Bicentennial year they served as a way of using creative drama to experience highlights of Rhode Island's history. They are now expanded to explore not only arts and the humanities, but science and technology as well.

Looking Glass Theatre, traveling since 1970, is now seeking to limit its touring and move into a permanent home. There the theatre will have the opportunity to refine and heighten present techniques and again produce experimental works.

Programs & Services: *Workshop Performing Group; internships; classes in creative dramatics, improvisation and movement; workshops; touring; united arts fund-raising; residencies;* Reflections, *annual newsletter.*

BERNICE BRONSON
Artistic Director
WENDY ANDREWS
Executive Director

The Casino, Roger Williams Park
Providence, Rhode Island 02907
(401) 781-1567

Founded 1965
Elaine Ostroff & Arthur Torg

Season
October – June

Schedule
Matinees
Monday – Friday

Budget
July 1, 1976 – June 30, 1977
Operating budget $117,627
Earned income $ 62,288
Unearned income $ 41,814

Touring contact
Wendy Andrews

Productions, 1975–76
A Midsummer Night's Dream, William Shakespeare
Desire Under the Elms, Eugene O'Neill
Tom Jones, Henry Fielding; adapted,
Larry Arrick; music, Barbara Damashek
A Memory of Two Mondays, Arthur Miller
Brandy Station, Davey Marlin-Jones
Once in a Lifetime, George S. Kaufman &
Moss Hart

Productions, 1976–77
Billy Budd, Herman Melville; adapted,
Louis O. Coxe & Robert Chapman
The Eccentricities of a Nightingale,
Tennessee Williams
The Beaux' Stratagem, George Farquhar
The House of Blue Leaves, John Guare
The Front Page, Ben Hecht &
Charles MacArthur

Margaret Winn in *The Eccentricities of a Nightingale*
by Tennessee Williams, directed by Davey Marlin-
Jones, sets by Atkin Pace, costumes by Bill Walker.
Photo: Michael Eastman.

Robert Darnell and Arthur A. Rosenberg in *A
Memory of Two Mondays* by Arthur Miller, directed
by Davey Marlin-Jones, sets by Grady Larkins,
costumes by Mary Strieff. Photo: Michael Eastman.

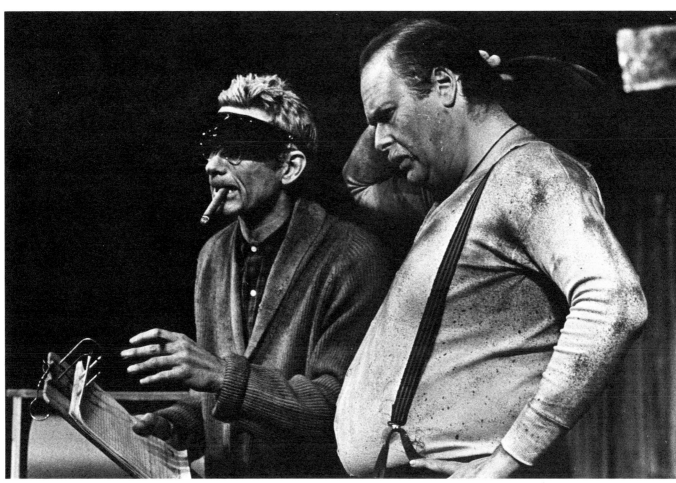

Loretto-Hilton Repertory Theatre

The Loretto-Hilton Repertory Theatre believes its primary task is to serve the community of St. Louis — to be a truly *regional* theatre. Loretto-Hilton is therefore committed to producing high-quality and artistically ambitious work that at the same time is meaningful to its large and varied audience. With the belief that theatre has a responsibility in the development of more sophisticated theatre tastes in its audience, the Loretto-Hilton has gradually introduced more "adventurous" plays with the ultimate objective of creating an intense, shared experience between audience and actors. The theatre aims to produce work which is distinguished by burning energy, the desire to communicate ideas and insights, and a dedicated enthusiasm for the art of theatre.

The theatre, committed to a resident company of actors, has worked to establish a nucleus of long-term company members supplemented by guest artists, many of whom return to the theatre frequently. One of the theatre's highest priorities is maintaining an environment that is pleasant, supportive and rewarding for the artist and technician, and which fosters a dedication to the theatre and its audience. Thus, the achievements of the company can be greater than the accomplishments of any one individual.

The theatre recognizes that no one company can be everything to everybody, so it has not hesitated to develop a distinctive style. Although the productions of the past five years encompass a great variety of plays, the emphasis has been on American works, especially those with large casts. Because of its resident company and its relationship with Webster College, which provides the theatre with trained and talented apprentices, the theatre is capable of producing more large-cast productions than most regional theatres are able to undertake.

In a continual search for an expanded audience and ways to serve the community, the theatre has developed a range of touring programs. Outstanding among these has been the work of the Imaginary Theatre Company, which tours to elementary and junior high schools and is now embarking on a program for senior citizens. This small company of actors creates its own material using the popular "story theater" technique. A distinctive style has evolved with a greater reliance on words and literature than most story theater groups.

The Loretto-Hilton Repertory Theatre is dedicated to making first-rate professional theatre an important element in the lives of as many people in its community as possible. The theatre is the only one of its kind in the St. Louis metropolitan area of 2.5 million people. It has been in operation as an independent corporation for just six years, during which time the mainstage subscription audience has increased from 3,000 to over 16,000.

Programs & Services: *Performances and lectures for students; children's theatre; touring; booked-in events; student, senior citizen and group discounts; benefit performances; united arts fund-raising; Backers of Loretto-Hilton; speakers bureau; bar; volunteers; On Cue, newsletter for subscribers and backers; post-performance discussions for backers; backstage tours.*

DAVID FRANK
Producing Director

P.O. Box 28030
St. Louis, Missouri 63119
Telephone (314) 968–0500, ext. 266
Box Office (314) 968–4925

Founded 1966
Webster College

Season
October – April

Schedule
Evenings
Tuesday – Sunday
Matinees
Saturday & Sunday

Facilities
130 Edgar Road
Seating capacity 500–900
Stage Thrust

Budget
June 1, 1976 – May 31, 1977
Operating budget $926,504
Earned income $674,814
Unearned income $261,449

Audience
Percent of capacity 83
Number of subscribers 16,500

Touring contact
Michael Talbott

Booked-in events
Commercial theatre productions

Operates on AEA LORT (B) contract.

Productions, 1976
The Reluctant Dragon, Kenneth Grahame;
adapted, David Visser
The Mechanical and Picturesque, David Visser

Productions, 1977
Ragtime and All That Jazz, David Visser
Love's the Best Doctor, Moliere

A surrealistic "lollipop mask" which is strapped to
the performer's shoulders, used in a production of
Aria Da Capo by Edna St. Vincent Millay.

Margo Lovelace with two masked actors manipulate
the ancient Japanese bunraku figure, whose
complex and delicate movements require the skill of
three operators.

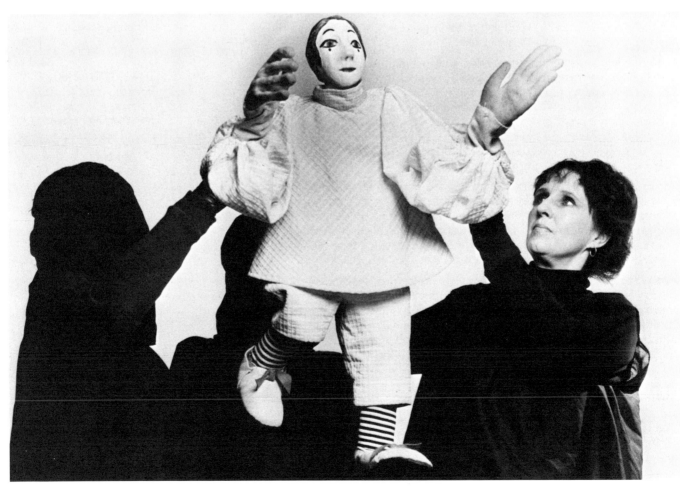

Lovelace Theatre Company

The Lovelace Theatre Company is dedicated to the exploration and development of puppet theatre as a valid and exemplary theatrical form in the United States. Working with a broad spectrum of dramatic materials, Lovelace productions have employed figures as common as the hand puppet and as unique as the ancient Japanese bunraku figures.

Founded by Margo Lovelace in 1964 as an outgrowth of the commercial operation she had headed for 15 years, the company has always held to the one main principle that each new production be approached as an experiment. Since no one yet knows the boundaries of puppet theatre, the field is ripe for bold and unique artistic exploration. Influenced strongly by the Central Puppet Theatre of the Soviet Union, one of Moscow's finest cultural assets, Ms. Lovelace opened the first professional puppet theatre in this country in 1964, located in the Shadyside area of Pittsburgh. A permanent puppet theatre seemed a most unlikely idea at that time, but it quickly caught the fancy of Pittsburgh audiences and the support of local foundations. The company presented eight full-length children's productions each season, and, in 1966, Ms. Lovelace was invited to Moscow to study with Sergei Obratzov, the artistic director of the Central Puppet Theatre. At this point, fundamental and far-reaching changes in the company's work began to appear. At first, emphasis was on stage design and technical aspects of production, developing more stylized, less naturalistic work for audiences. The company members were reluctant, however, to make changes in children's theatre too quickly. They decided that a production for adult audiences would be the best way to pull out all the stops and radically reshape any preconceptions about puppet theatre. As a result of that decision, the Lovelace Theatre has premiered experimental programs of Cocteau's *The Wedding on the Eiffel Tower*, Pinget's *Architruc*, Giraudoux's *Apollo of Belac* and de Ghelderode's *Christophe Colombe*. The company began to experiment with mime and mask theatre and life-size puppets, in addition to a wide variety of hand, rod, marionette and bunraku figures. Over the years, the adult productions have served as a testing ground for ideas that, proven successful, have been incorporated into the work for children.

The growth of the organization and the scope of its work eventually resulted in closing the Shadyside theatre. The 100-seat house and its limited stage facilities had simply become too small for the organization. Artistically, the company felt that it had explored everything possible within that limited space. Fortunately, an invitation to play in residence was forthcoming from the Carnegie Institute's Museum of Art. In the spring of 1977, Lovelace Theatre Company presented its first resident season at the Institute, performing two productions—an original piece entitled *Ragtime and All That Jazz* by David Visser and Moliere's one-act farce *Love's the Best Doctor*. The company also produced, in 1976, a 26-minute color film, *The Puppet Proposition*. With an overview of the history of puppet theatre, the film also examines a Lovelace production from conception to final curtain.

In addition to a subscription season, a touring program and residencies, the company has begun collaborative efforts with other regional theatres in an effort to integrate the unique production values of the puppet theatre with the more established "human theatre." In this direction, the company has worked with Mabou Mines from New York and with the Pittsburgh Public Theater on its production of Arbuzov's *Once upon a Time*.

Programs & Services: *Apprenticeships; Project Encompass, workshops for children; student, senior citizen and group ticket discounts; residencies; touring.*

MARGO LOVELACE
Producer-Director
TOM PECHAR
General Manager

5888½ Ellsworth Avenue
Pittsburgh, Pennsylvania 15232
(412) 361-4835

Founded 1964
Margo Lovelace

Season
February – May

Schedule
Matinees
Saturday & Sunday

Facilities
*Carnegie Institute Museum
of Art Theatre*
4400 Forbes Avenue
Seating capacity 188
Stage Proscenium

Budget
Oct 1, 1976 – Sept 30, 1977
Operating budget $83,498
Earned income $11,717
Unearned income $73,859

Audience
Percent of capacity 74
Number of subscribers 1,600

Touring contact
Tom Pechar

Productions, 1975-76

Cascando, Samuel Beckett; adapted,
JoAnne Akalaitis; music, Philip Glass
The Red Horse Animation, Lee Breuer;
music, Philip Glass
The Lost Ones, Samuel Beckett; adapted,
Lee Breuer; music, Philip Glass
Play and *Come & Go,* Samuel Beckett

Productions, 1976-77

Cascando, Samuel Beckett; adapted,
JoAnne Akalaitis; music, Philip Glass
The B-Beaver Animation, Lee Breuer
The Lost Ones, Samuel Beckett;
music, Philip Glass
Dressed Like an Egg; adapted, JoAnne
Akalaitis; music, Philip Glass

JoAnne Akalaitis in *The B-Beaver Animation,*
written and directed by Lee Breuer, sets/sculpture
by Tina Girouard. Photo: Bill Davis.

Mabou Mines production of *Dressed Like an Egg,*
conceived and directed by JoAnne Akalaitis,
costume sculpture by Ree Morton. Photo: Richard
Landry.

Mabou Mines

In 1964 in San Francisco, Lee Breuer, Ruth Maleczech and JoAnne Akalaitis began working together within the framework of a loose coalition of artists and performance groups, including Ann Halprin's Dancers' Workshop, Morton Subotnik and Pauline Olivero's San Francisco Tape Music Center and R.G. Davis' San Francisco Mime Troupe. Joined by composer Philip Glass and actor David Warrilow, the group continued to work together in Europe from 1966 to 1969. Mabou Mines, taking its name from a small town in Nova Scotia, was formed in 1969 and, in 1970, became a resident company of the La Mama Experimental Theatre Club in New York City. In 1973, the company left La Mama and established itself as an independent experimental theatre.

Mabou Mines' work is a synthesis of motivational acting, narrative acting and mixed media performance. In the area of motivational acting, the company focuses on an aspect of work that Stanislavski calls personalization and on Jerzy Grotowski's ideas about emotional parallels and visualization. The group has developed a variety of narrative techniques, often in the form of choral monologues, that have as their sources Brechtian acting, with its roots in commedia, mime, melodrama and oratory, and the narrative styles of the great Eastern dance theatres such as Kabuki and Kathakali. Mabou Mines' concern with process and visual communication enables it to cross the traditional lines between theatre and the art world.

Since 1970 the company has worked to create a style of presentation suitable for performance narrative and poetical texts, and at times takes sculptural, musical or movement process as a textual base for performance as well. When the company uses words, it is as a chorus of one — the storyteller. What is dramatized is not so much this character or that, but the personality of the language — not the author's words, but the perception of the author's metaphor. Mabou's work is always presented as a "two-scene" — a conversation between the character and the chorus or the character and the audience. In this conversation, the company members always try to say things more than one way, without repeating themselves, by speaking through music, sculpture and movement. They hope that each new way will elaborate and inform the text, as well as each other, because all are so differentially situated along the line stretching from the literal to the abstract.

The work of the company has been directed primarily toward the creation of their own original theatre pieces — the *Animations (Red Horse, B-Beaver* and *Shaggy Dog)* and innovative interpretations of works by Samuel Beckett (*Play, Come & Go, The Lost Ones, Cascando* and, scheduled for the spring of 1978, *More Pricks Than Kicks*). Their 1977 production, *Dressed Like an Egg*, is taken from the writings of Colette.

Programs & Services: *Touring; residencies.*

Collective Artistic Leadership
JANE M. YOCKEL
Administrator

Performing Artservices, Inc.
463 West Street
New York, New York 10014
(212) 989-4953

Founded 1970
Lee Breuer, Ruth Maleczech,
JoAnne Akalaitis, David
Warrilow, Philip Glass

Season
Varies

Budget
July 1, 1976 – June 30, 1977
Operating budget $134,931
Earned income $ 89,680
Unearned income $ 42,015

Touring contact
A Bunch of Experimental Theaters
105 Hudson Street
New York, New York 10013
(212) 966-0400

Productions, 1975–76
AC/DC, Heathcote Williams
The Pink Helmet and *The Grabbing of the Fairy,* Michael McClure
Angel City, Sam Shepard

Productions, 1976–77
Sexual Perversity in Chicago and *The Duck Variations,* David Mamet
Inacoma, Sam Shepard
Alfred Dies, Israel Horovitz
Hospital, Jock Reynolds & Suzanne Hellmuth
Are You Lookin'?, Murray Mednick

John Nesci and Jane Dornacker in Sam Shepard's *Inacoma,* in collaboration with the San Francisco Theatre Jazz Ensemble, directed by Sam Shepard, sets by Morgan Hall. Photo: Ron Blanchette.

John Nesci and Irving Israel in *The Duck Variations* by David Mamet, directed by Albert Takazauckas, sets by Donald Cate, costumes by Regina Cate. Photo: Ron Blanchette.

The Magic Theatre

In 1977, the Magic Theatre celebrated its tenth season under the direction of its founder, John Lion. The theatre, which was founded in Berkeley as an outgrowth of a University of California project on dadaist, surrealist, futurist and expressionist theatre, emphasizes the development of new American playwrights through the production of new American plays. Over the years, the theatre has developed an association with major playwrights of the alternative theatre movement that has resulted in premier productions of more than 75 original works. In 1977, the Magic Theatre engaged Martin Esslin as its literary manager.

Since its second season of production, the main thrust of the theatre's work has been attached to its playwright-in-residence program. The emphasis on the playwright's presence during rehearsals stems from the idea that the putting together of a dramatic event is the meshing of *all* the elements of production, regardless of the time which may be lost due to "creative conflict." Mr. Lion believes it is this very element of creative conflict which is at the center of a positive outlook in new theatre, as it assures against the dulling effect of "blueprint" productions, while moving the author, director and ensemble into new areas of theatrical exploration. During the past nine years, the Magic Theatre has had 20 resident playwrights, including Sam Shepard, Michael McClure, Israel Horovitz, Susan Yankowitz, James Schevill, Jeff Wanshel and Murray Mednick. Mr. Shepard himself directed the premier productions of his plays *Action* and *Killers Head* in 1975, and *Angel City* in 1976, and collaborated with the San Francisco Theatre Jazz Ensemble on an extended workshop piece entitled *Inacoma* in 1977.

The name Magic Theatre derives from its original home in a bar called Steppenwolf, named after the novel by Herman Hesse. In 1977–78, the theatre moved to a new facility at Fort Mason, San Francisco's newest community cultural center, located between the Marina and Ghirardelli Square. This space, built in a remodeled army warehouse, and housing two 99-seat theatres, will allow the Magic Theatre, for the first time, to expand its repertoire to include plays best suited to a flexible space. In 1977–78, in addition to its regular season, the theatre is inaugurating a Playwrights' Forum, designed to aid in the development of new talent and scripts. The Forum will provide space and technical assistance to artists in residence. Staged readings and productions of works in progress will be presented, fulfilling a long-range goal of a second stage, as a forum for in-process works and writers.

The Magic Theatre engages in a number of production activities outside of its main series of plays. The theatre sponsors a part-time training program, which offers classes in acting and directing for the stage and in acting for film and television, along with seminars on technical and administrative aspects of theatre.

The playwright-theatre association has resulted in the publication of a number of works, including *Gargoyle Cartoons* by Michael McClure. In 1972–73, Jeff Wanshel's *auto-destruct* was staged in New York by Mr. Lion as a special project, under the auspices of the Eugene O'Neill Memorial Theater Center, at the New York Cultural Center and the Manhattan Theatre Club. Michael McClure's *Snoutburbler* and his "sound creation," *Music Peace*, were produced for KPFA-radio in Berkeley. In 1976, Mr. McClure's play *Gorf* was published by New Directions, with photographs of the original production and an introduction by John Lion. In 1977, Sam Shepard's *Angel City and Other Plays* was published by Urizen Press, with an emphasis on his work created at the Magic Theatre.

Programs & Services: *Actor training program; student, senior citizen and group ticket discounts; playwrights in residence; bar; subscriber newsletter.*

JOHN LION
General Director
Building 314, Fort Mason
San Francisco, California 94123
(415) 441–8001

Founded 1967
John Lion

Season
October – July

Schedule
Evenings
Thursday – Sunday

Facilities
The Magic Theatre
Seating capacity 99
Stage ¾ Arena
The Magic Theatre Also
Seating capacity 99
Stage Flexible

Budget
July 1, 1976 – June 30, 1977
Operating budget $109,209
Earned income $ 34,334
Unearned income $ 88,332

Audience
Percent of capacity 85

*Operates under AEA
99-Seat Waiver.*

Productions, 1975–76
Jinxs Bridge, Michael Moran

Productions, 1976–77
A Thousand Nights and a Night, Gerald Bamman;
music, Bill Vanaver & Livia Drapkin
Between the Wars, Wilford Leach
The Room, Saskia Noordhoek Hegt &
Manhattan Project company; music,
Andrew Schloss

Gerry Bamman in *Endgame* by Samuel Beckett,
directed by Andre Gregory, designed by Jerry Rojo.
Photo: Babette Mangolte.

Gloria Maddox, Andrea Stonorov, Gerry Bamman,
Jim Carrington and Harsh Nayyar in *A Thousand
Nights and a Night* by Gerry Bamman, sets by
Lowell Detweiler, costumes by Nanzi Adzima.
Photo: Susan Opotow.

The Manhattan Project

The Manhattan Project is an artistic collective composed of Andre Gregory, Gerald Bamman, Saskia Noordhoek Hegt, Angela Pietropinto and John Holms, who receive help, collaboration and comfort from other artists and advisers too numerous to mention. It is a group devoted to experimentation in the theatre and performance.

In 1968, the Manhattan Project began as an experimental theatre, and there have been many times since then when the question arose as to whether convenient labels like "experimental," "avant-garde," "physical" or "environmental" still applied to this particular organization or, indeed, if they ever applied. The answer has always been that all such labels except for "experimental" can easily be relinquished. The word "experimental," however, is not so easy to let go. From the beginning, it has seemed important to be able to try anything, not knowing beforehand what the outcome may be, and not having the conclusions biased by prejudicial and extraneous factors such as the amount of money and time available, a fixed audience relationship, or any of the other rules and regulations that then, now and always seem to encumber and limit the theatre.

In the beginning, the need to experiment with the restrictions of normal rehearsal periods and the physical restraints of naturalism led to the Project's production of *Alice in Wonderland*. Subsequently, when the physical theatre developed its own vogue, and each and every practitioner was standing on his or her head, it was necessary to turn the experimentation toward language — working on the one hand with the classicism of Beckett's *Endgame*, and touching, on the other hand, on a whole new kind of language in Wallace Shawn's *Our Late Night*.

What are the questions now, in 1977? What are the assumptions that need to be challenged and experimented with? Questions of technique aside, the first is the nature of celebration itself and its relationship to our society. How does an art form that has its roots in social celebration and festivity resolve its position in this society as a cultural obligation? The second is the nature of performance itself. What is it and how does it relate to creativity? Mr. Gregory is conducting workshops in this country, Europe and the Mideast, in an attempt to establish the connection between the two, questioning whether or not true creativity can coexist with performance. Mr. Bamman is using his production *A Thousand Nights and a Night* and the legendary character Scheherazade as background to the question of what it means to be a performer, and Ms. Noordhoek Hegt, in a piece entitled *The Room*, is exploring the relationship between creativity and performance.

These are the ongoing questions. As yet, there are no answers, nor can one promise that there will be, for it is the nature of experiments that some succeed and some fail. Any company that calls itself "experimental" should take and be given that latitude.

> *Clov:* Do you believe in the life to come?
> *Hamm:* Mine was always that.

Programs & Services: *The Laboratory for Theatrical Interdisciplinary Human Research, workshops on theatrical and paratheatrical approaches to theatre; touring; student and senior citizen ticket discounts; voucher program; benefit performances; public forums, panel discussions with other members of A Bunch of Experimental Theaters of New York.*

ANDRE GREGORY
Artistic Director
GERALD BAMMAN
Treasurer

P.O. Box 811, Cooper Station
New York, New York 10003
(212) 674-7885

Founded 1968
Andre Gregory, Gerald Bamman,
Angela Pietropinto

Season
Varies

Budget
Sept 1, 1976 – Aug 31, 1977
Operating budget $101,373
Earned income $ 18,605
Unearned income $ 73,937

Touring contact
A Bunch of Experimental Theaters
105 Hudson Street
New York, New York 10013
(212) 966-0400

Productions, 1975–76
Golden Boy, Clifford Odets
Life Class, David Storey
The Blood Knot, Athol Fugard
The Son, Gert Hofmann; translated,
Jon Swan
In the Wine Time, Ed Bullins
Transformations, Anne Sexton
& Conrad Susa
Sea Marks, Gardner McKay
The Basement and *A Slight Ache,*
Harold Pinter
Geography of a Horse Dreamer,
Sam Shepard
Patrick Henry Lake Liquors,
Larry Ketron
The Voice of the Turtle, J. van Druten
Dearly Beloved, John Raymond Hart
The Pokey, Stephen Black
The Human Voice, Francis Poulenc &
Jean Cocteau; translated, Joseph Machlis

Productions, 1976–77
Children, A.R. Gurney
Ashes, David Rudkin
Boesman and Lena, Athol Fugard
The Gathering, Edna O'Brien
In the Summer House, Jane Bowles
Claw, Howard Barker
Ballymurphy, Michael Neville
Quail Southwest, Larry Ketron
Billy Irish, Thomas Babe
Statues and *Exhibition* and *The Bridge
at Belharbour,* Janet Neipris
The Last Street Play, Richard Wesley
The Wise Woman and the King, Carl Orff;
translated, H. Wesley Balk & Yale Marshall

Robert Christian and Frances Foster in *Boesman
and Lena* by Athol Fugard, directed by Thomas
Bullard, sets by Atkin Pace, costumes by Rachel
Kurland. Photo: Ken Howard.

Amy Nathan and Drew Snyder in *Quail Southwest*
by Larry Ketron, directed by Andy Wolk, sets by
James Joy, costumes by Susan Tsu. Photo: Ken
Howard.

Manhattan Theatre Club

The Manhattan Theatre Club was founded in 1970, by a group of private citizens, and is housed in the century-old Bohemian Hall on New York's upper east side. With the belief that there existed a crucial need to provide a forum for new talents to present and develop their work in a professional setting, an energetic young staff of four, headed by Lynne Meadow, produced a prolific first season in 1972, of over 65 events in its four performance spaces.

Though primarily dedicated to new work in the theatre, the MTC program also features revivals of the lesser-known classics, cabaret musical evenings, opera, a new composers series and a poetry series. The artistic philosophy behind production at the Manhattan Theatre Club is manifested by the unique opportunity to have work presented in a multitude of levels, depending on the stage of development of the work in question. Therefore, works are treated on one or more different levels, including staged readings, workshops and major productions.

The Manhattan Theatre Club affords the emerging artist the rare opportunity to work side-by-side with seasoned professionals and to participate in a practical learning situation. In these ways, the young artist is able to benefit from the professional experience gained at the theatre, and though there is no permanent company of artists at the MTC, artists are encouraged to return year after year.

Highlights of the MTC's first five seasons include Chekhov's *The Seagull*, adapted by Jean-Claude van Itallie and directed by Joseph Chaikin, *Life Class* by David Storey, *The Blood Knot* by Athol Fugard, *Transformations* by Anne Sexton and Conrad Susa, *Sirens* and *The Last Street Play* by Richard Wesley and *Bits and Pieces* by Corinne Jacker.

The Manhattan Theatre Club has also originated many shows which have gone on to other productions. Among the productions that have enjoyed runs beyond the MTC are *Ashes* by David Rudkin, directed by Ms. Meadow; *The Runner Stumbles* by Milan Stitt; *Sea Marks* by Gardner McKay; *Starting Here, Starting Now*, a musical revue by Richard Maltby, Jr., and David Shire; *Bad Habits* by Terrence McNally; and *The Wager* by Mark Medoff.

Although it is with pride that the Manhattan Theatre Club has been responsible for these productions, the theatre is primarily committed to providing a professional forum for a variety of material, regardless of its commercial potential. Many productions, unsuited for a commercial life in New York, are part of a regional repertoire. Through collaboration with other theatres, including the Mark Taper Forum, the Goodman Theatre and the New York Shakespeare Festival, many new plays have received multiple productions.

Programs & Services: *Internships; children's theatre productions; poetry and cabaret series; workshop productions; staged readings; student, senior citizen and group ticket discounts; free ticket program; voucher program; benefit performances; playwright-in-residence; bar; MTC Calendar, newsletter; post-performance discussions.*

LYNNE MEADOW
Artistic Director
BARRY GROVE
Managing Director

321 East 73rd Street
New York, New York 10021
Telephone (212) 288-2500
Box Office (212) 472-0600

Founded 1970
A.E. Jeffcoat, Peregrine Whittlesey,
Margaret Kennedy, Victor Germack,
Joseph Tandet

Season
October – June

Schedule
Evenings
Wednesday – Sunday
Matinees
Saturday & Sunday

Facilities
Downstage
Seating capacity 155
Stage Proscenium
Upstage
Seating capacity 100
Stage Thrust
Cabaret
Seating capacity 75
Stage Cabaret

Budget
Oct 1, 1976 – Sept 30, 1977
Operating budget $313,141
Earned income $155,531
Unearned income $158,580

Audience
Number of subscribers 1,700
Downstage
Percent of capacity 63
Upstage
Percent of capacity 79
Cabaret
Percent of capacity 45

Operates under AEA Showcase Code.

Productions, 1975-76
Once in a Lifetime, Moss Hart &
George S. Kaufman
Too Much Johnson, William Gillette;
adapted, Burt Shevelove
The Shadow Box, Michael Cristofer
The Duchess of Malfi, John Webster
The Three Sisters, Anton Chekhov;
translated, Michael Henry Heim
Ashes, David Rudkin
And Where She Stops Nobody Knows,
Oliver Hailey
Cross Country, Susan Miller

Productions, 1976-77
The Robber Bridegroom, Alfred Uhry &
Robert Waldman
Ice, Michael Cristofer
Vanities, Jack Heifner
Travesties, Tom Stoppard
The Importance of Being Earnest,
Oscar Wilde
A History of the American Film,
Christopher Durang
Angel City, Sam Shepard
Bugs and *Guns,* Doris Baizley;
music, Harry Aguado
Leander Stillwell, David Rush

Ron Rifkin and Britt Swanson in *Ice* by Michael
Cristofer, directed by Jeff Bleckner, designed by
John DeSantis. Photo: Steven Kuell.

Tom Rosqui, Simon Oakland and David Huffman in
William Gillette's *Too Much Johnson,* directed by
Gordon Davidson, sets by Robert Zentis, costumes
by Tom Rasmussen. Photo: Steven Kuell.

Mark Taper Forum

The Center Theatre Group/Mark Taper Forum, founded in 1967, was an outgrowth of the Theatre Group, a professional theatre which had been in residence at the University of California–Los Angeles since 1959.

The artistic program of the Mark Taper Forum, under the direction of Gordon Davidson, is divided into four interrelated parts: the major subscription season, the New Theatre For Now season, the Forum/Laboratory projects and affiliated community programs. The primary philosophy of the mainstage season is to provide audiences with a wide range of productions, including plays from the classical repertoire, but with an emphasis on the presentation of new works, as well as plays heretofore not produced in the United States or on the west coast. The repertory system was introduced into the major season in 1975 with the pairing of William Gillette's *Too Much Johnson* and the world premiere of Michael Cristofer's *The Shadow Box*. In the 1976–77 season, *The Importance of Being Earnest* played in repertory with Tom Stoppard's *Travesties*, and the Tenth Anniversary Repertory Festival paired the west coast premiere of Christopher Durang's *A History of the American Film* with Sam Shepard's *Angel City*, and the world premiere of David Rush's *Leander Stillwell* with two plays by Doris Baizley, *Bugs* and *Guns*.

The 1977–78 season marked the return of the New Theatre For Now program, which was an integral feature of the Taper from the theatre's birth until 1975, when economic pressures forced the suspension of the program. Pioneering in the development of new plays, playwrights and directors, NTFN explores unusual dramatic subjects and innovative staging concepts. Using the Taper stage for short runs, NTFN develops subscription-audience awareness of new voices in the theatre. Between 1967 and 1975, 67 original plays by 55 playwrights were produced. The Taper's commitment to the development of new theatre pieces of quality also finds expression through the Forum Laboratory. The Lab is a workshop which performs for an invited audience. Actors, writers, directors, composers and designers collaborate to develop projects in new modes of dramatic expression, free from any commercial or critical pressure. The 1976–77 Lab season presented 19 productions, including *Conjuring an Event* by Richard Nelson; *Jack Street*, based on a ballad by Joan Tewkesbury and adapted by the cast; *Convictions*, written and performed by the Terminal Island Correctional Institute Drama Workshop; *The Middle Ages* by A.R. Gurney; and *Gethsemane Springs* by Harvey Perr, the Taper's Rockefeller Foundation–supported playwright-in-residence.

Related community programs include the Improvisational Theatre Project and Artists-In-Prisons. ITP offers children innovative theatre experiences which call upon them to develop their imagination and creativity. ITP's material is created for the multiracial company by a resident writer and composer and also includes improvised stories based on audience suggestions. ITP tours locally and throughout the state, presenting performances and conducting workshops in schools and at the Mark Taper Forum. Artists-In-Prisons offers acting workshops for inmates of local correctional institutions. During the 1976–77 season, public performances were offered both in and out of the institutions.

The Mark Taper Forum's central location in the downtown area at the Los Angeles Music Center makes it reasonably accessible to the entire city and its many neighboring communities. Special discount ticket programs provide people who ordinarily could not afford standard prices an opportunity to experience live theatre at minimal cost.

Programs & Services: *Professional acting workshops; internships; performances, theatre tours, seminars and workshops for students; Improvisational Theatre Project, touring; New Theatre For Now, new play performance program; Forum Lab, development of new plays; Artists-In-Prisons; staged readings; booked-in events; student, senior citizen and group ticket discounts; benefit performances; playwright-in-residence; CTG Volunteers; The Paper Forum, quarterly newsletter; colloquies and seminars.*

GORDON DAVIDSON
Artistic Director
WILLIAM P. WINGATE
General Manager

135 North Grand Avenue
Los Angeles, California 90012
Telephone (213) 972-7353
Box Office (213) 972-7392

Founded 1967
Gordon Davidson

Season
July – June

Schedule
Evenings
Tuesday – Sunday
Matinees
Saturday & Sunday

Facilities
Mark Taper Forum
Seating capacity 742
Stage Thrust
Forum Laboratory
2580 Cahuenga, Hollywood
(213) 465-9039
Seating capacity 99
Stage Flexible

Budget
June 27, 1976 – July 2, 1977
Operating budget $2,797,384
Earned income $1,733,677
Unearned income $ 995,298

Audience
Percent of capacity 83
Number of subscribers 21,750

Touring contact
Susan E. Barton

Operates on AEA LORT (A) & (B) contracts.

Productions, 1975-76

A Grave Undertaking, Lloyd Gold
The Royal Family, George S. Kaufman &
Edna Ferber
Section Nine, Philip Magdalany
The Heiress, Ruth & Augustus Goetz
Awake and Sing, Clifford Odets
The Winter's Tale, William Shakespeare

Productions, 1976-77

A Streetcar Named Desire, Tennessee Williams
Major Barbara, George Bernard Shaw
The Night Of the Tribades, Per Olov Enquist;
translated, Ross Shideler
The Physicists, Friedrich Durrenmatt
Angel City, Sam Shepard
Design for Living, Noel Coward

Kathryn Walker, Donald Madden and Patricia Elliott
in *The Night Of the Tribades* by Per Olov Enquist,
directed by Michael Kahn, sets by Michael H.
Yeargan and Lawrence King, costumes by Jane
Greenwood. Photo: Cliff Moore.

Richard Gere and Morris Carnovsky in *Awake and
Sing* by Clifford Odets, directed by Kenneth Frankel,
sets by Marjorie Kellogg, costumes by Jeanne
Button. Photo: Cliff Moore.

McCarter Theatre

The McCarter Theatre's location has played a significant role in determining its unique character. The theatre, situated exactly midway between the major arts centers of New York City and Philadelphia, has a theatrically sophisticated and demanding audience within a 50-mile radius. McCarter's local community of Princeton, New Jersey, home of one of America's major educational institutions, provides it with an intellectual climate highly receptive to artistic experimentation and innovation. The theatre's location, therefore, has dictated a theatrical standard and challenge and has provided an intellectual and creative environment for responding to both. The most often repeated goal of the McCarter is to attain the highest standard of literary and theatrical quality possible. Plays are selected according to a programming policy which mandates in each season one innovative production of a classic, two or three new plays, and two or three lesser-known plays of major playwrights. This policy has resulted in a repertoire unlike those of most theatres in the country. McCarter's proximity to New York removes from its potential repertoire all plays recently produced on Broadway, as well as in the tri-state area of New York, New Jersey and Connecticut.

The company's season lasts from October through April and consists of six productions. Under the guidance of Michael Kahn, McCarter's producing director since 1974, the theatre has presented a number of premieres, among them Sam Shepard's *Angel City,* Philip Magdalany's *Section Nine* and Per Olov Enquist's *The Night Of the Tribades.* Over the past five seasons, both subscriptions and total attendance have doubled, the number of performances each season has tripled, and the number of yearly productions has increased by one. Since the 1974-75 season, McCarter productions have toured to Chicago, Washington, D.C., and Broadway. Each production is also presented for two weeks in Philadelphia under a residency program at the Annenberg Center for the Performing Arts.

In addition to its primary commitment to maintaining a resident acting company and producing a full season of plays, the McCarter plays host to a wide variety of booked-in attractions, including performances of classical, chamber, contemporary and jazz music, as well as programs of dance, film and special events for children.

Programs & Services: *Internships; performances and lectures for students; touring; film series; chamber music; dance performances and residencies; booked-in events; student and senior citizen ticket discounts; free ticket program; speakers bureau; McCarter Associates, volunteers; McCarter Calendar/Newsletter, quarterly; seminar series.*

MICHAEL KAHN
Producing Director
EDWARD A. MARTENSON
General Manager

Box 526
Princeton, New Jersey 08540
Telephone (609) 452-3617
Box Office (609) 921-8700

Founded 1972
Daniel Seltzer

Season
October – April

Schedule
Evenings
Tuesday – Sunday
Matinees
Sunday

Facilities
University Place & College Road
Seating capacity 1,077
Stage Proscenium

Budget
July 1, 1976 – June 30, 1977
Operating budget $1,435,603
Earned income $1,022,938
Unearned income $ 376,929

Audience
Percent of capacity 85
Number of subscribers 12,135

Touring contact
Edward A. Martenson

Booked-in events
Music, dance, children's & adult theatre productions

Operates on AEA LORT (B) contract.

Productions, 1975–76
A Midsummer Night's Dream, William
Shakespeare
Witness for the Prosecution,
Agatha Christie
Arms and the Man, George Bernard Shaw
The Little Foxes, Lillian Hellman
Relatively Speaking, Alan Ayckbourn
Under Milk Wood, Dylan Thomas
Born Yesterday, Garson Kanin
Yankee Ingenuity, Jim Wise &
Richard Bimonte

Productions, 1976–77
Man and Superman, George Bernard Shaw
The Night of the Iguana, Tennessee Williams
The School for Wives, Moliere;
translated, Richard Wilbur
When You Comin' Back, Red Ryder?,
Mark Medoff
Sleuth, Anthony Shaffer
The Merchant of Venice, William Shakespeare
The Show-Off, George Kelly
Dames at Sea, George Haimsohn, Robin
Miller, Jim Wise

Terence Marinan and Polly Rowles in *The Show-Off*
by George Kelly, directed by John Ulmer, sets by
Robert Joseph Mooney, costumes by Mary Lynn
Bonnell.

Robert Grossman, Susanne Peters and company in
A Midsummer Night's Dream by William
Shakespeare, directed by Terence Kilburn, sets by
Peter Hicks, costumes executed by Mary Lynn
Bonnell.

Meadow Brook Theatre

Meadow Brook Theatre is located on the campus of Oakland University in Rochester, Michigan, 30 miles from Detroit. Its audience is drawn from a wide area which includes the nearby suburbs, as well as the cities of Detroit and Flint, Michigan.

After opening in 1966, the first four seasons were presented under the leadership of John Fernald, former principal of the Royal Academy of Dramatic Art in London. During that time, the groundwork was laid for the building of an audience in a region where no professional theatre had previously existed.

In 1970, Terence Kilburn assumed the artistic leadership of the theatre and instigated a wider and more varied repertoire, which included the presentation of more contemporary and American plays. By offering a more diverse repertoire, Meadow Brook Theatre has been able to attract a wide audience from various segments of the community. Season subscription sales have grown steadily each season from 8,100 in 1970 to a projected 14,000 for the 1977-78 season.

The theatre itself, modern in decor with near-perfect acoustics, has a proscenium stage with an apron extending some 12 feet beyond the curtain line. This small thrust adds a feeling of intimacy to the playing area.

The acting company has developed in the 1970s into what is best described as a revolving resident company. Although each season brings a number of new actors to the theatre, many performers return each year to appear in three or four productions, and, oftentimes, a small nucleus of actors will appear in six or seven of the theatre's eight season productions. Mr. Kilburn feels that this system provides both stability and variety. For many of the actors who have frequently worked together at Meadow Brook, there has developed a sense of ensemble playing. The audience, too, shares in this sense of continuity, and at the same time has the stimulation provided by the introduction of new talent into the acting company. Mr. Kilburn directs three productions each season, with guest directors engaged for other productions.

MBT maintains an active school program, which is based on attendance by high school and junior high school students at matinee performances. In addition, teachers are invited to preview performances, study materials are available for each play, tours of the facilities are arranged, post-play discussions are conducted by cast members, and lectures on the technical aspects of the theatre are given by the staff.

In 1974, Meadow Brook Theatre instigated an in-state touring program. Regarded as a major step in the theatre's growth, the first tour took Meadow Brook Theatre to 11 towns in Michigan. The tour expanded to include 19 communities in the 1976-77 season. This program, sponsored by the Michigan Council for the Arts, is expected to continue to expand during the coming seasons. MBT has also established an internship program in conjunction with Oakland University, whereby selected students are given academic credit for their participation in Meadow Brook Theatre productions.

Programs & Services: *Touring; student, senior citizen and group ticket discounts; theatre support organization;* Marquee, *newsletter; post-performance discussions.*

TERENCE E. KILBURN
Artistic Director

Oakland University
Rochester, Michigan 48063
Telephone (313) 377-3310
Box Office (313) 377-3300

Founded 1966
Oakland University

Season
September – May

Schedule
Evenings
Tuesday – Sunday
Matinees
Wednesday

Facilities
Seating capacity 608
Stage   Proscenium

Budget
July 1, 1976 – June 30, 1977
Operating budget $807,715
Earned income $671,702
Unearned income $144,750

Audience
Percent of capacity 92
Number of subscribers 13,900

Touring contact
Frank Bollinger

Operates on AEA LORT (B) contract.

Productions, 1975–76
Medicine Show, Richard Schotter &
Medicine Show company
Glowworm, Medicine Show company

Productions, 1976–77
Glowworm, Medicine Show company
Frogs, Carl Morse & Medicine Show
company
Medicine Show, Richard Schotter &
Medicine Show company

Chris Brandt and James Barbosa in *Frogs,* company
created with Carl Morse, directed by James
Barbosa, costumes by Patricia McGourty. Photo:
Michael Hunold.

Gretchen Van Ryper, Chris Brandt and Barbara
Vann in *Frogs,* as performed at Lincoln Center Out-
of-Doors Festival, 1977. Photo: Michael Hunold.

Medicine Show

The Medicine Show Theatre Ensemble invites the audience to join its actors in the juggling of expectations and the reordering of experience to discover unconfined levels of thought and a potential for more expansive action. Theatre is held to be a living art, reflective of its time and anticipatory of new ways of seeing and being seen. Unconventional methods elicit multidimensional perceptions by mixing emotional truths with alien environments, combining cultural recall with juxtaposed performance styles and countering wit with humor. These combine to make a theatre adventure that awakens, compels, enchants, questions, confounds and exhilarates. A Medicine Show performance is at once immediate and a continuum. For audience and actor it is a transformation — a dialectic of action. The Medicine Show performer is a creative artist, integrating his knowledge of traditional theatre with imagination, physical and vocal strength, and the free exploration of inner space. Involved in the world outside the theatre, actors use the Ensemble as a conduit for their energies and ideas, creating a constant comic meditation.

The name Medicine Show is in homage to an entirely American popular art form which was inexpensive, deliberately itinerant and had pretensions to healing powers. The company continues the tradition of this popular performance theatre with high energy and with demanding, illuminating and comedic performances.

In 1970, when Joseph Chaikin's Open Theatre split into two separate groups, two company members, Barbara Vann and James Barbosa, formed the Medicine Show Theatre Ensemble with other Open Theatre members. Medicine Show has toured Europe and more than 30 campuses in the United States and Canada, played at street fairs and festivals, at Lincoln Center's Out-of-Doors Festival in New York City, in museums, prisons, large auditoriums, and very small rooms. The company's chance encounter with an unusual environment is as welcome as its regularly scheduled theatre performances.

The Ensemble's first production, Brecht's *Edward II*, confirmed the company's predilection for the historico-fantastical style that flourished in the three group-created works that followed: *Medicine Show*, a love-hate song to the American mythic consciousness; *Frogs*, the peril-fraught journey of spiritually dehydrating amphibians to new water and a happy ending; and *Glowworm*, an absurdist vaudeville with side trips to exotic isles, mixed with Italianate intrigue and very grand opera. The Ensemble's newer works, Shaw's *Don Juan in Hell* and *Ex Patria*, based on writings by Emma Goldman and Josephine Baker, were created in collaboration with leading visual artists and composers. These pieces experiment in sound and space and cross sensory boundaries, in an attempt to redefine song, speech, set, costumes and performance itself. Extravagance of technique and decor is coupled with the essential humanity of the actor's art. *Stages*, a piece which demonstrates the effect of using experimental methods in staging traditional repertoire, offers insight into methodology and process.

Medicine Show conducts workshops and residencies at all levels, both professional and educational, in the belief that the techniques developed and synthesized in more than a decade of continuous work are of inestimable value in clarifying life patterns and behavior, and in focusing and freeing individual energy. All workshops emphasize the mixture of craftsmanship and vitality, a combination which helps give the Ensemble its distinctive style. Medicine Show uses life as a model and a medium, probing its confusions and complexities. This investigation, though profound, is seldom serious.

Programs & Services: *Acting workshops; internships; performances and workshops for students; lecture-demonstrations for audience; guest artist workshops; touring and residencies; Miscellany Series, new music and dance programs; High School Workshop, development of performance piece; student, senior citizen and group ticket discounts; free ticket program; annual benefit party and flea market; Medicine Show Newsletter.*

BARBARA VANN
JAMES BARBOSA
Artistic Directors
ELLEN GREENBERG
Business Manager

45 East 20th Street
New York, New York 10003
(212) 982-2986

Founded 1970
Barbara Vann & James Barbosa

Season
September – June

Facilities
Cloudchamber
Seating capacity 75
Stage   Flexible

Budget
Aug 1, 1976 – July 31, 1977
Operating budget $26,668
Earned income $15,045
Unearned income $12,262

Audience
Percent of capacity 75

Touring contact
Ellen Greenberg

Booked-in events
New music & film, experimental dance companies, play readings

Productions, 1975–76
Quarry, Meredith Monk

Productions, 1976–77
Quarry, Meredith Monk
Paris, Meredith Monk &
Ping Chong
Venice, Meredith Monk &
Ping Chong
Chacon, Meredith Monk &
Ping Chong
Songs from the Hill, Meredith Monk
Tablet, Meredith Monk

Meredith Monk/The House company in *Quarry,*
written and directed by Meredith Monk.

Meredith Monk in *Anthology,* written and directed
by Ms. Monk, 1974–75.

Meredith Monk/The House

Meredith Monk/The House is a group of actors, musicians, dancers, writers and painters who believe in performance as a means of personal and, hopefully, social evolution. These performers, dedicated to the interdisciplinary approach to performance identified with Meredith Monk, create "composite theatre" works which combine elements of speech, vocal and instrumental music, dance movement, costume, objects, light, film and, most important, environment. These elements are blended into an artistically focused whole, in which everyone works together, with no performer taking precedence over any other. The effect is like a plotless, nonverbal, surrealistic opera. The company's work ranges from large operatic works requiring 20 to 50 performers to solos, duets and chamber works for 8 to 15.

Meredith Monk is a composer, choreographer, director, singer, dancer and actress. Since 1964, she has created more than 40 works using dance, theatre and music. Some of her works have included *Break* in 1964; *16 Millimeter Earrings* in 1966; *Juice: A Theatre Cantata* in 1969; *Vessel*, an epic opera, in 1971; *Education of the Girlchild* in 1973; and *Quarry* in 1976.

Besides developing her own work, Meredith Monk has, over the past three years, been collaborating with Ping Chong on a set of pieces called *The Travelogue Series*. The first one, *Paris*, created in 1974, was followed by *Chacon* in 1975 and *Venice* in 1976. The company is currently working on *Tangiers*.

The House has in its repertoire numerous vocal works which, in varying degree, combine music, dance movement and theatrical elements. These include *Our Lady of Late*, composed for solo voice and wine glass; *Raw Recital*, for solo voice and organ; and *Anthology*, which combines voice and dance. In *Songs from the Hill*, produced in 1976, the voice is totally alone, unaccompanied and unadorned. *Tablet*, originally composed for solo voice and piano in 1974, was extended in 1976 to include four voices, recorder and piano. Although in the past Ms. Monk has written duets, quartets and choral works for 25 to 80 voices, *Tablet* is the first extended composition with 4 equally complex vocal parts. All of Ms. Monk's music is an exploration of the voice as an instrument.

Meredith Monk/The House tours extensively as part of the National Endowment for the Arts Dance Touring Program and spends at least four weeks every year performing in Europe.

Programs & Services: *Acting workshops on Meredith Monk's interdisciplinary approach; performances, workshops and seminars for students; touring; benefit performances.*

MEREDITH MONK
Director
CATHERINE SMITH
Administrative Director

New Arts Management
47 West 9th Street
New York, New York 10011
(212) 691-5434

Founded 1969
Meredith Monk

Budget
July 1, 1976 – June 30, 1977
Operating budget $93,602
Earned income $21,100
Unearned income $67,961

Touring contact
New Arts Management

Productions, 1975-76
King Lear, William Shakespeare
Democracy, Romulus Linney
The School for Wives, Moliere; translated,
Richard Wilbur
The Visions of Simone Machard, Bertolt
Brecht & Lion Feuchtwanger; translated,
Carl Richard Mueller
Never a Snug Harbor, David Ulysses Clarke
My Sister, My Sister, Ray Aranha
Fanshen, David Hare
Out, Penelope Reed & Robert E. Ingham
Out to Sea, Slawomir Mrozek
Happy Days, Samuel Beckett

Productions, 1976-77
Death of a Salesman, Arthur Miller
The Trial of the Moke, Daniel Stein
A Christmas Carol, Charles Dickens;
adapted, Nagle Jackson
Private Lives, Noel Coward
Volpone, Ben Jonson
Vanities, Jack Heifner
The Dog Ran Away, Brother Jonathan, O.S.F.
The Birthday Party, Harold Pinter
In Memory Of, Kevin Schwartz
Domino Courts, William Hauptman

Mary Wright in *The Visions of Simone Machard* by
Bertolt Brecht and Lion Feuchtwanger, directed by
Nagle Jackson, sets by Christopher M. Idoine,
costumes by Elizabeth Covey. Photo: Ric Sorgel.

Jeffrey Tambor and Richard Risso in Moliere's *The
School for Wives*, directed by Nagle Jackson, sets by
Christopher M. Idoine, costumes by Elizabeth
Covey. Photo: Ric Sorgel.

Milwaukee Repertory Theater Company

Devoted to a diverse repertory of new and old works, the Milwaukee Repertory Theater Company is a regional theatre organization with a strong commitment to the community from which it has grown and the larger community of the American Midwest. Now nearing a quarter-century of continuous production, the company has experienced numerous changes since its inception in 1954 as the Fred Miller Theater.

During its first seven seasons, the theatre presented commercial productions primarily as vehicles for guest stars. In 1961 the organization became nonprofit and joined the blossoming regional theatre movement. Three years later the decision was made by the company's board of directors to change its name to the Milwaukee Repertory Theater Company. During the mid-sixties attendance at MRT productions increased dramatically, and as the company found broader avenues of community support it became apparent that its theatre building, a converted movie house with 384 seats, was inadequate. Plans were made to move into the proposed Milwaukee County Performing Arts Center, and in 1969 MRT established its main base of operations there in the Todd Wehr Theater.

Today more than 70 full-time professionals are at work for MRT. Its ensemble approach to theatre has grown through artistic directors Tunc Yalman (1966–1971) and Nagle Jackson (1971–1977), and continues under MRT's current artistic director, John Dillon. Mr. Dillon directs at least three of the company's six mainstage productions, with guest directors and directors from the company staging the remaining plays. Guest designers are employed for each production to work with resident technicians in the MRT shops, all of which are located at the Performing Arts Center.

Another important element of MRT's artistic goal lies in the company's belief that contemporary work must be included with the established repertoire. MRT searches constantly for new scripts and supports full-time writers in residence. Company-created pieces and full-length works commissioned by MRT are also a part of the theatre's commitment to the development of the American theatre.

The 99-seat Court Street Theater, established in 1973 in a converted warehouse, is an important part of MRT's overall program. With this second stage, MRT audiences and company members alike have an opportunity to experience new and different dramatic material. Indeed, MRT has continued over recent years to find numerous alternate spaces in which to perform. In 1974 the *English Mystery Plays* were presented in 41 churches, and in 1975 *The School for Wives* played to audiences throughout the five states of the upper Midwest. *Vanities* also toured the upper Midwest in 1977, and in 1978 Eugene O'Neill's *Ah, Wilderness!* and *Long Day's Journey Into Night* will tour nine states. Other MRT activities include an annual presentation of Charles Dickens' *A Christmas Carol*, sponsored by the Metropolitan Milwaukee Association of Commerce; tours of company-created pieces to local prisons and hospitals; and numerous outreach programs for secondary schools and colleges.

Programs & Services: *Internships; performances for students; technical workshops; actor-in-school program; touring; lecture series; student, senior citizen and group discounts; united arts fund-raising; Court Street sale of scenery, props and costumes; audiovisual programs; Laura Sherry League and MRT Committee for Business and Professions, support groups; Prologue, a publication for subscribers.*

JOHN DILLON
Artistic Director
SARA O'CONNOR
Managing Director

929 North Water Street
Milwaukee, Wisconsin 53202
(414) 273-7121

Founded 1954
Mary John

Season
September – May

Schedule
Evenings
Tuesday – Sunday
Matinees
Wednesday

Facilities
Todd Wehr Theater
Seating capacity 504
Stage ¾ Arena
Court Street Theater
315 West Court Street
Seating capacity 99
Stage Flexible

Budget
July 1, 1976 – June 30, 1977
Operating expenses $941,778
Earned income $728,825
Unearned income $286,744

Audience
Todd Wehr Theater
Percent of capacity 96
Number of subscribers 19,054
Court Street Theater
Percent of capacity 90

Touring contact
Susan Medak

Operates on AEA LORT (C) contract.

Productions, 1975

Born Yesterday, Garson Kanin
The Cherry Orchard, Anton Chekhov;
adapted, Vincent Dowling
Much Ado About Nothing, William Shakespeare
The Last Meeting of the Knights of the White Magnolia, Preston Jones
A Streetcar Named Desire, Tennessee Williams

Productions, 1976

The Rainmaker, N. Richard Nash
The Morgan Yard, Kevin O'Morrison
The Drunkard, W.H. Smith;
adapted, Francis J. Cullinan
Don Juan of Flatbush, Stanley Taikeff
The Great White Hope, Howard Sackler
The Heiress, Ruth & Augustus Goetz
Who's Afraid of Virginia Woolf?, Edward Albee
Once in a Lifetime, Moss Hart & George S. Kaufman

Robert Elliott, Al Christy and J.Q. Bruce, Jr.
interrogate Michael LaGue in *The Last Meeting of
the Knights of the White Magnolia* by Preston Jones,
directed by Thomas Gruenewald, sets by J. Morton
Walker, costumes by Barbara Medlicott.

Michael LaGue, Nina Furst and Walter Atamaniuk in
Edward Albee's *Who's Afraid of Virginia Woolf?*,
directed by James Assad, sets by Judie A. Juracek,
costumes by Barbara Medlicott.

Missouri Repertory Theatre

In 1977 Missouri Repertory Theatre marked its fourteenth season of resident productions in rotating repertory with eight plays presented in Kansas City and the surrounding region over a 24-week period. It was in 1964, with a two-play, two-week season, that MRT was inaugurated under the aegis of the University of Missouri-Kansas City in a converted Army barracks on the campus. MRT's founder-director Dr. Patricia McIlrath is also chairman of the university's drama department and director of university theatres.

The university concurred with Dr. McIlrath that the school's strong production-oriented academic theatre program provided the impetus for the creation of a parallel professional theatre serving the Kansas City metropolitan area of 1.5 million people, as well as the state and the region. Although the university views the performing arts as one of its three major areas of concentration and provides vital financial and administrative support, MRT is a separate and distinct entity. Mainstage and regional touring productions provide valuable professional experience for graduate students in theatre, many of whom participate in MRT's growing intern and apprentice programs.

In conjunction with a 7-week winter season of two plays in repertory and a 17-week schedule of six plays in rotating sequence, MRT reaches beyond Kansas City with its 5-week Vanguard Tour throughout Missouri in the spring and a somewhat shorter five-state regional tour in the fall. In 1976 paid admissions at the home playhouse totaled 35,954 persons, while another 35,017 persons saw touring presentations. The latter included extensive in-school programs, workshops and lectures.

John Houseman, Alex Minotis, Alan Schneider, John Reich, John O'Shaughnessy, Vincent Dowling, Harold Scott, Adrian Hall and Cyril Ritchard are among the distinguished guest directors that have helped attract a strong core of resident professional actors, interns and apprentices from throughout the country.

MRT presently finds itself in an evolutionary phase, influenced by the fact that the company, in early 1979, will take up residence in the Helen F. Spencer Theatre of the UMKC Performing Arts Center. In the new 800-seat theatre MRT expects to expand from the present 17 weeks to a 32-week mainstage season of both classical and new plays in repertory.

Programs & Services: *Internships; apprenticeships; performances and seminars for students; MRT Vanguard Tour; mainstage tour; in-school workshops; apprentice workshop productions; student, senior citizen and group discounts; free ticket program; speakers bureau; MRT Guild, support group; MRT Guild telethon; newsletter and play discussions for guild members.*

PATRICIA McILRATH
Producing Director

5100 Rockhill Road
Kansas City, Missouri 64110
Telephone (816) 276-2701
Box Office (816) 276-2705

Founded 1964
University of Missouri-Kansas City & Patricia McIlrath

Season
February &
July – October

Schedule
Evenings
Tuesday – Sunday
Matinees
Saturday & Sunday

Facilities
University Playhouse
51st and Holmes Streets
Seating capacity 501
Stage Proscenium

Budget
July 1, 1976 – June 30, 1977
Operating budget $353,166
Earned income $221,408
Unearned income $131,758

Audience
Percent of capacity 62
Number of subscribers 4,716

Touring contact
James Costin
MRT Vanguard Tour
(816) 276-1451

Booked-in events
Dance companies, chamber music groups, musical soloists, mime troupes & other small performing ensembles

Operates on AEA LORT (C) contract.

Productions, 1976
Nightclub Cantata, Elizabeth Swados
The Club, Eve Merriam

Productions, 1977
Viva Reviva, Eve Merriam
A Natural Death, Richard Howard
Three Music-Theatre Profiles,
Stanley Silverman, Francis Thorne,
Gunther Schuller

Elizabeth Swados in *Nightclub Cantata,* written and
directed by Ms. Swados, sets by Pat Woodbridge,
costumes by Kate Carmel. Photo: Martha Swope.

Ralph Bruneau, Kenneth Hamilton and Rinde Eckert
in *Viva Reviva* by Eve Merriam, directed by Graciela
Daniele, designed by Kate Carmel. Photo: Marc
Raboy.

Music-Theatre Performing Group/ Lenox Arts Center

The Music-Theatre Performing Group/Lenox Arts Center, entering its seventh year, is a laboratory engaged specifically in the development of new American music-theatre. The organization is pioneering the development of a music-theatre which fuses experimental theatre techniques with dance and a wide spectrum of musical forms, including contemporary music, opera and jazz. The group's direction is toward a cohesive meshing of theatre and music, not in the European tradition, but in a form indigenous to America.

MTPG/LAC operates on a year-round basis, spending nine months in New York and three in Stockbridge, Massachusetts. The organization's performing spaces are in Citizens Hall, a landmark building in Stockbridge, in June, July and August, and at the Theater of The Open Eye in Manhattan, from January through May. During the summer season, all staff and artists are housed in the theatre's artists' residence.

The driving force behind all the group's work is the creation of *new* music-theatre productions. The productions begin simply with extensive rehearsal periods in order that the artists may focus entirely on the work itself. The works then proceed to full production in New York or Stockbridge. Some of the company's productions have had an extended life both on and Off Broadway, in other cities throughout the country and in Europe.

The group is training a core of young performing artists skilled in all facets of the field, in order to develop a new music-theatre repertory company. MTPG/LAC has helped to foster the development of the following artists, in the following ways. Stanley Silverman and Richard Foreman's collaborative efforts have been nurtured through the production of their works, *Doctor Selavy's Magic Theater* and *Hotel for Criminals*. In the spring of 1978, MTPG/LAC plans to produce their latest piece, *The American Imagination*. Elizabeth Swados was given an opportunity to compose, direct and write for a piece of her own conception, entitled *Nightclub Cantata*, which has since played in Manhattan, Boston, Washington and Europe.

MTPG/LAC has sought to create fresh and dynamic collaborations by bringing together the "right" composer with the "right" director or writer. Many of these collaborators are people who have been working in other creative fields, some nontheatrical. For example, choreographer-performer Tommy Tune was given his first major chance to direct in the theatre, with a new piece compiled by Eve Merriam, entitled *The Club*. Richard Howard, Pulitzer Prize–winning poet, was brought into the theatre through the production of his play, *A Natural Death*, directed by Michael Feingold. Martha Clarke, a dancer and choreographer with the Pilobolus company, had her first opportunity to explore new theatre forms in her production, *Portraits*. And Charles Wuorinen, also a Pulitzer Prize winner, had some of his works presented in *Profile of Wuorinen*, as part of the theatre's Music-Theatre Profiles Series.

Over the theatre's six-year period of operation, the Music-Theatre Performing Group/Lenox Arts Center has developed and presented 32 innovative American music-theatre works.

Programs & Services: *Resident technicians and designers, training; poetry series; student ticket discounts; benefit performances; artist residencies; newsletter.*

LYN AUSTIN
MARY SILVERMAN
Executive Directors

18 East 68th Street
New York, New York 10021
(212) 371–9610

Citizens Hall
Stockbridge,
Massachusetts 01262
(413) 298–9463

Founded 1970
Lyn Austin

Season
New York
January – May
Stockbridge
June – August

Facilities
Theater of The Open Eye
316 East 88th Street
Seating capacity 100
Stage Flexible
Citizens Hall
Seating capacity 100
Stage Flexible

Budget
Jan 1, 1976 – Dec 31, 1976
Operating budget $132,585
Earned income $ 18,519
Unearned income $110,765

Audience
Percent of capacity 99

Touring contact
Lyn Austin

Productions, 1975–77
Soljourney Into Truth, Barbara Ann Teer

Hawk in *Soljourney Into Truth*, written and directed by Barbara Ann Teer, costumes by Larry LaGaspi and Judy Dearing.

The NBT company in *Soljourney Into Truth*.

National Black Theatre

The National Black Theatre (NBT), founded in 1968, is a multifaceted creative organization located in the heart of Harlem in New York City. It is a unique institution created by Barbara Ann Teer to expand the consciousness of the people it serves through a highly innovative theatrical form called "God-conscious art." This form allows each performer to express himself freely and spontaneously from within.

From this ideology flows a fresh, innovative and vibrant concept of theatre and performing, which goes beyond the standard definition and expectation of what theatre is, retires the conventional form of art and introduces the circular form of God-conscious art. Creative expression comes directly from that divine and omnipotent force within, which results in producing, for both performer and audience, vitality and joy.

NBT's theatrical activities are bolstered by its administrative programs. Both are designed to give people an opportunity to become spiritually and artistically knowledgeable and, at the same time, learn to master the skills of Western society's business world. The rewards the company experiences are based on the contribution each person makes to the institution, and to the community at large, as opposed to individual professional or monetary recognition.

The theatrical expression in which this art form is housed is called "ritualistic revivals." The ritual is musical and is designed to transmit to an audience an overwhelming creative force which provides a transforming, as well as entertaining, experience. NBT's ritualistic revivals are performed by a repertory company of 30 performers, all of whom have five to nine years of training and performing experience in God-conscious art. Spending an evening with the National Black Theatre performing company will give you a hand-clapping, soul-stirring experience of aliveness, celebration and joy.

In 1977, NBT was an official delegate of the North American zone to the Second Black and African Festival of Arts and Culture (FESTAC). During this exchange of cultural expression in Nigeria, NBT's performance was broadcast, via television and Telstar, all over the African continent. The impact that was made is a significant milestone in NBT's quest to reach and serve humanity.

Programs & Services: *Acting workshops; internships; touring; workshop productions; group ticket discounts; voucher program; benefit performances; Assistants Program, support group; NBT Newsletter, monthly publication.*

BARBARA ANN TEER
Executive Producer
FREDRICA TEER
Executive Director

9 East 125th Street
New York, New York 10035
(212) 427-5615

Founded 1968
Barbara Ann Teer

Season
Varies

Schedule
Evenings
Saturday & Sunday

Facilities
Seating capacity 110
Stage   Thrust

Budget
Nov 1, 1976 – Oct 31, 1977
Operating budget $134,690
Earned income $ 44,000
Unearned income $102,500

Audience
Percent of capacity 74

Touring contact
Keibu Faison

Productions, 1975–76
Parade, NTD company

Productions, 1976–77
Four Saints in Three Acts, Gertrude Stein
& Virgil Thomson; adapted, NTD company
The Harmfulness of Tobacco, Anton Chekhov;
adapted, NTD company
Children's Letters to God, anonymous children;
adapted, NTD company
Sir Gawain and the Green Knight; adapted, Dennis
Scott

*The Little Theatres of the Deaf presented
programs based on Aesop's fables
and stories by James Thurber.*

Timothy Scanlon in *The Dybbuk* by S. Ansky,
adapted by the NTD company and John Broome,
directed by Mr. Broome, 1974–75. Photo: David
Hays.

NTD company members in *Four Saints in Three
Acts* by Gertrude Stein and Virgil Thomson, directed
by David Hays, sets by Patricia Zipprodt, costumes
by Fred Voelpel.

184

National Theatre of the Deaf

David Hays formed the National Theatre of the Deaf in 1967, under the umbrella of the Eugene O'Neill Theater Center. From the outset, the principal goal was to create a new theatre form based upon visual language. By holding fast to that original concept, the NTD is now recognized throughout the world as one of America's most remarkable theatre companies. Using elements of speech, sign language, pantomime and dance, the NTD has developed a unique theatrical style that is readily understood by both hearing and deaf people.

Each summer, the NTD summer school is held at the O'Neill Center in Waterford, Connecticut, to extend and enhance the company's skills and to begin the training process of possible future company members. Along with this program, deaf community leaders from throughout the world are trained in various theatrical disciplines and production techniques. Each September, the company goes into rehearsal for a new production that will tour America and abroad throughout the following year. In between national and international tours of its major work, the company is divided into smaller units that tour to schools with a special repertoire for young people. These smaller units are called the Little Theatres of the Deaf.

In 1967, the NTD became the second professional theatre of the deaf in the world; the Russian theatre had existed since 1911. Now, only 10 years after its inception, the NTD has been instrumental in establishing professional theatres of the deaf in Great Britain, Sweden and Australia, and has encouraged and assisted in the formation of community theatres of the deaf in the United States. Due to the social impact of NTD's work, in city after city and country after country, the image of the deaf has been elevated. Old cliches, fears and misunderstandings concerning the deaf have been broken down. Hearing people, seeing the theatre for the first time, are astonished at the skill and artistic achievements of the company and at how easily the performances can be followed and understood without any knowledge of sign language. These social goals, although important and gratifying to the company, are, nevertheless, secondary goals. The theatre's primary thrust was, and is, the creation of a theatre of visual language, capable of holding its own alongside any theatre company in the world. The result is a theatre of extraordinary power and range, and exceptional and unique communication skills.

Since its inception, the NTD has completed 20 national tours, totaling more than 2,000 performances in 47 states, including two Broadway appearances. Over 100 million Americans have seen the NTD on television, most notably in the CBS Christmas special *A Child's Christmas in Wales*, co-starring Michael Redgrave. The company has also performed in 15 foreign countries in Europe, the Mideast and the South Pacific. In 1977, the NTD created a television special, *Who Knows One*, a Passover seder in sign language, which was shown nationally over the Public Broadcasting Service. The NTD was also commissioned by the Kennedy Center in Washington, D.C., to create a new work for young people. *Sir Gawain and the Green Knight*, adapted by Jamaican poet and playwright Dennis Scott, premiered at the Kennedy Center's Eisenhower Theater in April 1977. The theatre was also awarded a special Tony Award for theatrical excellence in 1977.

Fully four-fifths of the NTD audience are hearing people. By retaining its original emphasis on artistic goals, the NTD has made theatre of the deaf a new and exciting medium — a mixture of music, dance and speech, forged into a visual language readily comprehensible by all.

Programs & Services: *Professional School for Deaf Theatre Personnel; workshops on communication, visual theatre techniques, sign-mime, kinetic imagery and story telling; Little Theatre of the Deaf, children's touring production; touring; poetry readings; lecture-demonstrations of visual language; NTD Spotlight, newsletter.*

DAVID HAYS
Producing Director
JOSEPH KRAKORA
Executive Vice-President

O'Neill Theater Center
305 Great Neck Road
Waterford, Connecticut 06385
(203) 443-5378

Founded 1967
David Hays

Season
October – April

Budget
July 1, 1976 – June 30, 1977
Operating budget $561,647
Earned income $214,258
Unearned income $351,727

Touring contact
Mack Scism

Operates on AEA Guest Artist contract.

Productions, 1975–76
Eden, Steve Carter
Livin' Fat, Judi Ann Mason

Productions, 1976–77
The Brownsville Raid, Charles Fuller
The Great MacDaddy, Paul Carter Harrison;
music, Coleridge-Taylor Perkinson
Square Root of Soul, Adolph Caesar;
music, Jothan Callins

Reyno and Charles Weldon in *The Great MacDaddy*
by Paul Carter Harrison, directed by Douglas Turner
Ward, sets by William Ritman. Photo: Bert Andrews.

Douglas Turner Ward and Arthur French in Charles
Fuller's *The Brownsville Raid*, directed by Israel
Hicks, sets by Neil Peter Jampolis, costumes by
Mary Mease Warren. Photo: Bert Andrews.

The Negro Ensemble Company

The 1976–77 season climaxed the first 10 years of the Negro Ensemble Company's existence, during which time it literally changed the face of American theatre — painting it blacker. The NEC pioneered in establishing black drama as a dominant force in the cultural life of the nation by introducing new talents, developing new resources and exploring new aesthetic frontiers.

The NEC has an international reputation. It has toured Europe, giving performances in England, Germany and Italy. It has performed in Bermuda, the Virgin Islands and, more recently, at the Adelaide Festival in Australia. The company has also toured the United States extensively, and in New York has produced more than 40 plays, including *Song of the Lusitanian Bogey, Ceremonies in Dark Old Men, The Sty of the Blind Pig, The River Niger, The First Breeze of Summer, Eden,* and *The Brownsville Raid.*

If there is any one source to account for the achievements of the NEC, it is a commitment to excellence. From the beginning, excellence was stressed as a goal, and its attainment has been strived for ever since. In the process, risk taking has been cultivated as a programmatic norm. Upon entering its second decade, the NEC pursues fresh challenges — dares which promise unpredictable results, but are far more rewarding.

The NEC will launch its 1977–78 season with an innovation in programming, by mounting two new full-length plays by the same author, performed in repertory. These works, *The Offering* and *Black Body Blues* by Gus Edwards, will open individually, then alternate in repertory on a week-to-week basis.

In Gus Edwards, the NEC is introducing a playwright of great originality. Mr. Edwards' territory is the outer boundaries of the black experience. He portrays people isolated from the mainstream of Afro-American life, functioning on the borderline of existence; yet he depicts them with such compelling intensity and ferocious eloquence that they command primary attention. He is an important addition to the stellar roster of previously produced NEC playwrights like Lonne Elder III, Joseph A. Walker, Paul Carter Harrison, Leslie Lee, Phillip Hayes Dean, Derek Walcott, Wole Soyinka, Lennox Brown, John Scott, Silas Jones, Judi Ann Mason, Steve Carter and Charles Fuller. Following these productions, the company will do two more major productions of new plays, supplemented by a full training program and new play readings.

Rather than rest on its laurels, the NEC continues to press onward, with even more adventuresome explorations into the complexities of the black experience.

Programs & Services: *On-the-job professional theatre training; performances, workshops and seminars for students; touring; workshop productions and staged readings; student, senior citizen and group ticket discounts; free ticket program; benefit performances; "friends" organizations.*

DOUGLAS TURNER WARD
Artistic Director
FREDERICK GARRETT
Administrative Director

133 Second Avenue
New York, New York 10003
Telephone (212) 677-3939
Box Office (212) 674-3530

Founded 1967
Douglas Turner Ward,
Robert Hooks, Gerald Krone

Season
December – July

Schedule
Evenings
Tuesday – Sunday
Matinees
Saturday & Sunday

Facilities
St. Marks Playhouse
Seating capacity 145
Stage ¾ Arena

Budget
July 1, 1976 – June 30, 1977
Operating budget $644,705
Earned income $134,431
Unearned income $513,343

Audience
Percent of capacity 77
Number of subscribers 1,600

Touring contact
Coral Hawthorne

Operates on AEA LORT (D) contract.

Productions, 1975-76
Never a Snug Harbor, David Ulysses Clarke
The Last Christians, Jack Gilhooley
The Wolves and the Lamb, Frieda Lipp
Sister Sadie, Clifford Mason
Father Uxbridge Wants to Marry, Frank
Gagliano
The Resurrection of Jackie Cramer, Frank
Gagliano
Kerouac, Martin Duberman

Productions, 1976-77
The Brixton Recovery, Jack Gilhooley
Even the Window Is Gone, Gene Radano
The Wakefield Plays, Israel Horovitz
Bull Fight Cow, Allen Davis III
Berserkers, Warren Kliewer
Lust, Steven Somkin
A New World, Marian Winters; music,
Albert Hague
The Mute Who Sang, Gene Radano

*The New Dramatists also presented more than 60
cold and staged readings in the two-year period
from 1975 through 1977.*

Ed Crowley and Ruth Baker in a workshop staging of
Lust by Steven Somkin, directed by Andrew Harris,
sets by Letch Hudgins. Photo: Nicholas Levitin.

New Dramatist members Pat Staten, Eric
Thompson, Andrew Harris, Steven Somkin, William
Hauptman, Frieda Lipp and Bill Andrews at a
membership meeting.

The New Dramatists

The New Dramatists is a membership organization for New York area playwrights. Playwrights are accepted for membership on the basis of submitting two full-length plays that are not adaptations, collaborations or musicals. Evaluations of applicant plays are made by member playwrights, who read scripts without author identification.

Founded in 1949 by Richard Rodgers, Moss Hart, John Golden, Howard Lindsay, Oscar Hammerstein, John Wharton and Michaela O'Harra, the New Dramatists has provided a unique program of playwright development for more than 400 writers in more than a quarter-century of operation. These writers have been responsible for more than 200 plays presented on and Off Broadway, and include Robert Anderson, William Inge, Roger O. Hirson, Jack Gelber, William Gibson and Michael Stewart.

The membership presently includes 48 active members and 11 associates, each participating in the five-point Plan for Playwrights, which has formed the basis of the program since the organization's inception. The five-point plan includes workshop presentations of plays in progress, panel discussions of new plays, craft discussions with leading theatrical figures, free admission to most Broadway and Off Broadway shows, and production observerships which allow playwrights to observe a Broadway play from its first read-through to opening night. The most extraordinary aspect of the New Dramatists is that it provides a *community* for writers, which allows them to work on their plays in a laboratory situation, under the supervision of a professional staff and in collaboration with the other members of the organization.

The artistic temperament of the organization is best reflected in a statement by David Trainer, a present member: "It is the way the New Dramatists is devoted to playwrights that makes it so special. Quite simply, the place is a workshop in the purest sense of the word. In fact, it is almost a work*bench*. The playwright brings in the raw materials, the words, and is provided with the essential tools with which to shape these materials — actors, a director and a space. Nothing else is required to build a play, and that is all that anyone gets at the New Dramatists. Sets, costumes, all varieties of decoration are, of course, nice, but they are available elsewhere and, in fact, relate to presenting, not *creating*, a play. When a playwright thinks he has exhausted the resources of the organization, he can take his creation to market and sell it, or take it home and hide it. But the end result is irrelevant beside the fact that the resources of the New Dramatists, being almost entirely human, are also virtually limitless. There are no goals or objectives beyond improving one's *process*. It is significant, too, that the organization has almost no 'rules.' Given the tools, the writer can do anything he wants with them. The burden therefore falls on the writers to decide what they want, and to use their wits to achieve it."

The New Dramatists counts among its current membership such writers as Martin Duberman, William Hauptman, Alice Childress and Frank Gagliano. In 1976–77, among the plays that were developed at the New Dramatists and fed into the mainstream of American theatre through subsequent productions at other theatres, were Jack Gilhooley's *Brixton Recovery*, produced at the Indiana Repertory Theatre and at PAF Playhouse in Huntington, New York; Mr. Gilhooley's *Mummer's End*, produced commercially in Philadelphia, at the Asolo State Theater in Sarasota, Florida, and at the Folger Theatre Group in Washington, D.C.; Martin Duberman's *Visions of Kerouac*, produced at the Odyssey Theatre in Los Angeles and at the Lion Theatre Company in New York; Conn Fleming and Bland Simpson's *The Red Blue-Grass Western Flyer Show*, produced at the Goodspeed Opera House in East Haddam, Connecticut; and Rose Goldemberg's *Ghandiji*, produced at the Back Alley Theatre in Washington, D.C.

Programs & Services: *Internships; staged readings; workshop productions; craft and panel discussions for members; member newsletter.*

STEPHEN HARTY
Managing Director

424 West 44th Street
New York, New York 10036
(212) 757-6960

Founded 1949
Michaela O'Harra, John Golden,
Moss Hart, Oscar Hammerstein,
Richard Rodgers, Howard
Lindsay, John Wharton

Season
September – July

Facilities
Seating capacity 90
Stage Flexible

Budget
June 1, 1976 – May 31, 1977
Operating budget $89,046
Earned income $ 1,303
Unearned income $80,934

Productions, 1975-76

Toe Jam, Elaine Jackson
Section D, Reginald Johnson
For Colored Girls who have Considered Suicide When The Rainbow is Enuf,
Ntozake Shange
Showdown, Don Evans
Bargainin' Thing, Daniel Owens
Mondongo, Ray Ramirez; music, Willie Colon & David Barron; lyrics, Lon Ivey

Productions, 1976-77

The Defense, Edgar White
Perdido (Lost), Soledad
Divine Comedy, Owen Dodson
Macbeth, William Shakespeare; adapted, Orson Welles
Daddy, Ed Bullins
Season's Reason, Ron Milner; music, Charles Mason

George Fludd, Kim Sullivan and George Campbell in *Toe Jam* by Elaine Jackson, directed by Anderson Johnson. Photo: Bert Andrews.

Cast members of *A Recent Killing* by Imamu Amiri Baraka, directed by Irving Vincent, sets by Charles Mills, 1972. Photo: Bert Andrews.

New Federal Theatre
Henry Street Settlement

The New Federal Theatre was founded by Woodie King, Jr., at the Henry Street Settlement, in the summer of 1970. A small grant from the New York State Council on the Arts, coupled with funds from the Settlement, launched the theatre's first season in the basement of Saint Augustine's Church on Henry Street. Since then, the New Federal Theatre has carved a niche for itself in the theatrical world by bringing minority theatre to the audience for which the theatre was originally designed, the lower east side of Manhattan, as well as to the greater New York metropolitan area. At the same time, it has brought the work of minority playwrights and actors to national attention, as well as sponsored productions by various other ethnic theatres. In achieving its current status, the theatre has progressed from a shoestring budget of $7,500 to an annual investment of over $300,000, and from an essentially black ethnocentric effort, to a multiethnic endeavor presenting theatre productions by black, Jewish and Puerto Rican playwrights. The physical plant of the Settlement's Arts for Living Center includes three theatres, rehearsal studios and modern stage equipment, all of which is made available to NFT.

There are three main objectives of the New Federal Theatre. They are to provide promising playwrights with the opportunity of having their work produced; to provide its audiences with first-rate theatre that relates to the interests of various cultural groups; and to train minority people for employment in the theatre and theatre-related fields.

Six to ten showcase productions are offered each year, as well as approximately four play readings, which are designed to give playwrights the opportunity to review and improve a new work before possible production. For several years, the New Federal Theatre has had a Rockefeller Foundation – supported playwright-in-residence. In 1977–78, Ron Milner will be in residence and the theatre will be seeking additional funds to sponsor a writers' workshop and develop a new play, under Mr. Milner's direction. The theatre also sponsors vocational workshops two or three times a week, which offer people job training in black, Puerto Rican and experimental theatre, theatre management and technical theatre. Another program of NFT, the Hispanic Playwright Workshop, presents monthly readings of new plays. In 1976–77, these workshops attracted a large audience.

Over the past seven years, NFT has produced approximately 60 plays, bringing to public attention such playwrights as J.E. Franklin, Ron Milner, Ed Pomerantz, Joseph Lizardi and Ntozake Shange. In 1974–75, *The Taking of Miss Janie* by Ed Bullins, was the first play produced under a trial arrangement between NFT and Joseph Papp's New York Shakespeare Festival whereby plays are showcased first at Henry Street and then produced at one of the Shakespeare Festival's theatres. *For Colored Girls who have Considered Suicide When The Rainbow is Enuf* was the second play presented in association with the Shakespeare Festival and it subsequently moved on to a successful Broadway run. NFT productions also tour outside New York State; most recently, *Showdown* by Don Evans, toured to Washington, D.C., and Philadelphia.

The Henry Street Settlement's New Federal Theatre is in its eighth year. Its primary function is to serve new writers and, each year since its inception, the New Federal has brought attention to new American plays. In the 1977–78 season, the theatre will present six new plays in a total season of seven productions.

Programs & Services: *Acting and technical workshops in black and Hispanic theatre; internships; workshop productions; staged readings; all performances are free.*

WOODIE KING, JR.
Director

Henry Street Settlement
466 Grand Street
New York, New York 10002
Telephone (212) 766-9295
Box Office (212) 766-9334

Founded 1970
Woodie King, Jr.

Season
October – June

Facilities
Playhouse
Seating capacity 350
Stage   Proscenium

Budget
July 1, 1976 – June 30, 1977
Operating budget $260,000
Earned income $ 10,000
Unearned income $135,000

Audience
Percent of capacity 100

Touring contact
Woodie King, Jr.

Operates under AEA Showcase Code.

Productions, 1976

The Tempest, William Shakespeare
Henry V, William Shakespeare
The Best Man, Gore Vidal
The Devil's Disciple, George Bernard Shaw
Private Lives, Noel Coward
Stop the World — I Want to Get Off,
Leslie Bricusse & Anthony Newley
The Playboy of the Western World,
John Millington Synge
Of Mice and Men, John Steinbeck

Productions, 1977

Much Ado About Nothing, William Shakespeare
Titus Andronicus, William Shakespeare
Cyrano de Bergerac, Edmond Rostand;
translated, Brian Hooker
An Enemy of the People, Henrik Ibsen
The Hot l Baltimore, Lanford Wilson
The Glass Menagerie, Tennessee Williams

Geddeth Smith and Robin Leary in Shakespeare's
Titus Andronicus, directed by Paul Barry, sets by
Don A. Coleman, costumes by Jeffrey L. Ullman.
Photo: Blair Holley.

J.C. Hoyt, Robert Machray and Kenneth Gray in
The Best Man by Gore Vidal, directed by Paul Barry,
sets by David M. Glenn, costumes by Dean H.
Reiter. Photo: Blair Holley.

New Jersey Shakespeare Festival

The New Jersey Shakespeare Festival began in 1963 when its founder, Paul Barry, presented a single Shakespearean play, *The Taming of the Shrew*, as part of a 10-play stock season at the Cape May Playhouse. Mr. Barry gradually built a resident professional company, dedicated to the presentation of great plays primarily of the English, Irish and American traditions. Productions were performed in a nightly rotating repertory schedule, with at least two plays of Shakespeare produced each season, as standards of excellence against which other selections were measured.

By 1968, the Festival was producing a three-play repertoire in the midst of the stock season. In addition to 17 of Shakespeare's plays, the company presented a range of other works of quality, including *Rhinoceros, Rashomon, Night of the Iguana* and *The Devils*. Three fall seasons in Boston and two fall tours of New Jersey schools were mounted, in addition to the five summer seasons. In 1970, the company presented its first full season of plays as the nonprofit New Jersey Shakespeare Festival. In 1972, realizing that the resort economy of Cape May could never provide a year-round audience, the Festival moved north to Madison and accepted the invitation of Drew University to take up residence on its campus.

After six Madison seasons, the Festival now plays 19 to 23 weeks a year of five to eight plays in repertory, with 12 Monday Night Specials of guest attractions, which include dance, drama, mime and music performances. By 1977, the Festival had produced 113 productions, including 33 of Shakespeare's plays.

The New Jersey Shakespeare Festival is an actors' theatre, an ensemble led by one actor-manager-director, composed not of "stars" but of classical actors who want the experience of playing in rotating repertory. It is a theatre where actors are given great creative freedom in developing their roles. This freedom, along with the rare opportunity to work under a true repertory system and the selection of classic and contemporary plays performed back-to-back, are attractions which have created for the Festival a pool of actors who frequently return. The Intern Program, an intensive annual training regimen for 80 selected applicants, is a source of special pride and strength, as some interns become members of the Festival's resident company.

Festival seasons now combine the more popular plays of Shakespeare with his rarely produced works. The company hopes eventually to present Shakespeare's entire canon. Productions, although often innovative, are noted for clarity and loyalty to the playwright's intent. The Festival also strives for topicality. For example, Shakespeare's *Richard II* opened as another contemporary Richard was being driven from office, and *An Enemy of the People* by Ibsen was offered between two severe winters that forced a hard look at the nation's diminishing natural resources.

The Festival, like many regional theatres, is beset with financial concerns and the desire for artistic growth, but it is surviving, and statistical indications show that it is serving a wide audience as well. The number of contributors to the company has quadrupled in the past three years, subscribers come from more than 100 communities and audiences are at near-capacity levels.

Programs & Services: *Internships; performances and lectures for students; symposia on each production; Festival Intern Workshops, one production each year; Monday Night Specials, booked-in events; student and group ticket discounts; Festival Guild, volunteers; newsletter for guild members.*

PAUL BARRY
Artistic Director/Producer

Drew University
Madison, New Jersey 07940
Telephone (201) 377-5330
Box Office (201) 377-4487

Founded 1963
Paul Barry

Season
June – December

Schedule
Evenings
Tuesday – Sunday

Facilities
Seating capacity 238
Stage   Thrust

Budget
Jan 1, 1976 – Dec 31, 1976
Operating budget $232,965
Earned income $171,081
Unearned income $ 63,265

Audience
Percent of capacity 80
Number of subscribers 3,316

Booked-in events
Mime, drama, dance & music

Operates on AEA LORT (D) contract.

Productions, 1975–76
Bertie, Bernard Myers; music,
Thom Wagner
Mama of the Year, Edward H. Adams

Productions, 1976–77
Sirocco, Tim Grundmann & Ken Bloom
Gymnasium, H. Jones Baker, III
Hagar's Children, Ernest Joselovitz
Bride of Sirocco, Tim Grundmann
Fox against the Fence and *Gus and Company,*
John Sedlak
Canticle, Michael Champagne & William Penn

Fred Strother, Steve Wilson and Richard McNair in
Fox against the Fence by John Sedlak, directed by
Paul Hildebrand, Jr., sets by Robert Graham Small.
Photo: Doc Dougherty.

Tanis Roach, Jan Frederick Shiffman, Dana Vance
and A. David Johnson in *Bride of Sirocco* by Tim
Grundmann, directed by Ken Bloom, costumes by
Mary Kay McGregor. Photo: Doc Dougherty.

The New Playwrights' Theatre
of Washington

Under the direction of Harry M. Bagdasian since its inception in June 1972, the New Playwrights' Theatre of Washington (NPTW) has proven itself to be a vital and successful incubator for new plays and playwriting talent. Its founders were, and continue to be, staunch believers that Washington, D.C., as the nation's capital, should have a noncommercial theatre devoted exclusively to the creation and production of new plays, musicals and theatre pieces by American playwrights and composers.

For too many years, drama, as a performance art, has been taught as a subspecies of literature. It cannot be completely created at the typewriter and is best fostered in a noncommercial environment where raw materials are made readily available to its creators. To this end, Mr. Bagdasian, producing director along with Paul Hildebrand, Jr., artistic director, and Ken Bloom, associate producer, are working to build a center for such work in Washington, D.C. In addition to its mainstage performance series, and under the leadership of staff director, Robert Graham Small, the company is slowly developing a formal training and workshop program, where artists in all theatre-support fields can come together for advanced training and focus their energies on assisting in the development of new works.

The first two years of activity found the company operating in a 26-seat basement theatre, producing eight programs of new one-act plays, and slowly gaining the attention of the press and an audience of adventurous theatregoers. Over the following two years, the company led a nomadic existence, offering readings and simple productions in found spaces and borrowed stages throughout the city. The theatre settled in an old gymnasium in the Dupont Circle neighborhood and, in this location, NPTW has been working continuously with new dramatists to develop their works through its series of productions, staged readings and informal open workshop readings.

Because NPTW believes that it doesn't serve a new work to send the creator a polite reply along with a returned manuscript, many of the 248 playwrights served by NPTW since January 1976, have received either a careful, written evaluation of their material or a personal session with the staff. As with most theatres, the majority of submitted scripts are rejected, but those that are not enjoy the benefits of a variety of working performance situations.

In the past, many scripts developed at NPTW have enjoyed additional productions as a result of the exposure and development each one received before Washington audiences. Most recently, *Hagar's Children*, by San Francisco playwright Ernest Joselovitz, was produced, with its original NPTW cast and director, by Joseph Papp's New York Shakespeare Festival.

Programs & Services: *Internships; lectures for students; staged readings and informal reading series with discussions; student, senior citizen and group ticket discounts; free ticket program; Dramathon, annual fund-raising event; playwright residencies; Volunteers Program;* New Playwrights' Theatre, *bimonthly newsletter.*

HARRY M. BAGDASIAN
Producing Director
PAUL HILDEBRAND, JR.
Artistic Director

1742 Church Street, NW
Washington, DC 20036
(202) 232-1122

Founded 1972
Harry M. Bagdasian

Season
July – June

Schedule
Evenings
Wednesday – Sunday

Facilities
Seating capacity 80–120
Stage   Flexible

Budget
July 1, 1976 – June 30, 1977
Operating budget $153,744
Earned income $ 42,379
Unearned income $ 97,408

Audience
Percent of capacity 51

Productions, 1975–76

Hamlet, William Shakespeare
The Comedy of Errors, William Shakespeare
The Shoeshine Parlor, James Lee
Jesse and the Bandit Queen, David Freeman
Rich and Famous, John Guare
Apple Pie, Myrna Lamb; music, Nicholas Meyers
So Nice, They Named It Twice, Neil Harris
Rebel Women, Thomas Babe
For Colored Girls who have Considered Suicide When The Rainbow is Enuf, Ntozake Shange
Trelawney of the "Wells," Arthur Wing Pinero
Mrs. Warren's Profession, George Bernard Shaw
The Threepenny Opera, Bertolt Brecht & Kurt Weill; translated, Ralph Manheim & John Willett
The Shortchanged Review, Michael Dorn Moody
Streamers, David Rabe
The Leaf People, Dennis Reardon

Productions, 1976–77

Henry V, William Shakespeare
Measure for Measure, William Shakespeare
Mondongo, Ray Ramirez; music, Willie Colon & David Barron; lyrics, Lon Ivey
For Colored Girls who have Considered Suicide When The Rainbow is Enuf, Ntozake Shange
Marco Polo Sings a Solo, John Guare
Ashes, David Rudkin
Hagar's Children, Ernest Joselovitz
Creditors and *The Stronger*, August Strindberg
On the Lock-In, David Langston Smyrl
The Threepenny Opera, Bertolt Brecht & Kurt Weill; translated, Ralph Manheim & John Willett
The Cherry Orchard, Anton Chekhov; translated, Jean-Claude van Itallie; music, Elizabeth Swados
Agamemnon, Aeschylus; translated, Edith Hamilton; adapted, Andrei Serban & Elizabeth Swados; music, Elizabeth Swados
Streamers, David Rabe

Estelle Parsons in *Miss Margarida's Way*, written and directed by Roberto Athayde. Workshop production, 1977. Photo: Dan Asher.

Priscilla Smith, Irene Worth and Marybeth Hurt in *The Cherry Orchard* by Anton Chekhov, directed by Andrei Serban, sets and costumes by Santo Loquasto. Photo: Sy Friedman.

New York Shakespeare Festival

The New York Shakespeare Festival, under the leadership of Joseph Papp, has entered its second decade as one of the foremost theatres of the nation. Born as the Shakespeare Workshop in 1954, its chief accomplishment in its first decade was the establishment of "Free Shakespeare," as a civic amenity providing free performances each summer at the Delacorte Theater in Central Park. In order to pursue the audience to its own doorstep, the Festival designed and constructed a totally self-contained mobile theatre and performed in the streets, parks and playgrounds of the five boroughs of New York. In 1965, the theatre acquired the landmark Astor Library building in lower Manhattan and began converting it to the Public Theater, a complex of performing spaces used primarily for the production of new American plays.

The Festival has expanded, contracted and expanded again over the years, changing its shape and size but never its goals: the creation of a serious and enduring American theatre, available and responsive to a wide audience, and the development of a particular American style of producing Shakespeare and other classic works that regards tradition from a contemporary viewpoint. The Festival, which offers a life-support system for new American plays, encourages and presents new works that serve as a mirror of American spiritual and ethical life.

Over the years, the Festival has developed an extended program which interfaces with the commercial theatre as a means for both extending its audiences — in New York and across the country — and for providing a self-subsidy for its regular programs, which operate at a deficit. At present, this extended program includes three domestic companies of *A Chorus Line*, two of *For Colored Girls who have Considered Suicide When The Rainbow is Enuf*, and a production of *Miss Margarida's Way* on Broadway. Like all Festival shows that have reached Broadway and "the road," including *Two Gentlemen of Verona, Much Ado About Nothing, That Championship Season* and *Sticks and Bones*, these shows were first produced at the Delacorte or the Public Theater. The success of *A Chorus Line* has proved an extraordinary fiscal asset to the Festival, offering its chief means of support and insuring a measure of fiscal stability for the next two years.

In 1973, the Festival took over the operation, for four seasons, of the two theatre spaces at New York's Lincoln Center cultural complex — the Vivian Beaumont Theater and the Mitzi Newhouse Theater. With the Festival's departure from its Lincoln Center activities at the close of the 1976–77 season, energies have been refocused at the Public Theater. The theatre's six performing spaces will house more than 20 productions during the 1977–78 season, ranging from small workshops to major productions. A new theatre cabaret was opened in the fall of 1977, offering an increased variety of theatrical fare, and its renovation was the beginning of a program of improvement of all public facilities at the theatre. The twenty-second season of Free Shakespeare in Central Park will take place in 1978 in the recently rehabilitated Delacorte Theater; the Mobile Theater will continue its tour of New York City's boroughs; and Festival productions will be seen throughout New York and across the country.

Programs & Services: *Playwriting workshops; lecture-seminars for students; New York Dance Festival, annual summer event; workshop productions; staged readings; booked-in events; free and discount ticket programs; benefit performances; theatre companies in residence; restaurant; bar; post-performance discussions.*

JOSEPH PAPP
Producer
BERNARD GERSTEN
Associate Producer

Public Theater
425 Lafayette Street
New York, New York 10003
Telephone (212) 677-1750
Box Office (212) 677-6350

Founded 1954
Joseph Papp

Season
September – August

Schedule
Evenings
Tuesday – Sunday
Matinees
Saturday & Sunday

Facilities
Newman Theater
Seating capacity 299
Stage Proscenium
Anspacher Theater
Seating capacity 275
Stage ¾ Arena
Martinson Hall/Cabaret Theater
Seating capacity 191
Stage Flexible
LuEsther Hall
Seating capacity 135–150
Stage Flexible
Other Stage
Seating capacity 75–108
Stage Flexible
Old Prop Shop Theater
Seating capacity 55–93
Stage Flexible
Delacorte/Central Park
(212) 535-5630
Seating capacity 1,936
Stage Thrust
Mobile Theater
Seating capacity 1,500
Stage Flexible

Budget
July 1, 1976 – June 30, 1977
Operating budget $9,954,419
Earned income $5,583,254
Unearned income $2,143,809

Audience
Percent of capacity 80
Number of subscribers 9,500

*Operates on AEA Production, LORT (B),
Off-Broadway contracts & Showcase Code.*

Productions, 1975–76
Bitter Harvest
Sacco & Vanzetti

Productions, 1976–77
Hardtime Blues
Bitter Harvest
Sacco & Vanzetti

*All productions are created by
Marketa Kimbrell and the
New York Street Theatre Caravan.*

Company members in *Bitter Harvest*, adapted by
Marketa Kimbrell from Steinbeck's *The Grapes of
Wrath*, directed by Ms. Kimbrell.

New York Street Theatre Caravan in *Bitter Harvest*.

New York Street Theatre Caravan

Since its founding in 1970 — at the time of the United States' bombing of Cambodia — the New York Street Theatre Caravan has played primarily in strife-torn areas ranging from Appalachian coal mines to Indian reservations, from union halls to city streets. The company members have dedicated themselves to "living and participating in the struggle and historic change of working people," performing on a bare stage, or, as is even more customary, on the weather-beaten 8- by 10-foot platform of their flatbed International Harvester truck. Their repertoire of adaptations, like *Bitter Harvest* (from *The Grapes of Wrath*), and original scripts, such as *Sacco & Vanzetti*, speak to "oppressed workers," in whom the company seeks to engender a spirit of institutional questioning and self-determination.

The New York Street Theatre Caravan owes its roots and beginnings to the turmoil and battleground of the streets and ghetto neighborhoods of the 1960s. From these experiences the company has developed a work process uniquely its own, including expression through visual means of behavior and the use of time and space on a bare stage. After years of hard work and earning a reputation for professionalism and high standards, the theatre is now ready to take its place in the American theatre as a company whose work "breathes with the life of a whole nation."

In the company's own words: "We want nothing more on stage than our audiences can afford. To make something wonderful out of very little is our style. We believe acting is not putting on, but revealing. We believe in laying our souls bare through our work to our chosen audiences. Because we work largely for America's poor, we believe that their dignity is entrusted to our innermost expression, and our dignity — as honest artists searching for a common truth — is left intact. As a result, audiences will be free to confront questions with us and to make their own discoveries. We want to believe that art should make people less susceptible to manipulation and freer to ask crucial questions. It is for this reason we call ourselves a revolutionary theatre."

With the recent acquisition of a performing space in the Jamaica, Queens, Arts Centre, a converted office building operated by the Queens Council for the Arts, the company will have the opportunity to put down some roots and, hopefully, to begin to establish a core following among the poor and middle-class workers of the community. The touring will not stop, nor will the company ignore its responsibility to the less privileged across the country. For the New York Street Theatre Caravan, its new home is merely a new phase in its education of the American psyche.

Programs & Services: *Performances and workshops for students, prisoners and union workers; children's theatre productions; touring; group discount and free ticket programs; post-performance discussions; benefit performances.*

MARKETA KIMBRELL
Director

87–05 Chelsea Street
Jamaica, New York 11432
(212) 454–8551

Founded 1970
Marketa Kimbrell

Season
Year-round

Budget
July 1, 1976 – June 30, 1977
Operating budget $59,000
Earned income $15,000
Unearned income $44,000

Touring contact
Marketa Kimbrell

Productions, 1975–76
The Kid and *Love Scene* and *Rip Awake*,
Robert Coover
Soap, David Man; music, Aaron Egigian
The Adolf Hitler Show, Ron Sossi, Sam Eisenstein,
Odyssey Theatre Ensemble
Beauty & the Beast, Ron Sossi, Sam Eisenstein,
Odyssey Theatre Ensemble

Productions, 1976–77
Elizabeth One, Paul Foster; music, Joe Berland
& John Keller
America Hurrah, Jean-Claude van Itallie
Noonday Demons, Peter Barnes
A Theological Position, Robert Coover

Odyssey ensemble members in *Holy Shoot* by
Robert Coover, directed by Ron Sossi.

Ensemble members in *The Adolf Hitler Show* by Ron
Sossi, Sam Eisenstein and Odyssey Theatre
Ensemble, directed and designed by Mr. Sossi.
Photo: Ron Sossi.

Odyssey Theatre Ensemble

The Odyssey Theatre Ensemble was founded in 1968 as an alternative in a city which abounds in "industry showcase theatres" and large road-show commercial houses. Dedicated not only to creating theatre for its own sake in a film-oriented town, the Odyssey has consistently devoted itself to expanding the boundaries of live theatre possibilities in general. Experiments in both form and content have dominated the Ensemble's original works, as in the theatre's productions of *The Adolf Hitler Show, Soap* and *Holy Shoot*, as well as its popular radical treatments of such classics as *The Threepenny Opera, Peer Gynt* and *The Bacchae.*

In its past, the Odyssey has been heavily influenced by such innovators as Grotowski, Chaikin, Brook, Stanislavski and Michael Chekhov, but it has now evolved its own approach under artistic director Ron Sossi, though continuing ties with both Grotowski and Meyerhold are evident.

At the Odyssey the actor is central, with a commitment to acting and the acquisition of both the will and the technique to expose one's humanity through artistry. There is also a continual search for new possibilities in the live audience-performer relationship. The truest exploration, however, requires longevity — of purpose and personnel. The Polish Theatre Laboratory is an outstanding example of what can be achieved with such longevity. Thus, the Odyssey's dream is the creation of a regional experimental theatre, one with the resources and audience support to become one of the finest regional institutions, yet one with the freedom and daring of some of the best European and American "fringe" groups. The Odyssey believes that true experimentation need not be elitist, but rather is at once vital, exciting and, of its very nature, audience appealing.

Odyssey moved in 1973, from a small Hollywood theatre with 81 seats, into a flexible 99-seat space. In 1977, an additional 99-seat space, named Odyssey 2, was added, and the plan for 1978 is the final acquisition of the balance of a city block in West Los Angeles.

The stability and greater financial resources of such an enlarged facility will hopefully provide the Odyssey with the income necessary to leave behind the short-term and temporary idealism of the 1960s fringe theatre, in favor of the serious pursuit of theatre experimentation on a long-term basis.

Programs & Services: *Acting and directing workshops; administrative and technical internships; Jazz Monday Nights; Dance Showcase; booked-in events; student, senior citizen and group ticket discounts; free ticket program; post-performance seminars.*

RON SOSSI
Artistic Director

12111 Ohio Avenue
Los Angeles, California 90025
Telephone (213) 879-5221
Box Office (213) 826-1626

Founded 1968
Ron Sossi

Season
December – September

Schedule
Evenings
Monday – Sunday

Facilities
Odyssey 1
Seating capacity 99
Stage Flexible
Odyssey 2
Seating capacity 99
Stage ¾ Arena

Budget
July 1, 1976 – June 30, 1977
Operating budget $68,500
Earned income $36,000
Unearned income $32,500

Audience
Percent of capacity 65

Booked-in events
Experimental & children's theatre, dance companies, musical events

Operates under AEA 99-Seat Waiver.

Productions, 1975-77
Frankenstein; adapted, Tony McGrath
Three Little Pigs; adapted, Tony McGrath
Sinbad the Sailor; adapted, Tony McGrath
Beauty and the Beast; adapted, Tony McGrath
Cinderella; adapted, Tony McGrath
Little Red Riding Hood; adapted, Tony McGrath
Hansel and Gretel; adapted, Tony McGrath
Hope for Life, Stanley Seidman & Off
Center Theatre company

Tony McGrath in *Little Red Riding Hood*, adapted by
Tony McGrath and Jerry Chase, directed by Mr.
McGrath, sets by Nancy Marshall, costumes by
Karen Christeson. Photo: Diane Adams.

Company members in *Hope for Life* by Stanley
Seidman and Off Center Theatre Company, directed
by Tony McGrath, designed by the company. Photo:
Tana Ross.

Off Center Theatre

Off Center Theatre (OCT) was given its curious name in 1968, because of its original geographical location in the Good Shepherd Faith Church on 66th Street in Manhattan, next to the pit which was to become Lincoln Center. People would step into this tiny Off-Off Broadway house and ask, "Is this Lincoln Center?" The reply would be "No, this is off Lincoln Center," which eventually became shortened to "Off Center." Now OCT owns its own theatre complex on 18th Street in the Chelsea section of Manhattan. In the intervening 10 years, OCT has had many homes including 3 years at Westbeth, the artists' housing colony in Greenwich Village, and 5 years at the New York Ethical Culture Society where it still performs free weekly children's matinees.

Throughout its early years, OCT was similar to other Off-Off Broadway theatres in its presentation of experimental and avant-garde productions of original plays by little-known playwrights, along with classical pieces. In the last eight years, however, OCT has essentially been a "service" theatre, presenting specific shows for specific audiences — children's shows, plays for senior citizens, political awareness plays and "x-rated soap operas," performed outdoors in commercial districts for working people at lunchtime.

OCT began doing children's plays because of the large number of children in its neighborhood. The theatre began a series of plays based on the concept that children should be treated like human beings, a concept which seems so logical today but was, in 1969, revolutionary. OCT's children's theatre company has 15 productions in its repertoire, including *Cinderella, A Midsummer Night's Dream, Frankenstein* and *Noah and the Ark*. Children's productions are presented free of charge, year-round, either indoors or out, depending on the season. Each year since its inception, the children's theatre company has offered almost 200 free performances throughout every borough of New York City, in every neighborhood from 79th Street and Fifth Avenue to the burned-out Morrisania section of the Bronx. OCT believes that since children themselves cannot afford their own entertainment, it is a kind of discrimination, based on parents' income and values, to charge admission to kids. OCT's free admission policy is also based on the belief that theatre is a right, not a privilege.

OCT also has a street theatre company for adults which performs at lunchtime in areas where working people congregate. This company performs *Hope for Life*, a satirical, x-rated soap opera, which predated the television series *Mary Hartman, Mary Hartman* by two years and is presently being developed as a radio series. By 1976, more than 100 performances of 13 episodes of *Hope for Life* had been given throughout New York City.

The year 1977 marked the opening of OCT's new theatre building where the theatre will begin a 1977–78 subscription series of five plays by four American playwrights. It is believed that a small minority of the population currently attends theatre performances. OCT, with its roots in street theatre, performs before people from the majority of the population who are not among theatre's regular audience. Daily, OCT reaches people who find the commercial theatre neither affordable nor relevant. In more than 300 performances each year, OCT reaches an audience of well beyond 200,000 people. In 1977–78, the theatre will attempt to turn its throngs of street theatre viewers into "indoor" viewers, as well.

Programs & Services: *Free classes for neighborhood youth in street theatre techniques; summer internships; poetry workshops; seminars in schools for children with reading disabilities; touring; poetry and new play readings; lunchtime series; student, senior citizen and group ticket discounts.*

ANTHONY McGRATH
Executive Director
ABIGAIL ROSEN
Administrative Director

436 West 18th Street
New York, New York 10011
Telephone (212) 929–8299
Box Office (212) 691–0033

Founded 1968
Anthony McGrath

Season
October – August

Facilities
Seating capacity 100
Stage   Proscenium

Budget
July 1, 1976 – June 30, 1977
Operating budget $47,955
Earned income $ 5,748
Unearned income $43,819

Audience
Percent of capacity 80

Touring contact
Abigail Rosen

Booked-in events
Mime, children's theatre, dance companies, experimental groups

Productions, 1975-76
The Advocate, Robert Noah
Our Town, Thornton Wilder
The Hot l Baltimore, Lanford Wilson
The Pursuit of Happiness, Lawrence
& Armina Marshall Langner
Cat on a Hot Tin Roof, Tennessee Williams
U.S.A., John Dos Passos & Paul Shyre;
adapted, William Roesch
A Trip to Chinatown, Charles H. Hoyt;
adapted, Jack Bender & Paul Perkins
Winter Patriot, Frances Bardacke
*The Last Meeting of the Knights of
the White Magnolia,* Preston Jones
The Little Foxes, Lillian Hellman
Rodgers & Hart: A Musical Celebration;
adapted, Richard Lewine & John Fearnley
As You Like It, William Shakespeare
Troilus and Cressida, William Shakespeare
Othello, William Shakespeare

Productions, 1976-77
The Sea Horse, Edward J. Moore
Ring Around the Moon, Jean Anouilh
Play Strindberg, Friedrich Durrenmatt
Kennedy's Children, Robert Patrick
The Queen and the Rebels, Ugo Betti
Arms and the Man, George Bernard Shaw
Seascape, Edward Albee
Tango, Slawomir Mrozek
La Ronde, Arthur Schnitzler;
translated, J.D. Steyers
The Runner Stumbles, Milan Stitt
Charley's Aunt, Brandon Thomas
Timon of Athens, William Shakespeare
The Taming of the Shrew, William Shakespeare
Hamlet, William Shakespeare

John McMurtry and Richard Kneeland in *Timon of Athens* by William Shakespeare, directed by Eric Christmas, designed by Peggy Kellner. Photo: Bill Reid.

Mark Lamos, Eric Christmas and Byron Jennings in *Hamlet* by William Shakespeare, directed by Jack O'Brien, sets by Peggy Kellner, costumes by Robert Morgan. Photo: Bill Reid.

Old Globe Theatre

Having recently concluded its fortieth season as a nonprofit cultural institution in San Diego, the Old Globe Theatre continually strives to achieve the highest standards of excellence in meeting the theatrical needs of its community.

During the spring and summer of 1935 and 1936, San Diego residents viewed abridged versions of Shakespeare's plays in a replica of the original Globe Playhouse of London, which was built for the California-Pacific Exposition. From 1937 through 1949, the theatre joined with San Diego State University to coproduce a summer Shakespeare festival. In 1952, the Old Globe began on its own to produce the annual San Diego National Shakespeare Festival.

Since 1959, all major Festival roles have been performed by Actors' Equity members with smaller roles filled by actors on scholarship. The 1977 Festival of 15 weeks and three plays in repertory, performed to more than 53,000 persons, or 99 percent of the theatre's capacity, during its June through mid-September season. In the fall of 1977, the Festival was invited to perform *Hamlet* and *The Taming of the Shrew* at the Scottsdale Center for the Arts in Arizona. This program marks the first out-of-state tour for the Old Globe.

The Old Globe presents classical and contemporary comedy and drama during its fall and spring season, with 10 productions presented in the Old Globe Theatre and the adjacent Carter Centre Stage. The theatre offers its audiences a wide variety of theatrical presentations, in its two theatres and on tour, during its fall, spring and summer seasons. Attendance for the Old Globe Theatre's 1976–77 productions totaled more than 245,000 persons for the 778 performances of 16 productions. Eighty percent of the theatre's income is derived from ticket sales.

The Old Globe Theatre serves students of the community in several ways. During its summer Shakespeare season, 12 school preview performances are held for a total of 5,000 students. Discount tickets are also available for students during the fall and spring seasons in both theatres. During the fall and spring of 1976 and 1977, the fifth Globe Educational Tour presented over 200 performances to some 70,000 students during tours to schools in San Diego City and County, and neighboring Imperial County. In full productions, the carefully edited texts were presented to enrich the cultural experiences of children while introducing them to great world theatre. From 1975 through 1977, the Old Globe conducted its Regional Occupation Program, a statewide on-the-job training program, funded by the San Diego County Department of Education and administered by the San Diego City schools, which offered acting and technical theatre classes at the theatre.

Programs & Services: *Internships; performances and seminars for students; workshop performances; Globe Educational Tour; Shakespeare Film Festival; Play Discovery Project, staged readings; student, senior citizen and military ticket discounts; united arts fund-raising; Globe Guilders, support group; Zany, Guilder Gazette and Exposition, newsletters.*

CRAIG NOEL
Producing Director
ROBERT E. McGLADE
General Manager

P.O. Box 2171
San Diego, California 92112
Telephone (714) 231-1941
Box Office (714) 239-2255

Founded 1937
Community members

Season
October – September

Schedule
Evenings
Tuesday – Sunday
Matinees
October – May
Sunday
June – September
Wednesday, Saturday, Sunday

Facilities
El Prado, Balboa Park
Old Globe
Seating capacity 420
Stage   Modified Thrust
Carter Centre Stage
Seating capacity 245
Stage   Arena

Budget
Oct 1, 1976 – Sept 30, 1977
Operating budget $1,181,653
Earned income $1,156,116
Unearned income $ 117,371

Audience
Old Globe
Percent of capacity 96
Number of subscribers 11,351
Carter Centre Stage
Percent of capacity 88
Number of subscribers 6,454

Touring contact
Carole Marget

*Operates on AEA LORT (B)
contract.*

Productions, 1976

G.R. Point, David Berry
Benefit of a Doubt, Edward J. Clinton
A History of the American Film,
Christopher Durang
As to the Meaning of Words, Mark Eichman
Winds of Change, Barbara Field
Pirates, Amlin Gray
Secrets of the Rich, Arthur Kopit
Suckers, Werner Liepolt
Ladyhouse Blues, Kevin O'Morrison
The Sugar Bowl, Stanley Taikeff
Daddy's Duet, Clifford Turknett
The Defense, Edgar White

Productions, 1977

A Prayer for My Daughter, Thomas Babe
Two Small Bodies, Neal Bell
The Last American Dixieland Band,
Phillip Hayes Dean
The Elusive Angel, Jack Gilhooley
Eminent Domain, Percy Granger
Windfall Apples, Roma Greth
Custer, Robert E. Ingham
At the End of Long Island, Richard Lees
*Scooter Thomas Makes It to the Top of
the World*, Peter Parnell
Terra Nova, Ted Tally
Gazelle Boy, Ronald Tavel
Uncommon Women and Others, Wendy Wasserstein

John Seitz and Alan Rosenberg in Thomas Babe's
Prayer for My Daughter, directed by Robert
Ackerman at the 1977 National Playwrights
Conference.

A reading of *Benefit of a Doubt* by Edward J.
Clinton, directed by Lynne Meadow at the 1976
National Playwrights Conference. Photo: Roger
Christiansen.

O'Neill Theater Center

The O'Neill Theater Center was founded in 1964 by George C. White and has since spawned numerous programs in theatre research, development and education. The National Playwrights Conference was the first project undertaken by the Center and, under the artistic direction of Lloyd Richards, it has become one of the Center's best-known programs.

The purpose of the National Playwrights Conference is to assist playwrights in the evaluation of their creative work, as they interact with skilled theatre professionals on the production of their plays. Over the past 13 years, all efforts have been directed toward the achievement of the ideal artistic situation wherein experimentation, exploration and the unembellished creative experience form the basis of the work.

"New" is the key word in a description of the Conference's goals. The focus is on the discovery and nurturing of talented neophyte playwrights and on the exploration of new styles, techniques and forms by more established playwrights. The commercial success of a play, subsequent to its Conference premiere, is always welcome, but it is not a primary aim of the Conference. Rather, the Conference's goal is to reveal the original and unique voices in the American theatre for the playwrights themselves and the theatregoing public. Over the years the National Playwrights Conference has perfected a multi-step process of rehearsal, staged reading and critique, which permits "in-process" evaluation by experts and the exposure of the playwright to the finest available directors and actors, in a working situation.

In 1976, the National Playwrights Conference inaugurated the New Drama for Television Project which is designed to give talented playwrights an opportunity to conceive and develop original material specifically for television. Four scripts are selected for development during the Conference. During the one week of production devoted to each play, the playwright works with the director, the producer–story editor and a media writer consultant. At week's end, the material that has been taped is edited, so that the work can be viewed, discussed and critiqued by the participants.

In 13 years, the Conference has staged 176 new plays by 127 playwrights. Following the initial presentation at the Conference, many of these plays have been produced on and Off Broadway, as well as at regional and university theatres, through the Second Step program, which extends the O'Neill Center experience beyond the four-week summer Conference.

Concurrent with the Conference is the National Critics Institute, a professional workshop directed by Ernest Schier, which is designed to help critics explore the performing arts and to expand their writing skills. Another O'Neill program is the National Theatre Institute, a professional theatre training program. Since 1971, students from more than 60 colleges have received instruction in acting, directing, design, movement, puppetry, film and theatre management. The faculty, under the Institute's director, Dr. Lawrence J. Wilker, is made up of outstanding professional artists. Daily classes are augmented by a series of lectures and workshops with guest artists, and by trips to regional and New York theatres. The semester culminates in an original production that involves all 30 students and is toured for two weeks throughout the Northeast. Another training program sponsored by the O'Neill Center is the Creative Arts in Education Program, directed by Joyce Schmidt. The Center is also the home of the Monte Cristo Cottage Museum and Library, as well as the National Theatre of the Deaf and the Little Theatres of the Deaf, both under the direction of David Hays.

Programs & Services: *Creative Arts in Education; National Critics Institute; New Drama for Television Project; humanist lecture series; benefit performances; Friends of the O'Neill, volunteers; artists in residence;* The O'Neill Rialto, *quarterly newsletter for members;* National Playwrights Directory, *listing of over 400 playwrights.*

GEORGE C. WHITE
President
LLOYD RICHARDS
Artistic Director
National Playwrights Conference

1860 Broadway
Suite 1012
New York, New York 10023
(212) 246-1485

305 Great Neck Road
Waterford, Connecticut 06385
Telephone (203) 443-5378
Box Office (203) 443-1238
NY Direct Line:
(212) 925-5032

Founded 1964
George C. White

Season
July – August

Facilities
Waterford, Connecticut
Theatre Barn
Seating capacity 200
Stage   Thrust
Amphitheatre
Seating capacity 300
Stage   Thrust
Instant Theatre
Seating capacity 200
Stage   Arena
Barn El
Seating capacity 200
Stage   Flexible

Budget
July 1, 1976 – June 30, 1977
Operating budget $1,977,925
Earned income $ 972,682
Unearned income $1,021,045

Operates on AEA LORT (C) contract.

Productions, 1975–76
Rhoda in Potatoland

Productions, 1976–77
Book of Splendors (Part II) Book of Levers
Livre des Splendours

All productions are created by
Richard Foreman.

John Erdman and Kate Manheim in *Book of Splendors (Part II) Book of Levers*, written, directed and designed by Richard Foreman. Photo: Babette Mangolte.

Kate Manheim and John Erdman in *Book of Splendors (Part II) Book of Levers*. Photo: Babette Mangolte.

Ontological-Hysteric Theater

The Ontological-Hysteric Theater was founded by Richard Foreman in 1968. Since that time, it has produced 14 of Mr. Foreman's scripts, both here and abroad. In addition, Mr. Foreman has traveled to various universities and museums in the United States to mount productions of his work using local actors and technicians.

During the early years, the work of the company was based upon a sort of phenomenological analysis of act, gesture, speech and object. During the last few years, however, the focus of the work has shifted so that the pieces now document, with great rapidity in performance, the ever-shifting relations among the many and complicated production and textural elements.

Mr. Foreman's works are always created with the company rehearsing in the fully completed set for the entire rehearsal period. In the last three years, the theatre's unique stage shape (14 feet wide and 80 feet deep) has led to a variety of scenic innovations which play a major part in determining the style of performance.

Ontological-Hysteric Theater regularly performs one new piece each season in New York and another new piece each year in Europe. In addition, funds are currently being raised for the theatre to produce its first feature-length film, to be directed by Mr. Foreman.

The aesthetic roots and concerns of Ontological-Hysteric Theater have often been described as more closely related to twentieth-century painting, poetry and music than to existing theatrical traditions. While those relationships are true, to a certain extent, the fact remains that Mr. Foreman's work continues to manifest his own day-to-day efforts to evolve a completely new theatrical grammar — one that reflects the processes, difficulties and accidents of the consciousness-at-work.

A book on the theatre's work, *Richard Foreman, Plays and Manifestos*, has recently been published by New York University Press. In addition to the planned film, the company will be presenting two major new works by Mr. Foreman in 1977–78, *Blvd de Paris: I've got der Shakes*, in New York, and *Solidity Comes out of the Mouth*, in Rome and Berlin.

Programs & Services: *Lectures and seminars; touring.*

RICHARD FOREMAN
Artistic Director

Performing Artservices
463 West Street
New York, New York 10014
Telephone (212) 989-4953
Box Office (212) 966-7509

Founded 1968
Richard Foreman

Season
December – March

Facilities
491 Broadway
Seating capacity 70
Stage   Flexible

Budget
July 1, 1976 – June 30, 1977
Operating budget $91,874
Earned income $51,571
Unearned income $40,400

Audience
Percent of capacity 100

Touring contact
A Bunch of Experimental Theaters
105 Hudson Street
New York, New York 10013
(212) 966-0400

Productions, 1976
The Devil's Disciple, George Bernard Shaw
Brand, Henrik Ibsen; translated & adapted,
Jerry Turner
The Tavern, George M. Cohan
The Comedy of Errors, William Shakespeare
King Lear, William Shakespeare
Much Ado About Nothing, William Shakespeare
Henry VI, Part II, William Shakespeare
The Little Foxes, Lillian Hellman

Productions, 1977
The Merchant of Venice, William Shakespeare
Antony and Cleopatra, William Shakespeare
Henry VI, Part III, William Shakespeare
Measure for Measure, William Shakespeare
The Rivals, Richard Brinsley Sheridan
A Streetcar Named Desire, Tennessee Williams
Angel Street, Patrick Hamilton
A Taste of Honey, Shelagh Delaney
A Moon for the Misbegotten, Eugene O'Neill

Jerry Jones in *Henry IV, Part III* by William
Shakespeare, directed by Pat Patton, sets by
Richard L. Hay, costumes by Jeannie Davidson.
Photo: Hank Kranzler.

William Moreing and Mimi Carr in *The Rivals* by
Richard Brinsley Sheridan, directed by William
Glover, sets by Richard L. Hay, costumes by Jeannie
Davidson. Photo: Hank Kranzler.

Oregon Shakespearean Festival

The Oregon Shakespearean Festival was founded in 1935 by Angus L. Bowmer. The Festival opened with three performances each of *The Merchant of Venice* and *Twelfth Night*, as part of a Fourth of July celebration in Ashland. The stage was in the open air, built as a rough replica of an Elizabethan theatre and located within the walls of an abandoned theatre. Each play was produced without intermission in the manner inaugurated by William Poel and the Elizabethan Stage Society. In 1977, 42 years later, the Festival produced nine plays, four of them by Shakespeare, in three separate theatres, to an audience of nearly 235,000.

Three of the Festival's Shakespearean productions are staged in an outdoor Elizabethan Playhouse, fashioned after London's sixteenth-century Fortune Theatre, which was constructed in 1959 on the site of the original Festival stage. In 1970, the new and modern Angus Bowmer Theatre was built, thus enabling the company to expand into a spring season with a repertoire including Shakespeare, other classics, and plays from modern literature as well. In 1976, the intimate Black Swan Theatre was built to provide a showcase for less popular plays and theatrical experiments.

The Festival is dedicated to the production of all Shakespeare's plays in a manner consistent with Elizabethan practice. The Festival does not wish to create a theatrical museum, but rather to emphasize those values inherent in Shakespeare's theatre — the art of acting and the power of language. The Bowmer Theatre and the new Black Swan considerably expand the range of the repertoire and the variety of possible styles. Company members, supported by scholarships, are recruited from the best of the professional and college training programs. They work under professional conditions, with guest artists working under Actors' Equity contracts, and with respected professional directors and designers; and they perform in a rotating repertory schedule. The Festival is dedicated to the development of young talent through the rigors of professional discipline and great artistic demands. Most of the company is recruited for a year or more to maximize the ensemble effect of a group of players working and acting together in a variety of roles and styles.

Throughout the year, workshops and studio projects are encouraged to supplement the activities of public performance. The thrust of the Festival is classical without being stuffy, literary without being bookish, popular without being vulgar. The theatre is not a school, but it operates as a place of learning, where actor and audience can make discoveries together.

Programs & Services: *Acting workshops; internships; scholarships; performances and workshops for students; Actor/School Visit Program; Institute of Renaissance Studies; touring; lecture series; lunchtime series; workshop productions; staged readings; booked-in events; student, senior citizen and group ticket discounts; free ticket program; auction; benefit performances; Tudor Guild, support group; newsletter; post-performance discussions.*

JERRY TURNER
Producing Director
WILLIAM W. PATTON
General Manager

P.O. Box 158
Ashland, Oregon 97520
Telephone (503) 482-2111
Box Office (503) 482-4331

Founded 1935
Angus L. Bowmer

Season
February – May
June – September

Schedule
Evenings
Tuesday – Sunday (spring)
Daily (summer)
Matinees
Saturday & Sunday (spring)
Daily (summer)

Facilities
15 South Pioneer Street
Elizabethan Theatre
Seating capacity 1,173
Stage Thrust
Angus Bowmer Theatre
Seating capacity 599
Stage Flexible
Black Swan Theatre
Seating capacity 138–156
Stage Flexible

Budget
Oct 1, 1976 – Sept 30, 1977
Operating budget $1,497,028
Earned income $1,485,350
Unearned income $ 215,279

Audience
Elizabethan Theatre
Percent of capacity 100
Angus Bowmer Theatre
Percent of capacity 96
Black Swan Theatre
Percent of capacity 99

Touring contact
Sally White

Operates on AEA Guest Artist contract.

Productions, 1975-76
The Wonderful Ice Cream Suit, Ray
Bradbury
The Beckoning Fair One, Oliver Onions;
adapted, Bury St. Edmund; music,
Jonathan Pearthree
Switch Bitch, Roald Dahl;
adapted, Organic Theater company;
music, Jonathan Pearthree
*The Adventures of Huckleberry Finn, Parts One
and Two,* Mark Twain; adapted, Organic
Theater company

Productions, 1976-77
Switch Bitch, Roald Dahl;
adapted, Organic Theater company;
music, Jonathan Pearthree
Volpone, Ben Jonson
Cops, Terry Curtis Fox
The Sirens of Titan, Kurt Vonnegut;
adapted, Organic Theater company; music,
Richard Fire
Bleacher Bums, Organic Theater company

Joe Mantegna and Carolyn Purdy-Gordon in
Volpone by Ben Jonson, directed by Stuart Gordon,
sets by Dean Taucher, costumes by Maggie Bodwell.
Photo: Danny Rest.

Dennis Franz, Michael Saad and Joe Mantegna in
Cops by Terry Curtis Fox, directed by Stuart
Gordon, sets by Jim Maronek, costumes by the
company. Photo: Danny Rest.

Organic Theater Company

The Organic Theater Company is for people who otherwise "hate" the theatre — who find it pretentious, boring and expensive. In other words, when in Chicago, Organic Theater is the place to find "cheap thrills."

The company is made up of an odd assortment of theatre professionals, who share a similar vision as to what theatre should be and have stuck around for the past eight years to create an equally odd assortment of 20 original plays.

The Organic was formed in the fall of 1969 by Stuart Gordon, in Madison, Wisconsin, where he had been attending the University of Wisconsin. The decision to leave school was made for Mr. Gordon by the University after he was arrested for directing a satirical adaptation of *Peter Pan* with a nude dance sequence. Attempts to censor the company and harassments from the Madison city government convinced the Organic to accept Paul Sills' offer to move the company to Chicago. "They'll leave you alone here," he said, and he was right. With Mr. Sills' help the company set up shop in the Holy Covenant Church, and opened in March of 1970 with an original adaptation of George Orwell's *Animal Farm*. Later that year, Paul Sills took his production of *Story Theater* to Broadway and offered the Organic, for a few weeks, the use of his theatre on Lincoln Avenue at the Body Politic. The Organic remained at the Body Politic for three years, during which time the company presented seven productions in Chicago and traveled to New York for two engagements. In 1971, Joseph Papp invited the Organic to present its adaptation of Voltaire's *Candide* at the Public Theater, and in 1973, *Warp*, the world's first science fiction epic adventure play in serial form, was produced on Broadway.

In the fall of 1973, the Organic moved to the Leo Lerner Theater in the Uptown Center Hull House. This new home seemed to bring the company luck. Of the three shows premiered that year, *Bloody Bess* and *The Wonderful Ice Cream Suit* were invited by Amsterdam's Mickery Theater for a European tour, while the third play, David Mamet's *Sexual Perversity in Chicago*, has had several other productions including an extended Off Broadway run.

In 1975, the company created a two-part, five-hour adaptation of Mark Twain's *The Adventures of Huckleberry Finn*. The gimmick was that there were no gimmicks, as the actual book, bubbling over with its original satire, bile and violence, was used for the script. The production went on to tour the United States and Europe.

Success with literary adaptations encouraged the Organic to dramatize Roald Dahl's tales of "sexual one-upmanship," *Switch Bitch*, and Kurt Vonnegut's interplanetary search for the meaning of life, *The Sirens of Titan*. As a result, the company was able to meet both authors, who seemed quite pleased with the Organic's treatment of their work. During the last two seasons, the company has flirted with the supernatural in *The Beckoning Fair One* by *Warp* coauthor Bury St. Edmund; assaulted the audience with a police "shoot 'em up," in *Cops* by Terry Curtis Fox; and turned a production of Ben Jonson's *Volpone* into a Warner Brothers cartoon.

The Organic's future plans include west coast, Midwest and east coast tours; a feature film; and a new 450-seat, flexible theatre space, scheduled to open in the summer of 1978.

Programs & Services: *Directing, acting, management and stage combat workshops; From Page to Stage, workshop on adapting plays from novels; technical internships; residencies; workshops for students; student, senior citizen and group ticket discounts; voucher program; benefit performances; post-performance discussions.*

STUART GORDON
Artistic Director
REBECCA DITZLER
Managing Director

4520 North Beacon Street
Chicago, Illinois 60640
Telephone (312) 271-3010
Box Office (312) 271-2436

Founded 1969
Stuart Gordon

Season
October – September

Schedule
Evenings
Wednesday – Sunday

Facilities
Leo Lerner Theater
Seating capacity 159
Stage ¾ Arena

Budget
Oct 1, 1976 – Sept 30, 1977
Operating budget $209,878
Earned income $133,444
Unearned income $ 67,899

Audience
Percent of capacity 68

Touring contact
Herbert Barrett Management
1860 Broadway
New York, New York 10023
(212) 245-3530

Operates on AEA Chicago Off-Loop Theatre contract.

Productions, 1975–76
The 3rd Annual River Raft Revue,
Otrabanda company
The Doctor in Spite of Himself, Moliere
The 4th Annual River Raft Revue,
Otrabanda company

Productions, 1976–77
The 4th Annual River Raft Revue,
Otrabanda company
Glass, Mark J. Dunau & Otrabanda company
Louisiana Legong, David Dawkins &
Otrabanda company

Louise Smith and Stephen Stern in *Louisiana Legong* by David Dawkins and the Otrabanda company. Photo: Susan Horowitz.

Members of the Otrabanda Company rafting on the Mississippi River, summer of 1975. Photo: Susan Horowitz.

Otrabanda Company

The Otrabanda Company, a New Orleans–based collective which has been performing original productions for more than six years, seeks to bring its style of theatre to a wide variety of audiences. The company has performed in a large circus tent, as well as in theatres and halls throughout the United States, Europe and Southeast Asia.

The company was founded in 1971 on the Caribbean island of Curacao, where seven actors from America collaborated with Belgian playwright-director Tone Brulin, on a piece entitled *The Kaaka-Makaakoo.* Since then, Otrabanda has presented *Stump Removal, Barong Display,* Moliere's *The Doctor in Spite of Himself, Glass, Louisiana Legong,* and four vaudeville-like events, each called the *River Raft Revue.* Besides Curacao, the group has resided in Vermont, Ohio, Louisiana, Malaysia and on a raft, on the Mississippi River.

Otrabanda settled in New Orleans in the fall of 1975. Its activities there have included performances in public schools, parks, playgrounds, libraries and arts centers. It was also the first professional theatre company to perform in the Louisiana Superdome. When possible, the company performs outdoors with shows that are free to the public. Otrabanda intends to remain in New Orleans through its 1978 season, as it continues a residency at the city's new Contemporary Arts Center.

The project which has given the company its greatest national attention is the *River Raft Revue,* Otrabanda's annual tour by raft to communities and institutions along the Mississippi River. During the past five summers, the company has floated from St. Louis to New Orleans, offering free performances to thousands of people. Their most recent raft production, *Louisiana Legong,* is directed by a company member who lived and studied for more than a year in Southeast Asia. It is a unique spectacle, incorporating Asian and Western music, Balinese masks and circus clowning. It is possibly the first Western production to employ a full Balinese gamelan orchestra, which, in this case, is composed of actors.

Otrabanda is also the first theatre company to receive support from the National Science Foundation. A grant was provided for the production of *Glass,* a play which concerns changes in society promoted by scientific and technological development, from the invention of a clear and colorless glass to the Hiroshima bombing. During 1977–78, *Glass* will be presented in museums of science and technology, as Otrabanda seeks new environments and audiences for dramatic events.

Providing theatre for people in places that rarely experience live performances is a primary focus of Otrabanda. As the company continues, it hopes to serve New Orleans and the South, while continuing to receive inspiration from the rest of this country and the entire world.

Programs & Services: *Improvisational workshops; performances and training for students; performances in libraries and prisons; free children's productions; residencies; newsletter; post-performance discussions.*

ROGER BABB
Director
JOHN MAYNARD
Managing Director

301 Pacific Avenue
New Orleans, Louisiana 70114
(504) 566-7729

Founded 1971
Roger Babb, Diane Brown,
Nelson Camp, David Dawkins,
Graham Paul, Stephen Stern

Season
April – December

Facilities
Circus Tent
Seating capacity 250
Stage   Thrust
Contemporary Arts Center
900 Camp Street
Seating capacity 200
Stage   Flexible

Budget
Jan 1, 1976 – Dec 31, 1976
Operating budget $39,880
Earned income $19,230
Unearned income $16,300

Audience
Percent of capacity 63

Touring contact
Stephen Stern

Productions, 1975–76

Same Painted Pony, Don Tucker
To Kill a Mockingbird, Harper Lee;
adapted, Jay Broad
The Halloween Bandit, Mark Medoff
Vanities, Jack Heifner
The Zinger, Sandy Chapin, Brother
Jonathan O.S.F., Harry Chapin; music,
Steve Chapin
White Pelicans, Jay Broad

Productions, 1976–77

The Signalman's Apprentice, Brian Phelan
How to Rob a Bank, David S. Lifson
In Memory of Long John Silver, Jamie
Oliviero, William Pisarra, Zizi Roberts
Gemini, Albert Innaurato
Patrick Henry Lake Liquors, Larry Ketron
The Bright and Golden Land, Harry Granick
The Brixton Recovery, Jack Gilhooley

Jane Galloway in *Vanities* by Jack Heifner, directed
by Garland Wright, sets by John Arnone, costumes
by David James. Photo: Joan James.

Jose Ferrer and Christopher Lloyd in *White Pelicans*
by Jay Broad, directed by Mr. Broad, sets by David
Chapman, costumes by Diane DeBaun. Photo: Joan
James.

PAF Playhouse

PAF Playhouse, the only resident professional theatre on Long Island, is a 250-seat proscenium theatre in a converted warehouse facility. In August 1975, Jay Broad became PAF's producer and initiated a policy of staging only new or previously unproduced plays. Since that time, PAF has given full professional productions to over two dozen new works, including Mark Medoff's *The Halloween Bandit*, Jack Heifner's *Vanities*, Albert Innaurato's *Gemini*, and Mr. Broad's own *White Pelicans*. Two of these productions represent a unique collaborative effort among nonprofit theatres. *Gemini* was first given a showcase at Playwrights Horizons in New York; then, after rewrites and substantial recasting, it was presented at PAF; then at Circle Repertory Company in Manhattan; and then it moved to Broadway. *Vanities*, originally created by the Lion Theatre Company, found itself on a similar route with productions at Playwrights Horizons, PAF and the Chelsea Theater Center in New York.

The Playhouse does not maintain a resident company but casts each production on an individual basis. As the theatre is located only an hour from midtown Manhattan, it makes full use of New York's pool of directors, actors and designers.

The Long Island community's response to PAF's policy of new works has been outstanding. Beginning with a subscription audience of 2,000, when Mr. Broad first arrived in 1975, it has grown, in 1977–78, to close to 10,000 with capacity audiences at all 42 performances of each production. As a result, PAF plans to expand its theatre's seating capacity to 500 beginning in the fall of 1978.

PAF also operates an extensive Arts in Education program with fully professional Actors' Equity companies, including a resident youth theatre presenting primarily new works; a touring troupe which performs participatory dramas in both elementary and secondary schools; teams of artists in residence going into the classroom to work towards curriculum objectives; and a theatre institute which presents theatre-related courses for both students and adults. The object of the Arts in Education program is to make the performing arts an integral part of the educational system in over 150 schools throughout Long Island. PAF also operates one of eight national CEMREL Centers, a federally funded educational laboratory conducting research and development in aesthetic education.

Programs & Services: *Theatre Institute, community classes in directing and acting; internships; Theatre For Young People, resident and touring performances; Troupe Program, performance and individual artist work in schools; student, senior citizen and group ticket discounts; benefit performances; bar; The Subscriber Newsletter.*

JAY BROAD
Producer
JOEL WARREN
General Manager

185 Second Street
Huntington Station,
New York 11746
Telephone (516) 271–8319
Box Office (516) 271–8282

Founded 1966
Clint Marantz

Season
October – June

Schedule
Evenings
Tuesday – Sunday
Matinees
Varies

Facilities
Seating capacity 250
Stage   Proscenium
*PAF/McDonald's
Youth Theatre*
Seating capacity 300
Stage   ¾ Arena

Budget
July 1, 1976 – June 30, 1977
Operating budget $710,366
Earned income $355,861
Unearned income $292,465

Audience
Percent of capacity 83
Number of subscribers 5,745

Touring contact
Lynette Bianchi
Theatre For Young People
PAF Centre
97 Little Neck Road
Centerport, New York 11721
(516) 261–0050

*Operates on AEA LORT (D)
contract.*

217

Productions, 1975–76
Everybody, Everybody
Dandelion
Hot Feet

Productions, 1976–77
Everybody, Everybody
Grandpa

*All productions are created by Judith Martin
with music by Donald Ashwander.*

Jeanne Michels, Virgil Roberson, Judith Martin and
Irving Burton in *Grandpa*, written, directed and
designed by Judith Martin. Photo: Martha Swope.

Irving Burton in *Grandpa*. Photo: Martha Swope.

The Paper Bag Players

The Paper Bag Players produces original plays for children in a unique style that has brought the company international recognition as innovators in children's theatre. Judith Martin writes, designs and directs all of the shows for the company and Donald Ashwander composes the music. Ms. Martin collaborates with Mr. Ashwander while sketching ideas with Irving Burton, the company's leading actor, and using the entire cast in rehearsal, to develop theatre pieces that integrate story, music and dance with the dramatic use of paper props.

Ms. Martin's ideas deal with events and experiences that confront both children and adults in contemporary society. Her stories are, in fact, modern-day allegories, which use both extraordinary and commonplace situations. While most of her short plays are humorous, many are lyrical and all are fanciful — a bar of soap tries to persuade a little boy to take a bath; a girl milks a cardboard cow and out comes a carton of milk; a street cleaner falls in love with his trash; a pair of lips escape from a lipstick ad; a family is diverted from their summer vacation by a fruitless search for their dream hamburger. The stories are told in short cartoonlike scenes, with acting, dancing, singing and sometimes even painting on stage.

The Paper Bag Players is not only a theatre of allegories but very much a musical theatre. Its musicality comes from the inspiration of its composer, Donald Ashwander. His songs and musical ideas are an essential and basic part of all the Paper Bag plays. He is so much a part of each production that his actual presence on the stage, playing and performing, seems natural. He has chosen for his instrument the electric harpsichord, which when backed by a Rhythm Master and various small instruments for sound effects, has the volume and variety of a small orchestra. He is a one-man band, supplying the rhythmic drive, the lyric background and the contemporary sound that infuses every show.

Paper, cardboard, paints and crayons are, of course, basic elements in the Paper Bag Players' theatre. The props and scenery function in several ways — sometimes as a caricature of the image and sometimes as an abstraction. For example, a jagged piece of cardboard gives the impression of an alligator, and a refrigerator box represents a crowded tenement. Costumes or props are drawn, even constructed, by the actors on stage as part of the action. Sometimes loose paper that cannot be completely controlled is deliberately used, which gives the feeling that the paper is alive.

There is no set format in the Bags' approach to creating new pieces. Usually beginning with a rough idea, Ms. Martin starts to work alone in the studio. Donald Ashwander's musical ideas sometimes lead and sometimes follow the course of action. The company members then go about building the scene and eventually, various pieces are linked into a complete revue.

The Paper Bag Players has been in operation for 19 years. Working independently and outside the established theatrical scene, Judith Martin has created a theatre that is an expression of fantasy, clarity, humor and exuberance. The Paper Bag Players is a theatre as satisfying to the most demanding adult theatregoer as it is to its range of young audiences. The Paper Bag Players has performed in a variety of places, from Lincoln Center, Harlem and rural schools in Kentucky, to Israel, Iran, Egypt and London.

Programs & Services: *Workshops in Paper Bag Players' performance techniques; performances for students; free performances for handicapped and disadvantaged children; touring; residencies; Friends of the Bags, supporters.*

JUDITH MARTIN
Director
JUDITH LISS
Administrator

50 Riverside Drive
New York, New York 10024
(212) 362-0431

Founded 1958
Judith Martin, Remy Charlip,
Shirley Kaplan, Sudie Bond,
Daniel Jahn

Season
September – May

Budget
May 1, 1976 – Apr 30, 1977
Operating budget $237,544
Earned income $117,783
Unearned income $113,660

Touring contact
Judith Liss

Operates on AEA Guest Artist contract.

Productions, 1975–76

The Midnight Ride of Paul Revere,
Allan Cruickshank & John Allen; music,
Malcolm Dodds; lyrics, Jill Gorham
The Stars & Stripes Forever, Joseph
Robinette & Thomas Tierney
Young Abe Lincoln, Richard N. Bernstein &
John Allen; music, Victor Ziskin; lyrics,
Joan Javits & Arnold Sundgaard
Aesop and Other Fables, Marshall Izen
Freedom Train, Marvin Gordon
Young Ben Franklin, Allan Cruickshank &
John Allen; music, Albert Hague; lyrics,
Ray Errol Fox
Escape to Freedom, Ossie Davis
Invasion from the Planet of the Clowns,
Steven Taylor

Productions, 1976–77

The Stars & Stripes Forever, Joseph
Robinette & Thomas Tierney
Young Mark Twain, John Allen; music,
Mary Rodgers
The Midnight Ride of Paul Revere,
Allan Cruickshank & John Allen; music,
Malcolm Dodds; lyrics, Jill Gorham
Escape to Freedom, Ossie Davis
Aesop and Other Fables, Marshall Izen
Dinosaurs, Puppets & Picasso, Marshall Izen
Young Tom Edison and the Magic Why,
Robert K. Adams; music, Martin Kalmanoff
The Road to Camelot, Daniel Kinoy; lyrics,
Robert Joseph; music, Donald Siegal
Jim Thorpe, All-American, Saul Levitt;
music, Harrison Fisher
Give 'Em Hell, Harry!, Samuel Gallu

Tom McLaughlin, T.J. Boyle and Sam Blackwell in
Jim Thorpe, All-American by Saul Levitt, directed by
John Henry Davis, sets by Raymond C. Recht,
costumes by Joyce Aysta. Photo: Barry Kramer.

G. Wayne Hoffman, Mark Hattan and Stephen Scott
in *The Road to Camelot* by Daniel Kinoy, Robert
Joseph and Donald Siegal, directed by Rick Atwell,
sets by Richard B. Williams, costumes by Joyce
Aysta.

PART (Performing Arts Repertory Theatre)

The Performing Arts Repertory Theatre Foundation (PART) was incorporated in 1967. It was an outgrowth of Harnick-Adams Productions, founded in 1961 by Jay Harnick and Robert K. Adams, in recognition of the need for high-quality educational theatre. They believed that young people and their educators would respond to a theatre which brought history and its characters to life in an imaginative way. They set out to combine the best in professional theatre and education, by commissioning authors of excellence to write original scripts and scores, and by producing these original plays with professional designers, directors and performers.

The first Harnick-Adams production was *Young Abe Lincoln*, which became the first children's musical to play Broadway. *Lincoln* established an important precedent and reflects the artistic philosophy of the company. The play is concerned with Lincoln as a young man, rather than the elder stovepipe-hat statesman that every schoolchild knows. It shows Lincoln growing up, inhibited and making mistakes — "a failure at anything I ever tried." It ends with his overcoming self-doubts and making a decision to run for his first elective office. *Young Abe Lincoln* was sent on tour and played 59 performances in that first season. Since then, the company's growth has been rapid, with several new shows opening each season. Almost 30 productions have now been introduced, and, in 1975–76, 836 performances were given in 38 states. Approximately seven companies now tour during PART's September to June season. These tours travel from the Atlantic seaboard to the Rockies and have played to well over a half-million people.

One of PART's goals is to bring live professional theatre to young people all across the country, wherever they may be, particularly those in remote and rural areas. Therefore, PART tours with extremely adaptable freestanding sets, authentic costumes, original taped scores, and sound equipment, in order to adapt to any performing area in any community.

PART spends one to two years developing a new script with major playwrights. Typical is the development of *Jim Thorpe, All-American*, conceived in 1976 and produced in 1977. PART approached Saul Levitt, author of *The Andersonville Trial*, who became intrigued with the concept and set to work. To the author, Mr. Thorpe's loss of his Olympic medals and his fall from grace stood as a metaphor for the American Indian experience. The Alliance for Arts Education, at Washington's Kennedy Center, aided the project by supplying commission funds for Mr. Levitt, and *Jim Thorpe, All-American* premiered at the Kennedy Center in April 1977. In 1977–78 the show will play for almost 30 weeks and, in 1978–79, will tour in a wide arc throughout the midwestern and southwestern United States.

In 1970, PART added to its touring program a resident series in the 1,500-seat proscenium theatre of the New York Children's Theatre Center at Town Hall. This program features a season of low-priced performances during school hours for young people, who come by bus and subway to the theatre with their teachers, as well as performances for the general public. In succeeding years, PART has added extensions to the season at suburban locations around New York, and PART now hosts over 175,000 young people annually in the city's metropolitan area.

Programs & Services: *Performances, seminars and workshops for students; touring; group ticket discounts; newsletter.*

JAY HARNICK
Artistic Director
CHARLES HULL
Managing Director

P.O. Box 415, Cathedral Station
New York, New York 10025
(212) 866-9191

Founded 1967
Robert K. Adams, Jay Harnick,
Charles Hull

Season
September – June

Facilities
Town Hall
123 West 43rd Street
Seating capacity 1,500
Stage   Proscenium

Budget
Oct 1, 1976 – Sept 30, 1977
Operating budget $660,000
Earned income $610,000
Unearned income $ 50,000

Audience
Percent of capacity 75

Touring contact
Christine Prendergast

Operates on AEA Theatre for Young Audiences contract.

Productions, 1975–76
Sly Mourning, Performance Group Gay
Workshop company
Sakonnet Point, Spalding Gray &
Elizabeth LeCompte
The Tooth of Crime, Sam Shepard
The Marilyn Project, David Gaard
Mother Courage and Her Children,
Bertolt Brecht

Productions, 1976–77
Sakonnet Point, Spalding Gray &
Elizabeth LeCompte
Rumstick Road, Spalding Gray &
Elizabeth LeCompte
Mother Courage and Her Children,
Bertolt Brecht
Oedipus, Seneca; translated,
Ted Hughes

Spalding Gray and Ron Vawter in *Rumstick Road,*
written and directed by Mr. Gray and Elizabeth
LeCompte. Photo: Ken Kobland.

The Performance Group company members in
Mother Courage and Her Children by Bertolt
Brecht, directed by Richard Schechner, during a
performance in Calcutta, India, March 1976.

The Performance Group

The Performance Group is an environmental theatre and a collective. For each production the company starts with everything new except for its core of actors, who have been with the Group for 7 to 10 years. Most Group members fulfill several functions, including performing, directing, designing and managing. Weekly meetings are held to go over all Group business — artistic and fiscal. The board of directors are the workers in the theatre.

The work changes. When TPG began in 1967, it was concerned with the "group process" as reflected in encounter groups, confrontation and the expression of feelings. The exploration of this process led to group-created works like *Commune* in 1970. At present, the work appears to be going in three directions at once. Company members, Spalding Gray and Elizabeth LeCompte, are completing the trilogy *Three Places in Rhode Island*. Each of the plays — *Sakonnet Point, Rumstick Road* and *Nyatt School* (to be completed in 1978) — relate to Mr. Gray's autobiography, as he researches it with other members of the Group. The style is precise, visual and controlled.

Work which will be directed by Richard Schechner in 1977–78 — Ted Hughes' adaptation of Seneca's *Oedipus* and *Cops*, a new American play by Terry Curtis Fox — are more "traditional" environmental theatre. *Oedipus*, however, is also a new experience for TPG, because of its extremely dense and rich poetry. *Cops* is a neorealistic play set in an all-night diner. As in *The Marilyn Project*, the Group will attempt in *Cops* a style more at home in film than on stage. But, then, *Cops* will not be staged "on stage," but rather in a diner built upstairs at the Group's home, the Performing Garage. The environment for *Oedipus* is a set of six concentric circles making a perfect arena, built within the large downstairs theatre at the Garage. The dirt playing area is a circle, 16 feet in diameter and 3 feet deep. James Clayburgh designed both environments.

The third direction the Group is taking is the encouragement of its members to start their own projects — both inside and outside the Garage. Consequently, there is a membership structure looser than before. There is also more emphasis on collaboration with dancers, musicians and other theatre workers. An insularity that marked the first 10 years of TPG is now gone.

Perhaps these changes have come out of the Group's 1976 tour to India and the six months following, when many Group members were working by themselves in America and overseas. TPG was the first American professional theatre to perform in India. The company performed in the big cities of New Delhi, Calcutta and Bombay, but also in smaller places like Lucknow and Bhopal, and even in one village, Sinjole, far from any city. Everywhere, Brecht's *Mother Courage and Her Children* was well received Group members ran workshops in various Indian cities, and studied Indian folk theatre, dance and yoga.

Back in America, TPG began to do things differently. In May 1977, sponsored by Local 12 (a union of federal government workers) and American University, TPG presented *Mother Courage* as a five-part noontime serial in a cafeteria at the Labor Department. The Group still tours, teaches workshops and accepts residencies. TPG plans to do new American plays, compose its own works and explore the classics. The 1977–78 season of *Cops, Nyatt School* and *Oedipus* is reflective of these intentions.

Finally, and most important, TPG is a company: Stephen Borst, James Clayburgh, Spalding Gray, Libby Howes, Elizabeth LeCompte, Deborah Locitzer, Joan McIntosh, Bruce Porter, Bruce Rayvid, Leeny Sack, Richard Schechner and Ron Vawter.

Programs & Services: *Workshops; internships; performances and seminars in schools; touring; workshop productions and open rehearsals; student and senior citizen discount ticket program; free ticket program; residencies; post-performance discussions.*

RICHARD SCHECHNER
Executive Director
DEBORAH LOCITZER
General Manager
RON VAWTER
Producing Director

P.O. Box 654
Canal Street Station
New York, New York 10013
Telephone (212) 966–3652
Box Office (212) 966–3651

Founded 1967
Richard Schechner

Season
October – June

Facilities
The Performing Garage
33 Wooster Street
Seating capacity 200
Stage   Environmental
Upstairs
Seating capacity 100
Stage   Environmental

Budget
July 1, 1975 – June 30, 1976
Operating budget $149,928
Earned income $ 71,915
Unearned income $ 88,750

Audience
Percent of capacity 55

Touring contact
A Bunch of Experimental Theaters
105 Hudson Street
New York, New York 10013
(212) 966–0400

Booked-in events
Experimental theatre, dance and music groups

Productions, 1975–76
The Royal Family, George S. Kaufman &
Edna Ferber
The Glass Menagerie, Tennessee Williams
The Birthday Party, Harold Pinter
Hedda Gabler, Henrik Ibsen; adapted,
Christopher Hampton
The Miser, Moliere; adapted,
Miles Malleson

Productions, 1976–77
Heartbreak House, George Bernard Shaw
Enter a Free Man, Tom Stoppard
Five Finger Exercise, Peter Shaffer
Blithe Spirit, Noel Coward
Hamlet, William Shakespeare

Louise Troy and Edward Atienza in *Enter a Free Man* by Tom Stoppard, directed by Douglas Campbell, sets by John Kasarda, costumes by Dona Granata. Photo: Peter Lester.

John Glover as *Hamlet* by William Shakespeare, directed by Douglas Seale, sets by John Kasarda, costumes by Dona Granata. Photo: Peter Lester.

Philadelphia Drama Guild

The grass-roots community theatre movement precipitated the birth of the Philadelphia Drama Guild in 1956. Founded by Philadelphians who wished to participate in play production, the company soon settled on a classical repertoire, including plays by Shakespeare, Shaw, Sheridan, O'Casey and Chekhov. As local interest and involvement with the company grew, so did the quality of its productions. In 1971, the company turned professional and made the historic Walnut Street Theatre its permanent performing space.

At the end of its third professional season, James B. Freydberg was brought in as managing director, and the Guild decided to change from what had essentially been a "star system" to a resident company format. Plans were then laid to develop a company under the artistic direction of Douglas Seale, who had previously worked with major British, American and Canadian theatre companies. Positive local support for such a concept was dramatized by a 50 percent increase in 1975–76 subscriptions.

The goal of the Philadelphia Drama Guild is simply to produce the finest quality theatre possible. Its mainstage season presents a wide range of classics and the best modern works in dramatic literature. Mr. Seale is developing an acting company of sufficient flexibility to ensure the best possible casting, while sustaining the openness, harmony and receptivity characteristic of ensemble playing. Support and expansion continues under this concept. The 1976–77 season broke records in terms of ticket sales, dollar income and overall attendance. The Philadelphia Drama Guild currently covers 75 percent of its expenses through earned income; the balance of its expenses are met by private, corporate and government funding.

In 1977–78, the Guild will inaugurate a second stage for the presentation of previously untried works, one-man shows, cabaret offerings and other projects not currently produced on the main stage.

One of the major features of the Philadelphia Drama Guild has been its education program. Some 30,000 students attend Drama Guild productions each year. The theatre offers study guides, workshops, lectures and symposia, and both students and teachers receive ticket discounts. Community leaders, local foundations and corporations have been highly supportive in subsidizing large portions of student tickets.

A long-range goal of the theatre is the establishment of the Philadelphia Drama School, a conservatory with classes taught by professionals in the field.

As the company views it, Philadelphia is the ideal location for the Drama Guild. It is a large, cosmopolitan city, steeped in tradition, with a history of staunch support for the arts and attendance at the theatre. Philadelphia is the home of a number of other important cultural institutions, including several museums, a fine ballet company and a world-famous symphony orchestra.

Programs & Services: *Performances, workshops and seminars for students; Theatre Club Lectures, public lectures by theatre artists; student and senior citizen ticket discounts; benefit performances; Theatre Club, volunteers;* Backstage, *quarterly audience newsletter; post-performance discussions.*

DOUGLAS SEALE
Artistic Director
JAMES B. FREYDBERG
Managing Director

220 South 16th Street
Philadelphia, Pennsylvania 19102
Telephone (215) 546–6789
Box Office (215) 547–3550

Founded 1956
Sidney S. Bloom

Season
September – April

Schedule
Evenings
Tuesday – Sunday
Matinees
Wednesday & Saturday

Facilities
Walnut Street Theatre
9th & Walnut Streets
Seating capacity 1,052
Stage Proscenium

Budget
June 1, 1976 – May 31, 1977
Operating budget $770,266
Earned income $546,852
Unearned income $244,491

Audience
Percent of capacity 89
Number of subscribers 16,736

Operates on AEA LORT (A) contract.

Productions, 1975–76
A Memory of Two Mondays, Arthur Miller
27 Wagons Full of Cotton, Tennessee Williams
They Knew What They Wanted, Sidney Howard
Boy Meets Girl, Sam & Bella Spewack
Secret Service, William Gillette

Productions, 1976–77
Ladyhouse Blues, Kevin O'Morrison
Canadian Gothic and *American Modern,*
Joanna Glass
Marco Polo, Jonathan Levy
A Sorrow beyond Dreams, Peter Handke;
translated, Ralph Manheim; adapted,
Daniel Freudenberger
G.R. Point, David Berry
Scribes, Barrie Keeffe

Jo Henderson in *Ladyhouse Blues* by Kevin
O'Morrison, directed by Tony Giordano, sets by
James Tilton, costumes by Fred Voelpel. Photo:
Roger Greenawalt.

Len Cariou in *A Sorrow beyond Dreams* by Peter
Handke, directed by Daniel Freudenberger, sets by
James Tilton. Photo: Roger Greenawalt.

Phoenix Theatre

The Phoenix Theatre is committed to the development of new playwrights and their work. Its entire effort is focused on encouraging the developing playwright and creating opportunities for first-rate productions of new plays in protected, noncommercial situations.

Since its founding in 1953 by Norris Houghton and T. Edward Hambleton, the Phoenix has continually ventured into areas of theatrical activity that need to be explored. The projects that have grown out of the Phoenix have all been aimed at filling a void in the New York or national theatre repertoires. The original goal of the Phoenix was to create a broad-based, reasonably priced, popular "art theatre," which produced significant new plays too adventurous for commercial producers, as well as revivals of classics that the commercial theatre would not consider. Before the end of the decade the Phoenix had established itself Off Broadway with productions of new plays and musicals.

In 1958, with the conviction that the best work could only be done through the continuing interrelationship of artists dedicated to a common goal, the Phoenix embarked on a 15-year experiment in building a permanent ensemble company. With Stuart Vaughan as artistic director, the Phoenix Acting Company presented Off Broadway productions, including *The Taming of the Shrew, Who'll Save the Ploughboy,* and *Oh Dad, Poor Dad.* In 1964, the Phoenix and the APA, under the artistic leadership of Ellis Rabb, joined forces and, after a highly successful initial season, moved to Broadway for four years. The theatre produced, in repertory, an unusual array of plays like *You Can't Take It with You,* the Piscator adaptation of *War and Peace* and *Exit the King.* In 1972, the New Phoenix Repertory Company was formed with Harold Prince, Stephen Porter and Michael Montel as artistic directors. With a permanent group of actors, the company toured several universities, conducting seminars and offering classical and modern plays like *Love for Love* and *The Visit,* before opening a season on Broadway.

In 1976, under artistic director Daniel Freudenberger, the decision was made to devote the entire Phoenix operation to the working playwright by mounting productions of new works for limited runs. In its choice of plays, the Phoenix tries to capitalize on both its New York base and its long-standing ties to regional theatres across the country. In its first new-play season, there was close cooperation with the O'Neill Theater Center, the Music-Theatre Performing Group/Lenox Arts Center, and the Manhattan Theatre Club, in locating plays and playwrights. There was also flow outward to regional theatres. The Phoenix production of Peter Handke's *A Sorrow beyond Dreams* was moved to the Guthrie Theater in Minneapolis and to Center Stage in Baltimore. Kevin O'Morrison's *Ladyhouse Blues* went from the Phoenix to productions at many other theatres around the country. The Phoenix' newest thrust — developing and producing new work and actively aiding the playwright in finding further productions — is based on the premise that all theatres can gain by working together in the development of writers.

Ancillary efforts of the Phoenix are also aimed at developing new work for the theatre. The Staged Reading Series works with eight new scripts, presenting them to a special audience, followed by discussions with the authors. The Phoenix Community Project in New York public schools is geared to sparking theatrical creativity in student and teacher alike.

In all of its work, the Phoenix has had as its standard the maintenance of the special quality of fine theatre that will attract the most talented artists. It has been this uncompromising demand for excellence that has inspired the Phoenix in its many incarnations.

Programs & Services: *Internships; Phoenix Community Project, workshops with students and teachers; staged readings; benefit performances.*

T. EDWARD HAMBLETON
Managing Director
DANIEL FREUDENBERGER
Artistic Director
MARILYN S. MILLER
Executive Director

1540 Broadway
New York, New York 10036
Telephone (212) 730-0787
Box Office (212) 730-0794

Founded 1953
T. Edward Hambleton &
Norris Houghton

Season
October – June

Schedule
Evenings
Tuesday – Sunday
Matinees
Saturday & Sunday

Facilities
Marymount-Manhattan Theatre
221 East 71st Street
Seating capacity 249
Stage Proscenium

Budget
July 1, 1976 – June 30, 1977
Operating budget $393,102
Earned income $101,497
Unearned income $414,003

Audience
Percent of capacity 81
Number of subscribers 2,002

Operates on AEA Off-Broadway contract.

Productions, 1975–76
The Glass Menagerie, Tennessee Williams
One Flew Over the Cuckoo's Nest,
Ken Kesey; adapted, Dale Wasserman
Twelfth Night, William Shakespeare

Productions, 1976–77
Uncle Vanya, Anton Chekhov;
translated, Michael Henry Heim
Sizwe Bansi Is Dead, Athol Fugard,
John Kani, Winston Ntshona
King Henry 5, William Shakespeare

Carol Teitel in *The Glass Menagerie* by Tennessee
Williams, directed by Ben Shaktman, designed by
Peter Wexler. Photo: Jack Weinhold.

John Long and Leonard Nimoy in Shakespeare's
Twelfth Night, directed by Ben Shaktman, designed
by David Chapman. Photo: Jack Weinhold.

Pittsburgh Public Theater

With the birth of the Pittsburgh Public Theater in 1974, Pittsburgh acquired its own resident professional theatre company for the first time in 10 years. With Ben Shaktman, one of the theatre's founders, as general director, the Public Theater opened in September 1975 at the Allegheny Theater. This facility had been renovated by the city of Pittsburgh and was given to the Public on a rent-free basis.

From its inception, the theatre's founders and directors have made commitments to artistic excellence, community programs and broad-based popular and financial support. With an artistic formula for the first two seasons that included the selection of a modern classic, a contemporary drama and a Shakespearean play, the Public Theater has stimulated extraordinary community response and support.

The Public Theater space, which was created by Peter Wexler, provides a unique audience and stage concept. Within the frame of a flexible 336-seat arena performing space, the performers are enveloped by the audience, creating an intimate theatre experience. The theatre's two seasons have been produced and performed by a company of talented and respected actors, directors, designers and technicians.

During its inaugural year, the Pittsburgh Public Theater implemented three resident educational programs which focus primarily on Pittsburgh's inner-city community. The Open Stage introduces students from the city's public high schools and middle schools to live theatre, often for the first time. Students receive intensive and innovative in-class instruction in preparation for their attendance at a technical dress rehearsal. The theatre's training program, the only one of its kind in the country, offers inner-city residents the opportunity to receive vocational training in many areas of technical theatre production. Community Arts is a program offered free to schools, community, civic and neighborhood organizations, providing lectures, demonstrations and workshops specifically tailored to a group's particular needs. These education-oriented programs are bringing theatre to life for thousands of city residents who ordinarily would not have the opportunity to experience any aspect of theatrical production.

For its first two seasons, the Pittsburgh Public Theater has won the enthusiastic and popular support of near-capacity audiences, with over 90 percent of the audience composed of subscribers. The theatre has also added performances to its production schedule to accommodate the demands of additional theatregoers. Single-ticket sales have also grown. With this tremendous enthusiasm has come broad-based financial support through grants and donations from individual contributors, corporations and foundations, as well as federal, state and local government agencies.

Programs & Services: *Community Arts Program, lectures, demonstrations and workshops; on-the-job training; internships; Open Stage, workshops and performances for students; symposia; student and group ticket discounts; Volunteer Associates; Director's Forums for subscribers.*

BEN SHAKTMAN
General Director

300 Sixth Avenue Building
Suite 501
Pittsburgh, Pennsylvania 15222
Telephone (412) 765-3400
Box Office (412) 323-1900

Founded 1974
Joan Apt, Margaret Rieck,
Ben Shaktman

Season
September – March

Schedule
Evenings
Tuesday – Sunday
Matinees
Thursday, Saturday, Sunday

Facilities
Allegheny Theater
Allegheny Square
Seating capacity 336
Stage   Arena

Budget
July 1, 1976 – June 30, 1977
Operating budget $671,327
Earned income $256,342
Unearned income $348,355

Audience
Percent of capacity 89
Number of subscribers 10,800

*Operates on AEA LORT (C)
contract.*

Productions, 1975–76
The Piper Man, Robert Browning; adapted,
Play Group company; music,
Mac Pirkle
Cowboys #2, Sam Shepard
Every Alice, Lewis Carroll; adapted,
Play Group company
The Maids, Jean Genet; adapted,
Play Group Women's Ensemble
200 R.P.M., David McIntosh & Play Group
company; music, Si Kahn & Charlotte Brody

Productions, 1976–77
200 R.P.M., David McIntosh & Play Group
company; music, Si Kahn & Charlotte Brody
Myths 1–10, Play Group Women's Ensemble
Church, David McIntosh & Play Group company
The T-Rific Two, David McIntosh & Play
Group company
Smoke on the Mountains, David McIntosh,
Play Group company, Hunter Hills company

Mac Pirkle and Beth Stubblefield in *Snow White,
Blood Red, Ebony Black*, company developed,
1974–75. Photo: Dennie Cody.

Play Group company members in *200 R.P.M.* by
David McIntosh, directed by Tom Cooke. Photo:
Dennie Cody.

The Play Group

The Play Group's work springs from remembrances of child's play. Molded by vigorous explorations of the attitudes that permit play, their expression is a transgression of the rituals with which it is masked. The work, then, can best be seen by the child's eye, when it is within you: "The reflections you will see, child, are of a world in which wonder, and not salvation, is primordial."

The Play Group was formed in 1973 and is a nonprofit corporation, with a board composed of half the original company members and additional people from the community. The Group is in residence at the Laurel Theatre, a turn-of-the-century church building which the company has substantially renovated. The Group has been organized artistically, in the past, around specific projects, with the Play Group Ensemble now established as an ongoing collaborative company, with a writer, David McIntosh, and a director, Tom Cooke. Katharine Pearson is director of the Women's Ensemble, and administration is managed by LeAnn Davis, with the staff sharing office and building tasks.

The members of the company "work/play" for the pleasure of the people down the block, as well as the theatre connoisseurs of the big city. One of the strongest elements of the Group's survival is its commitment to touring. Definition is hard to come by. . . hard because the work is concerned with impulses which are no longer vital if they must fit into a predefined mold. Process is at the center of the company's work. Improvisationally based, actor impulses and reactions provide the basis for collaboration. Each piece has evolved into a unique definition of itself, while at the same time helping to redefine the Group.

Guests are welcomed from near and far to the Laurel Theatre, which functions as a center for dance, theatre, music, literature and community meetings. A period of time each year is devoted to performing in the schools of Knoxville and Knox County. The Group is also beginning work on a program called the Life History Project, with the intention of helping people to create their own plays.

The Play Group is one of the organizers of Alternate ROOTS, Regional Organization of Theatres–South, an organization which seeks to develop a cohesive, regional spirit among southern theatres, through the exchange of ideas, space, promotion and mutual awareness.

Programs & Services: *Acting workshops with visiting theatre companies; Life History Project, community workshops; children's theatre; touring; Laurel Theatre Festival, music, dance and theatre companies; poetry readings; writers' workshops; weekly music concerts; resident dance company; student, senior citizen and special group ticket discounts; free ticket program; residencies;* Play Group Newsletter, *quarterly.*

Collective Artistic Leadership
LE ANN DAVIS
Managing Director

1538 Laurel Avenue
Knoxville, Tennessee 37916
(615) 523-7641

Founded 1973
A group of artists

Season
Year-round

Schedule
Evenings
Friday – Sunday

Facilities
Seating capacity 100
Stage   Flexible

Budget
Oct 1, 1976 – Sept 30, 1977
Operating budget $47,500
Earned income $30,000
Unearned income $15,000

Audience
Percent of capacity 50

Touring contact
LeAnn Davis

Booked-in events
Mime, experimental, dance, small professional regional companies

Productions, 1975-76

Godspell, John-Michael Tebelak &
Stephen Schwartz
A Shot in the Dark, Marcel Achard;
adapted, Harry Kurnitz
Tobacco Road, Erskine Caldwell;
adapted, Jack Kirkland
The Fantasticks, Tom Jones &
Harvey Schmidt
Bus Stop, William Inge
Once upon a Mattress, Jay Thompson,
Marshall Barer, Dean Fuller, Mary Rodgers
*Jacques Brel Is Alive and Well and
Living in Paris,* Jacques Brel, Eric
Blau, Mort Shuman
An Evening of Soul, Erma Clanton

Productions, 1976-77

A Streetcar Named Desire, Tennessee Williams
Happy Birthday, Wanda June, Kurt Vonnegut
Two Gentlemen of Verona, William Shakespeare;
adapted, John Guare & Mel Shapiro; music,
Galt MacDermot
Hay Fever, Noel Coward
A Thurber Carnival, James Thurber
The Misanthrope, Moliere
The Threepenny Opera, Bertolt Brecht &
Kurt Weill
Candida, George Bernard Shaw
A School for Wives, Moliere
Of Mice and Men, John Steinbeck
Fallen Angels, Noel Coward

Maureen Burns and Donna Neuwirth in Moliere's
The Misanthrope, directed by Gene Wilkins, sets by
Mr. Wilkins, costumes by Charlote Cole. Photo:
Elbert Greer.

Michael Boyle in *The Threepenny Opera* by Brecht
and Weill, directed by Gene Wilkins, sets by Jackie
Nichols, costumes by Charlote Cole. Photo: Elbert
Greer.

Playhouse on the Square

Playhouse on the Square is the professional theatre of the Circuit Playhouse, a multi-operational organization originally founded in 1968, as a community theatre, by Jackie Nichols. The theatre's objectives include the presentation of a diversified program of quality older plays and challenging new works to an area that, in the past, has been quite traditional in its theatrical tastes. It has continually endeavored to produce as much original work as possible, while at the same time providing an exposure to the best in classical theatre and innovative work from on and Off Broadway.

In addition to Playhouse on the Square, which is a resident professional theatre company performing year-round, the Circuit Playhouse operation includes a Main Stage Series of new plays and original scripts; the Workshop Theatre, which provides training for young actors and directors and presents original material; a Youth Theatre company, which performs free to more than 8,000 schoolchildren a year; and a special theatre program for the deaf and handicapped. In addition, during the last two years, Circuit Playhouse has been instrumental in the establishment of two black performing arts groups in Memphis — the Harry Bryce Dance Company and the Beale Street Repertory Company.

Playhouse on the Square operates a convertible performing space, which alternates among arena, thrust and proscenium stage productions. The Playhouse has two bars and is located in the entertainment district of Overton Square, which consists of numerous shops and restaurants. A special events series is also offered to patrons, featuring one-act plays, jazz and blues concerts, and guest artist programs.

The Workshop Theatre program is designed to offer professional training to inexperienced individuals with acting potential, while at the same time giving new writers an opportunity to have their material staged. Free class instruction is also available in dance, improvisational acting, creative writing and creative dramatics for children. A new program for senior citizens has recently been added to the Workshop curriculum. The Theatre for the Deaf program works with audio-handicapped children and adults both as performers and as spectators.

The Circuit Playhouse program has also been energetic in providing the community with a variety of new and creative theatrical events. One of the most significant was the staging of Lanford Wilson's *Hot l Baltimore* in the lobby of the Hotel King Cotton, a decaying hotel in downtown Memphis. Circuit has also staged a production of *The Frogs* by Aristophanes in an outdoor swimming pool atop the Pilot House Motor Inn, overlooking the Mississippi River. Sets were executed by Mr. Dolph Smith, a well-known water colorist, and each evening's sunset was incorporated into the performance.

Programs & Services: *Internships; performances and discussions for students; theatre for the deaf; Teen Theatre Company; touring; New Play Series, workshop productions; student, senior citizen and group ticket discounts; free ticket program; benefit performances; united arts fund-raising; Backstage, support group;* Subscriber Newsletter, *monthly; post-performance discussions.*

JACKIE NICHOLS
General Manager

Circuit Playhouse
1947 Poplar Avenue
Memphis, Tennessee 38104
Telephone (901) 725-0776
Box Office (901) 726-4656

Founded 1968
Jackie Nichols

Season
September – August

Schedule
Evenings
Wednesday – Sunday

Facilities
2121 Madison Avenue
Seating capacity 235
Stage Flexible

Budget
Jan 1, 1976 – Dec 31, 1976
Operating budget $191,276
Earned income $165,994
Unearned income $ 14,250

Audience
Percent of capacity 95
Number of subscribers 2,100

Productions, 1976–77
The Crucible, Arthur Miller
All's Well That Ends Well,
William Shakespeare
A History of the American Film,
Christopher Durang
Once in a Lifetime, Moss Hart &
George S. Kaufman

Ronald Bishop and Bonnie Blake in *Once in a
Lifetime* by George S. Kaufman and Moss Hart,
directed by Tom Haas, sets by Rick Pike, costumes
by Bobbi Owen.

Frank Raiter, William Myers and Brian Keeler in
Shakespeare's *All's Well That Ends Well,* directed by
Tom Haas, sets by Rick Pike, costumes by Bobbi
Owen.

Playmakers Repertory Company

Playmakers Repertory Company is a resident theatre serving the Triangle area of Raleigh, Durham and Chapel Hill, North Carolina, attempting to meet the increasing entertainment and cultural needs of this rapidly growing community. Developing from the rich, 58-year legacy of its predecessor, the Carolina Playmakers, PRC's chief commitment is to provide a season of plays that speak from a contemporary viewpoint to modern audiences, and are reflective of the best work being done in professional theatres around the country. This commitment includes new plays, modern American plays and those classics which still speak to us with a fresh and contemporary voice.

In addition to service to its local community, PRC is committed to serving a larger audience — the people of North Carolina. This statewide goal is reflected in the company's 1978–79 plans for a touring program, which will combine mainstage productions and outreach programs such as classes, seminars and workshops.

Stemming from its association with the Eugene O'Neill Theater Center's National Playwrights Conference, one of PRC's most exciting commitments is to the development of new plays and playwrights in the American theatre. PRC provides a forum where new voices can be heard, and where playwrights have the opportunity to experience their work in production. For example, the company's recent production of *Isadora Duncan Sleeps with the Russian Navy*, by Jeff Wanshel, was first presented at the National Playwrights Conference, then staged by PRC, and later at the American Place Theatre in New York.

PRC is also devoted to the training of actors, directors, designers and technicians for careers in the professional theatre. Affiliated with the MFA program in dramatic art at the University of North Carolina at Chapel Hill, the professional theatre acts as a model of professional practices and standards. Furthermore, graduate students in the program, who have completed two years of training, will on occasion be invited to serve for a third year as apprentices in the professional company.

Playmakers Repertory Company defines itself as a modern American theatre — a theatre with a vision which will provide society with an up-to-date mirror of its problems, heartfelt concerns, issues and achievements. It is in the pursuit of this vision that the theatre serves the audiences of North Carolina, provides a forum for new plays and playwrights, and assists in the training of theatre artists. It is the pursuit of this vision which infuses the work of the Playmakers Repertory Company with excitement and vitality.

Programs & Services: *Graduate training through the University of North Carolina in acting, directing, design and technical theatre; internships; performances, workshops and seminars for students; touring; children's theatre production; playwrights in residence; Lab Theatre, workshop productions; student, senior citizen and group discount ticket programs; united arts fund-raising; Friends of the Playmakers, support group; benefit performances; quarterly subscriber newsletter; participant in O'Neill Theater Center's Second Step Program.*

ARTHUR L. HOUSMAN
Executive Director
TOM HAAS
Artistic Director
JOSEPH COLEMAN
Managing Director

207 Graham Memorial 052A
University of North Carolina
Chapel Hill, North Carolina 27514
Telephone (919) 933–1122
Box Office (919) 933–1121

Founded 1976
Arthur L. Housman

Season
September – April

Schedule
Evenings
Tuesday – Saturday
Matinees
Sunday

Facilities
Seating capacity 285
Stage   Proscenium

Budget
Jan 1, 1977 – June 30, 1977
Operating budget $216,874
Earned income $ 36,043
Unearned income $180,831

Audience
Percent of capacity 83
Number of subscribers 1,318

Touring contact
Martha Nell Hardy

Operates on AEA LORT (D) contract.

Productions, 1975-76
Clair and the Chair and *Professor George*, Marsha Sheiness
The Importance of Being Earnest, Oscar Wilde
A Quality of Mercy, Roma Greth
The Mikado, W.S. Gilbert & Arthur Sullivan
The Lymworth Millions, David Shumaker
Report to the Stockholders, Kevin O'Morrison
Julius Caesar, William Shakespeare
Guy Gauthier's Ego Play, Guy Gauthier
Misalliance, George Bernard Shaw
Vanities, Jack Heifner
Ocean Walk, Philip Magdalany
The Boor and *The Marriage* and
The Bank Jubilee and *The Marriage Proposal*,
Anton Chekhov
The Public Good, Susan Dworkin
The Spelling Bee, Marsha Sheiness
The Boss, Edward Sheldon
Perched on a Gabardine Cloud, Steven
Braunstein
Two for the Seesaw, William Gibson
Magritte Skies, Yale Udoff
George Washington Slept Here, George S.
Kaufman & Moss Hart
The Caseworker, George Whitmore
Cakes with the Wine, Edward M. Cohen
Dear Ruth, Norman Krasna
Paradise, Steven Shea
The Tavern, George M. Cohan
Born Yesterday, Garson Kanin

Productions, 1976-77
Babes in Arms, Richard Rodgers & Lorenz Hart
Boo Hoo, Philip Magdalany
The Dybbuk, S. Ansky
Rio Grande, Martin Sherman
The Rivals, Richard Brinsley Sheridan
Rebeccah, Karen Malpede
Gemini, Albert Innaurato
Hay Fever, Noel Coward
Stop the Parade, Marsha Sheiness
The Mousetrap, Agatha Christie
Fair Weather Friends, Kenneth Pressman &
Philip Magdalany
*Jacques Brel Is Alive and Well and Living
in Paris*, Jacques Brel, Eric Blau, Mort Shuman
For the Use of the Hall, Oliver Hailey
Stage Door, George S. Kaufman & Edna Ferber
Earthworms, Albert Innaurato
Cracks, Martin Sherman
The Gingerbread Lady, Neil Simon
The Playboy of the Western World,
John Millington Synge

Jonathan Frakes and Cara Duff-MacCormick in
Albert Innaurato's *Earthworms*, directed by David
Schweizer, sets by Christopher Nowak, costumes by
William Ivey-Long. Photo: Nathaniel Tileston.

Joseph Mays and Maria Cellario in *Stop the Parade*
by Marsha Sheiness, directed by Harold Scott, sets
by Paul Eads, costumes by Mary Alice Orito. Photo:
Nathaniel Tileston.

Playwrights Horizons/
Queens Festival Theater

The artistic mission of Playwrights Horizons, under the continuing direction of Robert Moss, is divided into three integrated activities — the mainstage New Playwrights Season and the Workshop Theater, both in Manhattan, and the Queens Festival Theater, six miles outside of Manhattan in the borough of Queens. In Manhattan, total emphasis is on living American playwrights actively working on new material. At the Queens Festival Theater, the emphasis is on the development of an audience sensibility through the presentation of a wide range of plays, both classic and modern, as well as a program of modern and ethnic dance.

In the spring of 1975, the New York City Department of Cultural Affairs invited Playwrights Horizons, founded in 1971, to expand its activities to the Queens Theater in the Park. PH accepted and has since produced more than 60 events there. As part of the ever-growing commitment to the Queens audience, the production schedule is eclectic and varied. It includes productions which offer new looks at standard classics, the work of new playwrights, and the presentation of modern dance companies. Expanding the perceptions and sensibilities of its audience is a major thrust of the Queens activity, and to this end, theatre patrons are regularly invited to meet with visiting theatre artists. A further extension of this concept is the Theater-in-Education program, which includes artists performing in Queens' high schools, professional theatre craftspeople going to the classrooms to discuss particular aspects of the craft, high school students attending special matinee performances, and seminars for students with the casts of PH productions. The commitment to the audience is constantly growing and changing as the artistic leadership further identifies the potential audience, its needs and its personality.

A major thrust of Playwrights Horizons' activities continues to be the ongoing encouragement, support and development of American playwrights. The theatre's resources include three artistic leaders — the artistic director, associate artistic director and the literary manager — and three different performing spaces. There are readings of plays — rehearsed, unrehearsed or staged, as well as workshops and full productions. There is constant feedback to the writer from one of the artistic trio who guide the activities of PH.

In the 60-seat Studio Workshop the entire emphasis is on the developing and emerging script, with scant attention paid to physical production. Energy is spent on getting the playwright's words moving three-dimensionally in space. Conferences between the playwright and the literary manager are constant, as the script moves off the page. As a rule, this is the playwright's first experience with theatre collaboration.

In the 99-seat mainstage theatre, where activity is shepherded by the artistic director, the playwright is often more experienced, and the script receives a more sophisticated treatment. Attention is paid to physical production, and the writer collaborates with other theatre artists. A larger audience is encouraged to attend and critics are invited.

A few new scripts move one more step in the PH process and are subsequently performed at the Queens Festival Theater. Here, the playwright and his vision meet a much larger community audience. The associate artistic director joins the collaborative process as the work is reshaped again. This last phase is the one most closely resembling the competitive arena in which the writer must ultimately participate. The Queens experience is the most advanced stage of PH support of the playwright. Some Playwrights Horizons plays have moved on to other productions, including Robert Patrick's *Kennedy's Children*, Jack Heifner's *Vanities* and Albert Innaurato's *Gemini*.

Programs & Services: *Internships; performances, discussions and seminars for students; dance series in Queens; staged readings; workshop productions; student and group ticket discounts; The Friends of Playwrights Horizons, support group; annual raffle.*

ROBERT MOSS
Artistic Director
PHILIP HIMBERG
Associate Artistic Director
JANE MOSS
Managing Director

416 West 42nd Street
New York, New York 10036
(212) 564-1235

P.O. Box 888
Forest Hills, New York 11375
(212) 699-1660

Founded 1971
Robert Moss

Season
October – July

Schedule
Evenings
Thursday – Sunday
Matinees
Sunday

Facilities
Mainstage
Seating capacity 99
Stage   Proscenium
Studio Workshop
Seating capacity 60
Stage   Flexible
Queens Festival Theater
Flushing Meadow Park
Seating capacity 500
Stage   Proscenium

Budget
July 1, 1976 – June 30, 1977
Operating budget $324,388
Earned income $153,304
Unearned income $167,400

Audience
Mainstage
Percent of capacity 66
Studio Workshop
Percent of capacity 57
Queens Festival Theater
Percent of capacity 55

Booked-in events
Dance companies

*Operates under AEA Showcase
Code.*

Productions, 1976
The Proposition, Allan Albert &
Proposition Workshop company
The Boston Tea Party, Allan Albert &
Proposition Workshop company
The Whale Show; adapted, Allan Albert
Corral; adapted, Allan Albert
Soap, Allan Albert; music, Margaret Ulmer

Productions, 1977
The Proposition, Allan Albert &
Proposition Workshop company
Soap, Allan Albert; music, Margaret Ulmer
Fable, Jean-Claude van Itallie; music,
Richard Peaslee
The Whale Show; adapted, Allan Albert
The Casino, Allan Albert

John Brownlee and Alaina Warren in *The Casino* by
Allan Albert, directed by Mr. Albert, sets by Cletus
Jackson, costumes by Carol Talkov. Photo:
Elizabeth Wolynski.

Company members in *Fable* by Jean-Claude van
Itallie and Richard Peaslee, directed by Allan Albert,
sets by Karen Schulz, costumes by Halliday Wallace.
Photo: Jeff Albertson.

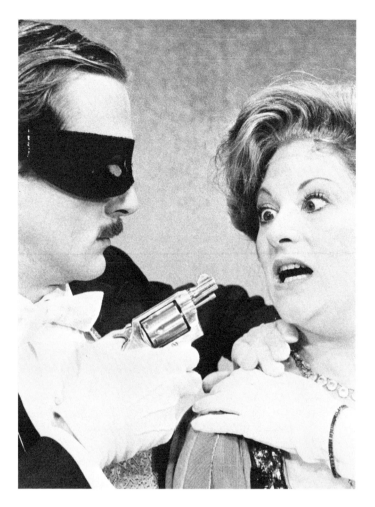

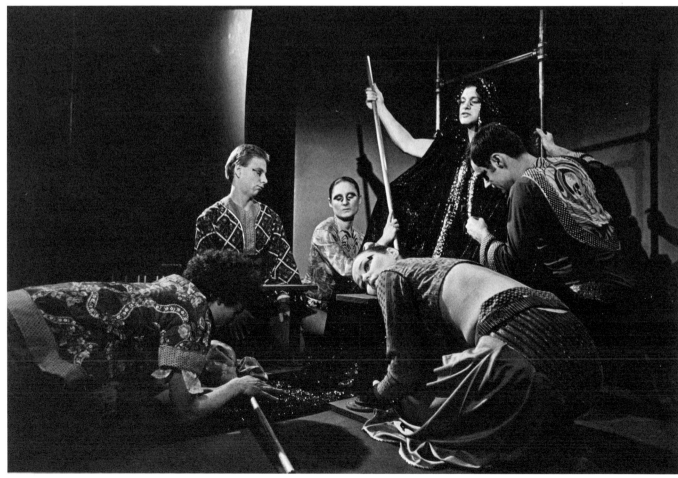

The Proposition Workshop

Since its founding in 1968, in a converted bakery on Inman Square in Cambridge, Massachusetts, the Proposition has grown from a part-time, student operation to a nationally recognized theatre. As artistic director since 1969, Allan Albert first conceived the Proposition as a fully improvised show but, through the techniques and ensemble work of improvisation, the company has been led to a series of scripted, documentary works. With the exception of two collaborations with writer Jean-Claude van Itallie and composer Richard Peaslee, these pieces have all been written, or conceived, and directed by Mr. Albert. In short, the structure of the Proposition is most akin to that of a choreographer's company.

The company's scripted pieces represent a body of nonfiction theatre, dealing with sociohistoric themes. *Corral*, the first of these pieces, was based on "tall tales" and songs from the era of the trail drives. From the start, each of these pieces has been marked with a special authenticity, such as the use of cowboy songs in traditional arrangements or costumes in the dusty sepia colors of old photographs. The second piece, *The Whale Show*, is darker in content — a depiction of the rigors of whale fishery in the 1800s. *Soap* is a look at the schizophrenia of actors and their soap-opera characters. *The Casino* is an evocation of the society typified by the Stockbridge, Massachusetts, Casino at the turn of the century. In this play, research sources, such as newspaper accounts and diaries, are combined with oral history, in the form of taped reminiscences from older residents of Stockbridge. *The Casino* also represents a distillation of the musical elements that were important in previous pieces, but are now elevated to a central focus.

This combination of music, oral history and research will be further pursued in three new pieces planned for the 1977–78 season: a piece on coal mining and unions in the 1930s with Appalachian folk music; a country and western trucking show; and a play about Jewish immigration. In order to pursue these projects, the Proposition is being restructured around a more project-oriented base. There will be no year-round performance schedule in Cambridge, but rather limited runs primarily in New York City. In 1977, Mr. Albert became artistic director of the Berkshire Theatre Festival, where the Proposition is in residence during the summer. New plays will be showcased in New York and elsewhere. Touring throughout the country will continue as a major activity, including a spring residency in South Carolina.

Children's theatre has been an important part of the Proposition's programs. Several Proposition adult productions have been recycled to create a number of children's versions, like *The Proposition Circus*. In 1976, the Museum of Modern Art in New York commissioned a new children's piece, *Taxi Tales*. Written by Mr. Albert, under a Young Audiences Play Commission Grant from the New York State Council on the Arts, with music by Don Sosin, *Taxi Tales* was performed in the summer of 1976 as part of the museum's Taxi Exhibit.

Programs & Services: *Improvisation workshops; touring and lecture-demonstrations in schools; improvised shows for children; staged readings; student and group ticket discounts; benefit performances; Proposition Props, support group; community residencies; What's Popping at the Prop?, quarterly flyer; post-performance discussions.*

ALLAN ALBERT
Artistic Director
CAROL LAWHON
Production Supervisor

1697 Broadway, Suite 701
New York, New York 10019
(212) 541–7643

Founded 1968
Jeremy Leven & C. Wendell Smith

Season
Berkshire Theatre Festival
June – August
Touring
September – May

Facilities
Berkshire Theatre Festival
Stockbridge, Massachusetts
Unicorn Theatre
Seating capacity 125
Stage Flexible
Proposition Theatre
Seating capacity 75
Stage Cabaret

Budget
Oct 1, 1976 – Sept 30, 1977
Operating budget $300,000
Earned income $250,000
Unearned income $ 40,000

Audience
Unicorn Theatre
Percent of capacity 72
Proposition Theatre
Percent of capacity 100

Touring contact
Carol Lawhon

Operates on AEA special contracts.

Productions, 1975–76

XA: A Vietnam Primer, Michael Monroe & Provisional Theatre company
America Piece, Susan Yankowitz, Don Opper, Provisional Theatre company
Voice of the People, Part One, Provisional Theatre company
Voice of the People, Part Two, Provisional Theatre company

Productions, 1976–77

Voice of the People, Part One, Provisional Theatre company
Voice of the People, Part Two, Provisional Theatre company
Songs and Speeches of the People, Provisional Theatre company
America Piece, Susan Yankowitz, Don Opper, Provisional Theatre company

Provisional company members in *Voice of the People, Part One*, ensemble created, directed and designed.

Company members in *America Piece* by the Provisional Theatre with Susan Yankowitz and Don Opper, directed and designed by the company.

Provisional Theatre

The Provisional Theatre is a touring theatre troupe, a family and a highly disciplined collective committed to the use of innovative and exciting theatre as a tool, to help reflect and change the world. The Provisional people are cultural workers, creating original dramatic pieces about the experience of living and working in a land where loneliness, alienation and cynicism are becoming all too familiar. Their works are about spirit, hope and potential.

In its five-year history, the Provisional has created five original pieces and is at work on a sixth. Its current repertoire includes *Voice of the People, Parts One and Two; America Piece;* a new untitled work; workshops and mobile performances. *Voice of the People* is an epical, alternative look, with traditional music, mime and huge puppets, at the history of the people of the United States — a view that is rarely taught in the schools. *America Piece* is a physical and vocal dramatization about what it feels like to be here, now, in American society. The new untitled piece centers on living and surviving inside the present environment and is filled with laughter, music and provocative questions.

The Provisional is basically an itinerant theatre, even at home in Los Angeles. It has no performing space of its own, so it is always "on tour." When traveling, the group looks for work in two kinds of places — schools and communities. The income from school residencies most often provides the minimal financial security necessary to allow the community work to happen.

In communities, the Provisional is sponsored by local groups and coalitions, who find the performance location, arrange for the performances, do the publicity, supply the technical needs, and mobilize a support group to bring the cultural event and a large number of people togther.

The Provisional puts energy into getting its theatre work out of *theatres*, to people who don't call themselves theatregoers — people who would feel ill at ease in traditional theatre situations. The group performs in churches, meeting halls, soup kitchens, community centers, outdoors — places where people go and already feel at home.

Workshops are an important part of the Provisional's tour activities. The members work with both theatre-oriented and community-active people in areas such as physical and vocal preparation, game theory, ritual exercises, singing and discussion. Workshops center on what people are doing with their lives and how that relates to theatre.

The hallmarks of the Provisional Theatre are discipline and a sense of humor, qualities which are often thought to be mutually exclusive. The company members work daily on their vocal and physical apparatus. Their original pieces are carefully polished, arranged and choreographed. Their singing is like that of a trained chorus, and their stage movement reflects the precision and grace of their martial arts training. An important ingredient in the company's work is what they learn from their audiences.

Programs & Services: *Workshops in Provisional techniques and group dynamics; performances and workshops for students; touring; prison workshops; lecture series and slide shows; poetry, music and dance programs; booked-in events; student and senior citizen ticket discounts; free ticket program; newsletter; post-performance discussions.*

Collective Leadership
Contact: Steven Kent, Candace Laughlin, Barry Opper

1816½ North Vermont Avenue
Los Angeles, California 90027
(213) 664-1450

Founded 1972
A group of artists

Season
Year-round

Budget
Jan 1, 1976 – Dec 31, 1976
Operating budget $86,402
Earned income $21,475
Unearned income $60,729

Touring contact
Cricket Parmalee

Productions, 1975–76
Windows (Las Ventanas), Roberto
Rodriguez; translated, Ignacio Perez
The Dinner Guest, Manuel Martinez
Mediero; translated, Ignacio Perez
*Everything Not Compulsory Is Strictly
Forbidden,* Jorge Diaz; translated,
Ignacio Perez
Eleuterio the Coqui, Tomas Blanco;
adapted, Pablo Cabrera, Miriam Colon,
Rosa Luisa Marquez

Productions, 1976–77
The Oxcart (La Carreta), Rene Marques
I Took Panama, Luis A. Garcia & El
Teatro Popular de Bogota; translated,
Tony Diaz; music, Galt MacDermot

Ernesto Gonzalez in *The Dinner Guest* by Manuel
Martinez Madeiro, directed by Alba Oms, sets by
Robert Strohmeier, costumes by Benito Gutierrez-
Soto. Photo: Joseph Griffith.

Daniel Faraldo, Tony Diaz and Juan Vaquer in *I
Took Panama* by Luis A. Garcia and El Teatro
Popular de Bogota, directed by Alba Oms, sets by
Carlos Carrasco, costumes by Maria Ferreira.
Photo: Ken Howard.

Puerto Rican Traveling Theatre

The Puerto Rican Traveling Theatre, a professional bilingual performing group, is now celebrating its tenth anniversary. From a tentative start as a street theatre, the Puerto Rican Traveling Theatre has developed into a multifaceted organization with a permanent theatre, a touring company and a training unit, where hundreds of youths from economically deprived homes have been trained free of charge.

The Puerto Rican Traveling Theatre has been a strong force in introducing to American audiences plays in English and Spanish, by Puerto Rican and Hispanic writers. The permanent theatre has also staged productions by important European and North American authors. Not only has it introduced works by Luis Rafael, Jaime Carrero, Piri Thomas, Rene Marques, Fernando Arrabal, Maxwell Anderson, Manuel Mendez Ballester and others, but it has been responsible for presenting adaptations of short stories and poetry. In addition, the theatre has commissioned and created new translations and introduced the talents of English-speaking professional Hispanic actors to New York audiences.

An important feature of the group is its touring company, which has played the streets, parks and playgrounds of New York's five boroughs, as well as Long Island, Buffalo, Rochester, New Jersey, Washington, D.C., Connecticut and Pennsylvania. This company tours with full lighting and sound equipment and a 20-square-foot stage on the back of a flatbed truck. Its work has been seen, at no cost, by tens of thousands of citizens in the less affluent regions of New York. Some of America's finest costume, set and lighting designers have designed for the touring company. Its actors come from various places, including Puerto Rico, Cuba, the Dominican Republic, Argentina, the United States, Panama, Chile, Colombia and Spain.

A third and most crucial aspect of the theatre is its six-year-old training unit. Some 800 students from low-income families have received free training in acting, dance, singing and speech.

The theatre has been fortunate in attracting the attention and support not only of the city, state and federal governments, but also of individual contributors and volunteers. In June 1977, the City of New York granted the Puerto Rican Traveling Theatre a long-term lease on an historic firehouse, in the heart of the Broadway theatre district. In this same year the theatre was awarded a National Endowment for the Arts Challenge Grant.

In its new home, the Puerto Rican Traveling Theatre has become a permanent Hispanic theatre located in the Broadway theatre district, introducing New York theatregoers to the riches and diversity of Latin American, Puerto Rican and European contemporary writers, both in English and Spanish.

Programs & Services: *Training Unit, classes for students in theatre arts; internships; Hispanic playwrights' workshop; touring and seminars in schools; booked-in events; student and group ticket discounts; free ticket program; voucher program; benefit performances.*

MIRIAM COLÓN EDGAR
Executive Director
ALLEN DAVIS III
Administrator

141 West 94th Street
New York, New York 10025
Telephone (212) 749-8474
Box Office (212) 354-1293

Founded 1967
Miriam Colon Edgar, George P. Edgar,
Anibal Otero, Jose Ocasio

Season
January – September

Facilities
304 West 47th Street
Seating capacity 74
Stage ¾ Arena

Budget
July 1, 1976 – June 30, 1977
Operating budget $170,254
Earned income $ 18,587
Unearned income $136,825

Audience
Percent of capacity 58

Touring contact
Allen Davis

Booked-in events
*Music concerts & Hispanic
theatre companies*

*Operates on AEA LORT (C)
contract and under
AEA Showcase Code.*

Productions, 1975–76
A Child's View of the Gaspee, Marc Kohler
The Abduction of General Prescott,
Marc Kohler
The Lamb's Christmas, Marc Kohler

Productions, 1976–77
The Carrot Story, Lynne Sutter,
Janice Alberghene, Marc Kohler,
Anne McCaffrey
The Incident at Chelmsford, Janice
Alberghene & Marc Kohler
The Bear's First Christmas, Marc Kohler &
Lynne Sutter
The Gork, Marc Kohler

The Tax Man and Judy in *Judy's Dream,* written and
directed by Marc W. Kohler, designed by Mr. Kohler
and Kevin Lima. Photo: Terrance Price.

Mr. Punch, The Schlunk and Judy in *The Landing of
the Schlunk,* written and directed by Marc Kohler,
designed by Marc Kohler and Kevin Lima. Photo:
Terrance Price.

The Puppet Workshop

Out of his employment as a puppeteer for the Providence Recreation Department grew Marc Kohler's commitment to the art form. He envisioned a permanent program of puppetry, which would become an established part of the lives of all Rhode Island citizens. In July 1972, the Puppet Workshop was incorporated with two paid staff members, who began implementing the excitement of puppet theatre in Rhode Island schools and libraries through performances and workshops.

The puppet plays, which form the core of the program, are all original pieces conceived and directed by Mr. Kohler and developed by the company, with original music created for each piece. The style of the work has evolved from a tradition that uses stock characters involved in contemporary situations, confronting personal growth crises. The situations come from the artists' life experiences and are translated into the struggles of the characters. Highly personal audience involvement, through verbal participation, allows children to take part in each event as a one-time-only experience. This technique, combining the improvisational nature of the commedia dell'arte style with current emotional reality in a structured setting, allows for a great amount of freedom. Each puppet play reinforces the illusion that the puppets are real people — alive with human fears, joys and hopes.

In addition to performing, the theatre's program includes workshops for children and adults. These workshops offer participants an in-depth study of the company's methods in all phases of puppet production — from sculpturing a head to performing with the finished puppet in a script evolved for the particular character. Each workshop's environment provides a structure for the participant to take the existential risks involved in projecting himself into a created object, portraying that projection, and taking responsibility for all aspects of it. Both with children and adults, this structure, and the resulting interaction with other characters, creates a new use of puppetry which provokes a dramatic reality rarely expected from the medium.

Each year the Puppet Workshop has explored new areas for the use of puppetry. In 1975, two members of the troupe traveled to Aracaju in the state of Sergipe, Brazil, to perform with puppets in Portuguese and to instruct at the University of Sergipe. Other special projects include puppet making and performance training for the Providence Police Department's Officer Friendly Program; script creation, stage and puppet construction, and performance training for the Rhode Island Center for Economic Education; construction of giant puppets and masks for the Rhode Island Feminist Theatre's production of *Anne Hutchinson: American Jezebel*; establishment of a year's residency of puppetry in hospitals, a special project funded initially by the Rhode Island State Council on the Arts and continued with the support of Rhode Island Hospital; establishment of a residency program at Meeting Street School, made possible by a grant from the Providence Rotary Club; and teaching a course, Puppetry in the Classroom, at the Attleboro campus of Lesley College.

The Puppet Workshop embraces art in all forms and is deeply committed to providing individual artists, in all mediums, with the skills and resources for full development of their art. The Store-Front Theatre Project, begun in the spring of 1977, offers a lunchtime performing arts series by Rhode Island artists who represent virtually every artistic medium.

Long-term goals of the Puppet Workshop include national touring, the establishment of a school of puppet arts, the exploration of additional residencies in institutions caring for people with special needs, and providing Providence with an "open space" for cultural events.

Programs & Services: *Apprenticeships; teacher workshops; internships; Puppetry in the Hospital; touring; workshops in making and using puppets for adults and children; Store-Front Theatre; booked-in events; lunchtime theatre; student and senior citizen discounts; free ticket program; united arts fund-raising; residencies.*

MARC W. KOHLER
Executive/Artistic Director

128 North Main Street
Providence, Rhode Island 02903
(401) 521-4250

Founded 1972
Marc W. Kohler

Facilities
Store-Front Theatre
Shepard's Building
Washington Street
Seating capacity 150
Stage   Flexible

Budget
July 1, 1976 – June 30, 1977
Operating budget $62,634
Earned income $30,104
Unearned income $31,102

Touring contact
Patricia Bessette

Booked-in events
Rhode Island performing arts groups and individual artists

Productions, 1975–76
Pasos, Lope de Rueda
Entremeses, Miguel de Cervantes
La Malquerida, Jacinto Benavente
Dona Rosita, La Soltera, Federico
Garcia Lorca
*Amor de don Perlimplin con Belisa en Su
Jardin*, Federico Garcia Lorca
Los Soles Truncos, Rene Marques
La Fiaca, Ricardo Talesnik
La Celestina, Fernando de Rojas
O.K., Isaac Chocron

Productions, 1976–77
La Maxima Felicidad, Isaac Chocron
La Dama Duende, Calderon de la Barca
La Fiaca, Ricardo Talesnik
*Amor de don Perlimplin con Belisa en Su
Jardin*, Federico Garcia Lorca
Dona Rosita, La Soltera, Federico
Garcia Lorca
O.K., Isaac Chocron
La Pipa Azul, Maggie Crespo
El Censo, Emilio Carballido
Cien Veces No Debo, Ricardo Talesnik
La Decente, Miguel Mihura
Vidas Privadas, Noel Coward; translated,
Eduardo Leyva
La Valija, Julio Mauricio
Don Juan Tenorio, Jose Zorrilla
Una Mujer Muy...Decente, Miguel Mihura
Los Fantastikos, Tom Jones & Harvey Schmidt;
translated, Rene Buch
La Celestina, Fernando de Rojas

Braulio Villar in *Dona Rosita, La Soltera* by Federico
Garcia Lorca, directed by Rene Buch, sets by Robert
Federico, costumes by Maria Ferreira. Photo: Gerry
Goodstein.

Blanquita Amaro and Chamaco Garcia in *Vidas
Privadas* by Noel Coward, directed by Rene Buch,
sets by Mario Arellano, costumes by Rene Sanchez.
Photo: Ruben Rubiera.

Repertorio Español

Although outside the mainstream of American theatre, Repertorio Espanol aspires to the same goal as major professional theatre groups: to produce good theatre. Dedicated to a theatre of texts, Repertorio Espanol concentrates on high artistic standards to attract audiences. Because of these standards, the company has become a force, offering a sense of identity and cultural esteem to Hispanics. What began informally in June 1968 has grown into a full-time company with resident theatres in Miami and New York, and with a stable company of actors trained in both the classical and modern styles. The diversity of the company members' roots and training is matched in the theatre's repertoire, which includes Spanish classic drama and contemporary Latin American plays, as well as international works.

A series of Spanish classics have included works by Calderon and Cervantes from the "Golden Age" and by Lorca and Benavente of the twentieth century. One production, *La Celestina*, has been in the company's repertoire since 1974, with more than 200 performances given throughout the United States and Mexico. *La Celestina* was also presented at theatre festivals in Guanajuato, Mexico, and El Paso, Texas, where it won all the awards in the professional theatre category.

Ever since its presentation of *Las Pericas* in 1969, Repertorio Espanol has been producing Latin American plays and, in 1973, the company began a series of Latin American theatre festivals. These plays, many receiving their American debuts, have provided audiences with a view of the Latin American theatre movement. For Hispanic-American audiences, the Latin American plays, in particular, have a relevance to their customs and culture. With the growing worldwide interest in Latin American literature, Repertorio Espanol has been invited to perform at many festivals and symposia of Latin American drama.

On occasion, Repertorio Espanol presents plays translated into Spanish to give both actors and audiences a change of pace. Diverse plays such as Edward Albee's *Who's Afraid of Virginia Woolf?*; *Private Lives* by Noel Coward; and *The Fantasticks* by Tom Jones and Harvey Schmidt were presented in Spanish. The production of Mr. Albee's play was selected for presentation at the Tapia Theatre in Puerto Rico during 1973.

Repertorio Espanol has been proud to present Spanish and Latin American guest artists and performing arts groups. Guest artists have included Amelia Bence and Carmen Montejo in Repertorio Espanol's own productions; and Estela Medina and China Zorrilla in one-woman shows. Groups have included El Nuevo Grupo from Venezuela, Once al Sur from Argentina and Aula de Teatro de Universidad de Valladolid from Spain.

Repertorio Espanol also sponsors three outreach programs designed to increase audiences and create theatre-lovers. In New York City's Hispanic neighborhoods, the company performs at social clubs and community organizations in order to introduce itself to new audiences and to make theatre more accessible. Nationally, Repertorio Espanol performs at theatres and universities to entertain the local Hispanic population and to acquaint students with Hispanic theatre culture. Through workshops in voice, movement and acting, Repertorio Espanol develops new members for its company.

To reach a larger audience and attract a broad cross section of the Spanish-speaking community, Repertorio Espanol initiated a "Year of the Comedy," in 1976-77, which introduced several new comedic plays to its repertoire. With these new plays which provide balance to *La Celestina, Los Soles Truncos* and the tragedies of Lorca, Repertorio Espanol now offers a wide variety of theatre for everyone.

Programs & Services: *Workshops in Spanish; performances for students; children's theatre; touring; Latin American theatre festivals; booked-in events; student, senior citizen and group discounts; voucher program; post-performance discussions.*

RENE BUCH
Artistic Director
GILBERTO ZALDIVAR
Producer

138 East 27th Street
New York, New York 10016
(212) 889-2850
2173 SW 8th Street
Miami, Florida 33135
(305) 688-4194

Founded 1969
Gilberto Zaldivar, Rene Buch,
Frances Drucker

Season
New York
October – June
Miami
September – August

Schedule
New York
Evenings
Friday – Sunday
Matinees
Sunday
Miami
Evenings
Friday – Sunday

Facilities
New York
Seating capacity 180
Stage Proscenium
Miami
Seating capacity 255
Stage Proscenium

Budget
Sept 1, 1976 – Aug 31, 1977
Operating budget $262,000
Earned income $160,000
Unearned income $100,000

Audience
New York
Percent of capacity 55
Miami
Percent of capacity 60

Touring contact
Gilberto Zaldivar

Booked-in events
Spanish-language performing artists and companies

Productions, 1975–76
Caprice

Productions, 1976–77
Der Ring Gott Farblonget
Stage Blood

All productions created by
Charles Ludlam.

Company members in *Der Ring Gott Farblonget*,
written, directed and designed by Charles Ludlam.

A scene from *Der Ring Gott Farblonget*.

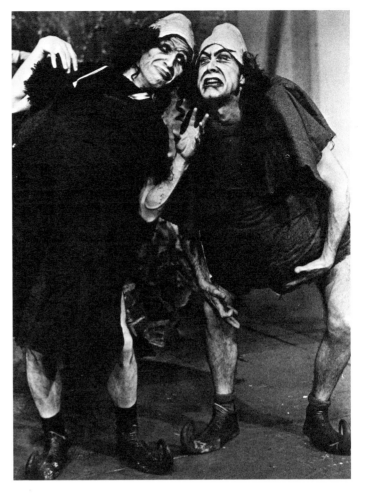

The Ridiculous Theatrical Company

The Ridiculous Theatrical Company was founded in 1967. Since then, the original members, Charles Ludlam, Lola Pashalinski, John Brockmeyer, Black-Eyed Susan and Bill Vehr, have worked together as an ensemble in unbroken continuity with Mr. Ludlam as artistic director, actor, designer and playwright-in-residence. The company has fused its style from widely disparate, yet historically popular, theatrical sources, including oriental theatre (the Kabuki and the Peking Opera), commedia dell'arte and Elizabethan theatre. These forms are combined with a style of ensemble playing that synthesizes wit, parody, vaudeville, farce, melodrama and satire, giving reckless immediacy to classical stagecraft.

The company teaches workshops in commedia dell'arte, acting, directing, puppetry and design. During the summer of 1975, the company taught extended workshops at American University in Washington, D.C. In the spring of 1976, Mr. Ludlam taught at New York University and, in 1977–78, is teaching a graduate course in playwriting at Yale University.

Together with the continuous development of its repertoire, touring and teaching, the company has been developing a children's theatre series. This series began in 1974 with Mr. Ludlam's *Professor Bedlam's Punch and Judy Show*. In 1975, Mr. Ludlam was commissioned through a New York State Council on the Arts Young Audience grant to write *Jack in the Beanstalk*. In 1977–78, the company plans to extend its children's series with a production entitled *The Enchanted Pig*.

In the 10 years since its inception, the company has created and produced 13 original works, including *Big Hotel* in 1967, *Conquest of the Universe/When Queens Collide* and *Whores in Babylon* in 1968, *Turds in Hell* and *The Grand Tarot* in 1969, *Bluebeard* in 1970, *Eunuchs of the Forbidden City* in 1971, *Corn* in 1972, *Camille* in 1973, and *Hot Ice* in 1974. Indicative of the unique style and flavor of the company is their recycling of old stories as in *Camille*, with Mr. Ludlam appearing as Marguerite Gautier, the lady of the camellias; *Stage Blood*, a parody of *Hamlet* and at the same time a parody of itself, featuring a troupe of actors presenting *Hamlet*; and the company's latest piece, *Der Ring Gott Farblonget*, an operatic spoof on Wagner's *The Ring of the Nibelungen*.

The Ridiculous Theatrical Company tours nationally and internationally. The company is planning a six-week Australian tour, beginning in February 1978 and concluding with a two-week tour of University of California campuses.

Programs & Services: *Workshops in acting, commedia dell'arte, directing, playwriting, puppetry and design; performances, workshops and lectures for students; children's theatre series; staged readings; student, senior citizen and group ticket discounts; benefit performances; post-performance discussions; touring.*

CHARLES LUDLAM
Director
CATHERINE SMITH
Administrative Director

New Arts Management
47 West 9th Street
New York, New York 10011
(212) 691–5434

Founded 1967
Charles Ludlam

Season
Year-round

Schedule
Evenings
Tuesday – Sunday
Matinees
Saturday

Budget
July 1, 1976 – June 30, 1977
Operating budget $77,098
Earned income $29,207
Unearned income $46,586

Touring contact
New Arts Management

Productions, 1975-76
American Buffalo, David Mamet
A View from the Bridge, Arthur Miller;
music, Alaric Jans
Sitcom, Julian Barry; music,
Wayne Wilentz & Ed Petersen

Productions, 1976-77
The Collected Works of Billy the Kid,
Michael Ondaatje; music, Elliott Delman
Mert & Phil, Anne Burr
Joplin, Kathleen Lombardo; music, Scott
Joplin & Robert Lombardo
Domino Courts, William Hauptman
A Slight Accident, James Saunders
The Water Engine, David Mamet

Gail Silver and William H. Macy in *The Water Engine*
by David Mamet, directed by Steven Schachter, sets
by David Emmons, costumes by Jessica Hahn.
Photo: James C. Clark.

Madonna Niles and Guy Barile as *Mert & Phil* by
Anne Burr, directed by Steven Schachter, sets by
Dean Taucher, costumes by Kaye Nottbusch.
Photo: Ed Krieger.

St. Nicholas Theater Company

The St. Nicholas Theater Company was founded in 1974 by David Mamet, Steven Schachter, William H. Macy and Patricia Cox. In just three seasons it has become one of Chicago's leading centers for the performing arts. The company is now housed in a three-story warehouse which has been converted to include a theatre, a dance studio, classrooms and administrative offices. St. Nicholas is dedicated to the production of new plays and the development of individual artists.

In its first season, St. Nicholas performed in various locations around the city, producing the world premieres of *Squirrels* and *The Poet and the Rent* by David Mamet, and a revival of O'Neill's *Beyond the Horizon*. Encouraged by growing audiences, the company scoured the city to find its current building, and the St. Nicholas Theater officially opened to the public in December of 1975. The first production in the new space was David Mamet's *American Buffalo*, which went on to be produced both on and Off Broadway.

During the 1976–77 season, St. Nicholas continued to expand its audience and artistic program by presenting a five-play subscription "season of premieres" to almost 1,200 new subscribers. The season featured the world premieres of *Joplin* by Kathleen Lombardo, and *The Water Engine* by Mr. Mamet who, in 1977–78, is St. Nicholas' official playwright-in-residence, under a grant from the Rockefeller Foundation. In 1976–77, St. Nicholas also welcomed Lily Tomlin for a pre-Broadway run of her one-woman show.

Another major activity of the theatre is its Children's Theater Program, which began in the spring of 1975 with the premiere of *The Adventures of Captain Marbles and His Acting Squad*, a serialized musical extravaganza about a young director and his eager, but rather unusual group of thespians. *Captain Marbles...* is now in its fourth episode and will tour Illinois in 1977–78, sponsored by the Illinois Arts Council.

Over the past three years, St. Nicholas has instituted several education and development programs, which are designed to encourage young writers and provide professional training for actors. St. Nicholas Theater's professional classes in theatre and dance began in 1975, with a roster of four classes and 25 students. The series now enrolls 2,000 students each year and offers classes in acting technique, movement, voice and speech, as well as numerous special seminars. It is the goal of the company to expand its education program to a full-time "trade school" in the next two years.

The Showcase Series, also begun in 1975, is designed to provide new writers, directors, designers and actors with the opportunity to work together on new scripts. Showcase productions are presented free to subscribers on the theatre's dark nights. For 1977–78, the Showcase Series has been revised and will offer five premier productions, performed by a resident company of 12 actors, most of whom have been selected from the professional classes.

St. Nicholas Theater Company is located on Chicago's north side and is part of the city's thriving Off Loop theatre movement.

Programs & Services: *Professional classes in theatre and dance; Showcase Series, productions of new plays; internships; summer workshop; Children's Theater Program; student, senior citizen and group discount ticket programs; benefit performances; playwrights in residence; St. Nicholas Support Group, volunteers; Sunday at Six, discussions.*

STEVEN SCHACHTER
Artistic Director
PETER SCHNEIDER
Managing Director

2851 North Halsted Street
Chicago, Illinois 60657
Telephone (312) 348-8415
Box Office (312) 281-1202

Founded 1974
David Mamet, Steven Schachter,
William H. Macy, Patricia Cox

Season
September – June

Schedule
Evenings
Thursday – Sunday
Matinees
Sunday

Facilities
Seating capacity 174
Stage   Thrust

Budget
Aug 1, 1976 – July 31, 1977
Operating budget $263,640
Earned income $185,000
Unearned income $ 65,600

Audience
Percent of capacity 63
Number of subscribers 1,110

Touring contact
Patricia Cox

Operates on AEA Chicago Off-Loop Theatre contract.

Productions, 1975-76

Cyrano de Bergerac, Edmond Rostand; translated, Brian Hooker
Jumpers, Tom Stoppard
Seven Keys to Baldpate, George M. Cohan
The Last Meeting of the Knights of the White Magnolia, Preston Jones
The Madwoman of Chaillot, Jean Giraudoux; translated, Maurice Valency
Private Lives, Noel Coward
Benito Cereno, Robert Lowell
Entertaining Mr. Sloane, Joe Orton
Made for TV, Mary Claire Zaslove & 2nd Stage company
Kennedy's Children, Robert Patrick
The Collected Works of Billy the Kid, Michael Ondaatje

Productions, 1976-77

Music Is, George Abbott; music, Richard Adler; lyrics, Will Holt
Anna Christie, Eugene O'Neill
The Mousetrap, Agatha Christie
Cat on a Hot Tin Roof, Tennessee Williams
The Show-Off, George Kelly
Equus, Peter Shaffer
Bingo, Edward Bond
Once upon a Time, Aleksei Arbuzov
Suzanna Andler, Marguerite Duras
Boesman and Lena, Athol Fugard
Vanities, Jack Heifner

Cast members of *The Last Meeting of the Knights of the White Magnolia* by Preston Jones, directed by Harold Scott, sets by Robert Dahlstrom, costumes by Lewis D. Rampino.

Farley Granger and Margaret Hall in Noel Coward's *Private Lives,* directed by Duncan Ross, sets by Robert Dahlstrom, costumes by Lewis D. Rampino.

Seattle Repertory Theatre

The Seattle Repertory Theatre was founded in 1963. As a result of the Seattle World's Fair, a new playhouse became available, a committee was formed, and an artistic director was hired. Thus, unlike earlier regional theatres founded by individuals who led the community in support, the Seattle Repertory Theatre was the direct result of citizen demand and effort.

The current artistic policy has been operative throughout the last seven years. Central to this policy is a belief in the theatre as a "coming together" of people — actors and audiences. Plays are regarded as blueprints for the imaginings of people. The theatre resists exploitation on one side, by those who would seek to use its vitality simply to entertain, while at the same time refusing to permit its repertoire to decline into a literary museum. It also resists those who would use the theatre as a forum for social and political change. The theatre believes that what is good will be popular and enduring, and that it is necessary to distinguish between art and fashion. There is nothing "new" to be invented in the theatre; but rather a continuous endeavor in each generation to rediscover the permanent imaginative values on which theatre is based. This rediscovery process involves a constant reworking of style as a response to the life of the people from whom theatre draws its vitality.

It is possible that there is a strong similarity between the present and the seventeenth century. Now, as then, there is a general emotional insecurity arising from the feeling that changes in the way science describes the world have altered the way in which man can view his nature as part of that world. But the choices open to people permit a sense of delight in the ridiculous, as well as an appreciation of alienation as a sign of maturity — a sense of "self" as distinct from "other." In short, a comedic attitude is always available and is the prevailing atmosphere at the Seattle Repertory Theatre.

The Seattle Repertory Theatre is entering its fifteenth year. The first phase of its development, a permanent place in the life of the community, has been achieved. The citizens of Seattle have recently voted funds for the building of a new theatre to be principally designed around the needs of the Seattle Repertory Theatre. The next phase in the theatre's development may be more difficult, as it may involve the examination of assumptions that have been laid down at earlier times. The attitudes and axioms developed in the stages of a pioneering adventure, when survival was almost the only consideration, may not be the most appropriate to meet the future.

Since 1975, the Seattle Repertory Theatre has served the state of Washington with a new concept of touring called "hub cities" touring. This method allows the company to settle in a town, on a residency basis, for several days and to present school and adult performances of a play from the mainstage season, exactly as it was presented in Seattle. A second company, touring in tandem with the main company, then has the capability of "spinning off" daily within a radius of approximately 70 miles for in-school performances. This concept was enlarged in 1976 when George M. Cohan's *Seven Keys to Baldpate* toured Washington, Oregon, Idaho, Nevada and Utah. An annual summer tour called Rep 'n Rap travels throughout the Puget Sound area performing in libraries, parks and any other place suitable for a group of 100–200.

The Seattle Repertory Theatre finished its 1976–77 season with 22,000 season-ticket holders for the mainstage Seattle Center series and 2,500 for its 2nd Stage program of innovative and experimental works, having presented 400 performances during the season to the citizens of Washington, for a total combined attendance of more than 250,000.

Programs & Services: *Directing and acting workshops; internships; performances, workshops and seminars for students; touring and residencies; free and discount ticket programs; auction; book fair; benefit performances; united arts fund-raising; Friends of the Rep, support group; Seattle Repertory Organization, volunteers; Repartee, subscriber newsletter; post-performance discussions.*

DUNCAN ROSS
Artistic Director
PETER DONNELLY
Producing Director

P.O. Box B
Queen Anne Station
Seattle, Washington 98109
Telephone (206) 447-4730
Box Office (206) 447-4764

Founded 1963
Citizens of Seattle

Season
October – May

Schedule
Evenings
Tuesday – Sunday
Matinees
Wednesday & Saturday

Facilities
Seattle Center Playhouse
225 Mercer Street
Seating capacity 894
Stage Proscenium
The 2nd Stage
1421 Eighth Avenue
(206) 447-4653
Seating capacity 342
Stage Thrust

Budget
July 1, 1976 – June 30, 1977
Operating budget $1,621,837
Earned income $1,172,272
Unearned income $ 381,582

Audience
Seattle Center Playhouse
Percent of capacity 100
Number of subscribers 22,180
The 2nd Stage
Percent of capacity 67
Number of subscribers 2,521

Touring contact
Jeffrey Bentley

*Operates on AEA LORT (B) &
(C) contracts.*

Productions, 1975–76

Jumpers, Tom Stoppard
Scenes from American Life, A.R. Gurney
The National Health, Peter Nichols
A Midsummer Night's Dream, William Shakespeare
Rubbers and *Yanks 3 Detroit 0 Top of
the Seventh*, Jonathan Reynolds
In Fashion, Jon Jory; music, Jerry Blatt;
lyrics, Lonnie Burstein

Productions, 1976–77

The Ruling Class, Peter Barnes
Saturday Sunday Monday, Eduardo de Filippo
Old Times, Harold Pinter
Two Gentlemen of Verona, William Shakespeare
Equus, Peter Shaffer
*Jacques Brel Is Alive and Well and Living in
Paris*, Jacques Brel, Eric Blau, Mort Shuman

Al Checco in Shakespeare's *A Midsummer Night's
Dream*, directed by Dan Sullivan, designed by Tom
Rasmussen. Photo: Phil Koenen.

Barbara Van Holt and Hal Landon, Jr. in *Saturday
Sunday Monday* by Eduardo de Filippo, directed by
Martin Benson, sets by Susan Tuohy, costumes by
Sondra Huber. Photo: Don Hamilton.

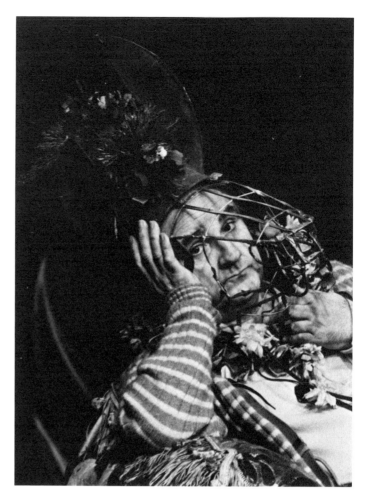

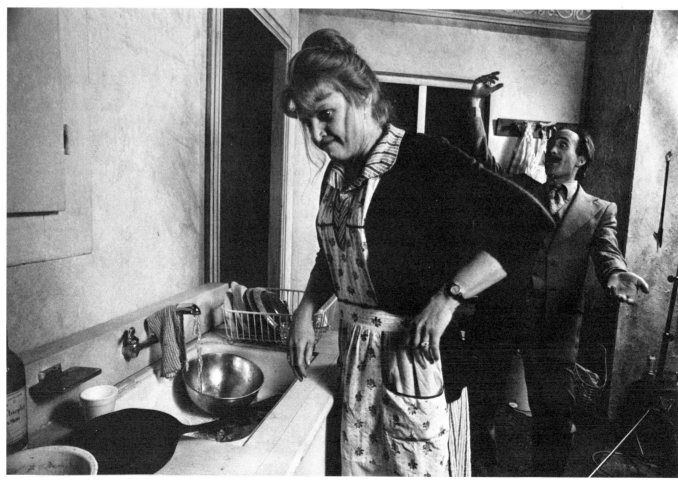

South Coast Repertory

South Coast Repertory was founded in 1964 by David Emmes and Martin Benson, both of whom still serve as artistic directors of the resident company. SCR is the professional resident theatre of Orange County, an area of southern California with close to 30 different cities and a population of more than 1.5 million. It is primarily from this area that the theatre draws its audience.

SCR began as an inadequately financed 12-member touring company, which played bookings in scattered parts of Orange County. In 1965, SCR opened a 75-seat endstage theatre in Newport Beach, California, and, during the following two-and-one-half years, experienced considerable artistic and organizational growth. At the same time, SCR's audience grew to an appreciable extent, and the theatre began to establish continuing community support. Responding to the pressures of this growth, SCR entered its next and current phase, with the opening of its Third Step Theatre in 1967, a 217-seat open-stage facility in Costa Mesa, California.

From the beginning, South Coast Repertory has been committed to the general aesthetic tenets of the resident theatre movement — a commitment to the artistic development of the American theatre, a belief in the decentralization and diversification of American theatre, and a commitment to serve its regional audience with stimulating and imaginative productions of works that represent, in balance and variety, the best plays in the repertoire of world theatre. To maximize ensemble opportunities and artistic continuity, SCR maintains a resident company, augmented each season by artists new to the company and, on occasion, by special artists on a per-production basis.

SCR also presents, in addition to the subscription season, a series of new or experimental works called the Expedition Series. Among those new works presented during the 1976–77 season were *The Daring Dardolases* by Ronald Boussom and Steve DeNaut, and *James Joyce's Women*, written and performed by Fionnuala Flanagan, and staged by Burgess Meredith. SCR was also one of five California theatres to receive a grant from the California Arts Council, which provided funding for a statewide tour of Jack Heifner's *Vanities* to prisons, halfway houses, community centers and colleges.

In addition to its regular season of plays, SCR provides an Educational Theatre Program which, during the 1976–77 school year, benefited more than 180,000 elementary, junior and senior high school students. SCR's combined touring programs presented 440 performances in 1976–77. SCR's Living Theatre Project, developed in cooperation with Orange County secondary schools, offers special study materials and conducts post-performance discussions. The Acting Conservatory offers year-round theatre classes for children, teenagers and adults, as well as an intensive summer actor-training session.

SCR is supported by the Friends of SCR Guilds, the volunteer arm of the theatre. The guilds represent four major areas of Orange County, with more than 240 family members. These guilds participate in the ongoing fund-raising activities of the theatre and serve as a communication conduit for SCR throughout the county.

For the upcoming 1977–78 season SCR has a record 9,400 subscribers. In the fall of 1978, SCR will open a new 506-seat theatre. This $2.8 million complex will house the administrative, technical and conservatory components of SCR and will also include a second performance space devoted to the production of new and experimental works.

Programs & Services: *SCR Acting Conservatory; master classes; performances for students; touring; pre-performance lectures; Expedition Series, new or experimental works; student, senior citizen and group ticket discounts; Friends of SCR Guilds, contributors and volunteers; speakers bureau;* SCR Subscriber Newsletter; Friends of SCR Newsletter; *post-performance discussions.*

DAVID EMMES
Executive/Artistic Director
MARTIN BENSON
Artistic Director

P.O. Box 335
Costa Mesa, California 92627
Telephone (714) 646-3252
Box Office (714) 646-1363

Founded 1964
David Emmes & Martin Benson

Season
September – July

Schedule
Evenings
Tuesday – Sunday
Matinees
Sunday

Facilities
1827 Newport Boulevard
Seating capacity 217
Stage   Thrust

Budget
July 1, 1976 – Aug 31, 1977
Operating budget $573,989
Earned income $508,812
Unearned income $ 96,937

Audience
Percent of capacity 96
Number of subscribers 7,269

Touring contact
Ellen Ketchum

Operates on AEA LORT (D) contract.

Productions, 1975–76
Tales of Carolina-South, Gerald Slavet,
Dick Goldberg, Stage South company
U.S.A., John Dos Passos & Paul Shyre

Productions, 1976–77
*Hoptoads, Hardheads and other Mountain
Beasties,* Stage South company
Green Pond, Robert Montgomery & Mel Marvin

Stephen James and Richard Ryder in *Green Pond* by
Mel Marvin and Robert Montgomery, directed by
David Chambers, sets by Marjorie Kellogg. Photo:
Pat Crawford.

Thom McCleister, Stephen Bordner and Mimi Strum
in *Hoptoads, Hardheads and other Mountain
Beasties,* company developed, directed by Grant
Stewart, designed by Vittorio Cappece. Photo: Pat
Crawford.

Stage South

Stage South, the state theatre of South Carolina, originated in 1973 as SCORE, the South Carolina Open Road Ensemble. In 1976, the theatre changed its name to reflect the increasingly regional and professional nature of its offerings. The South Carolina Arts Commission administers Stage South, with additional support provided by the federal government, private foundations and the business community. The theatre stages an educational tour each autumn, primarily for public school groups, and a community tour for the general public each spring. Workshops, conducted by cast members and support personnel, are scheduled in conjunction with individual bookings.

Hoptoads, Hardheads, and Other Mountain Beasties, the fall 1976 production, toured to Colombia, South America, through the United States State Department's Partners of the Americas exchange. Produced in story-theater format, *Hoptoads...* reflects the rich folklore and music of the Appalachian region. This show also toured the Appalachian area of North Carolina, through a grant from the Southern Federation of State Arts Agencies.

In the spring of 1977, Stage South toured the very successful world premier production of *Green Pond*, a musical by Mel Marvin and Robert Montgomery. Its success led to a sold-out run in Charleston, South Carolina, at "Spoleto, USA," the American counterpart of Gian-Carlo Menotti's "Festival of Two Worlds" held annually in Spoleto, Italy. This same production, directed by David Chambers, was presented at the Chelsea Theater Center in New York in the fall of 1977.

Sea Island Song, another original work based on the culture of the theatre's region, was Stage South's fall 1977 production. Actress-writer-director Alice Childress, a native of Charleston, wrote the play, with music composed by her jazz-trumpeter husband, Nathan Woodard. The play represents a fresh, nonstereotyped treatment of the lives and folkways of the black inhabitants of South Carolina's Sea Islands.

The production of work inspired by the indigenous culture of South Carolina and the surrounding area, has proved invaluable in Stage South's growth. Because many people in the Stage South audience have not yet developed a sense of — or prejudice against — theatre, Stage South believes it has an important opportunity to engage and excite these individuals, who have seen little, if any, live professional theatre.

Stage South Supporting Players, an auxiliary group including such honorary members as John Houseman, Joanne Woodward, Ben Vereen and chairperson Celeste Holm, is composed of a cross section of theatregoers from South Carolina and surrounding states. The group includes active volunteer committees in such areas as actor hospitality, touring, membership and special projects.

Future plans call for turning Stage South into a resident theatre operation with a four- or five-play mainstage season by 1980. Later, the theatre also hopes to develop an experimental theatre, a mobile theatre, a street theatre and an international theatre festival.

Programs & Services: *Performances and lecture-demonstrations for students; Stage South Supporting Players, support group; post-performance discussions; touring.*

DICK GOLDBERG
Producer
MERIBETH MEACHAM
General Manager

South Carolina Arts Commission
829 Richland Street
Columbia, South Carolina 29201
(803) 758–3442

Founded 1973
Wesley Brustad

Season
October – January
March – April

Schedule
Fall
Matinees
Monday – Saturday
Spring
Evenings
Thursday – Tuesday

Budget
July 1, 1976 – June 30, 1977
Operating budget $289,460
Earned income $ 72,350
Unearned income $217,110

Touring contact
Myrna Rodriguez

Operates on AEA Guest Artist contract.

Productions, 1975–76
Ah, Wilderness!, Eugene O'Neill
The Tempest, William Shakespeare
The Balcony, Jean Genet
The Country Girl, Clifford Odets
Design for Living, Noel Coward
Serenading Louie, Lanford Wilson

Productions, 1976–77
Sleuth, Peter Shaffer
You Can't Take It with You, George
S. Kaufman & Moss Hart
The Tooth of Crime, Sam Shepard
When We Dead Awaken, Henrik Ibsen;
translated, Michael Feingold
The Hot l Baltimore, Lanford Wilson
*Jaques Brel Is Alive and Well and Living in
Paris*, Jacques Brel, Eric Blau, Mort Shuman

Ray Aranha and Clyde Burton in *The Tooth of
Crime* by Sam Shepard, directed by Davey Marlin-
Jones, sets by Robert Alpers, costumes by Carr
Garnett. Photo: Alan R. Epstein.

Nancy Sellin, Steven Worth, Renos Mandis,
Christopher Romilly, Gwyllum Evans and Chris
Waering in Kaufman and Hart's *You Can't Take It
With You*, directed by Rae Allen, sets by Lawrence
King, costumes by Sigrid Insull. Photo: Alan R.
Epstein.

StageWest

In 1966, Stephen E. Hays approached Springfield's Chamber of Commerce with the idea of reviving professional theatre in that city. He was steered to the newly formed Springfield Theatre Arts Association in order to investigate the future of the arts of Springfield. Encouraged by the Association's interest, Mr. Hays applied for a grant from the Eastman Foundation and began a feasibility study. He discovered that the area could indeed support a resident professional theatre, but the business community had to be educated to the fact that a theatre is a deficit operation and could only exist with their support. That support was forthcoming, and StageWest opened its first season in November 1967, under the direction of the Springfield Theatre Arts Association. Under the leadership of Stephen Hays as producing director and James Cromwell as artistic director, the first season was artistically successful but financially disappointing, as the subscription goal was not reached and the repertoire did not encourage single-ticket sales.

With a more varied repertoire, subsequent seasons became progressively more successful as evidenced by greater attendance, more subscribers, larger budgets, higher earned income and increased grant support. In the fall of 1971, StageWest learned that it was to participate in a four-year Ford Foundation grant totalling $150,000, designed to help pay off half the theatre's founding deficit. Matching funds were raised by the community and the debt was paid. StageWest has operated since then on a balanced budget.

In its 10 years of operation, StageWest has developed a strong base of audience support. Under the guidance of John Ulmer, artistic director from 1969 through 1975, StageWest committed itself to serving the diverse audience of the greater Springfield community with contemporary plays and at least one classic each season. Also during Mr. Ulmer's tenure, several world premier productions were staged, including *This Agony, This Triumph* by Reginald Rose, *Count Dracula* by Ted Tiller, *The Good News* by Paul Enger, *Masquerade* by John Ulmer and Tom Babbitt, and *Marcus Brutus* by Paul Foster.

Rae Allen, an actress-turned-director, has served as artistic director since 1975. Since that time, StageWest's artistic policy has revolved around the creation of a larger resident acting company and the development of a permanent second company. The theatre's achievements under Ms. Allen's leadership have been many and include a mini-repertory season within the theatre's regular seven-play season; expanded touring, education and community service programs; a second company; and plans for a future move to a new permanent home.

StageWest is presently located on the Eastern States Exposition Grounds, just west of the Connecticut River. The theatre serves a half-million people within a 20-mile radius of Springfield. As an industrial city, Springfield is a melting pot of cultures and ideas, thereby adding new dimensions and challenges to the theatre experience at StageWest.

Programs & Services: *Acting workshops for children and adults; internships; performances and lectures for students; Young People's Theatre, touring; staged readings; student, senior citizen and group ticket discounts; auction; Theatre Guild, volunteers; bar; Backstage, quarterly subscriber newsletter; post-performance discussions.*

RAE ALLEN
Artistic Director
STEPHEN E. HAYS
Managing Director

1511 Memorial Avenue
West Springfield
Massachusetts 01089
Telephone (413) 781-4470
Box Office (413) 736-7092

Founded 1967
Stephen E. Hays

Season
November – April

Schedule
Evenings
Tuesday – Sunday
Matinees
Varies

Facilities
Seating capacity 351
Stage   Thrust

Budget
July 1, 1976 – June 30, 1977
Operating budget $462,186
Earned income $269,513
Unearned income $192,327

Audience
Percent of capacity 70
Number of subscribers 3,600

Touring contact
Laura Stinette

Operates on AEA LORT (C) contract.

Productions, 1975–76
The Verdict Is In, Richard Wesley
The Past Is the Past, Richard Wesley
Acts of Reality, C. Lester Franklin &
Comstock prison inmates
Moments of Loneliness, C. Lester Franklin &
Comstock prison inmates
Fish Eyes and Butterflies, Rebecca Ranson
Can't Stop Laughing, George Myles &
Greenhaven prison inmates
The Promise, C. Lester Franklin
The Corner, Ed Bullins
Sinderella, C. Lester Franklin &
Eastern Correctional Facility inmates
Getting Over, Rebecca Ranson
Choices, Taconic prison inmates

Productions, 1976–77
Aria Da Capo, Edna St. Vincent Millay
Choices, Taconic prison inmates
The Tavern, George M. Cohan
Inside/Outside, Warren Harry & Taconic
prison inmates

Dianne Bivens and Michael Kolba in *Aria Da Capo*
by Edna St. Vincent Millay, directed by C. Lester
Franklin.

Malik Smith, Sidney Rochester and Sidney Grimsley
in *Choices* by Taconic prison inmates, directed by
Nancy Gabor. Photo: Michael Kolba.

The Street Theater

The Street Theater, founded in 1970 by Gray Smith, offers theatre and writing workshops and performances to people in cultural settings where such opportunities do not normally exist. The theatre began as the Ossining Street Theater, serving primarily the black communities of New York's Westchester County. Increasingly, its work has focused on the confined "communities" of the New York State prison system, and the Westchester County Penitentiary. Out of the theatre's first Bedford Hills Correctional Facility workshop, the company now called The Family was developed. It has since received widespread attention for its production of *Short Eyes* by Miguel Pinero, whose work was first produced by the Street Theater in 1972 at Sing Sing prison while he was an inmate and, later the same year, at the Lincoln Center Street Theater Festival.

A number of other writers and actors have found their way into the professional theatre through the Street Theater's prison workshop program, which develops inmates' writing and acting skills. These workshops were conducted on a statewide level from 1974 through 1976, under the sponsorship of the Department of Corrections and the Street Theater, representing the first time this kind of programming had been implemented on a statewide basis by a corrections department. Some 30 productions were mounted by inmates in these workshops, half of which were original and developed through the workshop process. In addition to prison workshops and performances, the theatre has conducted workshops in four Westchester communities, maintained an experimental workshop for ex-inmates and professional actors that develops original plays, and sustained a professional touring company on a seasonal basis. The company also performs in the streets, at colleges, Off-Off Broadway and in other locations.

In the fall of 1977, the theatre will continue to focus its activities on Westchester County, from its new base of operations in downtown White Plains. Ex-inmates, professionals and community residents are working together in a variety of workshops to develop their potential as artists and teachers. Their goal is to provide extensive workshop and performance service to those audiences in Westchester County who have no other opportunity to explore their own artistic resources.

For its productions, the theatre continues to emphasize original plays, developed in workshops, which bring together the best directors from the experimental theatre with the best actors for this process — whether they be professionals, ex-inmates or community residents.

Programs & Services: *Training of ex-inmate writers and actors to become workshop leaders in the community; Community and Experimental Workshops, development of original pieces by professionals and ex-inmates; creative writing workshop, publication of magazine.*

GRAY SMITH
Executive/Artistic Director

10 Mitchell Street
White Plains, New York 10601
(914) 949-8558

Founded 1970
Gray Smith

Season
Year-round

Budget
June 1, 1976 – May 31, 1977
Operating budget $95,135
Earned income $ 2,837
Unearned income $94,122

Touring contact
Gray Smith

Productions, 1975–76
Butley, Simon Gray
Scapino, Moliere; adapted, Frank Dunlop &
Jim Dale
A Doll's House, Henrik Ibsen
Equus, Peter Shaffer
The Magic Show, Bob Randall & Stephen Schwartz
A Little Night Music, Hugh Wheeler &
Stephen Sondheim
Replika, Jozef Szajna

Productions, 1976–77
The Eccentricities of a Nightingale,
Tennessee Williams
Death of a Salesman, Arthur Miller
Vanities, Jack Heifner
Sizwe Bansi Is Dead, Athol Fugard, John
Kani, Winston Ntshona
Elizabeth the Queen, Maxwell Anderson
A Very Private Life, Neal Du Brock

David Selby and Betsy Palmer in *The Eccentricities
of a Nightingale* by Tennessee Williams, directed by
Edwin Sherin, sets by William Ritman, costumes by
Theoni V. Aldredge. Photo: Sy Friedman.

George Chakiris and Kim Hunter in *Elizabeth the
Queen* by Maxwell Anderson, directed by Tony
Tanner, sets by Scott Johnson, costumes by Clifford
Capone. Photo: Phototech Studios.

Studio Arena Theatre

Buffalo's Studio Arena Theatre, founded in 1927 as a school and community organization, is now a professional theatre serving the 1.5 million people in western New York. The largest theatre in the state, outside of New York City, it offers an annual subscription series of seven plays and, during the 12 years of its operation as a nonprofit professional theatre, has presented a total of 106 productions, encompassing new plays, musicals, contemporary dramas, comedies and classics. The selection of these plays is based on the merits of the scripts and their audience appeal. The artistic talent is selected for each individual production, which enables the theatre to maintain maximum flexibility and quality in casting, as well as maximum economy in production scheduling and expenditures throughout the season. An intrinsic part of the theatre's artistic program is the search for and presentation of new plays. The theatre has presented a total of 15 American or world premieres, including Lanford Wilson's *Lemon Sky*, Edward Albee's *Box-Mao-Box*, Anna Marie Barlow's dramatization of Truman Capote's *Other Voices, Other Rooms* and A.R. Gurney's *Scenes from American Life*.

Studio Arena Theatre has consistently attracted some of the country's foremost directors, designers and actors to its stage. Jose Quintero, Alan Schneider, Stephen Porter, Edward Parone, Milton Katselas, Paxton Whitehead, Joseph Hardy, Michael Kahn, Paul Giovanni, Edwin Sherin and Woodie King, Jr., have guided Studio Arena productions. Actors and actresses in the theatre's 12-year history have included James Daly, Colleen Dewhurst, Jon Voight, Celeste Holm, George Grizzard, Tammy Grimes, Jo Van Fleet, Pat Hingle, Betsy Palmer, Kim Hunter and Emlyn Williams. Recent artistic highlights were the presentation of Tennessee Williams' *The Eccentricities of a Nightingale*, which went on to a Broadway production, and the world premiere of Neal Du Brock's *A Very Private Life*.

In addition to its regular production schedule, the Studio Arena Theatre offers a Monday evening American Classic Film Series, special events and children's theatre productions during school holidays. The Studio Arena Theatre School, starting its fifty-first year, is an integral part of the theatre's activities. During the 1976–77 season, 250 students, ranging from preschool age to adults, participated in the year-round professional theatre training program in acting, speech, movement and technical theatre.

Programs & Services: *Studio Arena Theatre School, professional training for students and adults; technical theatre training; internships; workshops, seminars and theatre tours for students; speakers bureau; children's theatre production; film series; booked-in events; student, senior citizen and group discounts; free ticket program; voucher program; telethon; bar; women's committee;* Sightlines, *biannual newsletter.*

NEAL DU BROCK
Executive Producer
CHARLES W. RAISON
Director of Management

681 Main Street
Buffalo, New York 14203
Telephone (716) 856-8025
Box Office (716) 856-5650

Founded 1965
Neal Du Brock

Season
September – April

Schedule
Evenings
Tuesday – Sunday
Matinees
Thursday & Sunday

Facilities
Seating capacity 509
Stage   Thrust

Budget
June 1, 1976 – May 31, 1977
Operating budget $1,276,939
Earned income $ 625,028
Unearned income $ 485,832

Audience
Percent of capacity 65
Number of subscribers 7,288

Booked-in events
Mime & children's theatre

Operates on AEA Stock contract.

Productions, 1975–76
Morning's at Seven, Paul Osborn
No Exit, Jean-Paul Sartre
The Man with the Flower in His Mouth,
Luigi Pirandello
The Bear and *The Harmfulness of Tobacco*
and *The Marriage Proposal*, Anton
Chekhov; translated, Eric Bentley
Blithe Spirit, Noel Coward
Dynamo, Eugene O'Neill
A Flea in Her Ear, Georges Feydeau

Productions, 1976–77
A Quality of Mercy, Roma Greth
What the Butler Saw, Joe Orton
Twelfth Night, William Shakespeare
The Seagull, Anton Chekhov
Sleuth, Anthony Shaffer
A Streetcar Named Desire, Tennessee Williams

Nicholas Hormann in *What the Butler Saw* by Joe
Orton, directed by Marshall Oglesby, sets by Virginia
Dancy & Elmon Webb, costumes by Patricia
McGourty. Photo: Robert Lorenz.

Haskell Gordon, Tony Aylward, Stephanie Braxton,
Alan Rosenberg and Richard Pilcher in
Shakespeare's *Twelfth Night*, directed by Bill Ludel,
sets by Sandro La Ferla, costumes by Nanzi Adzima.
Photo: Robert Lorenz.

Syracuse Stage

Syracuse Stage opened in March 1974, with a short season of three plays, including the world premiere of William Gibson's *The Butterfingers Angel*, directed by founder and producing director Arthur Storch. Since then, Syracuse Stage has produced three seasons of six plays each, offered consecutively on four-week performance schedules.

In choosing and implementing each season, Mr. Storch and managing director James Clark are always guided by the complementary artistic principles of balance and excellence. Each season is intended as a harmonious blend of the finest representative comedy and drama from the classical, contemporary, foreign and American repertoires, as well as new plays of excellence by both established playwrights and talented new voices.

The theatre is housed in facilities contributed by Syracuse University and maintains an active association with the university's drama department, serving as a professional resource to that program. The theatre, with its open proscenium stage, offers artists and audience an intimate and comfortable atmosphere. As part of the Regent Theatre complex, Syracuse Stage is located on the periphery of the university campus, near downtown Syracuse. The city of Syracuse, a prosperous upstate New York community with a thriving cultural life, is not only home to a regional theatre, but to a major symphony, an art museum, and ballet and opera companies. Syracuse also hosts many special events which are sponsored by the university or the city's civic center.

The proximity of Syracuse Stage to New York City allows the theatre access to the large number of professional actors, directors, designers and technicians in the New York talent pool. Although the theatre does not maintain a resident company for the entire season, performers are often engaged for more than one production, which provides the theatre with a growing "family" of actors. Guest designers and directors are selected individually for each production.

Major support for the theatre comes from city, state and federal sources, as well as local contributors. Significant support is received from Syracuse University, which contributes facilities and a portion of the staff, as well as some operating funds. Public support of the theatre has grown at a rapid rate. During the 1976–77 season, attendance grew to a point where thousands of people had to be turned away. In order to accommodate this increasing ticket demand, the 1977–78 season has been expanded to a five-week performance schedule for each play.

The theatre has also been expanding its subsidiary programs. An annual state-wide tour of a mainstage production was inaugurated during the 1976–77 season. In order to fulfill its role as an educational resource, the theatre has planned specially designed tours to regional elementary and secondary schools for the 1977–78 season.

Despite the aesthetic advantages of the intimacy of its stage, the full potential of the present theatre's limited seating capacity has been realized. Therefore, future plans include the renovation of an existing 886-seat movie theatre in the Regent Theatre complex to create a 400- to 500-seat theatre for the company.

Programs & Services: *Apprenticeships; performances, discussions and backstage tours for students; Actors-to-the-Classroom program; touring; Monday night play readings; student, senior citizen and group ticket discounts; speakers bureau; bar; Syracuse Stage Guild, volunteers; Back Stage, monthly subscriber newsletter; Sunday Night Discussion Series.*

ARTHUR STORCH
Producing Director
JAMES CLARK
Managing Director

820 East Genesee Street
Syracuse, New York 13210
Telephone (315) 423-4008
Box Office (315) 423-3275

Founded 1974
Arthur Storch

Season
October – May

Schedule
Evenings
Tuesday – Sunday
Matinees
Varies

Facilities
Seating capacity 202
Stage Proscenium

Budget
July 1, 1976 – June 30, 1977
Operating budget $566,184
Earned income $202,520
Unearned income $374,627

Audience
Percent of capacity 97
Number of subscribers 4,544

Touring contact
Diane Malecki

Operates on AEA LORT (D) contract.

Productions, 1975–76
The Seagull, Anton Chekhov
The Wax Museum, John Hawkes
A Delusion of Grandeur, William Narducci
Jesse and the Bandit Queen, David Freeman
Signals I/II, Jack Sheedy
Seven White and the Snowed Dwarves,
Judy Johns
Old Times, Harold Pinter
A Slight Ache, Harold Pinter
Gas Heart, Tristan Tzara

Productions, 1976–77
The Stronger, August Strindberg
After Magritte, Tom Stoppard
The Good Doctor, Neil Simon
You Can't Take It with You, George S.
Kaufman & Moss Hart
The Unseen Hand, Sam Shepard
Eat Cake and *Almost Like Being,*
Jean-Claude van Itallie
Elevators, Denise Chavez

Paula Neal and Caroline Johnson in *The Stronger* by
Strindberg, directed by Marianne de Pury-
Thompson, designed by Suzanne Jamison. Photo:
Rudy Duran.

John Oldach, Rob Monroe, Julia Ordevahl, Caroline
Johnson and Coleman de Kay in *After Magritte* by
Tom Stoppard, directed by Elizabeth Harris,
designed by Coco de Forrest. Photo: Rudy Duran.

Theatre Arts Corporation

Theatre Arts Corporation is a small professional theatre—small in seating capacity and budget, but professional in the quality of its productions—which has been operating continuously since 1961. Founded by the late David Munn, in whose memory its playhouse was named, the theatre started in a coffee-house and grew from there.

Each season TAC presents new plays and playwrights, as well as established successes and classics. It conducts a yearly playwriting contest, with the three winning plays, two for adults and one for children, produced as part of the following season.

In addition to its theatre activities, TAC owns and operates a private club on premises adjacent to the theatre. Here members can indulge in activities ranging from dart tournaments to pool championships, or partake of "football evenings" with sauerkraut and sausages. In addition, the club sponsors music and poetry nights, as well as play readings, where playwrights can bring new works. It is a place where actors can maintain contact with other actors, and new theatre people in town are afforded an opportunity to meet their peers. The theatre itself, after regular performing hours, is available to any and all performers, directors and writers to experiment with new shows on an independent basis. On these occasions, TAC is always available to assist, and there are no restrictions as to what can be presented.

Theatre Arts is also getting involved in new types of activity. Touring plays are presented at senior citizen homes, recreation centers, schools and penitentiaries. Special plays are devised for children in various age groups and are performed, free of charge, all over Santa Fe County. Spanish-speaking theatre is not neglected, and local playwrights are encouraged to write in Spanish, as well as English, or even in "Spanglish," a mixture of the two which is indigenous to New Mexico.

Theatre Arts Corporation consists of a full-time professional staff, a volunteer group, a board of trustees and a general membership. It is currently searching for a larger theatre building which will allow an expansion of its programs.

Programs & Services: *Acting workshops; playwrights' workshops; performances for students; touring to senior citizen centers and prisons; children's theatre workshop; poetry, music and play readings; booked-in events; student, senior citizen, group and member ticket discounts; benefit performances; playwright residencies; bar; Theatre Arts in Santa Fe News, newsletter; post-performance discussions.*

MARIANNE DE PURY-THOMPSON
General Director

P.O. Box 2677
Santa Fe, New Mexico 87501
Telephone (505) 982-0252
Box Office (505) 983-9003

Founded 1961
David Munn

Season
September – July

Schedule
Evenings
Wednesday – Saturday
Matinees
Sunday

Facilities
Munn Theatre
905 South St. Francis Drive
Seating capacity 50
Stage Flexible
Armory for the Arts
1050 Old Pecos Trail
Seating capacity 200
Stage Flexible

Budget
July 1, 1976 – June 30, 1977
Operating budget $53,020
Earned income $36,188
Unearned income $24,684

Audience
Percent of capacity 95

Touring contact
Marianne de Pury-Thompson

Booked-in events
Mime & experimental theatre

Productions, 1975–76
Androcles and the Lion; adapted,
Aurand Harris; music, Glenn Mack
Angel Street, Patrick Hamilton
The Comedy of Shakespeare; adapted,
John S. Benjamin
Honey in the Rock, Kermit Hunter;
music, Ewel Cornett & Jack Kilpatrick
Hatfields & McCoys, Billy Edd Wheeler
& Ewel Cornett

Productions, 1976–77
The Emperor's New Clothes; adapted,
Charlotte Chorpenning
She Stoops to Conquer, Oliver Goldsmith
You're a Good Man, Charlie Brown,
Clark Gesner
Romeo and Juliet, William Shakespeare
Honey in the Rock, Kermit Hunter;
music, Ewel Cornett & Jack Kilpatrick
Hatfields & McCoys, Billy Edd Wheeler
& Ewel Cornett

Lisa Bansavage and Francois de la Giroday in
Androcles and the Lion, adapted by Aurand Harris,
directed by John S. Benjamin. Photo: Betty
Benjamin.

James McGuire, Francois de la Giroday and Jim
Klawin in *The Comedy of Shakespeare*, compiled by
John S. Benjamin, directed by Mr. Benjamin. Photo:
Betty Benjamin.

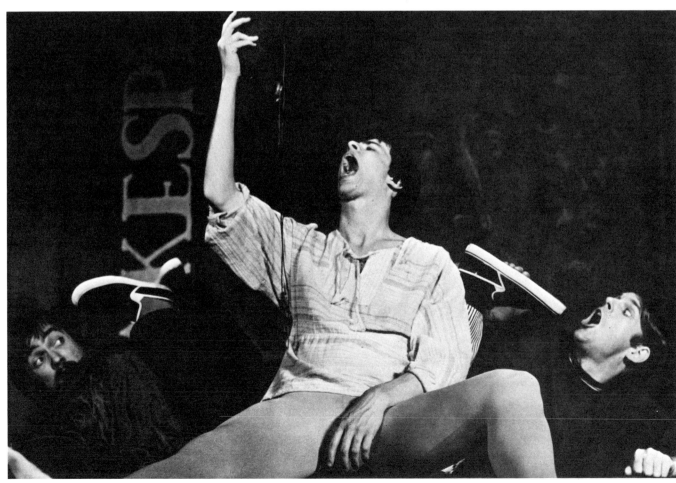

Theatre Arts of West Virginia

In the late 1950s, a courageous group of citizens in the small coal town of Beckley, West Virginia, organized the West Virginia Historical Drama Association to produce Kermit Hunter's play, *Honey in the Rock*. The Association soon grew into one of the largest arts institutions in the state and became the parent institution of West Virginia's resident professional theatre. In 1970, the production of Billy Edd Wheeler and Ewel Cornett's *Hatfields & McCoys* doubled the Association's audience and brought national visibility to the small theatre company. In 1972, John S. Benjamin founded Theatre West Virginia, a professional theatre that toured principally to the schools in the southern part of the state. Mr. Benjamin and his troupe found a home with the Drama Association.

With the return of producer Ewel Cornett to the organization in 1974, the corporation changed its name to Theatre Arts of West Virginia, and combined operations under one administrative structure. The company continued to grow and, from its meager beginning in 1961, when it produced one play at an annual cost of approximately $60,000, the company has expanded its operation to a minimum of six plays annually, on a budget of approximately a half-million dollars, and has increased its attendance from 30,000 to nearly 90,000 a year.

Theatre West Virginia tours its troupe, complete with full stage, lights and costumes, throughout West Virginia, Maryland, Ohio, Pennsylvania, Virginia, Kentucky, the District of Columbia, Indiana and Illinois. In 1977–78, the company will be in production for 44 weeks of the year, with rehearsals in June and September.

In addition to the touring company and the two summer productions presented in rotating repertory, a separate unit of puppeteers serves the elementary schools of the area with marionette productions. The puppet company also plays in libraries, museums, cultural centers, civic clubs and for community arts organizations throughout the region. A seven-week residency is scheduled at the Smithsonian Institution in Washington, D.C., during the 1977–78 season.

Theatre Arts of West Virginia believes that the arts are for everyone and are not reserved for an elite group of citizens. It is Theatre Arts' intention to bring to people the finest theatrical literature, produced at the highest professional quality possible. West Virginia is a frontier, free of artistic prejudices and established theatrical sophistication. It is refreshing to discover that Shakespeare is received as enthusiastically as a Broadway musical; that *She Stoops to Conquer* is as salable as *Angel Street* or *You're a Good Man, Charlie Brown*; that an original play is as welcome as a tried classic. Attendance figures have tripled over the years, reflecting the enthusiasm of the theatre's audience. By far the highest percentage of attendance is the blue-collar sector or middle social stratum of the theatre's community. In addition, it is the dedicated purpose of the company to establish an attractive atmosphere within which its artists can work, with the freedom of expression and creativity necessary to insure the highest possible quality of production.

Programs & Services: *Touring performances and lecture-demonstrations in schools; community residencies with performances and workshops; children's theatre productions; student, senior citizen and group ticket discounts; post-performance discussions.*

EWEL CORNETT
Producer
JOHN S. BENJAMIN
Artistic Director

P.O. Box 1205
Beckley, West Virginia 25801
(304) 253-8313

Founded 1961
Community of Beckley

Season
June – September
Touring
October – May

Schedule
Summer
Evenings
Tuesday – Sunday

Facilities
Cliffside Amphitheatre
Seating capacity 1,442
Stage   Proscenium

Budget
Oct 1, 1976 – Sept 30, 1977
Operating budget $457,052
Earned income $211,446
Unearned income $291,864

Audience
Percent of capacity 33

Touring contact
Bob Kovacevich

Productions, 1976
A Midsummer Night's Dream,
William Shakespeare
The Imaginary Invalid, Moliere;
translated, Robert Johanson
Antony and Cleopatra, William
Shakespeare
King Henry IV, Part I, William
Shakespeare

Productions, 1977
Twelfth Night, William Shakespeare
Othello, William Shakespeare
Measure for Measure, William
Shakespeare
She Stoops to Conquer, Oliver
Goldsmith

John H. Fields as Falstaff in Shakespeare's *Henry IV,
Part I,* directed by James J. Thesing, sets by Karen
Schulz, costumes by Joyce Aysta. Photo:
Imageworks/D.A. Fuller.

Lee McClelland, Verne Hendrick and John H. Fields
in *The Imaginary Invalid* by Moliere, directed by
Robert Johanson, sets by Karen Schulz, costumes
by Joyce Aysta. Photo: Imageworks/D.A. Fuller.

Theater at Monmouth

The Theater at Monmouth was founded in 1970 by Dr. Robert Joyce of the University of Wisconsin and by Richard Sewell, director of theatre at Colby College in Waterville, Maine. It is Maine's only professional classical repertory theatre and, in 1975, was officially designated the Shakespearean Theatre of Maine by the Maine legislature. The theatre's purpose from its inception has been to provide high-quality professional classical theatre to the "unjaded" audiences of central Maine's dairy and apple orchard country.

The theatre is housed in beautiful Cumston Hall, the ornate town hall of the little town of Monmouth, which is located between Lewiston and Augusta, not far off the well-worn tourist path of the Maine Turnpike. Cumston Hall, built in 1900 and on the National Register of Historic Places since 1973, is a castlelike structure with a stately tower, Romanesque stained-glass windows, and ceiling frescoes painted by the local architect-builder. The original purpose of the hall was service to the arts and, over the years, it has housed amateur productions of every kind, as well as a professional Gilbert and Sullivan company from 1952 through 1959.

The Theater at Monmouth is now operating on an Actors' Equity contract, with a summer season running from late May to early September. The company is composed of professional actors, supplemented by apprentices, many of whom are from colleges and universities.

In addition to the 10- to 14-week repertory season, the theatre sponsors an annual Elizabethan Crafts Festival and a touring program to Maine schools in the fall or spring months. Business and fund-raising activities are continuous year-round. The theatre utilizes a permanent administrative office in Lewiston to coordinate a large statewide volunteer group known as the Monmouth Theater Associates.

Programs & Services: *Touring; children's theatre productions; annual Elizabethan Crafts Festival; auction; benefit performances; Monmouth Theater Associates, volunteers; The Bauble, bimonthly newsletter.*

TOM MARKUS
Artistic Director
GLEN COOPER
Managing Director

P.O. Drawer 3047
124 Lisbon Street
Lewiston, Maine 04240
Telephone (207) 782-9784
Box Office (207) 933-2952

Founded 1970
Richard Sewell & Robert Joyce

Season
May – September

Schedule
Varies

Facilities
Cumston Hall
Monmouth, Maine
Seating capacity 300
Stage   Thrust

Budget
Jan 1, 1976 – Dec 31, 1976
Operating budget $130,000
Earned income $ 93,000
Unearned income $ 37,000

Audience
Percent of capacity 68
Number of subscribers 1,800

Touring contact
Glen Cooper

Operates on AEA LORT (D) contract.

Productions, 1975–76

Annie Get Your Gun, Irving Berlin, Herbert &
Dorothy Fields
The Country Girl, Clifford Odets
Silent Night, Lonely Night, Robert Anderson
The Owl and the Pussycat, Bill Manhoff
Starshine, John Clifton & Michael McGrinder
Bus Stop, William Inge
1776, Peter Stone & Sherman Edwards
The Music Man, Meredith Willson
The Fantasticks, Tom Jones & Harvey Schmidt

Productions, 1976–77

Company, Stephen Sondheim & George Furth
Anna Christie, Eugene O'Neill
The Mousetrap, Agatha Christie
Vanities, Jack Heifner
Afternoons in Vegas, Jack Gilhooley
Under Milk Wood, Dylan Thomas
Man with a Load of Mischief, John Clifton &
Ben Tarver
Guys and Dolls, Frank Loesser, Jo Swerling,
Abe Burrows
Carnival, Bob Merrill & Michael Stewart

Scott Weintraub in *Afternoons in Vegas* by Jack
Gilhooley, directed by Russell Treyz. Photo: James
McGuire.

Cast members of *Guys and Dolls* by Frank Loesser,
Jo Swerling and Abe Burrows, directed by Russell
Treyz. Photo: William Smith.

Theatre by the Sea

Throughout its 13-year history, Theatre by the Sea has been committed to providing a broad range of the best of dramatic art selected from the whole history of drama. Not unlike most arts institutions, Theatre by the Sea has wrestled with the ever-present and delicate dilemma of economic survival versus artistic quality. The exclusive production of popularized "stock" shows with broad commercial appeal, no matter how well done, is inconsistent with the philosophy of Theatre by the Sea; yet a schedule of only esoteric, avant-garde or experimental productions would attract few of the theatre's potential audience in the region. For years, through numerous educational and outreach programs, as well as through its performance seasons, Theatre by the Sea has developed a stable audience and financial base, which enables it to flex its artistic muscles and, each successive year, to push its capabilities to higher and higher levels.

Today Theatre by the Sea is recognized as a major cultural contributor in the northern New England area. As such, it is particularly important to provide a forum for new playwrights and to enhance the body of contemporary dramatic literature. The theatre also recognizes the wealth of available established material for the stage and strives to present fresh productions which reflect each playwright's intent.

In keeping with its commitment to introduce the best in original drama to the tri-state region of Maine, New Hampshire and Massachusetts, Russell Treyz, resident director, and Jon Kimbell, producing director, selected Jack Gilhooley's *Afternoons in Vegas* for the theatre's American premier production in 1977. A grant from the Ford Foundation's New Playwright Program helped defray costs of the original production. The script was written during the summer of 1975, while Mr. Gilhooley was a playwright-in-residence at the MacDowell Colony in Peterborough, New Hampshire. During the 1975-76 season, Theatre by the Sea produced another original play, *Starshine*, a musical by John Clifton and Michael McGrinder. The success of both productions — though vastly different in concept and form — demonstrated that the theatre's audiences share the excitement and responsibility that a small theatre can give to an untried work. These productions reflect a direction the theatre plans to continue in the future — the production of new, exciting, untried and thought-provoking theatre, as well as established drama that demonstrates some of the best quality of writing for theatre.

With the anticipated success of a planned fund appeal, Theatre by the Sea will be in a new home by the fall of 1978. A building has been secured, at a location two blocks from the present facility. The historic building, a nineteenth-century brewery, will retain the intimacy of the present 100-seat Ceres Street theatre, offer more comfortable accommodations for the audience, and provide sufficient shop, office and storage space for the theatre's production requirements. The architectural firm of Wright, Pierce and Whitmore of northern New England is developing the design of the 300-seat theatre.

The move to larger quarters is a serious one for the theatre's currently small operation. Great care has gone into choosing a season that will be artistically sound, as well as attractive to subscribers, in the new, expanded space. Most encouraging is the fact that, as the theatre nears its goal in terms of artistic quality, the support and enthusiasm of its audience is growing as well.

Programs & Services: *Acting workshops for adults and children; performances, workshops and lecture-demonstrations for students; student, senior citizen and group ticket discounts; street fair; volunteers; Guild of Theatre by the Sea, support group; On the Waterfront, bimonthly subscriber newsletter; post-performance seminars.*

JON KIMBELL
Producing Director
RUSSELL TREYZ
Resident Director
KATHLEEN KIMBELL
Manager

91 Market Street
Portsmouth, New Hampshire 03801
Telephone (603) 431-5846
Box Office (603) 431-6660

Founded 1964
Pat and C. Stanley Flower

Season
September – June

Schedule
Evenings
Tuesday – Saturday
Matinees
Wednesday & Sunday

Facilities
Ceres Street
Seating capacity 100
Stage   Thrust

Budget
Sept 1, 1976 – Aug 31, 1977
Operating budget $264,253
Earned income $118,600
Unearned income $143,056

Audience
Percent of capacity 94
Number of subscribers 2,300

Operates on AEA LORT (D) contract.

Productions, 1976–77
Woyzeck, Georg Buchner
Cat's Cradle, Kurt Vonnegut;
adapted, Bruce Pribram
Tuesday, Jewel Walker
Killing Game, Eugene Ionesco
Mimelite, Randy Kovitz &
J. Christopher O'Connor

Randy Kovitz and Randell Haynes in *Woyzeck* by
Georg Buchner, directed by Rina Yerushalmi, sets
by Ms. Yerushalmi, costumes by Caren Harder.
Photo: James Edmondson.

J. Christopher O'Connor in *Cat's Cradle* by Kurt
Vonnegut, adapted by Bruce Pribram, directed by
Ken Kuta, sets by Mr. Kuta, costumes by Caren
Harder. Photo: James Edmondson.

Theatre Express

Theatre Express was founded in 1975, by a group of alumni from the drama school at Carnegie Mellon University in Pittsburgh, Pennsylvania, to act as a testing ground for professional actors, directors, playwrights and designers interested in new repertory theatre.

The founders chose to operate as a touring repertory company, producing new and seldom-performed plays. The company also teaches master classes in residencies at colleges, arts centers and other professional and community theatres. Young actors, directors and playwrights work in close association with better-known and more experienced directors and writers, to nurture the development and growth of a true ensemble company.

The company is developing strong support in Pittsburgh, its home base, and plans for a dual program of national touring, coupled with extended Pittsburgh residencies, are presently underway. Tour residencies last from one day to two weeks and include nightly performances, combined with daily master classes in specialized dramatic techniques such as mime, stage combat, circus skills, yoga and vocal exercises.

A broad range of theatre is maintained in the repertoire at all times, to offer the most diverse program possible for both audiences and company alike. The repertoire emphasizes the unconventional, though not exclusively the avant-garde. The ensemble nature of the company encourages a flexible and diverse program of seldom-produced plays such as *Woyzeck* by Georg Buchner, *Killing Game* by Eugene Ionesco, and new plays, which include Kurt Vonnegut's *Cat's Cradle; Tuesday*, a mime play by Jewel Walker; *The Unlit Corridor*, a gothic horror story, written, scored and directed by William Turner; *Son of Arlecchino*, a commedia piece by Leon Katz and directed by Word Baker; and *The Marquis de Sade's Justine*, written by Leon Katz and directed by Jed Harris.

In the spring of 1977, Theatre Express moved its offices and studios to a large renovated warehouse called the Mattress Factory on Pittsburgh's north side. The Mattress Factory was created as a cooperative community of visual and performing artists interested in establishing an atmosphere of critical exchange and mutual support. Art forms such as cinematography, sculpture, weaving, painting and theatre find a positive environment in which to grow, develop and showcase. Artists are allowed to observe one another's creative process, and various joint projects are undertaken combining several disciplines. The atmosphere encourages growth and change in a repertory company that was designed to be flexible and constantly evolving.

Programs & Services: *Internships; performances and workshops for students; touring; student, senior citizen and group ticket discounts; free ticket program; residencies; newsletter.*

WILLIAM TURNER
Artistic Director
CAREN HARDER
General Manager

500 Sampsonia Way
Pittsburgh, Pennsylvania 15212
(412) 322–4671

Founded 1975
Caren Harder, Randell Haynes,
William Turner, Ken Kuta

Season
November – May

Budget
June 1, 1976 – Aug 31, 1977
Operating budget $75,297
Earned income $38,875
Unearned income $47,396

Touring contact
Caren Harder

Productions, 1975–76

Feast for Flies, Stanley Seidman
The Cuttlefish, Stanislaw Ignacy Witkiewicz;
translated, Daniel C. & Eleanor Gerould
The Tragedy Queen, Arthur Williams
Memphis Is Gone, Dick Hobson
Jesus Is a Junkie, Leo Rutman
The Only Good Indian . . ., Mario Fratti &
Henry Salerno
Baggage, Deborah Fortson
Emma!, Howard Zinn
The Warringham Roof, Donald Kvares
Day Old Bread, Arthur Sainer
Whale Honey, Diane di Prima
The Dinosaur Door, Barbara Garson
Cold Cuts, Shelley Valfer
The Colonization of America, Joan Durant
Berchtesgaden, Jacques Levy

Productions, 1976–77

Bravo Isabel!, Ga-Ga LeGault
Seed from the East, Geraldine Lust
New York Flesh and Fantasy, Lee Kissman
Winter Sunshine, Arthur Williams
Twenty Years after the Man in the Iron Mask,
Leo Rutman
High Infidelity, John Dooley
Seven Days of Shiva, Sidney S. Antebi
Carol in Winter Sunlight, Arthur Sainer
The Dinosaur Door, Barbara Garson
*Clay Campbell's Trip with the Elephant
Goddess, Popeye, Eleanor Roosevelt and
Others,* Tom LaBar
The Plebeians Rehearse the Uprising,
Gunter Grass; translated, Ralph Manheim
Turtles Don't Dream, H.M. Koutoukas

Christopher Allport and Stanley Greene in *Jesus Is a Junkie* by Leo Rutman, directed by Ronald Roston, designed by Ernest Allen Smith. Photo: Carrie Boretz.

Cast members of *The Time They Turned the Water Off* by Crystal Field, George Bartenieff and the TNC company, directed by Ms. Field, set by Donald L. Brooks, costumes by Edmond Felix. Photo: Amnon Ben Nomis.

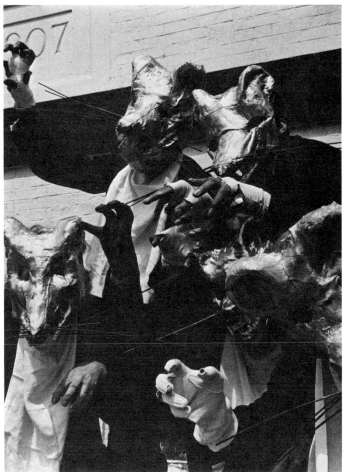

Theater for the New City

Theater for the New City was founded in 1970 as an alternative to the commercial theatre and as a place conducive to the development of talent and the intelligent communication between theatre and its audience. TNC aims at creating a real theatre community, composed of both artists and the people who come to see the artists work, develop and grow in scope, ability and style — a theatre that presupposes a bond between the general public and the avant-garde.

TNC's two primary objectives are to create a community-outreach theatre, physically and intellectually accessible to both new audiences and sophisticated theatregoers; and to create an innovative theatrical experience that integrates drama, dance, music, ritual, and verbal and nonverbal communication. In reaching these goals, TNC's productions invariably use artists trained in the newest styles of theatre, including music, dance, and classical drama as it relates to the avant-garde.

In its seven years of operation, TNC has become a generator of new experimental-developmental theatre works. It provides a cultural center, free of commercial pressures, where playwrights, actors and directors can explore and redefine their work, through professional performances before an audience. The heart of TNC is its resident theatre program, which annually premieres 9 or 10 new productions by contemporary American playwrights, both known and unknown. Their works include full-length plays, musicals and full-scale operas. Productions often employ large casts, original music and choreography, masks and multimedia components. TNC feeds new plays into the cultural mainstream, often providing the original arena for new American playwrights. TNC has produced plays by Arthur Sainer, Kenneth Bernard, Miguel Pinero, Ed Bullins and Maria Irene Fornes.

In the fall of 1977, TNC moved from the West to the East Village section of New York City. The change, however, did not halt TNC's work. It simply created more space for such programs as the presentation of special events. The Chamber Space will replace TNC's Backroom Theatre as a center for new trends, hosting many talented groups and individuals who are exploring the horizons of styles in the theatre experience. Surrealistic and abstract works by writers, sculptors and video artists, using various forms of "daylight theatre" and other multimedia effects, are presented in this space.

In 1976, TNC presented its Bicentennial program. This extensive two-part program, entitled *A Passage through Bohemia*, dramatized the history of Greenwich Village and portrayed Village life. TNC's children's theatre productions provide drama that speaks to the adult in each child. Original musical scores and choreography are featured in productions which sometimes include neighborhood parents and youngsters. A multimedia workshop offers a place for children to create costumes, sets, masks, video and slide effects.

TNC also offers a free street theatre program, which produces the annual Street Theater Tour. Original plays, developed by actors and directors in the Street Theater Workshop, tour the inner city during the summer, bringing dramatic spectacle, with original songs and live music, to the people in the streets, playgrounds and parks of disadvantaged neighborhoods. In addition to the free street theatre program, some 10 percent of TNC's theatre tickets are offered free to ex-offenders, recovering drug addicts, disadvantaged young people, senior citizens and foreign exchange students.

Programs & Services: *Street theatre, acting and stage managing workshops; apprenticeships; children's productions; Annual Street Theater Tour; avant-garde filmmakers series; poetry readings; new music and dance concerts; student, senior citizen and group ticket discounts; free ticket program; auctions; benefit performances; Annual Hallowe'en Costume Ball and Parade; TNC Newsletter; post-performance discussions.*

GEORGE BARTENIEFF
CRYSTAL FIELD
Artistic Directors

162 Second Avenue
New York, New York 10003
(212) 254–1109

Founded 1970
George Bartenieff, Crystal Field,
Lawrence Kornfeld, Theo Barnes

Season
July – June

Schedule
Evenings
Thursday – Sunday
Matinees
Varies

Facilities
James Waring Theater
Seating capacity 130
Stage Flexible
Joe Cino Theater
Seating capacity 140
Stage Proscenium
Chamber Space
Seating capacity 48
Stage Flexible

Budget
June 30, 1976 – July 1, 1977
Operating budget $105,470
Earned income $ 20,970
Unearned income $ 81,092

Audience
Percent of capacity 40

Touring contact
Mary Silverstein

Productions, 1975–76
Orphee, Jean Cocteau; translated, Stark Smith;
music, Teiji Ito
Sun Door; adapted, Dan Erkkila
Primordial Voices, Teiji Ito & Dan Erkkila
Moon Mysteries, William Butler Yeats;
music, Teiji Ito
Op Odyssey, Diane Wakoski; adapted,
Valerie Hammer, Doris Chase, George Gracey,
Robert Mahaffay

Productions, 1976–77
Gauguin in Tahiti, Jean Erdman & John
FitzGibbon; music, Teiji Ito & Wendy Erdman
Op Odyssey II, Diane Wakoski; adapted,
Valerie Hammer & Robert Mahaffay
Fontana, Valerie Hammer; music,
Robert Mahaffay
Raven's Dance; adapted, Eric Bass; music,
Robert Mahaffay, Didi Charney, Anne Sheedy

Kevin O'Connor and Kathy Paulo in *Gauguin in
Tahiti* by John FitzGibbon, created and directed by
Jean Erdman, sets by Frank Marsico, costumes by
Linda Letta. Photo: Roger Greenawalt.

Robert Townsend and Lola Smith in *Orphee* by Jean
Cocteau, directed by John FitzGibbon, designed by
Michael Massee. Photo: Marty Umans.

Theater of The Open Eye

Founded in 1972 by Jean Erdman and the creative members of its first production, *Moon Mysteries* by W.B. Yeats, the Theater of The Open Eye has evolved into a permanent association of dancers, actors, musicians and designers whose raison d'etre is the creation and production of original works of "total theatre." At the base of all endeavors of the theatre's parent organization, the Foundation for The Open Eye, and most evident in the theatre's repertoire, is an interest in those insights into the roots of human thought and feeling revealed through mythic and poetic images. This requires an art of visual and musical, as well as verbal, forms. Thus, Open Eye productions are inspired by works of poets and visual artists and are staged with a fusion of all the performing arts. The company's production of *Gauguin in Tahiti* told the story of an original spokesman for those spiritual values in life and art that are most endangered by Western civilization, while *Primordial Voices* was a celebration, expressed in the poetry and sacred ritual music of the arctic existence of the Eskimo. Both productions were brought to life by The Open Eye through an interweaving of dramatic scenes, dance, musical motifs, and projected light and pictorial effects, justified aesthetically by the multidimensional images to be expressed.

Companion projects of the Theater of The Open Eye all further this kind of involvement. The Children's Theater of The Open Eye presents works in this same interdisciplinary arts style, featuring the exciting use of puppetry. The theatre treats its young audiences as imaginative theatregoers who can respond to the symbolic imagery of folktales from the world's cultures. In another vein, the Foundation offers a seminar series, "Realms of the Creative Spirit," which, under the leadership of Joseph Campbell, has grown into a year-round presentation of weekend workshops, experiential sessions, and lecture-seminars that deal with philosophical, psychological, artistic and mythical subjects from the Open Eye perspective. These offerings are complemented by programs reaching out to the community-at-large. Fostered by the National Endowment for the Arts' Dance Touring Program, the Theater of The Open Eye has appeared in residencies at universities in numerous states from Maine to Hawaii, involving academic communities in its total-theatre approach, through workshops, lecture-demonstrations, master classes and performances. In order to help support other theatre companies that have evolved their own points of view, the Theater of The Open Eye has developed as a pilot project a Shelter Program which, in 1977–78, will provide space to three theatre companies.

The Theater of The Open Eye continues to stress its exploration of diverse artistic directions and to emphasize the production of original total-theatre works. Future plans include an international tour of a newly produced multimedia work for dancers and kinetic sculpture, titled *Op Odyssey II*, as well as a repertory season of new works and old, presented in the Foundation's two theatre spaces facing the garden of New York's Church of the Holy Trinity.

Programs & Services: *Touring Residency Program, performances and lecture-demonstrations to schools and community centers; Children's Theater of The Open Eye; works-in-progress program; Realms of the Creative Spirit, seminar series; new music and dance concerts; Open Eye Shelter, space for theatre companies; group ticket discounts; voucher program; benefit performances.*

JEAN ERDMAN
Artistic Director

316 East 88th Street
New York, New York 10028
Telephone (212) 534-6363
Box Office (212) 534-6909

Founded 1972
Jean Erdman & Joseph Campbell

Season
September – June

Schedule
Evenings
Wednesday – Sunday
Matinees
Saturday & Sunday

Facilities
Seating capacity 145
Stage Flexible

Budget
July 1, 1976 – June 30, 1977
Operating budget $259,201
Earned income $111,086
Unearned income $114,756

Audience
Percent of capacity 60

Touring contact
George Gracey

Booked-in events
Dance and innovative dramatic productions

Operates under AEA Showcase Code.

Productions, 1975-76
Morning's at Seven, Paul Osborn
Old Times, Good Times, James P. Farrell
The Big Reward, Rosemary Foley &
Brian O'Connor
The Cat and the Fiddle, Jerome Kern &
Otto Harbach
The Garden, Albert Asermely

Productions, 1976-77
Jo Anne!, Ed Bullins
Bread & Roses, Marisa Gioffre
The Double Inconstancy, Marivaux;
translated, Albert Asermely
Sweet Talk, Michael Abbensetts
Cocteau; adapted, Roy Finamore
Tuscarora, Joe Waddington

I.M. Hobson and Robbie McCauley in *Jo Anne!* by
Ed Bullins, directed by Carl Weber, sets by Karl
Eigsti, costumes by Mary Brecht. Photo: Mark 6.

Max Cole, Chet Doherty, Vera Visconti-Lockwood,
Dorothi Fox, Glenn Kezer and Robert Davis in *Old
Times, Good Times* by James P. Farrell, sets by
Thom Edlun, costumes by Pat Goldman. Photo:
Mark 6.

Theatre of the Riverside Church

The goal of the Theatre of the Riverside Church (TRC) is to become a performing arts and cultural resource center for the upper west side of Manhattan. To that end, TRC is composed of a threefold program: the Performing Cooperative, a season of four new or experimental plays; the Riverside Dance Festival, a series of dance performances; and the Community Arts Resource Program.

TRC has developed a policy of presenting new plays, new playwrights and new forms of established plays under its Performing Cooperative program, which completed its fourth professional season in 1976–77. TRC continually seeks to present valid, humanistic plays, as exemplified by such past productions as *Are You Now or Have You Ever Been*, a history of the House Un-American Activities Committee; *Short Eyes*, a real look at prison life; and *Jo Anne!*, the story of the life and trial of Joan Little. Based on its conviction that new forms can and should be developed not only for new plays, but for established plays as well, TRC has staged an innovative production of the 1931 musical *The Cat and the Fiddle* and the Marivaux classic *The Double Inconstancy*. During the past four seasons, over 50 percent of TRC's works have had subsequent productions at other theatres. In 1977, a special program was initiated that is designed to aid and train young theatre companies by giving them the opportunity to work with TRC's staff and to perform in one of the theatre's two spaces.

The Riverside Dance Festival offers 24 weeks of dance performances, including classical, ethnic and modern dance. TRC encourages participation from young choreographers and new groups, as well as established companies, but all groups are selected on the basis of high artistic quality. TRC provides maximum support and services, in an effort to create the best possible performing environment at the lowest possible cost to the performing company. The Festival presents groups from outside the New York City area, as well as local companies.

Through the Community Arts Resource Program, TRC serves Manhattan's culturally diverse upper west side, which includes large Hispanic, black and senior citizen populations, as well as international student groups from Columbia University, Barnard College and the Union Theological Seminary. The Community Arts Resource Program strives to serve each of these groups in ways that are uniquely beneficial to each. The program includes instruction and training designed to provide a basic understanding and background for children and young people interested in theatre; lecture-demonstrations for audience members, with playwrights, directors, actors, choreographers and dancers; theatre workshops aimed primarily at the adult semiprofessional, retired professional or amateur artist who is interested in the reading and presentation of plays. The Community Arts Resource Program also encompasses a variety of events offered free to the community, including a children's theatre workshop; poetry, creative writing and playwriting workshops; master dance classes; and a young artist series of musical presentations.

In residence at TRC are the Pumpernickel Players with Norman Ader, artistic director; a black-light dance troupe for children, who perform twice weekly throughout the season; and The Family, a theatrical performing group of ex-inmates, headed by Marvin Felix Camillo.

Programs & Services: *Children's drama, dance and voice classes; creative writing, poetry and playwriting classes and workshops; Community Arts Resource Program, lecture-demonstrations, master classes, performances; Riverside Dance Festival; resident arts companies.*

ANITA L. THOMAS
Artistic Director
DAVID DONADIO
Managing Director

490 Riverside Drive
New York, New York 10027
Telephone (212) 749–7000,
ext. 126 & 127
Box Office (212) 864–2929

Founded 1965
Gertrude Fagan

Season
October – June

Schedule
Evenings
Tuesday – Saturday
Matinees
Sunday

Facilities
120th Street & Riverside Drive
Cloister Theatre
Seating capacity 180
Stage Proscenium
10th Floor Theatre
Seating capacity 84
Stage ¾ Arena

Budget
Sept 1, 1976 – Aug 31, 1977
Operating budget $105,706
Earned income $ 26,297
Unearned income $ 78,485

Audience
Percent of capacity 60

Booked-in events
Dance companies

Operates under AEA Showcase Code.

Productions, 1976–77
Come True!, Fred Gordon
Jenny and the Phoenix, Daniel Mark Epstein

*Theatre Project hosted 105 performing groups
and artists in the two-year period from
1975 through 1977.*

Flora Coker in the Theatre X production of *The
Wreck* at the Theatre Project, February 1977. Photo:
Jody Weiseman.

The Play Group performing *Voices II* at the Theatre
Project, October 1975. Photo: Michael Baish.

Theatre Project

The Theatre Project is a community performing arts center, founded by Philip Arnoult in 1971 as a learning laboratory for Antioch College's Baltimore Center. It became independent of its parent institution in 1976. From the start, the Theatre Project was designed as an experiment in making the performing arts accessible to the large percentage of city residents who do not usually attend the theatre. To that end, no admission is charged for any performance, although donations are collected after each show. By the close of its sixth season, the Theatre Project had offered some 3,000 *free* performances by presenting touring theatre, dance and music groups from this country and abroad.

The Theatre Project serves two main constituencies: residents of Baltimore, for whom it provides an open, accessible place for interaction with a wide variety of artists; and touring artists, for whom it provides a flexible, hospitable performing space, and technical and administrative support. The theatre's current programs are directed toward broadening its services to this second constituency, by extending artists' residencies in Baltimore through other performance and teaching venues.

In January 1977, the Theatre Project began an association with Baltimore with the city's support of a theatre training program for 30 inner-city high school students. This collaboration continued in the summer of 1977 with the Baltimore Neighborhood Arts Circus, which began as a summer program of continuous performances and participatory events for eight "five-day weeks" — one week in each of eight Baltimore neighborhood clusters. The program has continued with expanded training in theatre skills throughout the school year, and further research is being conducted to develop other ways of extending the Theatre Project's artistic resources into Baltimore's neighborhoods.

Throughout its six years, the Theatre Project has rented an 80-year-old brick building that provides studio and office space, as well as two theatres — a large environmental space with modular platforms and an 80-seat studio theatre. Major support from the city came in 1976, with the passage of an urban renewal bill which enabled the city to buy the theatre building and sell it to the Theatre Project for a nominal sum. The city also purchased four townhouses adjacent to the theatre, which it makes available for the Theatre Project's use. This acquisition provides the theatre with an additional 24,000 square feet of space to be developed into a third theatre, artists' housing, and studios for theatre and dance training and research.

Although the Theatre Project has at various times provided a home for producing companies, including William Russo's Peabody Rock Opera, the Otrabanda Company and the Iowa Theater Lab, it has had no permanent resident company and has rarely mounted its own productions. However, with the renovation of its basement into a studio theatre during 1976–77, the Theatre Project began producing new plays and making the space available for long-term collaborations between directors and playwrights. Fred Gordon's *Come True!* and *Jenny and the Phoenix*, a first play by Daniel Mark Epstein, who recently received the Prix de Rome in poetry, were mounted in the studio theatre as pilot projects of the Playwright's Unit.

Programs & Services: *Acting and dance classes; workshops for inner-city students; Playwright's Unit, new play productions; performances and lecture-demonstrations of avant-garde music; admission by donation; auction; benefit performances; Baltimore Neighborhood Arts Circus; member of NAPNOC (Neighborhood Arts Program National Organizing Committee); newsletter; post-performance discussions.*

PHILIP ARNOULT
Director

45 West Preston Street
Baltimore, Maryland 21201
Telephone (301) 539-3091
Box Office (301) 539-3090

Founded 1971
Philip Arnoult

Season
October – June

Schedule
Evenings
Thursday – Sunday
Matinees
Varies

Facilities
Main Space
Seating capacity 250
Stage Flexible
Studio Theater
Seating capacity 80
Stage ¾ Arena

Budget
Oct 1, 1976 – Sept 30, 1977
Operating budget $353,000
Earned income $ 27,000
Unearned income $300,000

Booked-in events
Mime, alternative & children's theatre groups, avant-garde dance & music companies

Productions, 1975–76

Razor Blades, John Schneider &
Theatre X company; music, Sigmund
Snopek III
The Unnamed, John Schneider & Theatre X
company; music, Sigmund Snopek III
The Children's Revolt, Frederick Feirstein

Productions, 1976–77

Oh Wow! Nancy Drew, John Schneider &
Theatre X company
The Wreck, John Schneider & Theatre X
company; music, Mark Van Hecke
Razor Blades, John Schneider &
Theatre X company; music, Sigmund
Snopek III
The Unnamed, John Schneider & Theatre X
company; music, Sigmund Snopek III
Offending the Audience, Peter Handke;
translated, Michael Roloff

John Schneider in *The Wreck* by John Schneider
and Theatre X, directed by Sharon Ott, sets by John
Kishline and Willem Dafoe, costumes by Arleen
Kalenich. Photo: Mark Avery.

Flora Coker in *The Wreck*. Photo: Mark Avery.

Theatre X

Theatre X is a collective whose membership includes actors, directors, designers, administrators and a resident writer, each with a strong voice in all of its activities. Its major purpose is the creation of new plays, from within the membership, plays which are innovative yet accessible. The theatre's secondary purpose lies in its commitment to the community, the city of Milwaukee, where it operates a three-story art center which includes performance space for itself, along with two additional resident theatre companies, poets, musicians, touring theatre companies, dance groups, a noncommercial art gallery, and Wisconsin's only bookstore that specializes in small press publications and local writers.

Part of the company's work in the community is to lead others through the process of creating original theatre pieces. Such projects have been done with ex-offenders and the mentally ill. The company's most recent work involves the development of a piece with multiracial high school students, dealing with their experiences and the integration of the Milwaukee public school system, to be performed for the general public and toured to the area high schools. The company works closely with Artreach, Milwaukee, a division of Hospital Audiences, Inc., by donating tickets, touring performances to institutions and conducting workshops for institutionalized people.

But the main expression of community commitment is performance, creation of original pieces, sharing demons in the light of the times. Tribal shamans exorcise demons by putting on their faces. They may become manageable, seen in the light. If fears can be shared, a community can form, and one feels less alone.

The collective decision-making process involves trying to separate business ends from artistic ends. There are many voices from the company: "Theatre X makes personal myths and impugns them." "The company is a dreamer conscious of the act of dreaming, turning the dream and the dreamer criminal, nostalgic, and absurd." "It is not practical, spiritually or financially, to do more than one original piece per year." "Touring has become artistically invigorating and largely financially disadvantageous. But the company has always, and will continue to involve itself in national and international touring." "We will produce scripts by other than company members, new plays, known or unknown, as well as the classics." "We are also experimenting with film and video." "A reasonable goal for this year is fundamental survival — perhaps by way of a popular farce, maybe a fresh look at *Spin and Marty*." "Anything which seems by instinct right and true. . . ." "In practice, the major problem is to make certain one communicates the right information to the right people in time — it has worked for eight years." The voice of the future: "Theatre X is. . . ."

Programs & Services: *Performances and workshops for students; Integration Project, development of a play with high school students; residencies; workshops in institutions; touring; booked-in events; student, senior citizen and group discounts; free ticket program; coupons; benefit performances; newsletter; post-performance discussions.*

Collective Artistic Leadership
IRENE M. APALSCH
Business Manager

P.O. Box 92206
Milwaukee, Wisconsin 53202
(414) 278-0555

Founded 1970
Conrad Bishop, Ron Gural,
Denyce Gallagher

Season
Year-round

Schedule
Evenings
Thursday – Sunday

Facilities
Water Street Arts Center
1245–47 North Water Street
Seating capacity 99
Stage   Flexible

Budget
Jan 1, 1976 – Dec 31, 1976
Operating budget $40,776
Earned income $17,024
Unearned income $22,324

Audience
Percent of capacity 60

Touring contact
Stephen Wardwell

Booked-in events
Mime, experimental & children's theatre, dance companies, poetry readings

Productions, 1975–76
Cathedral of Ice, James Schevill;
music, Richard Cumming
Another Part of the Forest, Lillian Hellman
The Little Foxes, Lillian Hellman
Two Gentlemen of Verona, William Shakespeare;
adapted, John Guare & Mel Shapiro; music,
Galt MacDermot
Bastard Son, Richard Lee Marks
Eustace Chisholm and the Works, James
Purdy; adapted, Adrian Hall & Richard
Cumming

Productions, 1976–77
Seven Keys to Baldpate, George M. Cohan
A Flea in Her Ear, Georges Feydeau
Of Mice and Men, John Steinbeck
Knock Knock, Jules Feiffer
The Boys from Syracuse, George Abbott,
Richard Rodgers, Lorenz Hart
Rich and Famous, John Guare
King Lear, William Shakespeare
Bad Habits, Terrence McNally

Richard Kavanaugh and Richard Kneeland in
Eustace Chisholm and the Works by Richard
Cumming and Adrian Hall, directed by Mr. Hall, sets
by Eugene Lee, costumes by Betsey Potter. Photo:
William L. Smith.

George Martin in James Schevill's *Cathedral of Ice,*
directed by Adrian Hall, sets by Eugene Lee,
costumes by Franne Lee and Betsey Potter. Photo:
Dana Duke.

Trinity Square Repertory Company

Trinity Square Repertory Company is a continually evolving theatrical organization. Initially founded to serve the greater Rhode Island theatregoing community, it has conscientiously developed new audiences, including students and senior citizens, and increased attendance figures from approximately 20,000 in its charter year of 1964, to more than 100,000 during the 1976–77 season. A major source of new audiences has come through the Project Discovery program, initiated under the Laboratory Theatre Project, which was jointly funded by the National Endowment for the Arts and the United States Office of Education.

As the only professional producing organization of its type in the region, Trinity accepts its responsibility to stage the best examples of theatrical material, including the classics, contemporary revivals and new works. The maintenance of a resident company is a primary feature of Trinity Square and is both a restricting and a liberating force toward the realization of its mandate. The composition of the acting company dictates, on one hand, which classics and revivals can be staged in a given season but, at the same time, provides authors, designers and composers greater direction and insight in the creation of new work. The existence of the resident ensemble, which includes many actors who have been with the company for 6 to 10 years, enables the creators of new work to know at the outset who will bring their work to life. Thus, under the guidance of founding director Adrian Hall, composer-in-residence Richard Cumming, resident designer Eugene Lee, properties mistress Sandra Nathanson, and a host of other permanent artistic, technical and administrative personnel, original material has been developed that reflects who and where we are as a nation and a people, using the specific talents of an indigenous artistic entity to provide maximum impact.

In 1970, Trinity Square and Adrian Hall were presented the Margo Jones Award for outstanding work in encouraging new American playwrights, through the company's continuing program of new play production. Trinity's national and international reputation for its presentation of new work continues to grow, as the company has begun to expand its audience through the transformation of material from stage to television. Trinity's work in this direction has included television productions of *Feasting with Panthers*, created by Messrs. Hall and Cumming, and Robert Penn Warren's *Brother to Dragons*, on the WNET-TV series, *Theater in America*. In 1976–77, *Life Among the Lowly*, a piece created specifically for television by Messrs. Hall and Cumming, and filmed in Rhode Island with Trinity's resident company, was presented as a part of the KCET-TV *Visions* series. The company hopes to continue the exploration of translating stage work to film through the establishment of permanent facilities in Rhode Island where work of this kind can continue as an ongoing program of the theatre.

Without the devoted, sensitive and provocative audiences of its Rhode Island and surrounding New England community, Trinity Square, as it has evolved, would cease to exist. Exposure and recognition beyond Rhode Island stimulates the necessary support which enables Trinity to continue its present level of service to local audiences. A major goal, then, is to balance, with utmost diligence and a 52-week annual commitment, these two demanding, but equally important, constituencies.

Programs & Services: *Internships; Project Discovery, performances for students; dance festival; student, senior citizen and group ticket discounts; free ticket program; auction; Friends of Trinity Square, support group; Friends Newsletter; touring.*

ADRIAN HALL
Artistic Director
G. DAVID BLACK
Administrator

201 Washington Street
Providence, Rhode Island 02903
Telephone (401) 521–1100
Box Office (401) 351–4242

Founded 1964
Adrian Hall

Season
October – June

Schedule
Evenings
Tuesday – Sunday
Matinees
Wednesday, Saturday, Sunday

Facilities
Upstairs Theatre
Seating capacity 485
Stage   Flexible
Downstairs Playhouse
Seating capacity 297
Stage   Thrust

Budget
July 1, 1976 – June 30, 1977
Operating budget $1,010,965
Earned income $ 569,567
Unearned income $ 373,575

Audience
Upstairs Theatre
Percent of capacity 74
Number of subscribers 4,145
Downstairs Playhouse
Percent of capacity 69
Number of subscribers 4,280

Touring contact
G. David Black

Booked-in events
Dance companies

Operates on AEA LORT (C) contract.

Productions, 1975–1976

I'm Laughin' but I Ain't Tickled;
conceived, Vinnette Carroll;
music, Micki Grant
The Ups and Downs of Theophilus Maitland;
conceived, Vinnette Carroll;
music, Micki Grant
All the King's Men, Robert Penn Warren;
adapted, Vinnette Carroll

Productions, 1976–77

Play Mas, Mustapha Matura;
music, George Broderick & Vann Gibbs
The Ups and Downs of Theophilus Maitland;
conceived, Vinnette Carroll;
music, Micki Grant
I'm Laughin' but I Ain't Tickled;
conceived, Vinnette Carroll;
music, Micki Grant
Alice, Lewis Carroll; adapted,
Vinnette Carroll; music, Micki Grant

Neville Richen and Jayant Blue in *Play Mas* by
Mustapha Matura, directed by Vinnette Carroll, set
by Marty Kappel, costumes supervised by William
Schroeder. Photo: Ken Howard.

Jayant Blue, Marie Thomas, Neville Richen and
Every Hayes in *Play Mas.* Photo: Ken Howard.

Urban Arts Corps Theatre

In 1977–78, the Urban Arts Corps will commence its tenth year as a professional company. As stated by Vinnette Carroll, Urban Arts Corps' founder and artistic director: "The Urban Arts Corps must deal with human experiences and human concepts. It must be enriched by drawing on the resources of the entire artistic community — relentless in its pursuit of excellence, and in its pursuit of values that will sustain the artist at times when it may seem futile for him to develop his craft." Throughout its development from a grass-roots training program to a professional company, the Corps has evolved guidelines based on the goals articulated in Ms. Carroll's statement.

The company was established in 1967 as an offshoot of the New York State Council on the Arts' Ghetto Arts Program, in order to train young black and Puerto Rican artists for professional involvement in the theatre. During that stage in the Corps' development, it generated strong bonds with the communities throughout New York City, which hosted UAC productions in schools, playgrounds and parks, and from which UAC drew its artists. In 1968, the UAC was extended from a summer project to a year-round professional program; however, community ties remain important in the life of the company. In 1968, the UAC was commissioned to tour the city by Mayor John Lindsay's Urban Task Force. The following year, the company toured the Virgin Islands with a production of Erroll John's *Moon on a Rainbow Shawl*, before settling in its present home in the Chelsea district of Manhattan.

Although two Broadway shows, *Don't Bother Me, I Can't Cope* and *Your Arms Too Short to Box with God*, were originally produced at the Urban Arts Corps, the theatre considers itself an alternative to, rather than an incubator for, commercial theatre.

In 1977–78, as in the past, the Corps will be focusing on exposing its participants, both actors and audience, to a variety of theatrical voices and genres. This exposure has proved especially important to minority actors, who still face commercial stereotyping which limits access to the broad range of materials necessary in refining their skills.

Material under consideration for the 1977–78 season includes new looks at the classics, musicals, dramas and adaptations. Many of these pieces convey the complexity and variation within what is broadly classified as the black experience, while addressing themselves to an illumination of human issues. Adaptations derived from folktales are attractive to the UAC because, as Julius Lester has written, folktales "give people a way of communicating with each other about each other — dreams, hopes, fantasies, fears. They teach children who their parents are, and who they will become." Folktales also possess an eloquence accessible to audiences on all levels and from all backgrounds. Folk adaptations developed by the Corps have included *Croesus and the Witch* and *The Ups and Downs of Theophilus Maitland*.

Original works in progress will also figure prominently in the season. Production of these pieces is designed to support the exploration and intensive examination of the script by the actors, writer and director. Commitment to exploration extends from rehearsals through the run of the piece, since time and experimentation are essential in developing theatrically viable dramatic literature. The Urban Arts Corps looks forward to continued development as a forum for artists of all theatrical disciplines and as a theatre where audiences feel welcome and involved.

Programs & Services: *Apprenticeships; student preview performances; works in progress; booked-in events; senior citizen and group ticket discounts; volunteers; post-performance symposia.*

VINNETTE CARROLL
Artistic Director
ANITA MacSHANE
Managing Director

26 West 20th Street
New York, New York 10011
(212) 924-7820

Founded 1967
Vinnette Carroll

Season
September – June

Schedule
Evenings
Thursday – Sunday
Matinees
Sunday

Facilities
Seating capacity 66
Stage   Endstage

Budget
July 1, 1976 – June 30, 1977
Operating budget $83,935
Earned income $43,027
Unearned income $36,000

Audience
Percent of capacity 90

Operates under AEA Showcase Code.

Productions, 1975–76
Endgame, Samuel Beckett
The Cage, Rick Cluchey
Strangle Me, Frank Shiras
Dreams, Tom Sharkey
Three Women, Cynthia Baker Johnson,
Sandy Lipton, Roberta Maguire,
Cecil O'Neal
The Caretaker, Harold Pinter
The Benevolent Devil, P.D. Ouspensky;
adapted, June Pyskacek
All I Want, Bruce Hickey

Productions, 1976–77
Volpone, Ben Jonson
Jesse and the Bandit Queen, David
Freeman
The Blood Knot, Athol Fugard
Dreams, Tom Sharkey
Some Kind of Life, Bruce & Brian Hickey
All I Want, Bruce Hickey

Linda Clink-Scale and Bobby DiCicco in *All I Want,*
written and directed by Bruce Hickey, sets by
Michael Merritt, costumes by Shirlie Hickey. Photo:
Daniel Rest.

Alan Wade in *I from the Prose of Samuel Beckett,*
directed by Dennis Zacek, designed by Mr. Wade
and Mr. Zacek. An experimental workshop
production in 1976–77. Photo: Daniel Rest.

Victory Gardens Theater

Victory Gardens Theater was founded in 1974 by eight Chicago theatre artists — Warren Casey, Cordis Fejer, Stuart Gordon, Roberta Maguire, Mac McGinnes, Cecil O'Neal, June Pyskacek and David Rasche — to promote and develop Chicago theatrical talent, as well as to provide locally based, professional theatre for the Chicago community. Located on the upper floor of the Northside Auditorium Building, the facility includes a 150-seat theatre and a flexible studio space that seats 84.

Presently under the artistic direction of Dennis Zacek, Victory Gardens operates four major programs. The theatre actively seeks new scripts for production in its theatre and studio. Of the 23 plays produced at Victory Gardens in the past three years, 12 were original works. Scripts of outstanding merit, which have been presented elsewhere, are selected for production as revivals at Victory Gardens in either of its two spaces. These may be works not yet seen in Chicago, plays considered noncommercial or experimental, or scripts considered challenging to Chicago artists and audiences. Victory Gardens' Readers Theater presents free readings, by professional and student actors, of previously unproduced scripts, to introduce the Chicago community to new plays. The playwright is present to hear the script read and see the audience response. Thirteen plays have been given readings and several of these have been selected for full production at Victory Gardens. The Victory Gardens Theater Center offers classes, lasting from 8 to 10 weeks, in all aspects of theatre, taught by professional theatre artists who have backgrounds in education and teaching. In addition to the above major programs, Victory Gardens presents discussion circles, children's theatre productions, and tours of the Midwest.

Victory Gardens Theater is working to develop talent and audiences in Chicago. Auditions for each production are open to all actors; the theatre solicits new scripts; and each production's designers and directors are selected from available artists. Sizable ticket discounts are offered to students, senior citizens, community groups and halfway houses; and regular ticket prices are kept to a minimum. In addition, the theatre offers its facilities to community groups to encourage attendance and familiarity with the theatre.

Programs & Services: *Theater Center, eight-week classes in theatre arts; performances for students; touring; summer film series; Readers Theater, staged readings; student and senior citizen ticket discounts; free ticket program; volunteers; post-performance discussions.*

DENNIS ZACEK
Artistic Director
MARCELLE McVAY
General Manager

3730 North Clark Street
Chicago, Illinois 60613
(312) 549-5788

Founded 1974
A group of artists

Season
September – May

Schedule
Evenings
Wednesday – Sunday
Matinees
Sunday

Facilities
Mainstage
Seating capacity 150
Stage   Thrust
Studio
Seating capacity 84
Stage   Flexible

Budget
July 1, 1976 – June 30, 1977
Operating budget $164,172
Earned income $107,343
Unearned income $ 42,467

Audience
Mainstage
Percent of capacity 67
Studio
Percent of capacity 50

Touring contact
Marcelle McVay

Operates on AEA Chicago Off-Loop Theatre contract.

291

Productions, 1975–76
Guys and Dolls, Frank Loesser, Jo Swerling,
Abe Burrows
Sherlock Holmes in Scandal in Bohemia, Arthur
Conan Doyle; adapted, Ken Letner
The Member of the Wedding, Carson McCullers
The Crucible, Arthur Miller
Children, A.R. Gurney
The Emperor Jones, Eugene O'Neill
The Contrast, Royall Tyler; adapted,
Ken Letner & William Stancil

Productions, 1976–77
The Country Wife, William Wycherley
The Mousetrap, Agatha Christie
Oh Coward!, Noel Coward; devised,
Roderick Cook
The Caretaker, Harold Pinter
Hamlet, William Shakespeare
Childe Byron, Romulus Linney
A Christmas Carol, Charles Dickens;
adapted, Keith Fowler

Jeremiah Sullivan in *Childe Byron* by Romulus
Linney, directed by Keith Fowler, sets by Sandro La
Ferla, costumes by Paige Southard.

Steven Andresen, James Kirkland, Mark Hattan and
Jeremiah Sullivan in *The Country Wife* by William
Wycherley, directed by Keith Fowler, sets by Terry
A. Bennett, costumes by Frederick M. Brown.

Virginia Museum Theatre

The Virginia Museum Theatre occupies a unique place in its community. Although it has undergone a considerable number of changes since its inception in 1955, it has remained a solid and major division of the Virginia Museum of Fine Arts. The museum itself operates a diverse number of cultural activities, which encourage active exchange between its community and local artistic and educational institutions. The Museum Theatre is a vital part of these activities. From 1955 through 1969, it employed a professional staff of directors, designers and management personnel, who directed amateur performers and technicians. After 1969, the resident company was supplemented with Actors' Equity performers. Subsequently, a training program, open to the community and many of the state schools, evolved as an integral part of VMT activity. In 1972, VMT formed its own Actors' Equity company and undertook its first fully professional season. Under a succession of professional directors, including Robert Telford, James Dyas and especially Keith Fowler, VMT's artistic program has grown consistently, a fact supported by the steady increase in audience to more than 60,000 patrons each season.

VMT's offerings fall basically into three categories. The mainstage season consists of a selection of classical and new plays, revivals or new adaptations of standards, and musicals. Interspersed throughout the regular program, VMT offers a series of International Star Attractions, featuring well-known companies in dance, music, mime and related performing arts, who bypass the large civic auditoriums. Another important aspect of VMT's operation consists of its apprentice and internship programs, which offer training in theatre arts. The apprenticeship program offers, besides practical experience, seminar classes in acting, design, construction and management. This program is accredited on an undergraduate level by a number of state universities, including Virginia Commonwealth University. The internship program is designed for graduate students. In laboratory programs, the professional actors and directors are invited to work side by side with students, in experimenting with scenes, one-acts or new works.

The theatre's budget is based on income from ticket sales, donations and support from the Virginia Museum. VMT receives no state funds directly; however, a program providing free tickets to Virginia school children for special matinee performances is supported by the Virginia State Department of Education with matching funds from the Virginia Museum Corporate Patrons.

A professional regional theatre, VMT sees as its purpose the presentation of productions which link personal and cultural, present and historic, external and imaginative experiences, created through the immediacy of drama. The significance of the theatre's purpose is known, and the process is directed toward the goals it has outlined, but the theatre's direction is also growing in breadth. VMT subscribes to Margo Jones' legacy to regional theatres, expressed in her desire to have the present be a "golden age." She longed to be ". . . part of a civilization which is constantly being enriched . . . in an age when there is great theatre everywhere."

Programs & Services: *Resident Apprentice Program, acting, directing, technical and design training; internships; performances and workshops for students; International Star Attractions, booked-in events; student and group discount ticket programs.*

L. BRADFORD BOYNTON
Producer-Managing Director
LORAINE SLADE
General Manager

Boulevard & Grove Avenues
Richmond, Virginia 23221
Telephone (804) 786-6333
Box Office (804) 786-6331

Founded 1955
Virginia Museum of Fine Arts

Season
September – March

Schedule
Evenings
Tuesday – Sunday
Matinees
Saturday

Facilities
Seating capacity 500
Stage   Proscenium

Budget
July 1, 1976 – June 30, 1977
Operating budget $404,876
Earned income $330,025
Unearned income $ 53,612

Audience
Percent of capacity 93
Number of subscribers 8,985

Booked-in events
*Dance, music, mime &
other performing arts groups*

*Operates on AEA LORT (C)
contract.*

Productions, 1976

Luv, Murray Schisgal
In One Bed and Out the Other,
Jean de Letraz; translated & adapted,
Mawby Green & Ed Feilbert
In Praise of Love, Terence Rattigan
Li'l Abner, Norman Panama & Melvin Frank;
lyrics & music, Johnny Mercer & Gene de Paul
In Spite of All, Steele MacKaye; adapted,
Lou Furman; music, William L. Farlow
The Widow's Plight, Louis Helliwell &
Marion H. Willoughby; adapted, Lou Furman;
music, William L. Farlow
Man with a Load of Mischief, John Clifton &
Ben Tarver; adapted, Ashley Dukes

Productions, 1977

The Fourposter, Jan de Hartog
Wait Until Dark, Frederick Knott
She Stoops to Conquer, Oliver Goldsmith
Once upon a Mattress, Jay Thompson, Marshall
Barer, Dean Fuller, Mary Rodgers
Bus Stop, William Inge
Man of La Mancha, Dale Wasserman; music,
Mitch Leigh; lyrics, Joe Darion

Patti Allison and Ryan Hilliard in *Man with a Load of
Mischief* by John Clifton and Ben Tarver, directed by
Norman Gevanthor, sets by Kathleen Armstrong,
costumes by Nancy Thun. Photo: Lou Furman.

Cast members of *She Stoops to Conquer* by Oliver
Goldsmith, directed by William Koch, sets by
Richard B. Williams, costumes by Karen Kinsella.
Photo: Lou Furman.

Wayside Theatre

Wayside Theatre celebrated its fifteenth anniversary season during the summer of 1977 and continues to expand its programs in its Middletown, Virginia, home, a town of fewer than 600 inhabitants and about a dozen commercial enterprises.

For the newly inaugurated winter series program for college students, the 262-seat theatre draws its audiences from a 60-mile radius of its Shenandoah Valley region. For the summer theatre program, audiences travel even greater distances, seeking the rural atmosphere of Middletown. In the spring and fall, Wayside's touring program travels to its audiences — schoolchildren and young adults all over Virginia and in neighboring states.

The oldest of Wayside's three current performing programs is the summer series of six plays, produced during a 13- or 14-week season from early June until Labor Day. The summer program presents varied theatrical fare, including two musicals, a classical comedy, an American standard, a recent Broadway comedy and "something different." With this program, Wayside is committed to bringing the finest theatre possible to the northern Shenandoah Valley, taking into account production costs and available revenues. Since its opening in 1962, Wayside has produced over 100 shows in its summer program and played to more than 200,000 people. During this time, the summer resident company has hired more than 1,100 actors, directors, musicians and support personnel.

Since its inception in the spring of 1971, Wayside Theatre on Tour, the educational arm of the theatre, has performed in 622 schools and communities, the Smithsonian Institution and Wolf Trap Farm Park for the Performing Arts, and has reached 184,050 people in its short five-year span of operation. WTOT creates original productions with music, intended to be mainly entertaining and only incidentally educational. The extensive teachers' guides and workshops which precede the productions into the schools, however, emphasize the educational potential of each production. WTOT's objective is to train, motivate and demonstrate to educators how to seek and use alternate methods of awakening students' awareness of themselves and their environment. The 1977–78 production, *Once upon a Hedley Kow*, is based on international folktales. Four of its stories are performed by Wayside's five actor-musicians in the "story theater" style and the fifth by the ensemble, intermingled with audience members in a participation-theatre undertaking. WTOT's performances are frequently the only professional theatre to which many of these predominantly rural students have been exposed.

Wayside's Winter Series, begun in 1975, hosts productions by colleges and universities, allowing the schools to participate in a central showcase while furthering Wayside's sponsorship of cultural activities in its community. Initiated with productions by Shenandoah College and Conservatory of Music and Madison College, the 1976–77 Winter Series also included performances by Virginia Polytechnic Institute and State University, and the University of Virginia. Lynchburg College joins this series in 1977–78, which will bring the total to five productions presented during the winter season.

Programs & Services: *Internships; Wayside on Tour, performances and workshops in schools; Wayside Winter Season, showcase for college and university productions; student and group ticket discounts; Le Beau Geste, volunteers; Wayside Theatre News, newsletter.*

JAMES KIRKLAND
Producing Director
BARBARA SWINK
Associate Director

Middletown, Virginia 22645
Telephone (703) 869–1782
Box Office (703) 869–1776

Founded 1962
Leo Bernstein

Season
June – September

Schedule
Evenings
Tuesday – Sunday
Matinees
Wednesday & Saturday

Facilities
Seating capacity 262
Stage   Proscenium

Budget
Oct 1, 1976 – Sept 30, 1977
Operating budget $162,568
Earned income $113,629
Unearned income $ 37,057

Audience
Percent of capacity 55

Touring contact
Barbara Swink

Booked-in events
*College & university
productions*

*Operates on AEA CORST (Z)
contract.*

Productions, 1975-76
More Stately Mansions, Eugene O'Neill
You Can't Take It with You, George S.
Kaufman & Moss Hart
The Price, Arthur Miller
Orpheus Descending, Tennessee Williams

Productions, 1976-77
The Rose Tattoo, Tennessee Williams
Three Men on a Horse, John Cecil Holm &
George Abbott
The Maids, Jean Genet; translated,
Bernard Frechtman
The Lover, Harold Pinter
The School for Wives, Moliere; translated,
Richard Wilbur
Berlin to Broadway with Kurt Weill;
devised, Gene Lerner

Apollo Dukakis and Jessica Allen in *The School for
Wives* by Moliere, directed by Bernard Hiatt, sets by
Ernie Schenk, costumes by Veronica Deisler. Photo:
Keith Scott Morton.

Apollo Dukakis and Maggie Abeckerly in Harold
Pinter's *The Lover,* directed by Ernie Schenk, sets
by Raymond C. Recht, costumes by Julie Schwolow.
Photo: Keith Scott Morton.

The Whole Theatre Company

The Whole Theatre Company was founded in 1970 when a group of actors, directors and designers from diverse backgrounds in the commercial and noncommercial theatre began meeting in New York City to share ideas about ways of working, both individually and collectively. Their concern was growth as artists and as people. Three years later, after an intensive period of working together and sharing techniques, the group moved toward the formation of an ensemble and chose the name the Whole Theatre Company. They decided to leave New York and settle in Montclair, New Jersey, where they created a small proscenium theatre with 94 seats, in the back of the First Baptist Church. A special developmental contract with Actors' Equity Association was arranged and has since acted as a model for other beginning theatre companies.

In the fall of 1973, the company opened its first season with *Our Town*. Subsequent productions have included the works of O'Neill, Williams, Genet, Pinter, Kaufman and Hart, Beckett, Weill and Chekhov, as well as the American premiere of the first English translation of Feydeau's *Before Her Time* and a multimedia adaptation of Pirandello's *Six Characters in Search of an Author*.

The Whole Theatre Company has also become involved in a wide variety of educational and social service programs, including the Arts Alternative Program of creative dramatics in the public schools, traditional theatre courses at local colleges, and a specially designed communications curriculum for halfway houses. The company offers its own classes in acting, dance and stagecraft, and sponsors an internship program in technical theatre for area high school and college students.

The company itself is composed of eight married couples, who collectively determine and shape the aims and goals of the company. It is this sharing of privileges, rights and responsibilities that has sustained the company and caused it to grow at such a rapid rate. There is no artistic director, but the company has chosen one of its members to act as its artistic manager. The role of this manager is to work with each production as the representative of the company's artistic policy, so that each play is consistent in concept and quality.

The company is a resident theatre in the fullest sense of the word. All of its members live in Montclair and have become an integral part of the community. The company has assumed a leadership role in the area because of its concern for the quality of cultural life in New Jersey. The region has responded by increasing subscription sales each year, and by creating the New Jersey Theatre Foundation, a community organization which has purchased a new and permanent home for the Whole Theatre Company. In 1977, the Whole Theatre Company moved into a bank building that is being renovated into a flexible stage theatre. The new facility will eventually seat 311 and will have the capability of being transformed into a proscenium, arena, three-quarter arena, thrust or environmental stage space. With the new space will come a broadening of artistic experience. The company wants to maintain its commitment to the classics, both traditional and modern, while beginning to explore new plays and imaginative new treatments of existing works.

Programs & Services: *Acting workshops; classes in stagecraft and dance; internships; Artists in the Classroom; Arts Alternative Program, classes in creative dramatics; programs in social service centers; poetry readings; workshop productions; student, senior citizen and group ticket discounts; free ticket program; residencies; speakers bureau; Producer's Club, support group; newsletter; Sunday Speakeasies, post-performance discussions.*

Collective Artistic Leadership
OLYMPIA DUKAKIS
Artistic Manager
KAREN ANN SHAFER
Managing Director

544 Bloomfield Avenue
Montclair, New Jersey 07042
Telephone (201) 744-2996
Box Office (201) 744-2989

Founded 1970
A group of artists

Season
October – June

Schedule
Evenings
Wednesday – Sunday
Matinees
Saturday & Sunday

Facilities
Seating capacity 190
Stage Flexible

Budget
July 1, 1976 – June 30, 1977
Operating budget $170,730
Earned income $ 93,950
Unearned income $ 76,780

Audience
Percent of capacity 84
Number of subscribers 1,222

297

Productions, 1976
Heartbreak House, George Bernard Shaw
Orpheus Descending, Tennessee Williams
Born Yesterday, Garson Kanin
Our Town, Thornton Wilder
The Three Sisters, Anton Chekhov
A Touch of the Poet, Eugene O'Neill
Sleuth, Anthony Shaffer

Productions, 1977
Misalliance, George Bernard Shaw
Sherlock Holmes, Arthur Conan Doyle;
adapted, William Gillette
The Learned Ladies, Moliere; translated,
Richard Wilbur
Equus, Peter Shaffer
After the Fall, Arthur Miller
Platonov, Anton Chekhov; translated,
Steve Lawson & Nikos Psacharopoulos

Geraldine Fitzgerald and Steve Lawson in Thornton
Wilder's *Our Town,* directed by Tom Moore, sets by
Roger Meeker, costumes by Rachel Kurland. Photo:
C.G. Wolfson.

Second Company members in *Tartuffe* by Moliere,
directed by Harold DeFelice, designed by David
George. Photo: C.G. Wolfson.

Williamstown Theatre Festival

Since 1955, the Williamstown Theatre Festival has presented on its main stage 154 plays in nearly 190 weeks of production. Originally founded to provide the northern Berkshire area of Massachusetts with a summer theatre operation to complement dance activities at Jacob's Pillow and music performances at Tanglewood, the theatre became professional in 1957 and began to attract major theatre artists to supplement the original cadre of young Yale and New York nonprofessionals who had been the theatre's mainstay for the first two seasons. As the theatre approached its tenth season in 1964, it began to extend its repertoire from light continental plays and the American classics of Williams, Miller, Wilder and O'Neill, to the works of such writers as Chekhov. In the decade since, plays by Moliere, Sheridan, Ibsen, O'Casey, Pirandello, Gorky, Brecht, Pinter and Orton have proved remarkably successful.

Founded in 1972, both as an alternative to the more elaborate mainstage offerings and as a means of touring free theatre to people who might otherwise not get the chance to witness a live performance, Williamstown's Second Company presents productions of rejuvenated classics, experimental works and new plays or adaptations. The company has traveled to prisons, hospitals, drug rehabilitation centers and camps in western New England and eastern New York State. In 1977, the Second Company was the beneficiary of a Ford Foundation grant, which enabled it to produce a repertoire of seven new and experimental plays by American writers, including David Mamet, Sam Shepard, Len Jenkin, Ronald Tavel and John Ford Noonan.

The Festival also sponsors an Apprentice Workshop, founded 20 years ago to provide comprehensive training in acting, directing and production to gifted students intent on professional careers. This program has provided an impetus to such artists as designer Santo Loquasto, actor-director Austin Pendleton and actress Laurie Kennedy. The Festival's Cabaret takes late-night musical-satiric revues each week to various area restaurants, and the General Assistants Program presents staged readings and rejuvenated classics in the Festival's experimental theatre space. The Special Events Series presents Sunday afternoon entertainment, including poetry, one-man shows and musical events, at the Clark Arts Institute in Williamstown. Recent special events have included Frank Langella and Blythe Danner in Steve Lawson's adaptation of *The Fitzgeralds*; one-man shows by Eric Bentley, Geraldine Fitzgerald and Milo O'Shea; and Mildred Dunnock and E.G. Marshall in *Wilder's Women*.

In recent years, the Festival has enjoyed several "firsts": it is the only summer theatre to have a production taped for the Public Broadcasting Service's *Theater in America* television series — *The Seagull* in 1974–75; it is the first summer operation to receive a three-year grant for the training of young directors at Williamstown during the summer and at other regional theatres during the winter; it presented the world premiere of Richard Wilbur's new translation of Moliere's *The Learned Ladies*, and, in 1977, the first production of a new English version of Chekhov's *Platonov*, which featured Joel Grey and Carrie Nye. Since it opened, WTF has been the summer home for some 2,500 artists playing to more than a half-million people.

Programs & Services: *Apprentice Workshop, work-study program in acting and production; internships; Second Company, touring; Playwrights' Program, staged readings and full productions of new plays; Special Events Series, poetry readings and music concerts; Cabaret, late-night musical-satiric revues; student and group discount ticket programs; auction; benefit performances; WTF Volunteers; bar; post-performance discussions.*

NIKOS PSACHAROPOULOS
Artistic-Executive Director

P.O. Box 517
Williamstown, Massachusetts 01267
(413) 458-8146

Founded 1955
Area residents

Season
June – August

Schedule
Evenings
Tuesday – Saturday
Matinees
Thursday & Saturday

Facilities
Adams Memorial Theatre
Seating capacity 479
Stage   Proscenium
Pine Cobble School
Seating capacity 120
Stage   ¾ Arena
Experimental Theatre
Seating capacity 150
Stage   Flexible

Budget
Dec 1, 1976 – Nov 30, 1977
Operating budget $333,911
Earned income $222,350
Unearned income $111,744

Audience
Adams Memorial Theatre
Percent of capacity 75
Pine Cobble School
Percent of capacity 94

Touring contact
Nikos Psacharopoulos

Operates on AEA Stock (Y) contract.

Productions, 1975–76
Dignity, David Beaird
The Merchant of Venice, William Shakespeare
The Wizard of Id, David Beaird
The Threepenny Opera, Bertolt Brecht &
Kurt Weill

Productions, 1976–77
The Wager, Mark Medoff
Oedipus Rex, Sophocles
Twelfth Night, William Shakespeare
Of Mice and Men, John Steinbeck

Gregg Flood in *Oscar Wilde: In Person* by Gregg
Flood, directed by David Beaird, sets by David
Emmons. Photo: Charles Seton.

Colleen Dodson and Gregory C. Williams in *Of Mice
and Men* by John Steinbeck, directed by Robert
Falls, sets by James Maronek. Photo: Jennifer
Girard.

The Wisdom Bridge Theatre

In 1974, actor-director David Beaird and designer David Emmons, both graduates of the Goodman School of Drama, converted a second-floor loft into the 150-seat Wisdom Bridge Theatre. The theatre facility, located on the far north side of Chicago, had housed, at one time or another, a Chinese restaurant, a karate studio and an occult bookstore. In June of 1974, the first season opened with William Hanley's *Slow Dance on the Killing Ground.*

Following that first successful production, Wisdom Bridge gained a city-wide reputation for its imaginative stagings of both classical and original plays. Among the original works that premiered at Wisdom Bridge were Mr. Beaird's *The Wizard of Id,* based on the comic strip by Johnny Hart and Brant Parker, and *Oscar Wilde in Person,* a one-man show written and played by Gregg Flood and directed by Mr. Beaird.

In the fall of 1975, Wisdom Bridge established itself in the vanguard of the Chicago Off Loop theatre movement by becoming the first non-downtown theatre to offer a subscription program. Wisdom Bridge was also a founding member of the Chicago Alliance for the Performing Arts, a service organization which now includes more than 100 Chicago area performing arts groups.

Wisdom Bridge entered a second phase of its development when, in the autumn of 1977, Robert Falls succeeded Mr. Beaird as artistic director. Mr. Falls heads a greatly expanded staff that was made possible through funding by the Comprehensive Employment and Training Act (CETA). The fall of 1977 was also marked by the initiation of a space-renovation program to facilitate the expanded projects begun by the theatre. These projects include a Chicago playwrights' workshop, where local authors can introduce and develop new works under the auspices of Wisdom Bridge; a children's theatre, which performs at the theatre and conducts workshops in area schools; and a program which brings theatre to senior citizens.

The Wisdom Bridge Theatre maintains a continuing commitment to the presentation of both important new works and imaginative interpretations of classical works through the exploration of a variety of acting, directing and design techniques. Everything presented at Wisdom Bridge is produced with an eye toward creating a unique theatrical experience for every audience member who enters the performance space.

Programs & Services: *Apprenticeships; workshops for students; booked-in events; gallery, visual arts exhibits; student, senior citizen and group ticket discounts; free ticket program; Wisdom Bridge Wizards, volunteers; newsletter; post-performance discussions.*

ROBERT FALLS
Artistic Director
LISA LEE MELKUS
Managing Director

1559 West Howard Street
Chicago, Illinois 60626
Telephone (312) 743-7442
Box Office (312) 743-6442

Founded 1974
David Beaird

Season
October – May

Schedule
Evenings
Thursday – Sunday

Facilities
Seating capacity 150
Stage   Thrust

Budget
Aug 1, 1976 – July 31, 1977
Operating budget $53,509
Earned income $28,672
Unearned income $22,103

Audience
Percent of capacity 68

Touring contact
Lisa Lee Melkus

Booked-in events
Mime, experimental theatre, dance companies

Productions, 1975–76

A Thurber Carnival, James Thurber
The Importance of Being Earnest, Oscar Wilde
The Brewster Papers, Marc P. Smith
The Comedy of Errors, William Shakespeare
Dial "M" for Murder, Frederick Knott
The Unrest Cure, Saki; adapted, Marc P. Smith
The Diary of Anne Frank, Frances Goodrich & Albert Hackett
See How They Run, Phillip King
Dunnigan's Daughter, S.N. Behrman
Ten Nights in a Barroom, William W. Pratt; adapted, Richard Kinter

Productions, 1976–77

Send Me No Flowers, Norman Barasch & Carroll Moore
Amphitryon 38, Jean Giraudoux; adapted, S.N. Behrman
Anastasia, Guy Bolton
Twelfth Night, William Shakespeare
My Three Angels, Sam & Bella Spewack
The Lion in Winter, James Goldman
Blithe Spirit, Noel Coward
Angel Street, Patrick Hamilton
The Last Great Nipmuc, Marc P. Smith
6 Rms Riv Vu, Bob Randall

David Hinchman and Kristine Johnson in *The Comedy of Errors* by William Shakespeare, directed by Kricker James, sets by Brian Marsh, costumes by Anne Fletcher. Photo: Terence Finan.

Brent Hopkins and Paul Mayberry in *Ten Nights in a Barroom* by William Pratt, adapted by Richard Kinter, directed by S. Harris Ross, sets by Lindon E. Rankin, costumes by Anna Mae Gravel and Priscilla Eighme. Photo: Terence Finan.

Worcester Foothills Theatre Company

The Worcester Foothills Theatre Company is a resident professional company located in downtown Worcester in the heart of central New England. The company was founded in 1974 with the goal of establishing a regional repertory theatre that would be as generic to its region as the Abbey Theatre is to Ireland and the Comedie Francaise is to France.

Fascinated by the area's eventful 300-year history and by the fact that so many well-known Americans were natives of the region, the Worcester Foothills Theatre attempts to integrate and reflect the background of its community in its work. Therefore, the company produces at least one play each season that either focuses on some aspect of Worcester's past and current history, or was written by a Worcester author. These works, which reflect and illuminate the theatre's region, comprise the Worcester Series.

In addition, each of the theatre's 10-play seasons includes a diverse selection of classics from the American and European stage, both comedies and dramas, as well as contemporary works and premier productions. Presentations have included Oscar Wilde's *The Importance of Being Earnest*, the world premiere of Marc P. Smith's *The Brewster Papers*, Ibsen's *Hedda Gabler*, Shakespeare's *Twelfth Night*, Guy Bolton's *Anastasia*, Frances Goodrich and Albert Hackett's *The Diary of Anne Frank*, Bob Randall's *6 Rms Riv Vu*, and Richard Kinter's adaptation of William Pratt's *Ten Nights in a Barroom*.

Foothills' audience represents a wide range in age, background and socio-economic levels. In addition to its performances, the company reaches out into the community in a variety of ways. Theatre internships are offered to area high school and college students; a Boy Scout Explorers' post in theatre is available with merit badges awarded through work with the company; courses are offered in acting, playwriting, technical theatre and acting for young people; props and costumes are loaned to schools and social service organizations.

The presence of this full-time theatre has been a revitalizing catalyst in the economic growth of the central city. An independent report released by the Worcester Area Chamber of Commerce in the spring of 1976 concluded that the economic impact of WFTC on the downtown area represented $420,000. Economic impact is calculated on the basis of direct spending by those who are employed by the company, as well as by business generated from the audience's use of other services such as parking garages, specialty shops and restaurants. WFTC's attendance has grown from 15,800 in 1974-75, to 31,000 in 1976-77.

Programs & Services: *Acting, technical, audio and design training; internships; Worcester Series, new plays written by or about area residents; student, senior citizen and group ticket discounts; Meet-the-Company Night, post-performance discussions; newsletter.*

MARC P. SMITH
Executive Producer

P.O. Box 236
Worcester, Massachusetts 01602
Telephone (617) 754-3314
Box Office (617) 754-4018

Founded 1974
Marc P. Smith

Season
September – April

Schedule
Evenings
Wednesday – Sunday
Matinees
Thursday, Saturday, Sunday

Facilities
6 Chatham Street
Seating capacity 200
Stage   Thrust

Budget
June 1, 1976 – May 31, 1977
Operating budget $165,195
Earned income $142,516
Unearned income $ 46,500

Audience
Percent of capacity 95

Productions, 1975-76

A Midsummer Night's Dream, William
Shakespeare; music, Otto-Werner Mueller
Don Juan, Moliere; translated & adapted,
Kenneth Cavander; music, Richard Peaslee
Dynamite Tonite!, Arnold Weinstein; music,
William Bolcom
Walk the Dog, Willie, Robert Auletta; music,
Carol Lees
Bingo, Edward Bond
General Gorgeous, Michael McClure; music,
Paul Schierhorn
Troilus and Cressida, William Shakespeare;
music, Krzysztof Penderecki

Productions, 1976-77

Julius Caesar, William Shakespeare; music,
Kirk Nurock
Suicide in B^b, Sam Shepard; music,
Lawrence Wolf
Ivanov, Anton Chekhov; translated, Jeremy Brooks
& Hunter Blair
*The Vietnamization of New Jersey
(A American Tragedy),* Christopher Durang
The Durango Flash, William Hauptman
Mister Puntila and His Chauffeur Matti,
Bertolt Brecht; translated, Gerhard Nellhaus;
music, William Bolcom; lyrics adapted,
Michael Feingold
White Marriage, Tadeusz Rozewicz;
translated, Adam Czerniawski
The Banquet Years, Carmen de Lavallade,
Robert Gainer, Joe Grifasi, Jonathan Marks

Ben Halley, Jr., in *Mister Puntila and His Chauffeur
Matti* by Bertolt Brecht, directed by Ron Daniels,
sets by David Lloyd Gropman, costumes by Dunya
Ramicova. Photo: Eugene Cook.

Carol Williard and Blanche Baker in *White Marriage*
by Tadeusz Rozewicz, directed by Andrzej Wajda,
designed by Krystyna Zachwatowicz. Photo: Eugene Cook.

Yale Repertory Theatre

The Yale Repertory Theatre is a professional repertory company in residence at Yale University. The company was formed in 1966, growing out of the Yale School of Drama, the renowned conservatory for professional theatre training. Productions at the Yale Repertory Theatre are generally chosen from three categories: neglected works of the past that, aside from their historical value, are of special interest to contemporary audiences; more familiar classical work, reinterpreted for our time by means of a suggestive new metaphor or adaptation; and the most exciting and daring new plays available, usually by American playwrights. Over the past few years, however, another area of endeavor has been explored — the rediscovery of certain works of musical theatre. Recent productions have included Bertolt Brecht and Kurt Weill's *The Rise and Fall of the City of Mahagonny* and *Happy End*, and Brecht's *Mister Puntila and His Chauffeur Matti*. The theatre has also combined, for the first time, scores by Henry Purcell with Shakespeare's *The Tempest* and *A Midsummer Night's Dream*. With the appointment of director Andrei Serban to the theatre staff in 1977–78, the company will engage in more experimental projects.

Since its inception, the theatre has presented more than 80 productions, including 30 world premieres by American playwrights, 11 American premieres, and 6 new translations. The YRT offers a 40-week season of seven productions, on a subscription basis. Since 1971, plays have been performed by the company on a rotating repertory schedule.

In 1969, the company moved from its original home in the University Theatre to the Calvary Baptist Church, converted for the theatre's use. After six years' residency in this theatre, the building was completely renovated in 1975 to provide a permanent home for the company with vastly improved technical facilities.

The close relationship between the professional company and the conservatory at the School of Drama is demonstrated by the fact that most YRT members also teach in the School of Drama, and selected drama students are invited to join either the staff or the company following their graduation. Founded in 1924 as an undergraduate department of drama, the department was reorganized in 1955 as a separate graduate professional school. Although the School of Drama is organized on the graduate level and offers the majority of students a three-year course toward a Master of Fine Arts degree, the main objective of the program is to train the students for professional work in the theatre and allied fields.

In addition to the major production season at the Yale Repertory Theatre, other performance activities include a Sunday series of staged readings of plays; a film series; School of Drama activities, including student mainstage and studio productions and acting projects; the Yale Cabaret, a late-night weekend coffeehouse featuring satiric and comic sketches, one-act plays, musical revues, and other forms of cabaret-style entertainment.

The Yale Repertory Theatre is located a few blocks from downtown New Haven, on the edge of the Yale University campus. The theatre serves the greater New Haven area, including the university community.

Programs & Services: *Performances for students; touring slide presentation; Sunday film series; staged readings of new plays; booked-in events; cabaret; student and group ticket discounts; resident playwriting fellowships; speakers bureau; bar;* YRT Newsletter; *Wednesday Seminar Series, post-performance discussions.*

ROBERT BRUSTEIN
Director
ROBERT J. ORCHARD
Managing Director

222 York Street
New Haven, Connecticut 06520
Telephone (203) 436–1587
Box Office (203) 436–1600

Founded 1966
Robert Brustein

Season
September – May

Schedule
Evenings
Monday – Saturday
Matinees
Saturday

Facilities
1120 Chapel Street
Seating capacity 491
Stage   Thrust

Budget
July 1, 1976 – June 30, 1977
Operating budget $1,020,799
Earned income $ 265,317
Unearned income $ 755,482

Audience
Percent of capacity 80
Number of subscribers 5,068

Booked-in events
Experimental theatre groups

Operates on AEA LORT (C) contract.

Directors and Designers

PRODUCTION	DIRECTOR	SETS	COSTUMES	LIGHTS
A Contemporary Theatre				
Sizwe Bansi Is Dead	Gregory A. Falls	William Forrester	Sally Richardson	Richard Devin
The Time of Your Life	Gregory A. Falls	Jerry Williams	Sally Richardson	Phil Schermer
Scapino	Gregory A. Falls	Jerry Williams	Sally Richardson	Al Nelson
Desire Under the Elms	Robert Loper	Jerry Williams	Sally Richardson	Phil Schermer
Relatively Speaking	Paul Lee	William Forrester	Sally Richardson	Phil Schermer
Boccaccio	Gregory A. Falls	William Forrester	Sally Richardson	Al Nelson
A Christmas Carol	Gregory A. Falls	Shelley Henze Schermer	Sally Richardson	Phil Schermer
As You Like It	Gregory A. Falls	Karen Gjelsteen	Sally Richardson	Phil Schermer
Travesties	Bill Ludel	William Forrester	Sally Richardson	Phil Schermer
Ladyhouse Blues	Kent Paul	Shelley Henze Schermer	Sally Richardson	Al Nelson
Streamers	M. Burke Walker	Jerry Williams	Sally Richardson	Paul W. Bryan
The Club	Judith Haskell	Karen Gjelsteen	Sally Richardson	Phil Schermer
Absurd Person Singular	Raymond Clark	William Forrester	Sally Richardson	Jody Briggs
Academy Festival Theatre				
A Streetcar Named Desire	Jack Gelber	John Wulp	Laura Crow	Lowell Achziger
Hughie	Jose Quintero	Eric Head Mary Weaver	Laura Crow	Lowell Achziger
Dirty Jokes	Lee Sankowich	Eric Head	Laura Crow	Lowell Achziger
Misalliance	Austin Pendleton	Eric Head	Laura Crow	Lowell Achziger
Too True to Be Good	Philip Minor	Fred Kolouch	Laura Crow	Fred Kolouch
The Landscape of the Body	John Pasquin	John Wulp	Laura Crow	Jennifer Tipton
Tobacco Road	Marshall W. Mason	John Lee Beatty	Laura Crow	Dennis Parichy
Old Times	Marshall W. Mason	John Lee Beatty	Laura Crow	Dennis Parichy
Academy Theatre				
The Fantasticks	Frank Wittow	Dorset Noble	Corinne Anderson	John McCormick
The Merchant of Venice	Frank Wittow	Ezra Wittner	Ezra Wittner	Jane Eberle Cindy Bonsteel
Of Mice and Men	Frank Wittow	Dorset Noble	Fay Pruitt	Jane Eberle Cindy Bonsteel
Sticks and Bones	Frank Wittow	Dorset Noble	Fay Pruitt	Jane Eberle
America Hurrah	Frank Wittow	Dorset Noble	Abigail Murray	Jane Eberle Lorraine Lombardy
As You Like It	Frank Wittow	Dorset Noble	Suzan Anderson	Jane Eberle
Waiting for Godot	Frank Wittow	Dorset Noble	Cathy Brown Sammy Knox	Lorraine Lombardy
The Blood Knot	Frank Wittow	Dorset Noble	Margie Murch	Jane Eberle
Marat/Sade	Frank Wittow	Dorset Noble	Abigail Murray	Lorraine Lombardy
The Acting Company				
Arms and the Man	Edward Payson Call	John Lee Beatty	John David Ridge	David F. Segal
The Robber Bridegroom	Gerald Freedman	Douglas W. Schmidt	Jeanne Button	David F. Segal
The Time of Your Life	Jack O'Brien	Douglas W. Schmidt	Nancy Potts	David F. Segal
She Stoops to Conquer	Stephen Porter	Robert U. Taylor	Jane Greenwood	David F. Segal
The Way of the World	Norman Ayrton	Douglas W. Schmidt	Barbara Matera	David F. Segal
Diary of Adam and Eve	Gerald Gutierrez			David F. Segal
The Three Sisters	Boris Tumarin	Douglas W. Schmidt	John David Ridge	David F. Segal
Edward II	Ellis Rabb	Douglas W. Schmidt	Nancy Potts	David F. Segal
The Taming of the Shrew	Gerald Gutierrez	Douglas W. Schmidt	Carrie Robbins	David F. Segal
Camino Real	Gerald Freedman	Douglas W. Schmidt	Jeanne Button	David F. Segal
The Kitchen	Boris Tumarin	Douglas W. Schmidt	John David Ridge	David F. Segal
Love's Labour's Lost	Gerald Freedman	Douglas W. Schmidt	Theoni V. Aldredge	David F. Segal
The Duck Variations	Gerald Gutierrez	John Lee Beatty	John David Ridge	David F. Segal
Rosemary	Gerald Gutierrez	John Lee Beatty	John David Ridge	David F. Segal
Actors Theatre of Louisville				
Arms and the Man	Jon Jory	Paul Owen	Kurt Wilhelm	Geoffrey T. Cunningham
The Hot l Baltimore	Charles Kerr	Grady Larkins	Kurt Wilhelm	Geoffrey T. Cunningham
Ten Little Indians	Adale O'Brien	Paul Owen	Kurt Wilhelm	Geoffrey T. Cunningham
Oedipus the King	Jon Jory	Paul Owen	Kurt Wilhelm	Geoffrey T. Cunningham
Scapino	Christopher Murney	Anne A. Gibson	Kurt Wilhelm	Geoffrey T. Cunningham
The Last Meeting of the Knights of the White Magnolia	Jon Jory	Paul Owen	Kurt Wilhelm	Paul Owen
The Sunshine Boys	Clifford Ammon	Paul Owen	Kurt Wilhelm	Vincent Faust
Dear Liar	Ray Fry	Paul Owen	Kurt Wilhelm	Geoffrey T. Cunningham
Scott and Zelda	Elizabeth Ives	Kurt Wilhelm	Kurt Wilhelm	Geoffrey T. Cunningham
Measure for Measure	Charles Kerr	Paul Owen	Kurt Wilhelm	Paul Owen
The Sea Horse	Charles Kerr	Paul Owen	Kurt Wilhelm	Geoffrey T. Cunningham
The Best Man	Jon Jory	Paul Owen	Kurt Wilhelm	Vincent Faust

PRODUCTION	DIRECTOR	SETS	COSTUMES	LIGHTS
Sexual Perversity in Chicago	Charles Kerr	Paul Owen	Kurt Wilhelm	Vincent Faust
Vanities	Charles Kerr	Paul Owen	Kurt Wilhelm	Vincent Faust
Reunion	Ray Fry	Paul Owen	Kurt Wilhelm	Vincent Faust
Medal of Honor Rag	Elizabeth Ives	Paul Owen	Kurt Wilhelm	Vincent Faust
Tea with Dick and Jerry	Eric A. Brogger			
Much Ado About Nothing	Jon Jory	Paul Owen	Kurt Wilhelm	Paul Owen
A Christmas Carol	Robert Brewer	Richard Kent Wilcox	Kurt Wilhelm	Vincent Faust
The Resistable Rise of Arturo Ui	Jon Jory	Paul Owen	Kurt Wilhelm	Ronald Wallace
The Matchmaker	Jon Jory	Paul Owen	Paul Owen	Vincent Faust
Who's Afraid of Virginia Woolf?	Daniel Sullivan	Paul Owen	Kurt Wilhelm	Vincent Faust
The Diary of Anne Frank	Israel Hicks	Paul Owen	Kurt Wilhelm	James E. Stephens
The Gin Game	Steven Robman	Paul Owen	Kurt Wilhelm	Paul Owen
Indulgences in the Louisville Harem	Patrick Henry	Paul Owen	Kurt Wilhelm	Paul Owen
Table Manners	Jon Jory	Richard Gould	Kurt Wilhelm	Paul Owen
Round and Round the Garden	Elizabeth Ives	Richard Gould	Kurt Wilhelm	Paul Owen
The Rainmaker	Ken Frankel	Paul Owen	Kurt Wilhelm	Paul Owen

Alaska Repertory Theatre

PRODUCTION	DIRECTOR	SETS	COSTUMES	LIGHTS
Scapino	Robert J. Farley	Jamie Greenleaf	Jamie Greenleaf	E. Allen Kent
Private Lives	Lee Salisbury	Jamie Greenleaf	Jamie Greenleaf	E. Allen Kent
Clarence Darrow	Robert J. Farley	Jamie Greenleaf	Jamie Greenleaf	E. Allen Kent

Alley Theatre

PRODUCTION	DIRECTOR	SETS	COSTUMES	LIGHTS
Indians	Beth Sanford	William Trotman	Barbara C. Cox	Jonathan Duff
The Front Page	Robert E. Leonard	John Kenny	Michael Olich	Matthew Grant
The Last Meeting of the Knights of the White Magnolia	Robert E. Leonard	John Kenny	Michael Olich	Matthew Grant
Juno and the Paycock	Beth Sanford	Michael Olich	Barbara C. Cox	Jonathan Duff
The Show-Off	Robert E. Leonard	John Kenny	Barbara C. Cox	Jonathan Duff
The Cocktail Party	Nina Vance	William Trotman	Barbara C. Cox	Jonathan Duff
Tiny Alice	Nina Vance	William Trotman John Kenny	Barbara C. Cox	Matthew Grant
A Christmas Carol	William Trotman	William Trotman		Barry Reed
Scenes from American Life	William Trotman		Barbara C. Cox	
Purgatory	Robert Symonds			Jonathan Duff
The Harmful Effects of Tobacco	Robert Symonds			Jonathan Duff
The Sty of the Blind Pig	Beth Sanford	Matthew Grant	Michael Olich	Jonathan Duff
You Never Can Tell	Ted Follows	Matthew Grant	Michael Olich	Jonathan Duff
The Corn Is Green	Leslie Yeo	John Kenny	Julie Jackson	Jonathan Duff
The Runner Stumbles	Beth Sanford	Matthew Grant	Michael Olich	Jonathan Duff
How the Other Half Loves	Pat Brown	Michael Olich	Julie Jackson	Barry Reed
The Collection	Nina Vance	John Kenny	Julie Jackson	Matthew Grant
The Dock Brief	Nina Vance	John Kenny	Julie Jackson	Matthew Grant
Loot	Beth Sanford	Michael Olich	Michael Olich	Matthew Grant
Endgame	Robert Symonds	John Kenny	Julie Jackson	Matthew Grant

Alliance Theatre Company

PRODUCTION	DIRECTOR	SETS	COSTUMES	LIGHTS
The Last Meeting of the Knights of the White Magnolia	Fred Chappell	Michael Stauffer	Patricia McMahon	Michael Layton
The Miracle Worker	Fred Chappell	Michael Stauffer	Patricia McMahon	Michael Layton
To Be Young, Gifted and Black	Tina Sattin	Michael Stauffer	Patricia McMahon Patricia Sweet	Michael Layton
The Skin of Our Teeth	Fred Chappell	Michael Stauffer	Patricia McMahon	Michael Layton
The Member of the Wedding	Fred Chappell	Michael Layton	Patricia McMahon	Carol Graebner
The Tempest	Fred Chappell	Michael Stauffer		Cassandra Henning
Scapino	Fred Chappell	Michael Stauffer	Martha Kelly	Michael Stauffer
Hedda Gabler	Kent Paul	Philipp Jung	Martha Kelly	Michael Stauffer
Come Back to the 5 and Dime, Jimmy Dean, Jimmy Dean	Fred Chappell	Michael Stauffer	Martha Kelly	Michael Stauffer
Misalliance	Harold Scott	Philipp Jung	Martha Kelly	Michael Stauffer
All the Way Home	Fred Chappell	Michael Stauffer	Michael Stauffer	Cassandra Henning
Henry IV, Part I	Fred Chappell			
Who's Afraid of Virginia Woolf?	Charles Kerr			

AMAS Repertory Theatre

PRODUCTION	DIRECTOR	SETS	COSTUMES	LIGHTS
The Ragtime Blues	Jay Binder	Jeffrey Schissler	Patricia McGourty	Phillip A. Evola
The Big Knife	Rosetta LeNoire	Arthur Soyk	Kenneth McPherson	Daniel Snyder
Godsong	Tad Truesdale	Arthur Soyk		Vernon Enoch
Bojangles!	Ira Cirker	Michael Meadows	Sydney Lee Brooks	Paul Sullivan
The Mikado AMAS	Irving Vincent	Michael Meadows	Bruce Beckwith	Paul Sullivan
Save the Seeds Darling	Arthur Whitelaw	Michael Meadows	David Graden	Paul Sullivan
Come Laugh & Cry with Langston Hughes	Rosetta LeNoire	Michael Meadows	Bruce Beckwith	Paul Sullivan

American Conservatory Theatre

PRODUCTION	DIRECTOR	SETS	COSTUMES	LIGHTS
Tiny Alice	William Ball	Ralph Funicello	Robert Morgan	F. Mitchell Dana
The Matchmaker	Laird Williamson	Richard Seger	Robert Fletcher	F. Mitchell Dana
Desire Under the Elms	Allen Fletcher	Robert Blackman	Cathy Edwards	Dirk Epperson
General Gorgeous	Edward Hastings	Ralph Funicello	Robert Morgan	F. Mitchell Dana
The Merry Wives of Windsor	Jon Jory	Robert Blackman	Dorothy Jeakins	F. Mitchell Dana
This Is (an Entertainment)	Allen Fletcher	John Jensen	Robert Morgan	F. Mitchell Dana
Equus	William Ball	Robert Blackman	Robert Morgan	F. Mitchell Dana
Peer Gynt	Allen Fletcher	Ralph Funicello	Robert Blackman	Dirk Epperson

PRODUCTION	DIRECTOR	SETS	COSTUMES	LIGHTS
The Taming of the Shrew	William Ball	Ralph Funicello	Robert Fletcher	F. Mitchell Dana
Cyrano de Bergerac	William Ball	Robert Blackman	Robert Fletcher	F. Mitchell Dana
Othello	Allen Fletcher	Richard Seger	Robert Fletcher	F. Mitchell Dana
Man and Superman	Jack O'Brien	Robert Dahlstrom	Robert Morgan	F. Mitchell Dana
A Christmas Carol	Laird Williamson	Robert Blackman	Robert Morgan	F. Mitchell Dana
Knock Knock	Tom Moore	Robert Dahlstrom	Robert Blackman	Dirk Epperson
The Bourgeois Gentleman	William Ball	Richard Seger	Robert Fletcher	Richard Devin
Valentin and Valentina	Edward Hastings	Robert Blackman	Cathy Edwards	F. Mitchell Dana
Travesties	Nagle Jackson	John Jensen	Robert Morgan	Dirk Epperson

American Place Theatre				
Gorky	Dennis Rosa	David Jenkins	Shadow	Roger Morgan
Every Night When the Sun Goes Down	Gilbert Moses	Kert Lundell	Judy Dearing	Richard Nelson
The Old Glory		John Wulp	Willa Kim	Neil Peter Jampolis
Endecott and the Red Cross	Brian Murray			
My Kinsman, Major Molineaux	Brian Murray			
Benito Cereno	Austin Pendleton			
Jack Gelber's New Play: Rehearsal	Jack Gelber			Edward M. Greenberg
Domino Courts and Comanche Cafe	Barnet Kellman	Henry Millman	Carol Oditz	Edward M. Greenberg
Isadora Duncan Sleeps with the Russian Navy	Tom Haas		Bobbie Owen	
Cold Storage	Joel Zwick	Kert Lundell	Ruth Morley	Edward M. Greenberg

Arena Stage				
Long Day's Journey Into Night	Martin Fried	Karl Eigsti	Gwynne Clark	William Mintzer
An Enemy of the People	Zelda Fichandler	Grady Larkins	Marjorie Slaiman	Hugh Lester
Once in a Lifetime	Tom Moore	Karl Eigsti	Carol Luiken	Allen Hughes
The Tot Family	Edward Payson Call	John Lee Beatty	Marjorie Slaiman	Hugh Lester
Heartbreak House	John Pasquin	Santo Loquasto	Marjorie Slaiman	William Mintzer
Waiting for Godot	Gene Lesser	Ming Cho Lee	Marjorie Slaiman	Hugh Lester
Dandelion Wine	Martin Fried	Karl Eigsti	Marjorie Slaiman	William Mintzer
Death of a Salesman	Zelda Fichandler	Karl Eigsti	Marjorie Slaiman	Hugh Lester
The Front Page	Edward Payson Call	Karl Eigsti	Marjorie Slaiman	Hugh Lester
Our Town	Alan Schneider	Ming Cho Lee	Marjorie Slaiman	Hugh Lester
Saint Joan	Martin Fried	Karl Eigsti	Marjorie Slaiman	Hugh Lester
Saturday Sunday Monday	Norman Gevanthor	Karl Eigsti	Marjorie Slaiman	William Mintzer
Streamers	David Chambers	Tony Straiges	Jennifer von Mayrhauser	William Mintzer
The Autumn Garden	Martin Fried	Grady Larkins	Marjorie Slaiman	Hugh Lester
Catsplay	Edward Payson Call	Karl Eigsti	Linda Fisher	Hugh Lester
The Lower Depths	Liviu Ciulei	Santo Loquasto	Marjorie Slaiman	Hugh Lester
A History of the American Film	David Chambers	Tony Straiges	Marjorie Slaiman	William Mintzer
Forever Yours, Marie-Lou	David Chambers	Sally Cunningham	Marjorie Slaiman	Hugh Lester
Play and That Time and Footfalls	Alan Schneider	Zack Brown	Zack Brown	William Mintzer

Arizona Civic Theatre				
The Dybbuk	Sandy Rosenthal	Reagan Cook	William Damron, Jr.	Russell Stagg
The Sunshine Boys	Arthur Loew	Cynthia Beeman	William Damron, Jr.	Russell Stagg
Rashomon	Sandy Rosenthal	Reagan Cook	William Damron, Jr.	Russell Stagg
Diamond Studs	Sandy Rosenthal	Reagan Cook	Sandra Mourey	Russell Stagg
The Sea Horse	David Gardiner	Johnny Walker	Sandra Mourey	Russell Stagg
The Devil's Disciple	Robert Brewer	Reagan Cook	Sandra Mourey	Russell Stagg
In Fashion	David Pursley	Reagan Cook	Sandra Mourey	Dan T. Willoughby
Sizwe Bansi Is Dead	Dean Irby	John Walker, Cynthia Beeman	Sandra Mourey	Dan T. Willoughby
Ah, Wilderness!	David Pursley	Reagan Cook	Sandra Mourey	Dan T. Willoughby
Hamlet	Robert Ellenstein	Peter Wexler	Sandra Mourey	Peter Wexler
Vanities	Ryland Merkey	Reagan Cook	Sandra Mourey	Dan T. Willoughby
Jacques Brel Is Alive and Well and Living in Paris	Sandy Rosenthal	Reagan Cook	Sandra Mourey	Dan T. Willoughby

Asolo State Theater				
The New York Idea	John Ulmer	Holmes Easley	Catherine King	Martin Petlock
Hogan's Goat	William Woodman	Joseph Nieminski	Flozanne John	Martin Petlock
Going Ape	Robert Strane	Bennet Averyt	Catherine King	Martin Petlock
Boy Meets Girl	Howard J. Millman	Jim Chesnutt	Catherine King	Martin Petlock, Dan Gwin
A Streetcar Named Desire	Neal Kenyon	Peter Harvey	Flozanne John	Martin Petlock
The Quibbletown Recruits	Robert Strane	John Scheffler	Catherine King	Martin Petlock
The Music Man	Jim Hoskins	David Chapman	Catherine King, Flozanne John	Martin Petlock, Dan Gwin
Look Homeward, Angel	Richard G. Fallon	Robert C. Barnes	Catherine King	Martin Petlock, Dan Gwin
Win With Wheeler	Bradford Wallace	Bennet Averyt	Catherine King	Martin Petlock, Dan Gwin
The Ruling Class	Robert Strane	John Scheffler	Catherine King	Martin Petlock
Mummer's End	Peter Maloney	John Scheffler	Flozanne John	Martin Petlock
Cat on a Hot Tin Roof	Amnon Kabatchnik	John Scheffler	Catherine King	Martin Petlock
The Waltz of the Toreadors	Bradford Wallace	John Scheffler	Catherine King	Martin Petlock
Desire Under the Elms	Howard J. Millman	John Scheffler	Catherine King	Martin Petlock
My Love to Your Wife	Neal Kenyon	John Scheffler	Catherine King	Martin Petlock
Cyrano de Bergerac	John Ulmer	John Scheffler	Catherine King	Martin Petlock, Paul D. Romance
Saturday Sunday Monday	Robert Strane	Sandro La Ferla	Catherine King	Martin Petlock, David Loftin
Cromwell	Richard G. Fallon	Robert C. Barnes	Catherine King	Martin Petlock

PRODUCTION	DIRECTOR	SETS	COSTUMES	LIGHTS
Knock Knock	Howard J. Millman	Ray Perry	Catherine King	Martin Petlock
The Sea Horse	Isa Thomas	John Scheffler	Catherine King	Dan Gwin
Oh Coward!	Jim Hoskins	John Scheffler	Catherine King	David Loftin
Two for the Seesaw	Philip Le Strange	Jeff Dean	Sally A. Kos	Jim Rynning
Serenading Louie	Stephen Rothman	John Scheffler	Sally A. Kos	Jim Rynning

Back Alley Theatre

PRODUCTION	DIRECTOR	SETS	COSTUMES	LIGHTS
A Raisin in the Sun	John Collison	John Collison Paul Wahler		Paul Wahler
Payments	Frank Akers	Leslie Montgomery	Kim Peter Kovac	Kim Peter Kovac
Doomed Love	Kim Peter Kovac	Mike Stepowany	Wallace G. Lane, Jr.	Mike Stepowany
The Taking of Miss Janie	Fredric Lee	Paul Wahler	Theetta Bell	Tony Ebon Reid
Woyzeck	Kim Peter Kovac	Kim Peter Kovac	Kim Peter Kovac	Michael Foley
Design for Living	Fredric Lee	Ted Ciganik	Theetta Bell	Ted Ciganik
Small Craft Warnings	Frank Akers	Ted Ciganik	Kim Peter Kovac	
Short Eyes	Fredric Lee	Ted Ciganik		Ted Ciganik
Gandhiji	Kim Peter Kovac	Kim Peter Kovac	Pat Presley	Kim Peter Kovac
The Sun Always Shines for the Cool	Fredric Lee	Kim Peter Kovac		Kim Peter Kovac

BAM Theatre Company

PRODUCTION	DIRECTOR	SETS	COSTUMES	LIGHTS
The New York Idea	Frank Dunlop	William Ritman	Nancy Potts	F. Mitchell Dana
The Three Sisters	Frank Dunlop	William Ritman	Nancy Potts	F. Mitchell Dana

Barter Theatre

PRODUCTION	DIRECTOR	SETS	COSTUMES	LIGHTS
You Can't Take It with You	Charles Maryan	Bennet Averyt	Carr Garnett	Don Coleman
The Diary of Anne Frank	Owen Phillips	Bennet Averyt	Sigrid Insull	Don Coleman
Ten Nights in a Barroom	John Olon-Scrymgeour	Bennet Averyt	Sigrid Insull	Don Coleman
Biography	John Going	Bennet Averyt	Sigrid Insull	Don Coleman
The Glass Menagerie	Owen Phillips	James Franklin	Carr Garnett	Don Coleman
The Threepenny Opera	John Going	Bennet Averyt	Sigrid Insull	Don Coleman
Democracy	John Olon-Scrymgeour	Bennet Averyt	Elizabeth Covey	Don Coleman
The Matchmaker	Rex Partington	Bennet Averyt	Sigrid Insull	Don Coleman
Relatively Speaking	Owen Phillips	Parmelee Welles	Sigrid Insull	Don Coleman
Sweet Mistress	Charles Maryan	Bennet Averyt	Sigrid Insull	Don Coleman
Beyond the Fringe	Dorothy Marie	Carr Garnett	Carr Garnett	Don Coleman
The Matchmaker	Rex Partington	Bennet Averyt	Sigrid Insull	Tony Partington
The Taming of the Shrew	Owen Phillips	Bennet Averyt	Sigrid Insull	Grant Clifford Logan
All My Sons	John Olon-Scrymgeour	Parmelee Welles	Sigrid Insull	Grant Clifford Logan
Hay Fever	Dorothy Marie	Parmelee Welles	Carr Garnett	Tony Partington
The Playboy of the Western World	John Beary	Bennet Averyt	Sigrid Insull	Grant Clifford Logan
Man with a Load of Mischief	Ada Brown Mather	Parmelee Welles	Sigrid Insull	Grant Clifford Logan
Bubba	John Olon-Scrymgeour	Don Coleman	Sigrid Insull	Grant Clifford Logan
The Mousetrap	Dorothy Marie	Bennet Averyt	Carr Garnett	Tony Partington
Never Too Late	Owen Phillips	Bennet Averyt	Carr Garnett	Tony Partington

Berkeley Repertory Theatre

PRODUCTION	DIRECTOR	SETS	COSTUMES	LIGHTS
Seven Keys to Baldpate	Douglas Johnson	Lesley Skannal	Lesley Skannal	Joan Liepman
The Iceman Cometh	Michael Leibert	Jeff Whitman	Diana Smith	Matthew Cohen
Arsenic and Old Lace	Michael Addison	Ron Pratt Gene Angell	Lesley Skannal	Joan Liepman
Cat on a Hot Tin Roof	Douglas Johnson	Ron Pratt Gene Angell	Diana Smith	Joan Liepman
Of Mice and Men	Michael Leibert	Jeff Whitman	Lesley Skannal	Joan Liepman
Yankee Doodle	Douglas Johnson	Lesley Skannal	Lesley Skannal	Matthew Cohen
Rope	Michael Leibert	Jeff Whitman	Diana Smith	Matthew Cohen
The Importance of Being Earnest	Michael Addison	Lesley Skannal	Diana Smith	Matthew Cohen
Candida	Michael Leibert	Lesley Skannal	Lesley Skannal	Matthew Cohen
Bus Stop	Douglas Johnson	Jeff Whitman	Lesley Skannal	Matthew Cohen
Twelfth Night	Michael Addison	Lesley Skannal	Lesley Skannal	Matthew Cohen
The Philanthropist	Douglas Johnson	Jeff Whitman	Lesley Skannal	Matthew Cohen
Mann Ist Mann	Michael Leibert	Andrew DeShong	Diana Smith	Matthew Cohen
The Country Wife	Michael Addison	Gene Chesley	Lesley Skannal	Matthew Cohen
Private Lives	George Kovach	Gene Angell Ron Pratt	Marie Anne Chiment	Matthew Cohen
Our Town	Douglas Johnson	Gene Angell Ron Pratt	Lesley Skannal	Matthew Cohen

Berkeley Stage Company

PRODUCTION	DIRECTOR	SETS	COSTUMES	LIGHTS
Smack	Robert Goldsby	Andrew DeShong	Eliza Chugg	Sue Daly
Beclch	Robert Silvey	Bruce Keeler	Shelley Hischier Janice Weingrod Eliza Chugg	Jim Curtis Sue Daly
High on Pilet's Bluff	Warren Travis	Warren Travis	Eliza Chugg	Sue Daly
Coyote	John O'Keefe	Jim Curtis	Eliza Chugg Barr Chugg	Sue Daly
Pontifex	Angela Paton	Ariel	Eliza Chugg	Sue Daly
Kaspar	Tony Arn		Anton Haas	Jim Curtis
Winterspace	Drury Pifer	Jack Kostelnik	Sherrell Biggerstaff	George Ulnic
Feedlot	David Ostwald	Jim Curtis		Jim Curtis
Womansong	Angela Paton			
The Sea	John Vickery	Richard Reynolds	Beverly Schor	Richard Reynolds
The IX John Paul	John O'Meara	Emery Rogers	Elizabeth Hawk Deborah Gould	Joseph Broido
Three Sons	Martin Berman	Richard Mason	Eliza Chugg	Paul Murgatroyd

PRODUCTION	DIRECTOR	SETS	COSTUMES	LIGHTS
The Caucasian Chalk Circle	Tony Arn	Andrew E. Doe Tony Arn	Beverly Schor	Jack White
Safe House	Angela Paton	Angela Paton	Beverly Schor	Suresa Dundes
Earthworms	Robert Goldsby	Ariel	Ariel	Toshiro Ogawa

Bil Baird Theater

PRODUCTION	DIRECTOR	SETS	COSTUMES	LIGHTS
Alice in Wonderland	Paul Leaf	Howard Mandel	Bil Baird Susanna Baird	Peggy Clark
Winnie the Pooh	Bil Baird	Howard Mandel	Bil Baird Susanna Baird	Peggy Clark
Davy Jones' Locker	Bill Dreyer	Bil Baird Susanna Baird	Bil Baird Susanna Baird	Peggy Clark

The Body Politic

PRODUCTION	DIRECTOR	SETS	COSTUMES	LIGHTS
Philosophers in Skirts	Kirk Denmark	Eric Gustafson	Mary Dale	Eric Gustafson
Orpheus Descending	June Pyskacek	Eric Gustafson	Mary Dale	Eric Gustafson
As I Lay Dying	Sharon Phillips David Moore	Sharon Phillips	Sharon Phillips	Eric Gustafson
Heritage	Jim Shiflett		Geri Atwood	Robert S. Gold
Your Own Thing	Derek Evans	Eric Gustafson	Mary Dale	Eric Gustafson
The Real Inspector Hound and After Magritte	Ned Schmidtke	Gerry Stephens	Julie A. Nagel	Robert S. Gold
Who's Happy Now	Joseph Slowik	Dean Taucher	Susan T. Gayford	Robert S. Gold
Knock Knock	Anthony Petito	Dean Taucher	Kaye Nottbusch	Eric Strand
Johnnie Will	Ned Schmidtke	Nels Anderson	Julie A. Nagel	Nels Anderson

California Actors Theatre

PRODUCTION	DIRECTOR	SETS	COSTUMES	LIGHTS
Our Town	James Dunn	Ronald E. Krempetz	Marcia Frederick	Stephen F. Cherry
Ernest in Love	Milton Lyon	Ralph Fetterley	Marcia Frederick	Stephen F. Cherry
The Imaginary Invalid	John Reich	Ronald E. Krempetz	Marcia Frederick	Ray Garrett
The Three Sisters	James Dunn	Ronald E. Krempetz	Marcia Frederick	Ray Garrett
Enrico IV	John Reich	Steven Howell	Marcia Frederick Gini Vogel	
What Price Glory?	James Dunn	Ronald E. Krempetz		Ray Garrett
A Very Gentle Person	Peter Nyberg	Peter Nyberg	Gini Vogel	Ray Garrett
A Midsummer Night's Dream	Jack Bender	Russell Pyle	Gini Vogel	Ray Garrett
Hamlet	James Dunn	Ronald E. Krempetz	Barbara Affonso	Ray Garrett
Blithe Spirit	Terry Wills	Ronald E. Krempetz	Barbara Affonso	
The Good Woman of Setzuan	James Dunn	Ronald E. Krempetz	Barbara Affonso	Robert Klemm
The Odd Couple	G.W. Bailey	Ronald E. Krempetz	Sarah Godbois	Robert Klemm
The Rainmaker	James Dunn	Ronald E. Krempetz	Barbara Affonso	Robert Klemm
The Innocents	Anne McNaughton	Ronald E. Krempetz	Barbara Affonso	Robert Klemm
Rashomon	Kurtwood Smith	Ronald E. Krempetz	Barbara Affonso	Robert Klemm
Bierce Takes on the Railroad	James Dunn	Ronald E. Krempetz	Barbara Affonso	Robert Klemm

The Cambridge Ensemble

PRODUCTION	DIRECTOR	SETS	COSTUMES	LIGHTS
Deathwatch	Joann Green	Joann Green Paul D'Amato	Joann Green	Joann Green
Gulliver's Travels	Joann Green	Joann Green	Joann Green	Gayle Youngman
Judgement	Joann Green	Joann Green	Joann Green	Joann Green
Best of Chelm	Joann Green	Lisa Conley	Joann Green	
Oresteia	Joann Green	Joann Green	Joann Green	Len Schnabel Hilary Crosby
The Scarlet Letter	Joann Green	Joann Green	Joann Green	Hilary Crosby
Br'er Rabbit and His Friends	Joann Green	Joann Green	Joann Green	

Carolina Regional Theatre

PRODUCTION	DIRECTOR	SETS	COSTUMES	LIGHTS
Illustrated Sports	John W. Morrow, Jr.	John W. Morrow, Jr.	Judy Adamson	Gene Achols
Appalachia Sounding	John W. Morrow, Jr.	John W. Morrow, Jr.	Judy Adamson	John W. Morrow, Jr.
The Great American Fourth of July Parade	John W. Morrow, Jr.	John W. Morrow, Jr.	Judy Adamson	John W. Morrow, Jr.

Center Stage

PRODUCTION	DIRECTOR	SETS	COSTUMES	LIGHTS
Tartuffe	Jacques Cartier	David Jenkins	Nancy Potts	Roger Morgan
Busy Bee Good Food All Night Delicious	Jacques Cartier	Kert Lundell	Kert Lundell	Roger Morgan
Borders	Charles Eastman	Kert Lundell	Kert Lundell	Roger Morgan
Dream on Monkey Mountain	Albert Laveau	Eugene Lee	Robert Wojewodski	Roger Morgan
Old Times	Stanley Wojewodski, Jr.	Peter Harvey	Elizabeth P. Palmer	Ian Calderon
The Cherry Orchard	Jacques Cartier	John Jensen	John Jensen	Gilbert V. Hemsley, Jr.
The Real Inspector Hound and Black Comedy	Stanley Wojewodski, Jr.	Peter Harvey	Liz Covey	Ian Calderon
She Stoops to Conquer	Stanley Wojewodski, Jr.	Eldon Elder	Dona Granata	Ian Calderon
When You Comin' Back, Red Ryder?	Stanley Wojewodski, Jr.	Charles Cosler	Walker Hicklin	Charles Cosler
Misalliance	Arne Zaslove	Peter Harvey	Robert Wojewodski	Ian Calderon
Toys in the Attic	Stanley Wojewodski, Jr.	Peter Harvey	Elizabeth P. Palmer	Ian Calderon
The First Breeze of Summer	Woodie King, Jr.	Charles Cosler	Elizabeth P. Palmer	Charles Cosler
Knock Knock	John Henry Davis	Charles Cosler	Elizabeth P. Palmer	Arden Fingerhut
A Sorrow beyond Dreams	Daniel Freudenberger	James Tilton		James Tilton

The Changing Scene

PRODUCTION	DIRECTOR	SETS	COSTUMES	LIGHTS
Dummies and F-Yoo-Hoo and Dragons in the Wall	Teresa Marffie-Evangelista	Denny Horvath		Dale Jordan

PRODUCTION	DIRECTOR	SETS	COSTUMES	LIGHTS
Cracks	Richard Lore	Denny Horvath		Dale Jordan
Alferd Packer: A Colorado Ritual	David Ode	Randal Martines	Bethe Busey	Randal Martines
Freebies	Neil Yarema	Peter Nielson	Kathlean Bradley	Peter Nielson
Coupling	Alfred Brooks	Chuck Parsons	Alfred Brooks	Peter Nielson
Webs	Peter Nielson		Mari Zevin	E. Michael Miller
Music for Crumhorn & Sackbutt and	Don Katzman	Peter Nielson		Peter Nielson
George & Franz: Taking Sides in the Boer War		Becky Hill		
Requiem...1/1	Ralph Palasek	Ralph Palasek		Peter Nielson
The Longest Way Home	Ralph Palasek	Ralph Palasek		Peter Nielson
Cowgirl Ecstasy	Michael Smith	Chuck Parson	Bethe Busey	Peter Nielson
The Quannapowitt Quartet	Richard Lore	Chuck Parson	Rebecca Hill	Dale Jordan
The Gift of a Doll	Alan Deans	Peter Nielson		Peter Nielson
The Begonia and the Bygones	Bonnie J. Eckard	Peter Nielson	Becky Howard	Eric Rivedal
Hey, Rube	Bob Berkel	Peter Nielson	Lynne Walker	Peter Nielson
Stitches	Alfred Brooks	Greg Carr	Maxine Munt	Peter Nielson

Chelsea Theater Center

PRODUCTION	DIRECTOR	SETS	COSTUMES	LIGHTS
By Bernstein	Michael Bawtree	Lawrence King Michael H. Yeargan	Lawrence King Michael H. Yeargan	Marc B. Weiss
The Family	Barry Davis	Lawrence King	Jeanne Button	Daniel Flannery
Ice Age	Arne Zaslove	Wolfgang Roth	Ruth Morley	Daniel Flannery
The Boss	Edward Gilbert	Lawrence King	Carrie F. Robbins	William Mintzer
Vanities	Garland Wright	John Arnone	David James	Patrika Brown
The Prince of Homburg	Robert Kalfin	Christopher Thomas	Ruth Morley	Marc B. Weiss
Lincoln	Carl Weber	Lawrence King		William Mintzer
The Crazy Locomotive	Des McAnuff	Douglas W. Schmidt	Carol Oditz	Burl Hash
Happy End	Michael Posnick	Robert U. Taylor	Carrie F. Robbins	Jennifer Tipton

The Children's Theatre Company

PRODUCTION	DIRECTOR	SETS	COSTUMES	LIGHTS
Treasure Island	John Clark Donahue	Dahl Delu	Gene Davis Buck	Jon Baker
The Little Match Girl	John Clark Donahue	Gene Davis Buck Jay Bush	Gene Davis Buck	Jon Baker
Mother Goose	Myron Johnson	Steven M. Rydberg	Steven M. Rydberg	Jon Baker
The Snow Queen	John Clark Donahue	Dahl Delu	Dahl Delu	Karlis Ozols
The Seagull	Bain Boehlke	Bain Boehlke Dahl Delu	Gene Davis Buck Bain Boehlke	Jon Baker
Twelfth Night	Charles Nolte	Dahl Delu	Gene Davis Buck	Jon Baker
A Room in Paradise	John Clark Donahue	Dahl Delu	Gene Davis Buck	Jon Baker
Goldilocks and the Three Bears and	Myron Johnson	Steven M. Rydberg	Joseph S. Rusnock	Karlis Ozols
Little Red Riding Hood				
The Adventures of Tom Sawyer	John Clark Donahue	Dahl Delu	Dahl Delu	Jon Baker
Cinderella	Bain Boehlke	Edward Haynes	Gene Davis Buck	Jon Baker
The Dream Fisher	John Clark Donahue	Donald Pohlman	Gene Davis Buck	Jon Baker
Oliver!	Myron Johnson	Dahl Delu	Gene Davis Buck	Jon Baker
The Importance of Being Earnest	Gene Davis Buck	Gene Davis Buck Jay Bush	Gene Davis Buck Deborah L. Rusnock	Jon Baker
Romeo and Juliet	John Clark Donahue	Jack Barkla	Jack Barkla	Jon Baker
Variations on a Similar Theme (An Homage to Rene Magritte)	John Clark Donahue	John Clark Donahue	Gene Davis	Karlis Ozols

Cincinnati Playhouse in the Park

PRODUCTION	DIRECTOR	SETS	COSTUMES	LIGHTS
Death of a Salesman	Michael Murray	Neil Peter Jampolis	Annie Peacock Warner	Neil Peter Jampolis
Relatively Speaking	John Going	Eric Head	Annie Peacock Warner	Mark Kruger
The Little Foxes	Israel Hicks	Neil Peter Jampolis	Annie Peacock Warner	Neil Peter Jampolis
What the Butler Saw	Michael Bawtree	Neil Peter Jampolis	Annie Peacock Warner	Neil Peter Jampolis
The Contrast	Michael Murray	John Lee Beatty	Elizabeth Covey	Mark Kruger
Where's Charley?	Michael Murray	Neil Peter Jampolis	Annie Peacock Warner	Neil Peter Jampolis
Cat on a Hot Tin Roof	Michael Murray	Paul Shortt	Annie Peacock Warner	Neil Peter Jampolis
Oliver!	John Going	Neil Peter Jampolis	Annie Peacock Warner	Jane Reisman
A Month in the Country	Michael Murray	John Lee Beatty	Elizabeth Covey	Neil Peter Jampolis
When You Comin' Back, Red Ryder?	Robert Brewer	Karl Eigsti	Annie Peacock Warner	Neil Peter Jampolis
Heartbreak House	Michael Murray	John Lee Beatty	Annie Peacock Warner	Dennis Parichy
The Hostage	Geoff Garland	Neil Peter Jampolis	Annie Peacock Warner	Neil Peter Jampolis
Vanities	John Going	Neil Peter Jampolis	Jill Hamilton	Neil Peter Jampolis

Circle in the Square

PRODUCTION	DIRECTOR	SETS	COSTUMES	LIGHTS
Ah, Wilderness!	Arvin Brown	Steven Rubin	Bill Walker	Ronald Wallace
The Glass Menagerie	Theodore Mann	Ming Cho Lee	Sydney Brooks	Thomas Skelton
The Lady from the Sea	Tony Richardson	Rouben Ter-Arutunian	Rouben Ter-Arutunian	Thomas Skelton
Pal Joey	Theodore Mann	John J. Moore	Arthur Boccia	Ronald Wallace
Days in the Trees	Stephen Porter	Rouben Ter-Arutunian	Rouben Ter-Arutunian	Thomas Skelton
The Night of the Iguana	Joseph Hardy	H.R. Poindexter	Noel Taylor	H.R. Poindexter
Romeo and Juliet	Theodore Mann	Ming Cho Lee	John Conklin	Thomas Skelton
The Importance of Being Earnest	Stephen Porter	Zack Brown	Ann Roth	John McLain
The Club	Tommy Tune	Kate Carmel	Kate Carmel	Cheryl Thacker

Circle Repertory Company

PRODUCTION	DIRECTOR	SETS	COSTUMES	LIGHTS
The Elephant in the House	Marshall W. Mason	John Lee Beatty	Jennifer von Mayrhauser	Dennis Parichy
Dancing for the Kaiser	Marshall Oglesby	Atkin Pace	Jennifer von Mayrhauser	Dennis Parichy
Knock Knock	Marshall W. Mason	John Lee Beatty	Jennifer von Mayrhauser	Dennis Parichy
Who Killed Richard Cory?	Leonard Peters	John Ferenchak	Gary Jones	Arden Fingerhut

PRODUCTION	DIRECTOR	SETS	COSTUMES	LIGHTS
Serenading Louie	Marshall W. Mason	John Lee Beatty	Jennifer von Mayrhauser	Dennis Parichy
Mrs. Murray's Farm	Neil Flanagan Marshall W. Mason	John Lee Beatty	Jennifer von Mayrhauser	John P. Dodd
The Farm	Marshall W. Mason	John Lee Beatty	Laura Crow	Dennis Parichy
A Tribute to Lili Lamont	Marshall W. Mason	John Lee Beatty	Jennifer von Mayrhauser	Dennis Parichy
My Life	Marshall W. Mason	David Potts	Kenneth M. Yount	Dennis Parichy
Gemini	Peter Mark Schifter	Christopher Nowak	Ernest Allen Smith	Larry Crimmins
Exiles	Rob Thirkield	David Potts	Jennifer von Mayrhauser	Dennis Parichy
Unsung Cole	Norman Berman	Peter Harvey	Carol Oditz	Arden Fingerhut

		Cleveland Play House		
In Celebration	Larry Tarrant	Richard Gould	Harriet Cone	Richard Coumbs
First Monday in October	Jerome Lawrence	Richard Gould	Estelle Painter	Richard Coumbs
The Prague Spring	J Ranelli	Robert Steinberg	Estelle Painter	Robert Steinberg
Bingo	Jonathan Bolt	Richard Gould	Joe Dale Lunday	Richard Coumbs
Caesar and Cleopatra	Paul Lee	Robert Steinberg		Robert Steinberg
Abigail Adams	Edith Owen Evie McElroy		Estelle Painter	John Volpe
Relatively Speaking	Evie McElroy	Richard Gould	Joe Dale Lunday	Russell Lowe
Dr. Jekyll and Mr. Hyde	Paul Lee	Richard Gould	Estelle Painter	Richard Coumbs
The Dark at the Top of the Stairs	Larry Tarrant	Timothy Zupancic	Joe Dale Lunday	Richard Coumbs
Get-Rich-Quick Wallingford	Paul Lee	Richard Gould	Estelle Painter	Russell Lowe
The Last Meeting of the Knights of the White Magnolia	Larry Tarrant	Barbara Leatherman	Joe Dale Lunday	R.O. Wulff Timothy Zupancic
Of Mice and Men	Evie McElroy	Richard Gould	Harriet Cone	Richard Coumbs
Scapino	Paul Lee	Timothy Zupancic	Richard Gould	Richard Coumbs
The World of Carl Sandburg	Jonathan Farwell	Richard Gould	Estelle Painter	John Volpe
The Sunshine Boys	Larry Tarrant	Richard Gould	Harriet Cone	Richard Gould
The Cat and the Fiddle	Jack Lee Eddie Gasper	James Tilton	Richard Gould	Joseph P. Tilford
Are You Now or Have You Ever Been	Larry Tarrant	Timothy Zupancic	Harriet Cone	Timothy Zupancic
A Moon for the Misbegotten	Dorothy Silver	Maura Smolover	Maura Smolover	Joseph P. Tilford
The Yellow Jacket	William Rhys	Richard Gould	Estelle Painter	Richard Gould
Man and Superman	Paul Lee	Joseph P. Tilford	David Smith	Joseph P. Tilford
Ladyhouse Blues	Larry Tarrant	Richard Gould	Richard Gould	Richard Gould
Macbeth	John Dillon	Stuart Wurtzel	Estelle Painter	Arden Fingerhut
Table Manners	Paul Lee	Richard Gould	Harriet Cone	Richard Gould

		Cohoes Music Hall		
The Cast Aways	Anthony J. Stimac	Clarke W. Thornton	Dean Reiter	Clarke W. Thornton
Abie's Irish Rose	Garland Wright			
The Subject Was Roses	William Guild	Bil Mikulewicz	Dean Reiter	Clarke W. Thornton
Arsenic and Old Lace	Anthony J. Stimac	Bil Mikulewicz	Dean Reiter	Clarke W. Thornton
Of Mice and Men	David William Kitchen	Michael Tomko	Dean Reiter	Michael Tomko
Life with Father	Nancy Kulp	Inge Dunn	Marianne Powell-Parker	Scott Walrath
Babes in Arms	David William Kitchen	Inge Dunn	Marianne Powell-Parker	Greg Dunn
Blithe Spirit	Kent Paul	Inge Dunn	Marianne Powell-Parker	T. Winberry
Death of a Salesman	Peter Thompson	Inge Dunn	Marianne Powell-Parker	Harry Silverglat
The Importance of Being Earnest	Robert Mandel	Michael Anania	Robert Wojewodski	Patricia Collins

		Colonnades Theatre Lab		
Second Wind	Michael Lessac	Robert U. Taylor	Joan Ferenchak Donato Moreno	Joe Kaminsky
A Month in the Country	Michael Lessac	Robert U. Taylor	Joan Ferenchak	Joe Kaminsky
Reflections	Michael Lessac	Robert U. Taylor	Joan Ferenchak Donato Moreno	Joe Kaminsky
Cinema Soldier	Tom Tammi			Joe Kaminsky
Warbeck	Michael Lessac	Robert U. Taylor	Kenneth M. Yount Bill E. Noone	Joe Kaminsky
Reflections	Michael Lessac	Robert U. Taylor	Joan Ferenchak Kenneth M. Yount	Joe Kaminsky
A Flea in Her Ear	Krikor Latamain	Robert U. Taylor	John Hegerson	Joe Kaminsky
A Servant of Two Masters	A.G. Brooks	Thimothy Miles	Timothy Miles	Joe Kaminsky

		The Cricket Theatre		
The Journey of the Fifth Horse	Howard Dallin	Dick Leerhoff	Patty Facius	Dick Leerhoff
6 Rms Riv Vu	Howard Dallin	Dick Leerhoff	Patty Facius	Dick Leerhoff
Snow White Goes West	Thom Guthrie	Dick Leerhoff	Patty Facius	Dick Leerhoff
When You Comin' Back, Red Ryder?	Arif Hasnain	Dick Leerhoff	Patty Facius	Dick Leerhoff
It Strikes a Man	Howard Dallin	Dick Leerhoff	Patty Facius	Dick Leerhoff
The Sea Horse	Lou Salerni	Thom Guthrie	Patty Facius	Thom Guthrie
The Martian Chronicles	Howard Dallin	Dick Leerhoff	Patty Facius	Dick Leerhoff
Artichoke	Lou Salerni	Dick Leerhoff	Dick Leerhoff	Dick Leerhoff
Subject to Fits	Lou Salerni	Dick Leerhoff	Laraine Lee	Dick Leerhoff
The Mound Builders	Rustin Greene	Dick Leerhoff	Laraine Lee	Dick Leerhoff
And Where She Stops Nobody Knows	Lou Salerni	Jack Barkla	Christopher Beesley	Jack Barkla Dick Leerhoff

PRODUCTION	DIRECTOR	SETS	COSTUMES	LIGHTS
The Last Meeting of the Knights of the White Magnolia	Lou Salerni	Dick Leerhoff	Christopher Beesley	Dick Leerhoff
A Tribute to Lili Lamont	Lou Salerni	Jerry Williams	Christopher Beesley	Phillip Billey
				Mark Carlson
Who's Afraid of Virginia Woolf?	Lou Salerni	Thom Roberts	Christopher Beesley	Phillip Billey
				Mark Carlson

CSC Repertory

PRODUCTION	DIRECTOR	SETS	COSTUMES	LIGHTS
The Homecoming	Christopher Martin	Christopher Martin	Christopher Martin	Christopher Martin
Hedda Gabler	Christopher Martin	Clay Coyle	Donna Meyer	Christopher Martin
Antigone	Christopher Martin	Christopher Martin	Christopher Martin	Christopher Martin
A Country Scandal	Stuart Vaughan	Clay Coyle	Donna Meyer	Joel Grynheim
School for Buffoons and Escurial	Christopher Martin	Christopher Martin	Evelyn Thompson	Christopher Martin
Measure for Measure	Christopher Martin	Clay Coyle	Kristen Watson	Joel Grynheim
Hound of the Baskervilles	Christopher Martin	Christopher Martin	Linda Shannon	Christopher Martin
La Celestina	Rene Buch	Clay Coyle	Evelyn Thompson	Christopher Martin
Heartbreak House	Christopher Martin	Christopher Martin	Kay Pathanky	Christopher Martin
Tartuffe	Christopher Martin	Clay Coyle	Donna Meyer	Christopher Martin
			Christopher Martin	
Bingo	Christopher Martin	Christopher Martin	Evelyn Thompson	Christopher Martin
The Homecoming	Christopher Martin	Christopher Martin	Christopher Martin	Christopher Martin
		David Chapman	David Chapman	David Chapman
The Balcony	Christopher Martin	Christopher Martin	Christopher Martin	Christopher Martin
		Harry Lines	Harry Lines	Harry Lines

The Cutting Edge

PRODUCTION	DIRECTOR	SETS	COSTUMES	LIGHTS
Croon	Andrea Balis			
untitled work	Andrea Balis			

Dallas Theater Center

PRODUCTION	DIRECTOR	SETS	COSTUMES	LIGHTS
Saturday Sunday Monday	David Healy	Mary Sue Jones	Randolf Pearson	Allen Hibbard
Manny	Dolores Ferraro	Sam Nance	Gina Taulane	Sam Nance
A Place on the Magdalena Flats	Ken Latimer	Yoichi Aoki	Susan A. Haynie	Randy Moore
Much Ado About Nothing	Robin Lovejoy	John Henson	Kathleen Latimer	Allen Hibbard
Stillsong	Paul Baker	Virgil Beavers	Gina Taulane	Randy Moore
Sherlock Holmes and the Curse of the Sign of Four	Ken Latimer	John Henson	Cheryl Denson	Linda Blase
Sam	Bryant J. Reynolds	Steve Wallace	Pamela Jensen	Randy Moore
Once in a Lifetime	Ryland Merkey	John Henson	Cheryl Denson	Robin Crews
Scapino	Robyn Flatt	Yoichi Aoki	Denise Drennen	Sally Netzel
The Three Sisters	Ken Latimer	Kathleen Latimer	Pamela Jensen	Randy Moore
Something's Afoot	John Henson	Peter Wolf	Paul Buboltz	Randy Moore
Santa Fe Sunshine	John Logan	Yoichi Aoki	Michael Krueger	Wayne Lambert
Equus	Ryland Merkey	Sallie Laurie	Cheryl Denson	Robyn Flatt
Absurd Person Singular	Ken Latimer	Yoichi Aoki	Rodger M. Wilson	Linda Blase

Dell'Arte

PRODUCTION	DIRECTOR	SETS	COSTUMES	LIGHTS
As You Like It	Jael Weisman	Alan Choy	Jill K. Peterson	Alain Schons
The Contrast	Joanne Ruth Klein	Alan Choy	Susan Beth Klein	Alain Schons
Girl Crazy	Alexander Kinney	Alan Choy	Jill K. Peterson	Alain Schons
Tom Sawyer	John J. Collins	Alan Choy	Jill K. Peterson	Alain Schons
Babes in Arms	Jane Mazzone-Clementi	Chad Aiton		Chad Aiton
The Dell'Arte Clown Circus	Donny Osman			
The Loon's Rage	Jael Weisman	Alain Schons	Nancy Malsie	Jon' Paul Cook

Dinglefest Theatre Company

PRODUCTION	DIRECTOR	SETS	COSTUMES	LIGHTS
Goosebumps	Byron Schaffer, Jr.		Karen Elise Swanson	
Vacuum Pact	Byron Schaffer, Jr.			
Chautauqua	Byron Schaffer, Jr.		Tim Stevenson	Jack O'Connor
	Ruth E. Higgins			
Cap Streeter	Byron Schaffer, Jr.		Teri Brown	
Fresh or Frozen	Byron Schaffer, Jr.		Teri Brown	
Split the Differents	Thomas M. Doman	Jon Gantt	Teri Brown	Thomas Herman
Young Bucks	Byron Schaffer, Jr.		Teri Brown	Mary Fran Loftus

East West Players

PRODUCTION	DIRECTOR	SETS	COSTUMES	LIGHTS
The Chickencoop Chinaman	Mako	Rae Creevey	Rene Gendron	Rae Creevey
	Rae Creevey			
Nobody on My Side of the Family Looks Like That	Alberto Isaac	Rae Creevey		Rae Creevey
The Three Sisters	Norman Cohen	Jiro Saito	Beverly Innen	Rae Creevey
The Asian American Hearings	Rae Creevey	Rae Creevey	Rae Creevey	Rae Creevey
That's The Way The Fortune Cookie Crumbles	Dom Magwili	Rae Creevey	Denice Kumagai	Rae Creevey
And the Soul Shall Dance	Mako	Rae Creevey	Betty Muramoto	Rae Creevey
	Alberto Isaac			
Gee Pop	Rae Creevey	Rae Creevey	Valerie Dunlap	Rae Creevey

El Teatro Campesino

PRODUCTION	DIRECTOR	SETS	COSTUMES	LIGHTS
El Fin del Mundo (El Huracan)	Luis Valdez			
La Virgen del Tepeyac	Socorro Valdez Cruz			
Pastorela	Luis Valdez			
El Fin del Mundo II	Luis Valdez			
Rose of the Rancho	Luis Valdez			
La Carpa de los Rasquachis	Luis Valdez			

PRODUCTION	DIRECTOR	SETS	COSTUMES	LIGHTS
The Empty Space Theater				
Ronnie Bwana, Jungle Guide	John Aylward	Karen Gjelsteen	Sally Richardson	Jim Royce
Vampire	Tom Towler	Phil Schermer	Sally Richardson	Phil Schermer
Gertrude	Julian Schembri	Jim Royce	Debbie Gilbert	Jim Royce
Dandy Dick	M. Burke Walker	Karen Gjelsteen	Sally Richardson	James Verdery
Bullshot Crummond	Megan Dean	Karen Gjelsteen	Donna Eskew	Jim Royce
The Sea	Lori Larsen	Karen Gjelsteen	Sally Richardson	Phil Schermer
Molly Bloom	Randi Douglas	Karen Gjelsteen	Celeste Cleveland	Jim Royce
Pilk's Madhouse	Jeff Steitzer		Celeste Cleveland	Jim Royce
Yanks 3 Detroit 0 Top of the Seventh	Julian Schembri	Karen Gjelsteen	Celeste Cleveland	Jim Royce
Gammer Gurton's Needle	Lori Larsen	Karen Gjelsteen		
American Buffalo	M. Burke Walker	Karen Gjelsteen	Celeste Cleveland	Phil Schermer
Knuckle	Jeff Steitzer	Karen Gjelsteen	Michael Murphy	Scott Hawthorn
Heat	Lori Larsen	Karen Gjelsteen	Marian Cottrell	Phil Schermer
School for Clowns	Diane Schenker Jim Monitor	Karen Gjelsteen		Jeff Robbins
Butley	M. Burke Walker	Karen Gjelsteen	Celeste Cleveland	Jeff Robbins
Sexual Perversity in Chicago and	Jim Monitor	Ronald Erickson	Nanrose Buchman	Jeff Robbins
Squirrels	M. Burke Walker	Ronald Erickson	Nanrose Buchman	Jeff Robbins
Jesse and the Bandit Queen	Kurt Beattie	Walter Kurtz	Michael Murphy	Jeff Robbins
Klondike!	John Kauffman	Karen Gjelsteen	Wyn Roll	Martin Pavloff
Born to Maximize	John Kauffman	Karen Gjelsteen	Carol Hanford	Frank Simons
The Amazing Faz, or Too Good To Be Twoo	John Kauffman	David Butler	Marian Cottrell	
Ensemble Studio Theatre				
The Shortchanged Review	Richard Southern	Steve Duffy	T.L. Tubbs	Cheryl Thacker
Getting Through The Night	James Hammerstein	Joan Ferenchak	David Murin	Toni Goldin
Possession	James Hammerstein	Peter Larkin	David Murin	Pat Stern
Adam's Rib	Jessica James	Patricia Woodbridge	Patricia Woodbridge	Patricia Woodbridge
Money	Jan Eliasberg	Tracy Killam	David Murin	David Kissel
The Contest	Paul Austin	Patricia Woodbridge	Christina Weppner	Beverly Emmons
Good-By And Keep Cold	James Hammerstein	Joan Ferenchak	Donato Moreno	Sara Schrager
How Do You Do It?	Barbara Tarbuck			
Reflections of a China Doll	Barbara Tarbuck	Christopher Nowak	Laura Crow	Marc D. Weiss
The Soft Touch	John Bettenbender	Calvin Churchman	Margo La Zaro	Bill Motyka
Relationships	Shauneille Perry	C. Richard Mills	Judy Dearing	William Otterson
The Evanston Theatre Company				
The Duck Variations	Gregory A. Kandel	Patricia L. Dunbar Robert A. Atkins	Patricia L. Dunbar Robert A. Atkins	Patricia L. Dunbar Robert A. Atkins
Jumpers	Frank Galati	Patricia L. Dunbar Robert A. Atkins	Patricia L. Dunbar Robert A. Atkins	Patricia L. Dunbar Robert A. Atkins
The Au Pair Man	Gregory A. Kandel	Harriet Mintzer	Wendy Kheel Robert Berdell	Samuel C. Ball
Nourish the Beast	Mike Nussbaum		Wendy Kheel Robert Berdell	Jeff Davis
Candida	Robert Strane	David Emmons	Julie A. Nagel	Robert Shook
A Day in the Death of Joe Egg	Dennis Zacek	Maher Ahmad	Robert Berdell	Geoffrey Bushor
The Birthday Party	Gregory A. Kandel	Robert Ellsworth	Robert Ellsworth	Robert Shook
Seascape	George Keathley	David Emmons	Jessica Hahn	Maher Ahmad
The Little Hut	Dennis Zacek	Maher Ahmad	Jessica Hahn	Mark Mongold
The First All Children's Theatre Company				
A Whinny and A Whistle	Meridee Stein Cheryl Scammon	Ken Holamon	Ken Holamon	Charles Willmott
Alice Through the Looking Glass	Meridee Stein Cheryl Scammon	Denise Weber Kathy Kunkel	Patricia Kraft	
Guess Again	Meridee Stein	Kathy Kunkel Denise Weber	Patricia Kraft Cheryl Blalock	Charles Willmott
Who's Next?	Meridee Stein	Kathy Kunkel Denise Weber	Cheryl Blalock	Charles Willmott
Adventures of Pinocchio	Meridee Stein	Kathy Kunkel Denise Weber	Cheryl Blalock	Charles Willmott
Alice Through the Looking Glass	Meridee Stein Cheryl Scammon	Denise Weber Kathy Kunkel	Patricia Kraft Cheryl Blalock	Charles Willmott
Three Tales at a Time	Meridee Stein	Kathy Kunkel Denise Weber	Cheryl Blalock	Charles Willmott
Dorothy & the Wizard of Oz	Meridee Stein	Kathy Kunkel Denise Weber	Patricia Kraft	Rick Belzer
Florida Studio Theatre				
Caspar Hauser	Jon Spelman			
Mime, Etc.	Jon Spelman			
The Judicial Woes of Peter Bowes	S.C. Hastie	Paul D. Romance		
Endgame	Jon Spelman	Rick Pike	Pamela Hartford	
Florida: Feast of Flowers	Jon Spelman			Paul D. Romance
Insight Out	Jerry Brown		Terri Mastrobuono	
Extremities	Jon Spelman			
Folger Theatre Group				
The Collected Works of Billy the Kid	Louis W. Scheeder	David Chapman	Randy Barcelo	Hugh Lester
The Comedy of Errors	Jonathan Alper	Stuart Wurtzel	Robert Wojewodski	Arden Fingerhut
Medal of Honor Rag	David Chambers	Raymond C. Recht	Deborah Walther	Betsy Toth

315

PRODUCTION	DIRECTOR	SETS	COSTUMES	LIGHTS
Henry V	Louis W. Scheeder	David Chapman	David Chapman Carol Oditz	Betsy Toth
All's Well That Ends Well	Jonathan Alper	Raymond C. Recht	Robert Wojewodski	Arden Fingerhut
The Fool: Scenes of Bread and Love	Louis W. Scheeder	Raymond C. Recht	Robert Wojewodski	Arden Fingerhut
Much Ado About Nothing	Jonathan Alper	Raymond C. Recht	Jennifer von Mayrhauser	Hugh Lester
Mummer's End	Louis W. Scheeder	David Chapman	Robert Wojewodski	Betsy Toth
Black Elk Speaks	Jonathan Alper	John Kasarda	Karen M. Hummel	Arden Fingerhut
A Midsummer Night's Dream	Harold Scott	Franco Colavecchia	Robert Wojewodski	Betsy Toth

Frank Silvera Writers' Workshop

Laboratory readings				

Frederick Douglass Creative Arts Center

Sonata	Bill Duke	Jean Hays	Judy Dearing	Keith Harewood
The Secret Place	Bill Duke	Karl Eigsti	Judy Dearing	Shirley Prendergast
NOT	Bill Duke	Jean Hays	Judy Dearing	Gwendolyn M. Gilliam
Emily T.	Kimako Baraka	Carole Byard	Linda Lee	Gwendolyn M. Gilliam
Transcendental Blues	Kimako Baraka	Carole Byard	Linda Lee	Gwendolyn M. Gilliam

Free Street Theater

All productions	Patrick Henry			

George Street Playhouse

Luv	Dick Shepard	Howard Kessler	Linda Reynolds	Howard Kessler
Fortune and Men's Eyes	Dino Narizzano	Cliff Simon	Linda Reynolds	Francis Roefaro
Till Eulenspiegel's Merry Pranks	Eric Krebs	Howard Kessler	Linda Reynolds	Howard Kessler
Count Dracula	Robert Hall	Howard Kessler	Jane Tschetter	Francis Roefaro
The Glass Menagerie	Peter Bennett	Cliff Simon	Marilyn Pulawski	Francis Roefaro
The Threepenny Opera	Peter Bennett	John Herochik	Liz Diamond Kathy Fredricks	Paul Prasek
That Championship Season	Robert Hall	Cliff Simon	Liz Baldwin	Frank Webb
Brothers	Dino Narizzano	Allen Cornell		Allen Cornell
Oh Coward!	David Rubinstein	Allen Cornell	Linda Reynolds	Allen Cornell
A Midsummer Night's Dream	Eric Krebs	Eric Krebs	Linda Reynolds	Francis Roefaro
The Mousetrap	Peter Bennett	Allen Cornell	Laura Crow Linda Reynolds	Allen Cornell
The Memoirs of Charlie Pops	Robert Hall	Cliff Simon	Linda Reynolds	Allen Cornell
Waiting for Godot	Peter Bennett	Allen Cornell	Laura Crow	Allen Cornell

GeVa Theatre

Arms and the Man	Donald MacKechnie	David Herwitz		David Herwitz
A Thurber Carnival	Donald MacKechnie	David Herwitz	David Herwitz	David Herwitz
Play Strindberg	Donald MacKechnie	David Herwitz	David Herwitz	David Herwitz
Who Dunnit?	Donald MacKechnie	David Herwitz	David Herwitz	David Herwitz
The Contrast	Donald MacKechnie	David Herwitz	David Herwitz	David Herwitz
Private Lives	Donald MacKechnie	David Herwitz	David Herwitz	David Herwitz
Sleuth	Donald MacKechnie	David Herwitz	David Herwitz	David Herwitz
Much Ado About Nothing	Donald MacKechnie	Donald MacKechnie	Madeline Cohen	Donald MacKechnie
Tartuffe	Gary Reineke	David Herwitz	Danica Eskind	David Herwitz
The Birthday Party	Gideon Y. Schein	David Herwitz	Danica Eskind	David Herwitz
Relatively Speaking	Gideon Y. Schein	David Herwitz	Danica Eskind	David Herwitz
I Do! I Do!	Gideon Y. Schein	David Herwitz	Danica Eskind	David Herwitz

Goodman Theatre

Our Town	George Keathley	Joseph Nieminski	James Edmund Brady	Gilbert V. Hemsley, Jr.
Benito Cereno	Michael Montel	David Jenkins	James Edmund Brady	Gilbert V. Hemsley, Jr.
Mourning Becomes Electra	William Woodman	John Jensen	James Edmund Brady	F. Mitchell Dana
The Last Meeting of the Knights of the White Magnolia	Harold Stone	Joseph Nieminski	John David Ridge	F. Mitchell Dana
Our Father's Failing	John Dillon	Stuart Wurtzel	John David Ridge	Arden Fingerhut
The Devil's Disciple	William Woodman	James E. Maronek	Virgil C. Johnson	Pat Collins
American Buffalo	Gregory Mosher	Michael Merritt		Robert Christen
Three Plays of the Yuan Dynasty	June Pyskacek	Rick Paul Uta Olson	Uta Olson	Robert Christen
Chicago	Dennis Zacek	Paul K. Basten	Marsha Kowal	Robert Christen
The Local Stigmatic	Gary Houston	Paul K. Basten	Marsha Kowal	Paul K. Basten
Dandelion Wine	William Woodman	Michael Merritt	Maggie Bodwell	Robert Christen
Statues and The Bridge at Belharbour	Gregory Mosher	Brian Laczko	Marsha Kowal	Robert Christen
Design for Living	William Woodman	Joseph Nieminski	James Edmund Brady	Pat Collins
Long Day's Journey Into Night	George Keathley	Joseph Nieminski	Virgil C. Johnson	F. Mitchell Dana
The Show-Off	Gene Lesser	Marjorie Kellogg	James Edmund Brady	Pat Collins
Richard III	William Woodman	John Jensen	James Edmund Brady	F. Mitchell Dana
Streamers	Gregory Mosher	Joseph Nieminski	Marsha Kowal	Pat Collins
Don Juan	William Woodman	Joseph Nieminski	Virgil C. Johnson	Gilbert V. Hemsley, Jr.
Sizwe Bansi Is Dead	Gregory Mosher	Beverly Sobieski	Michelle R. Demichelis	Robert Christen
The Sport of My Mad Mother	Dennis Zacek	Dean Taucher	Marsha Kowal	Robert Christen
A Life in the Theatre	Gregory Mosher	Michael Merritt	Marsha Kowal	Robert Christen
Kaspar	Gary Houston	Maher Ahmad	Michelle R. Demichelis	Robert Christen
George Jean Nathan in Revue	Sidney Eden	Michael Merritt	Marsha Kowal	Robert Christen

Goodspeed Opera House

Going Up	Bill Gile	Edward Haynes	David Toser	Peter M. Ehrhardt
Dearest Enemy	Bill Gile	W. Oren Parker	David Toser	Peter M. Ehrhardt
Annie	Martin Charnin	Edward Haynes	David Toser	Peter M. Ehrhardt
Sweet Adeline	Bill Gile	Edward Haynes	David Toser	Peter M. Ehrhardt

PRODUCTION	DIRECTOR	SETS	COSTUMES	LIGHTS
Hit the Deck	Dan Siretta	John Lee Beatty	David Toser	Peter M. Ehrhardt
The Red Blue-Grass Western Flyer Show	John Cullum	John Lee Beatty	David Toser	Peter M. Ehrhardt

Great Lakes Shakespeare Festival

PRODUCTION	DIRECTOR	SETS	COSTUMES	LIGHTS
The Tempest	Vincent Dowling	John Ezell	Susan Tsu	Mark Kruger
Dear Liar	Vincent Dowling	David Cunningham	Susan Murar	Mark Kruger
Ah, Wilderness!	John Dillon	John Ezell	Susan Tsu	Mark Kruger
The Devil's Disciple	Vincent Dowling	John Ezell	Susan Tsu	Mark Kruger
Romeo and Juliet	William Glover	John Ezell	Susan Murar	William Plachy
Hamlet	Vincent Dowling	John Ezell	Michael Olich	Richard Coumbs
Peg o' My Heart	Vincent Dowling	John Ezell	Michael Olich	Richard Coumbs
In a Fine Frenzy	Roger Hendricks Simon		Michael Olich	Richard Coumbs
The Glass Menagerie	Vincent Dowling	John Ezell	Michael Olich	Richard Coumbs
The Importance of Being Oscar	Roger Hendricks Simon	John Ezell		Richard Coumbs
The Taming of the Shrew	Daniel Sullivan	John Ezell	Algesa O'Sickey	Richard Coumbs

The Guthrie Theater

PRODUCTION	DIRECTOR	SETS	COSTUMES	LIGHTS
Arsenic and Old Lace	Thomas Gruenewald	Jack Barkla	Lewis Brown	Duane Schuler
The Caretaker	Stephen Kanee	Jack Barkla	Lewis Brown	Duane Schuler
A Streetcar Named Desire	Ken Ruta	Jack Barkla	Lewis Brown	Duane Schuler
Loot	Tom Moore	John Jensen	John Jensen	Duane Schuler
Private Lives	Michael Langham	Jack Barkla	Jack Edwards	Duane Schuler
Under Milk Wood	Kenneth Welsh	Robert T. Ellsworth	Jack Edwards Robert T. Ellsworth	Duane Schuler
Mother Courage and Her Children	Eugene Lion	Jack Barkla	Nancy Potts	Duane Schuler
A Christmas Carol	Stephen Kanee	Jack Barkla	Jack Edwards	Duane Schuler
Measure for Measure	Michael Langham	Desmond Heeley	Desmond Heeley	Duane Schuler
The Matchmaker	Michael Langham	Desmond Heeley	Desmond Heeley	Duane Schuler
Cat on a Hot Tin Roof	Stephen Kanee	John Conklin	Jack Edwards	Duane Schuler
Doctor Faustus	Ken Ruta	Ralph Funicello	Robert Morgan	Duane Schuler
An Enemy of the People	Adrian Hall	Sam Kirkpatrick	Sam Kirkpatrick	Duane Schuler
Rosencrantz & Guildenstern Are Dead	Stephen Kanee	John Conklin	John Conklin	Duane Schuler
The Winter's Tale	Michael Langham	Desmond Heeley	Desmond Heeley	Duane Schuler
The National Health	Peter Nichols Michael Langham	Sam Kirkpatrick	Sam Kirkpatrick	Duane Schuler

Hartford Stage Company

PRODUCTION	DIRECTOR	SETS	COSTUMES	LIGHTS
Awake and Sing	Irene Lewis	Santo Loquasto	Linda Fisher	Ian Calderon
All Over	Paul Weidner	Marjorie Kellogg	Claire Ferraris	David Chapman
Oh Coward!	Roderick Cook	Hugh Landwehr	Caley Summers	Arden Fingerhut
The Estate	Paul Weidner	Marjorie Kellogg	Claire Ferraris	Arden Fingerhut
Dream on Monkey Mountain	Charles Turner	Hugh Landwehr	Caley Summers	David Chapman
Born Yesterday	Irene Lewis	Hugh Landwehr	Claire Ferraris	Peter Hunt
The Glass Menagerie	Irene Lewis	Santo Loquasto	Santo Loquasto	Ian Calderon
The Blood Knot	Paul Weidner	Hugh Landwehr	Claire Ferraris	David Chapman
The Waltz of the Toreadors	Paul Weidner	John Conklin	Caley Summers	Peter Hunt
Counting the Ways and Listening	Edward Albee	David Jenkins	Robert Mackintosh	John McLain
A History of the American Film	Paul Weidner	Hugh Landwehr	Claire Ferraris	John McLain
Candida	John Going	Hugh Landwehr	Claire Ferraris	Steve Woodring

Hartman Theatre Company

PRODUCTION	DIRECTOR	SETS	COSTUMES	LIGHTS
The Government Inspector	Byron Ringland	Peter Harvey	Dona Granata	John McLain
The Hostage	John Beary	John Wright Stevens	Rachel Kurland	John McLain
The Runner Stumbles	Austin Pendleton	Robert Verberkmoes	James Berton Harris	Cheryl Thacker
Tom Jones	Larry Arrick	Akira Yoshimura	Rachel Kurland	Roger Meeker
Joan of Lorraine	Alan Arkin	Robert Verberkmoes	Rachel Kurland	Roger Meeker
Portrait of a Madonna and 27 Wagons Full of Cotton and I Rise in Flame, Cried the Phoenix	Del Tenney	Robert Verberkmoes	Rachel Kurland	Roger Meeker
Catch 22	Larry Arrick	Akira Yoshimura	J.D. Ferrara	Roger Meeker
The Reason We Eat	Mel Shapiro	Akira Yoshimura	Gerda Proctor	John McLain
Arsenic and Old Lace	Jerry Blunt	J.D. Ferrara	Gerda Proctor	David McWilliams
Tartuffe	Del Tenney	Zack Brown	Zack Brown	Roger Meeker
As to the Meaning of Words	John Dillon	Akira Yoshimura		Roger Meeker
Death of a Salesman	Del Tenney	Robert Verberkmoes	Gerda Proctor	John McLain
He Who Gets Slapped	Larry Arrick	Akira Yoshimura	David Murin	Roger Meeker

Hippodrome Theatre Workshop

PRODUCTION	DIRECTOR	SETS	COSTUMES	LIGHTS
Scuba Duba	Gregory Hausch	Carlos Asse		Chuck Haddad
Line	Marshall New			Grant Carrington
Ravenswood	Marilyn Wall			Grant Carrington
A Midsummer Night's Dream	Bruce Cornwell Kerry McKenney	Kerry McKenney	Fernando Fonseca	Jennifer Lane Kevin McTigue
Catch 22	Mary Hausch			Sarah Ochs
Frankenstein	Kerry McKenney	Bruce Cornwell John Page		Gregory Hausch
The Ruling Class	Marshall New	John Page Marshall New	Mary Hausch	Kerry McKenney
Tom Jones	Gregory Hausch		Cindy Duffin	Carlos Asse
The Real Inspector Hound	Mary Hausch			Gregory Hausch
Two Gentlemen of Verona	Bruce Cornwell	John Page	Mary Hausch	Peter Theoktisto Paul Pavelka
Feiffer's People	collective direction and	design		
In the Boom Boom Room	Marshall New	John Page	Marilyn Wall	Chuck Haddad Mary Hausch

PRODUCTION	DIRECTOR	SETS	COSTUMES	LIGHTS
Rubbers	Kerry McKenney		Mary Hausch	Gregory Hausch
The Duck Variations	Kerry McKenney			Gregory Hausch
Vanities	Gregory Hausch			Richard Fleming
Butley	Kerry McKenney			Mary Hausch
Steambath	Mary Hausch	Kerry McKenney		Kerry McKenney

Honolulu Theatre for Youth

PRODUCTION	DIRECTOR	SETS	COSTUMES	LIGHTS
The Hobbit	Wallace Chappell	Charles Walsh	Linda Letta	Charles Walsh
Maui the Trickster	Wallace Chappell	Charles Walsh	Linda Letta	Charles Walsh
A Christmas Carol	Wallace Chappell	Richard Mason	Richard Mason Katherine James	Charles Walsh
Tanuki	Jim Nakamoto	Charles Walsh	Frances Ellison	Charles Walsh
The Cotton Blossom Floating Palace Theatre	George Herman			
Hamlet	Wallace Chappell	Charles Walsh	Sandra Finney	
The Mirrorman	Wallace Chappell	Charles Walsh	Linda Letta	Charles Walsh
Marco Polo	Wallace Chappell	Charles Walsh	Linda Letta	Charles Walsh
The Tragical History of Dr. Faustus	Wallace Chappell	Charles Walsh	Linda Letta	Charles Walsh
The Lion, the Witch and the Wardrobe	Wallace Chappell	Charles Walsh	Linda Letta	Charles Walsh
Tales of the Pacific	Wallace Chappell	Charles Walsh	Linda Letta	Charles Walsh
The Magic Circle	Wallace Chappell	Charles Walsh	Linda Letta	

The Hudson Guild Theatre

PRODUCTION	DIRECTOR	SETS	COSTUMES	LIGHTS
Ceremonies in Dark Old Men	Craig Anderson	Joe Gandy	Leslie Day	Ron Daley
Who's Happy Now?	Craig Anderson	Sandi Marks	David James	Beth Glick
The Disintegration of James Cherry	David Kerry Heefner	Frank Kelly	Mary Ann Tolka	John Gisondi
Where's My Little Gloria?	Ernest Martin	Harold Watson	Mark Barnhart	Rick Belzer
The Diary of Anne Frank	Craig Anderson	Tom Warren	Michele Suzanne Reisch	Rick Belzer
The Admirable Crichton	Craig Anderson	Mary Beth Mann	Michele Suzanne Reisch	Rick Belzer
Creditors and Miss Julie and The Stronger	James Kendell Rip Torn	John Wright Stevens	Madeline O'Connor	John Wright Stevens Rick Belzer
Savages	Gordon Davidson	Sally Jacobs	Sally Jacobs	John Gleason
Dance on a Country Grave	Robert Brewer	Tom Warren	Donna Meyer	Curt Ostermann

Impossible Ragtime Theatre

PRODUCTION	DIRECTOR	SETS	COSTUMES	LIGHTS
The American Stickball League	George Ferencz	Ryan Hilliard		Ron Daley
Rondelay	Ted Story	Charles Miller	Michele Cohen	Ira Landau
The Hairy Ape	George Ferencz	Ron Daley George Ferencz	Sally J. Lesser	John Gisondi
Ivanov	Ted Story	Ron Daley	Margo LaZaro	Terry Byrne
Caesar	George Ferencz	John Gisondi	Sally J. Lesser	John Gisondi
Please Hang Up and Dial Again	Ted Story	Bill Stabile	Jonathan Foster	John Gisondi
The Dark at the Top of the Stairs	Jonathan Foster	Jeffrey Robin Modereger	J. Brent Porter	Preston Yarber
Dynamo	George Ferencz	Bill Stabile	Sally J. Lesser	John Gisondi
Macbeth	Ted Story	Ron Daley	J. Brent Porter	William D. Anderson
The Dybbuk	Stephen Zuckerman	Franco Colavecchia	Sally J. Lesser Kathleen Smith	Gary Porto
Jungle of Cities	George Ferencz	George Ferencz	Sally J. Lesser	Cheryl Thacker
Stage Door	Jonathan Foster	Leslie Rollins		Preston Yarber
The Refrigerators	Ted Story	George Ferencz	Linda Joan Vigdor	Cheryl Thacker

The Independent Eye

PRODUCTION	DIRECTOR	SETS	COSTUMES	LIGHTS
All productions	collective direction and	design		

Indiana Repertory Theatre

PRODUCTION	DIRECTOR	SETS	COSTUMES	LIGHTS
That Championship Season	Edward Stern	Raymond C. Recht	Sherry Mordecai	Raymond C. Recht
Arms and the Man	Vincent Dowling	John Ezell	Susan Tsu	Michael Watson
Long Day's Journey Into Night	Thomas Gruenewald	John Lee Beatty	Barbara Medlicott	Michael Watson
The Envoi Messages	Edward Stern	Raymond C. Recht	Linda Fisher	Raymond C. Recht
The Real Inspector Hound	Edward Stern	Bill Stabile	James Edmund Brady	Jody Boese
Black Comedy	Edward Stern	Bill Stabile	James Edmund Brady	Jody Boese
The Tavern	John Going	William Schroder	William Schroder	Michael Watson
The Sea Horse	Bernard Kates	Keith Brumley	Florence L. Rutherford	Carl Roetter
The Caretaker	Edward Stern	Keith Brumley	Thomas W. Schmunk	Timothy K. Joyce
The Old Jew	Jack L. Davis	Keith Brumley	Florence L. Rutherford	Allen Cornell
The Harmfulness of Tobacco	Edward Stern	Keith Brumley	Florence L. Rutherford	Allen Cornell
The Man with the Flower in His Mouth	Edward Stern	Keith Brumley	Florence L. Rutherford	Allen Cornell
The Last Meeting of the Knights of the White Magnolia	John Going	Raymond C. Recht	Carol H. Beule	Ralph John Merkle
When You Comin' Back, Red Ryder?	Edward Stern	Van Phillips	Carol H. Beule	Ralph John Merkle
The Threepenny Opera	Arne Zaslove	John Doepp	Susan Tsu	Michael Watson
The Tempest	Leland Moss	Christopher Hacker	Susan Denison	Michael Watson
Private Lives	Edward Stern	Eric Head	Carol H. Beule	Timothy K. Joyce
Sleuth	Edward Stern	Ursula Belden	Carol H. Beule	Ralph John Merkle
Who's Afraid of Virginia Woolf?	Charles Kerr	Thomas Taylor Targownik	Carol H. Beule	Charles Gotwald
The Brixton Recovery	Edward Stern	Thomas Taylor Targownik	Carol H. Beule	Susan Dandridge Bridget Beier
Miss Julie	William Guild	Thomas Taylor Targownik	Florence L. Rutherford	Joel Grynheim

PRODUCTION	DIRECTOR	SETS	COSTUMES	LIGHTS
INTAR, International Arts Relations				
La Dama Boba	Francisco Morin	Julio Matilla	Julio Matilla	Francis Roefaro
Cap-a-Pie II	Maria Irene Fornes	Robert Joyner		Curt Ostermann
La Herencia Puertorriquena	Steven-Jan Hoff	Steven-Jan Hoff	Steven-Jan Hoff	Steven-Jan Hoff
Yoruba	Doris Castellanos	Antonio Alvarez	Demetrio Alfonso	Candice Dunn
La Cencicienta	Manuel Martinez	Steve Sullivan	Steve Sullivan	Candice Dunn
Greta Garbo de la calle 42	Max Ferra	Ken Holamon	Ken Holamon	Sally Locke
Nuestro New York!	Max Ferra	Ken Holamon	Ken Holamon	Sally Locke
			Jo Goiran	
The House of Bernarda Alba	Max Ferra	Sally Locke	Betty Chlystek	Sally Locke
Lolita en el Jardin	Maria Irene Fornes	Beth Kuhn	Beth Kuhn	Joe Ray
Interart Theatre				
The First of April	Margot Lewitin	Patricia Woodbridge	Mary Alice Orito	Cheryl Thacker
Matushka-Barynya	Margot Lewitin	Patricia Woodbridge	Mary Alice Orito	Cheryl Thacker
Video Toys	Wendy Clarke	Wendy Clarke	Wendy Clarke	Wendy Clarke
Acrobatics	Joyce Aaron	Patricia Woodbridge	Mary Alice Orito	Cheryl Thacker
Crab Quadrille	Margot Lewitin	Patricia Woodbridge	Mimi Berman Maxmen	Cheryl Thacker
Still Life	Rhea Gaisner	Christina Weppner	Susan Tsu	Patricia Moeser
The Expelled	Rhea Gaisner	Christina Weppner	Susan Tsu	Patricia Moeser
New Roots	Margot Lewitin		Maria Irene Fornes	Rebecca Binks
Cross Country	Elinor Renfield	Christina Weppner	Margo LaZaro	Pat Stern
Quarry	Meredith Monk	Ping Chong	Lanny Harrison	Beverly Emmons
		Jean-Claude Ribes		
Intiman Theatre Company				
Arms and the Man	Stephen Rosenfield	Charles Kading	Donna Eskew	Cynthia J. Hawkins
Elektra	Margaret Booker	Robert A. Dahlstrom	Donna Eskew	Cynthia J. Hawkins
Anatol	Margaret Booker	Charles Kading	Donna Eskew	Cynthia J. Hawkins
Bus Stop	Pat Patton	Karen Gjelsteen	Stephanie Poire	Cynthia J. Hawkins
The Northwest Show	Margaret Booker	Ronald Erickson	Donna Eskew	Cynthia J. Hawkins
		Ted D'Arms	Stephanie Poire	
Toys in the Attic	Margaret Booker	Robert A. Dahlstrom	Nanrose Buchman	Richard Devin
The Importance of Being Earnest	Clayton Corzatte	Karen Gjelsteen	Nanrose Buchman	James Verdery
Ghosts	Margaret Booker	Michael Miller	Nanrose Buchman	Cynthia J. Hawkins
The Playboy of the Western World	Pat Patton	Robert A. Dahlstrom	Ronald Erickson	Cynthia J. Hawkins
A Moon for the Misbegotten	Margaret Booker	Robert A. Dahlstrom	Ellen M. Kozak	James Verdery
The Invisible Theatre				
Dauntless	Molly McKasson	Peter Conway	Peter Conway	Mark Betz
Noises	Page Burkholder	Peter Conway	Peter Conway	
Echoes	Susan Claassen	Peter Conway	Peter Conway	
Vienna Play	Page Burkholder	Rory McCarthy	Peter Conway	
Let Us Now Praise the Good Old Days	Greg McCaslin	Keith Dick	Peter Conway	Russell Stagg
	Susan Claassen			
Sideshow	Molly McKasson	Joseph Calvin	Kit Winslow	Jay Smith
Weeds	Susan Claassen	Jack Schwanke	Deb Walker	Russell Stagg
A Midsummer Night's Dream	Page Burkholder	Reagan Cook	Jan Olson	Melissa Davis
Iowa Theater Lab				
The Naming	Ric Zank			
Dancer without Arms	Ric Zank			
Moby Dick	Ric Zank			
Sweetbird	Ric Zank			
Judas-Pax	Christopher Amato			
	Ric Zank			
Passage	Ric Zank			
Jean Cocteau Repertory				
Twelfth Night	Eve Adamson	James S. Payne	James S. Payne	James S. Payne
Brecht on Brecht	Eve Adamson	James S. Payne	James S. Payne	James S. Payne
Desire Under the Elms	Eve Adamson	James S. Payne	James S. Payne	James S. Payne
The Importance of Being Earnest	Eve Adamson	James S. Payne	James S. Payne	James S. Payne
Endgame	Eve Adamson	James S. Payne	James S. Payne	James S. Payne
The Count of Monte Cristo	Eve Adamson	James S. Payne	James S. Payne	James S. Payne
Vera	Eve Adamson	James S. Payne	James S. Payne	Craig Smith
Winterset	Eve Adamson	James S. Payne	James S. Payne	James S. Payne
The Lesson	Eve Adamson	James S. Payne	James S. Payne	Craig Smith
Macbeth	Eve Adamson	James S. Payne	James S. Payne	Craig Smith
Rhinoceros	Eve Adamson	James S. Payne	James S. Payne	James S. Payne
Androcles and the Lion	Eve Adamson	James S. Payne	James S. Payne	James S. Payne
The Caretaker	Eve Adamson	James S. Payne	James S. Payne	James S. Payne
The Cenci	Eve Adamson	Douglas McKeown	James S. Payne	James S. Payne
She Stoops to Conquer	Eve Adamson	Douglas McKeown	James S. Payne	James S. Payne
Salome	Eve Adamson	Douglas McKeown	Douglas McKeown	James S. Payne
The Brass Butterfly	Eve Adamson	Douglas McKeown	James S. Payne	James S. Payne
Joseph Jefferson Theatre Company				
Rip Van Winkle	William Koch	Gerald Weinstein	Hugh Sherrer	Richard B. Williams
Thunder Rock	William Koch	Richard B. Williams	John Scheffler	Robby Monk
April Fish	Christopher Cox	Cliff Simon	A. Christina Giannini	Francis Roefaro
The Wooing of Lady Sunday	Bill Herndon	Cliff Simon	A. Christina Giannini	Francis Roefaro
Memory of a Large Christmas	William Koch			
Morning's at Seven	Cathy Roskam	Gerald Weinstein	Cindy Polk	Robby Monk

PRODUCTION	DIRECTOR	SETS	COSTUMES	LIGHTS
John	Cyril Simon	Kenneth Shewer	Susan Hilferty	Jennifer Herrick Jebens
Jack Fallon Fare Thee Well	Cathy Roskam	Cynthia Hamilton Gerald Weinstein	Marsha Imhof	Susan Hilferty Susan Sudert
U.S.A.	John Henry Davis	Raymond C. Recht	A. Christina Giannini	Francis Roefaro
The Well	Julianne Boyd	Bill Groom	Bill Groom	Boyd Masten
Johnny Belinda	William Koch	Gerald Weinstein	Cindy Polk	Richard B. Williams
Skaters	Bill Herndon	Bill Groom	A. Christina Giannini	Ronald B. Lindholm
The Second Man	Marvin Einhorn	Raymond C. Recht	Vittorio Capecce	William Stallings

Julian Theatre

PRODUCTION	DIRECTOR	SETS	COSTUMES	LIGHTS
Home Free	Alma Becker	Linda Hauswirth	Linda Hauswirth	Steve Rehn
Margaret, Goodbye	Edward Weingold	Edward Weingold	Edward Weingold	Steve Rehn
The CIA Makes a Hit	Edward Weingold	Edward Weingold	Edward Weingold	Steve Rehn
A Very Gentle Person	Richard Reineccius Edward Weingold	Richard Reineccius		John Albert
Documents from Hell	Richard Reineccius	Richard Reineccius	Shoshonah Dubiner	Marcia Pesce
The Mound	Edward Weingold	Bill Wulf		Bonnie Barbarini
Rumpelstiltskin and the Magic Eye	Brenda Berlin Reineccius	Janet Lipkin	Regina Cate	
Ralph Who Must Run and	Robert Woodruff	Ron Madonia	Linda Hauswirth	Tom Ames
The Temptations of Sister Aimee Semple McPherson	Edward Weingold	Michael Kroschel	Linda Hauswirth	Tom Ames
The Maids	Alma Becker	Linda Hauswirth	Linda Hauswirth	Alma Becker
Hamlet	Richard Rekow	Dale Altvater	Regina Cate	Dale Altvater
The Architect and the Emperor of Assyria	Lewis Brown	Linda Hauswirth	Linda Hauswirth	Bonnie Barbarini
Along the Garlic Route	Barbara Graham	Steve Rehn	Linda Hauswirth	Bonnie Barbarini
The Inheritance	Edward Weingold	Steve Rehn	Linda Hauswirth	Bonnie Barbarini
Daddies	Alma Becker	Ron Madonia	Linda Hauswirth	Ron Madonia
The Long Voyage Home and	Richard Reineccius	Dale Altvater	Alice Truscott	Dale Altvater
The Rope and	Brenda Berlin Reineccius			
Where the Cross Is Made and Ile	Richard Reineccius			
Awake and Sing	Edward Weingold	Michael Kroschel Ron Madonia	Linda Hauswirth	Ron Madonia

Living Stage

PRODUCTION	DIRECTOR	SETS	COSTUMES	LIGHTS
All performances are improvisations created by the company	Robert Alexander			

Long Wharf Theatre

PRODUCTION	DIRECTOR	SETS	COSTUMES	LIGHTS
Artichoke	Arvin Brown	David Jenkins	Bill Walker	Ronald Wallace
The Show-Off	Peter Levin	Kenneth Foy	Linda Fisher	Jamie Gallagher
What Every Woman Knows	Kenneth Frankel	Steven Rubin	Jania Szatanski	Judy Rasmuson
Streamers	Mike Nichols	Tony Walton	Bill Walker	Ronald Wallace
On the Outside	Arvin Brown	David Jenkins	Jania Szatanski	Ronald Wallace
On the Inside	Arvin Brown	David Jenkins	Jania Szatanski	Ronald Wallace
The House of Mirth	Waris Hussein	Marjorie Kellogg	Bill Walker	Judy Rasmuson
Daarlin' Juno	Arvin Brown	David Jenkins	Bill Walker	Ronald Wallace
Alphabetical Order	Steven Robman	Marjorie Kellogg	Carrie F. Robbins	Ronald Wallace
The Autumn Garden	Arvin Brown	David Jenkins	Bill Walker	Judy Rasmuson
Home	Michael Lindsay-Hogg	Steven Rubin	Mary Strieff	Jamie Gallagher
The Shadow Box	Gordon Davidson	Ming Cho Lee	Bill Walker	Ronald Wallace
Saint Joan	Martin Fried	Marjorie Kellogg	Bill Walker	Ronald Wallace
Absent Friends	Eric Thompson	Edward Burbridge	Michele Suzanne Reisch	Ronald Wallace
The Rose Tattoo	Steven Robman	John Conklin	Bill Walker	Judy Rasmuson
The Gin Game	Mike Nichols	David Mitchell	Bill Walker	Ronald Wallace

Looking Glass Theatre

PRODUCTION	DIRECTOR	SETS	COSTUMES	LIGHTS
Tjupak	John Emigh			
How That Incredible Rhode Island Jonnycake...	Bernice Bronson	Stephen Pollock	Betsey Sherman	
Earthwatch	Bernice Bronson	Joseph Geran	Joseph Geran Jean Matthewson	
Alice in the American Wonderland	Bernice Bronson	Robert D. Soule	Betsey Sherman	

Loretto-Hilton Repertory Theatre

PRODUCTION	DIRECTOR	SETS	COSTUMES	LIGHTS
A Midsummer Night's Dream	David Frank	John Kavelin	John Carver Sullivan	Peter E. Sargent
Desire Under the Elms	Davey Marlin-Jones	Grady Larkins	Bill Walker	Peter E. Sargent
Tom Jones	Larry Arrick	John Kavelin	John Carver Sullivan	Glenn Dunn
A Memory of Two Mondays	Davey Marlin-Jones	Grady Larkins	Mary Strieff	Stephen Ross
Brandy Station	Davey Marlin-Jones	Grady Larkins	Grady Larkins	Stephen Ross
Once in a Lifetime	Jack O'Brien	John Kavelin	John Carver Sullivan	Peter E. Sargent
Billy Budd	David Frank	John Kavelin	John Carver Sullivan	Peter E. Sargent
The Eccentricities of a Nightingale	Davey Marlin-Jones	Atkin Pace	Bill Walker	Peter E. Sargent
The Beaux' Stratagem	Harold Scott	John Kavelin	John Carver Sullivan	Glenn Dunn
The House of Blue Leaves	Carl Schurr	John Kavelin	Catherine Reich	Peter E. Sargent
The Front Page	Davey Marlin-Jones	Karen R. Connolly	John Carver Sullivan	Glenn Dunn

Lovelace Theatre Company

PRODUCTION	DIRECTOR	SETS	COSTUMES	LIGHTS
The Reluctant Dragon	Jewel Walker	Tim Joswick Tina Haatainen	Margo Lovelace	Tim Joswick Tina Haatainen
The Mechanical and Picturesque	Margo Lovelace	Tim Joswick Tina Haatainen	Margo Lovelace	Tim Joswick Tina Haatainen

PRODUCTION	DIRECTOR	SETS	COSTUMES	LIGHTS
Ragtime and All That Jazz	David Visser	Margo Lovelace	Margo Lovelace	Norman Beck
Love's the Best Doctor	Richard McElvain	Laurence Sammons	Margo Lovelace	Norman Beck

Mabou Mines

PRODUCTION	DIRECTOR	SETS	COSTUMES	LIGHTS
Cascando	Jo Anne Akalaitis			
The Red Horse Animation	Lee Breuer			Jene Highstein
The Lost Ones	Lee Breuer	Thom Cathcart		Thom Cathcart
Play and Come & Go	Lee Breuer	Jene Highstein	Anne Frank	
The B-Beaver Animation	Lee Breuer	Tina Girouard		Thom Cathcart
Dressed Like an Egg	Jo Anne Akalaitis	Jo Anne Akalaitis	Dru-Ann Chukram	Robin Thomas
			Ann Farrington	
			Sally Rosen	

The Magic Theatre

PRODUCTION	DIRECTOR	SETS	COSTUMES	LIGHTS
AC/DC	John Lion	Jock Reynolds		Dan Swain
The Pink Helmet and	John Lion	Donald Cate	Regina Cate	Dave Goodno
The Grabbing of the Fairy				
Angel City	Sam Shepard	Morgan Hall		Dave Goodno
Sexual Perversity in Chicago and	Albert Takazauckas	Donald Cate	Regina Cate	Dennis J. Breen
The Duck Variations				
Inacoma	Sam Shepard			John Chapot
Alfred Dies	John Lion	Donald Cate		Richard Reynolds
Hospital	Suzanne Helmuth	Suzanne Helmuth	Suzanne Helmuth	Suzanne Helmuth
	Jock Reynolds	Jock Reynolds	Jock Reynolds	Jock Reynolds
Are You Lookin'?	Robert Woodruff	Larry Beard		John Chapot

The Manhattan Project

PRODUCTION	DIRECTOR	SETS	COSTUMES	LIGHTS
Jinxs Bridge				Victor En Yu Tan
A Thousand Nights and a Night	Gerry Bamman	Lowell Detweiler	Nanzi Adzima	Will Morrison
Between the Wars	Wilford Leach	Wilford Leach	Wilford Leach	Wilford Leach
The Room	Saskia Noordhoek Hegt			

Manhattan Theatre Club

PRODUCTION	DIRECTOR	SETS	COSTUMES	LIGHTS
Golden Boy	Lynne Meadow	John Lee Beatty	Vittorio Capecce	William D. Anderson
Life Class	Robert Mandel	Marjorie Kellogg	Jennifer von Mayrhauser	Arden Fingerhut
The Blood Knot	Thomas Bullard	Patricia Woodbridge	Kenneth M. Yount	Arden Fingerhut
The Son	Stephen Pascal	Raymond C. Recht	Vittorio Capecce	Raymond C. Recht
In the Wine Time	Robert Macbeth	Steven Rubin	Grace Williams	Spencer Mosse
Transformations	David Shookhoff	Patricia Woodbridge	Ken Holamon	Spencer Mosse
Sea Marks	Steven Robman	Marjorie Kellogg	Kenneth M. Yount	Arden Fingerhut
The Basement and	David Kerry Heefner	Sandi Marks	Louis Pshena	Patricia Moeser
A Slight Ache				
Geography of a Horse Dreamer	Jacques Levy	T. Winberry	Kenneth M. Yount	Frank R. Kelly
Patrick Henry Lake Liquors	Ronald Roston	Ernest Allen Smith	Ernest Allen Smith	John Gisondi
The Voice of the Turtle	Julianne Boyd	Bill Groom	Danny Mizell	Patricia Moeser
Dearly Beloved	Paul Schneider	Vittorio Capecce	Margo Bruton Elkow	Paul Kaine
The Pokey	Lynne Meadow	Raymond C. Recht	Margo Bruton Elkow	William D. Anderson
The Human Voice	Thomas Bullard	Vittorio Capecce	Ann Wolff	John Gisondi
Children	Melvin Bernhardt	Marjorie Kellogg	Patricia McGourty	Arden Fingerhut
Ashes	Lynne Meadow	John Lee Beatty	Jennifer von Mayrhauser	Dennis Parichy
Boesman and Lena	Thomas Bullard	Atkin Pace	Rachel Kurland	Spencer Mosse
The Gathering	Austin Pendleton	Patricia Woodbridge	Kenneth M. Yount	Cheryl Thacker
In the Summer House	Stephen Hollis	John Kasarda	Rachel Kurland	Dennis Parichy
Claw	Stephen Pascal	Bill Byrd, Jr.	Rachel Kurland	John Gisondi
Ballymurphy	Ronald Roston	Ernest Allen Smith	Joyce Aysta	Cheryl Thacker
Quail Southwest	Andy Wolk	James Joy	Susan Tsu	Toni Goldin
Billy Irish	Barry Marshall	Eugene Warner	Kenneth M. Yount	Cheryl Thacker
Statues and *Exhibition* and	Stanley Wojewodski, Jr.	David Potts	Robert Wojewodski	Ian Calderon
The Bridge at Belharbour				
The Last Street Play	Thomas Bullard	David Potts	Judy Dearing	Dennis Parichy
The Wise Woman and the King	David Shookhoff	Steven Rubin	Steven Rubin	Dennis Parichy

Mark Taper Forum

PRODUCTION	DIRECTOR	SETS	COSTUMES	LIGHTS
Once in a Lifetime	Edward Parone	Jim Newton	Pete Menefee	Tharon Musser
Too Much Johnson	Gordon Davidson	Robert Zentis	Tom Rasmussen	H.R. Poindexter
The Shadow Box	Gordon Davidson	Robert Zentis	Tom Rasmussen	H.R. Poindexter
The Duchess of Malfi	Howard Sackler	Paul Sylbert	Dorothy Jeakins	John Gleason
The Three Sisters	Edward Parone	Sally Jacobs	Sally Jacobs	F. Mitchell Dana
Ashes	Edward Parone	Sally Jacobs	Julie Weiss	F. Mitchell Dana
And Where She Stops Nobody Knows	Gordon Davidson	Sally Jacobs	Julie Weiss	F. Mitchell Dana
Cross Country	Vickie Rue	Sally Jacobs	Julie Weiss	F. Mitchell Dana
The Robber Bridegroom	Gerald Freedman	Douglas W. Schmidt	Jeanne Button	David F. Segal
Ice	Jeff Bleckner	John DeSantis	John DeSantis	John DeSantis
Vanities	Garland Wright	John Arnone	David James	F. Mitchell Dana
Travesties	Edward Parone	Ralph Funicello	Peter J. Hall	Tharon Musser
The Importance of Being Earnest	Edward Parone	Ralph Funicello	Peter J. Hall	Tharon Musser
A History of the American Film	Peter Mark Schifter	John Conklin	Joe I. Tompkins	F. Mitchell Dana
Angel City	Robert Calhoun	John Conklin	Joe I. Tompkins	F. Mitchell Dana
Bugs and Guns	John Dennis	Charles Berliner	F. Mitchell Dana	Charles Berliner
Leander Stillwell	John Dennis	Charles Berliner	F. Mitchell Dana	Charles Berliner

321

PRODUCTION	DIRECTOR	SETS	COSTUMES	LIGHTS
McCarter Theatre				
A Grave Undertaking	Michael Kahn	Paul Zalon	Lawrence Casey	John McLain
The Royal Family	Ellis Rabb	Oliver Smith	Ann Roth	John Gleason
Section Nine	Michael Kahn	Kert Lundell	Jeanne Button	John McLain
The Heiress	Michael Kahn	David Jenkins	Jane Greenwood	L.B. Achziger
Awake and Sing	Kenneth Frankel	Marjorie Kellogg	Jeanne Button	John McLain
The Winter's Tale	Michael Kahn	John Conklin	Jane Greenwood	John McLain
A Streetcar Named Desire	Michael Kahn	Michael H. Yeargen Lawrence King	Jane Greenwood	John McLain
Major Barbara	Kenneth Frankel	Marjorie Kellogg	Carrie F. Robbins	Pat Collins
The Night Of the Tribades	Michael Kahn	Michael H. Yeargen Lawrence King	Jane Greenwood	John McLain
The Physicists	Gene Lesser	Tony Straiges	Jeanne Button	John McLain
Angel City	Michael Kahn	David Jenkins	Laura Crow	John McLain
Design for Living	Stephen Porter	Zack Brown	Zack Brown	John McLain
Meadow Brook Theatre				
A Midsummer Night's Dream	Terence Kilburn	Peter Hicks	Mary Lynn Bonnell	Larry A. Reed
Witness for the Prosecution	Terence Kilburn	Peter Hicks	Mary Lynn Bonnell	Robert Neu
Arms and the Man	Terence Kilburn	Nancy Thompson	Mary Lynn Bonnell	Jeffrey Schissler
The Little Foxes	Charles Nolte	C. Lance Brockman	Mary Lynn Bonnell	Jean A. Montgomery
Relatively Speaking	Terence Kilburn	Peter Hicks	Mary Lynn Bonnell	Larry A. Reed
Under Milk Wood	Michael Montel	Larry A. Reed	Mary Lynn Bonnell	Robert Neu
Born Yesterday	Anthony Mockus	Thomas A. Aston	Mary Lynn Bonnell	Fred Fonner
Yankee Ingenuity	Terence Kilburn	Peter Hicks	Mary Lynn Bonnell	Larry A. Reed
Man and Superman	Terence Kilburn	Peter Hicks	Mary Lynn Bonnell	Nancy Thompson
The Night of the Iguana	Charles Nolte	C. Lance Brockman	Mary Lynn Bonnell	Jean A. Montgomery
The School for Wives	Terence Kilburn	Peter Hicks	Mary Lynn Bonnell	Fred Fonner
When You Comin' Back, Red Ryder?	Charles Nolte	C. Lance Brockman	Mary Lynn Bonnell	Nancy Thompson
Sleuth	Vincent Dowling	Larry A. Reed	Mary Lynn Bonnell	Larry A. Reed
The Merchant of Venice	Terence Kilburn	Peter Hicks	Mary Lynn Bonnell	Larry A. Reed
The Show-Off	John Ulmer	Robert Joseph Mooney	Mary Lynn Bonnell	Fred Fonner
Dames at Sea	Don Price	Peter Hicks	Mary Lynn Bonnell	Larry A. Reed
Medicine Show				
Medicine Show	Barbara Vann		Patricia McGourty	
Glowworm	Barbara Vann	Brozgold	Patricia McGourty	Linnaea Tillett
Frogs	James Barbosa		Patricia McGourty	
Meredith Monk/The House				
Quarry	Meredith Monk	Ping Chong Jean-Claude Ribes	Lanny Harrison	Beverly Emmons
Paris	Meredith Monk Ping Chong	Meredith Monk Ping Chong	Meredith Monk Ping Chong	Meredith Monk Ping Chong
Venice	Meredith Monk Ping Chong	Meredith Monk Ping Chong	Meredith Monk Ping Chong	Meredith Monk Ping Chong
Chacon	Meredith Monk Ping Chong	Meredith Monk Ping Chong	Meredith Monk Ping Chong	Meredith Monk Ping Chong
Songs from the Hill	Meredith Monk	Meredith Monk	Meredith Monk	Meredith Monk
Tablet	Meredith Monk	Meredith Monk	Meredith Monk	Meredith Monk
Milwaukee Repertory Theater Company				
King Lear	Nagle Jackson	Christopher M. Idoine	Elizabeth Covey	Christopher M. Idoine
Democracy	John Olon-Scrymgeour	R.H. Graham	Elizabeth Covey	R.H. Graham
The School for Wives	Nagle Jackson	Christopher M. Idoine	Elizabeth Covey	Christopher M. Idoine
The Visions of Simone Machard	Nagle Jackson	Christopher M. Idoine	Elizabeth Covey	Christopher M. Idoine
Never a Snug Harbor	John Dillon	R.H. Graham	Ellen M. Kozak	R.H. Graham
My Sister, My Sister	Paul Weidner	Christopher M. Idoine	Ellen M. Kozak	Christopher M. Idoine
Fanshen	Barry Boys	Johniene Papandreas	Ellen M. Kozak Holly Olson Susan Perkins	Christopher M. Idoine
Out	Robert Lanchester	James Wolk	Ellen M. Kozak	Frances Aronson
Out to Sea	William McKereghan	James Wolk	Ellen M. Kozak	Frances Aronson
Happy Days	Montgomery Davis	Valerie Kuehn	Joanne Karaska	Charles Gotwald
Death of a Salesman	Nagle Jackson	R.H. Graham	Ellen M. Kozak	R.H. Graham
The Trial of the Moke	Robert Lanchester	Christopher M. Idoine	Ellen M. Kozak	Christopher M. Idoine
A Christmas Carol	Nagle Jackson	Christopher M. Idoine	Elizabeth Covey	Christopher M. Idoine
Private Lives	William Glover	R.H. Graham	Ellen M. Kozak	R.H. Graham
Volpone	Nagle Jackson	Christopher M. Idoine	Linda Fisher	Christopher M. Idoine
Vanities	Kent Paul	R.H. Graham	Ellen M. Kozak	R.H. Graham
The Dog Ran Away	Nagle Jackson	Christopher M. Idoine	Ellen M. Kozak	Christopher M. Idoine
The Birthday Party	Sanford Robbins	Pete Davis	Rosemary Ingham	R.H. Graham
In Memory Of	Daniel Mooney	Sam Garth	Joanne Karaska	Seth Price
Domino Courts	Walter L. Schoen	Valerie Kuehn	Ellen M. Kozak	Seth Price
Missouri Repertory Theatre				
Born Yesterday	Robin Humphrey	James Hart Stearns	Judith Dolan	Curt Ostermann
The Cherry Orchard	Vincent Dowling	John Ezell	Vincent Scassellati	Joseph Appelt
Much Ado About Nothing	James Assad	Michael J. O'Kane	Judith Dolan	Joseph Appelt
The Last Meeting of the Knights of the White Magnolia	Thomas Gruenewald	J. Morton Walker	Barbara E. Medlicott	Joseph Appelt
A Streetcar Named Desire	Francis J. Cullinan	John Ezell	Vincent Scassellati	Curt Ostermann
The Rainmaker	James Assad	G. Philippe de Rosier	Vincent Scassellati	Joseph Appelt

PRODUCTION	DIRECTOR	SETS	COSTUMES	LIGHTS
The Morgan Yard	Kevin O'Morrison	Max A. Beatty	Vincent Scassellati	Joseph Appelt
The Drunkard	Francis J. Cullinan	James L. Joy	Vincent Scassellati	Joseph Appelt
Don Juan of Flatbush	Thomas Gruenewald	James L. Joy	Barbara E. Medlicott	Joseph Appelt
The Great White Hope	John O'Shaughnessy	G. Philippe de Rosier	Vincent Scassellati	Joseph Appelt
The Heiress	John Reich	John Ezell	Baker S. Smith	Curt Ostermann
Who's Afraid of Virginia Woolf?	James Assad	Judie A. Juracek	Barbara E. Medlicott	Curt Ostermann
Once in a Lifetime	Thomas Gruenewald	Frederic James	Barbara E. Medlicott	Curt Ostermann

Music-Theatre Performing Group/Lenox Arts Center

Nightclub Cantata	Elizabeth Swados	Patricia Woodbridge	Kate Carmel	Cheryl Thacker
The Club	Tommy Tune	Tommy Tune	Kate Carmel	Cheryl Thacker
Viva Reviva	Graciela Daniele	Kate Carmel	Kate Carmel	Cheryl Thacker
A Natural Death	Michael Feingold	Michael Feingold	Kate Carmel	Cheryl Thacker

National Black Theatre

Soljourney Into Truth	Barbara Ann Teer		Larry LeGaspi Judy Dearing	Omowale Harewood

National Theatre of the Deaf

Parade	Linda Bove David Hays	David Hays	Fred Voelpel	Guy Bergquist
Four Saints in Three Acts	David Hays	Patricia Zipprodt	Fred Voelpel	David Hays
The Harmfulness of Tobacco	Mack Scism	Patricia Zipprodt	Fred Voelpel	David Hays
Children's Letters to God	Bernard Bragg	Patricia Zipprodt	Fred Voelpel	David Hays
Sir Gawain and the Green Knight	Mack Scism	David Hays	Fred Voelpel	David Hays

The Negro Ensemble Company

Eden	Edmund Cambridge	Pamela S. Peniston	Edna Watson	Sandra L. Ross
Livin' Fat	Douglas Turner Ward	Mary Mease Warren	Mary Mease Warren	Sandra L. Ross
The Brownsville Raid	Israel Hicks	Neil Peter Jampolis	Mary Mease Warren	Sandra L. Ross
The Great MacDaddy	Douglas Turner Ward	William Ritman	Arthur McGee	Sandra L. Ross
Square Root of Soul	Perry Schwartz			Perry Schwartz

The New Dramatists

Never a Snug Harbor	Tom Ligon	Clay Coyle	Clay Coyle	Gregg Marriner
The Last Christians	Clint Atkinson	Clay Coyle	Clay Coyle	Clay Coyle
The Wolves and the Lamb	Christopher Adler	Clay Coyle	Ari DeGangotena	Clay Coyle
Sister Sadie	Clifford Mason	Guy J. Smith		Guy J. Smith
Father Uxbridge Wants to Marry	Frank Gagliano	Clay Coyle		Gary C. Porto
The Resurrection of Jackie Cramer	J Ranelli	Clay Coyle		Gary C. Porto
Kerouac	Kenneth Frankel	Clay Coyle		Clay Coyle
The Brixton Recovery	Cliff Goodwin	Ken Fillo		Greg Buch
Even the Window Is Gone	Shan Covey	Ken Fillo	Linda Roots	Jo Mayer
The Wakefield Plays	John Dillon	Bil Mikulewicz	Susan Tsu	Arden Fingerhut
Bull Fight Cow	Warren Kliewer	Ken Fillo	Veronica Deisler	Ken Fillo
Berserkers	Cliff Goodwin	Douglas F. Lebrecht	Linda Roots	Priscilla Cooper
Lust	Andrew Harris	Letch Hudgins	June Lowe	Ken Fillo
A New World	Marian Winters			Ned Hallick
The Mute Who Sang	Frank Scaringi	Robert Lewis Smith		Robert Lewis Smith

New Federal Theatre

Toe Jam	Anderson Johnson, Jr.	C. Richard Mills	Georgia Ellis	Ira Landau
Section D	Anderson Johnson, Jr.	C. Richard Mills	Kathy Roberson	Sandra L. Ross
For Colored Girls who have Considered Suicide When The Rainbow is Enuf	Oz Scott	Ifa Iyaun	Judy Dearing	Victor En Yu Tan
Showdown	Shauneille Perry	C. Richard Mills	Judy Dearing	George Greczylo
Bargainin' Thing	Harold Scott	C. Richard Mills	Ornyece Prince	Sandra L. Ross
Mondongo	Dean Irby	Joseph Gandy	Elsie Rodriguez	George Greczylo
The Defense	Dennis Scott	C. Richard Mills	Judy Dearing	George Greczylo
Perdido (Lost)	Reggie Life	C. Richard Mills	Barbara Lee Maccarone	George Greczylo
Divine Comedy	Clinton Turner Davis	C. Richard Mills	Judy Dearing	Sandra L. Ross
Macbeth	Edmund Cambridge	C. Richard Mills	Edna Watson	Shirley Prendergast
Daddy	Woodie King, Jr.	Karl Eigsti	Judy Dearing	Shirley Prendergast
Season's Reason	Ron Milner	C. Richard Mills	Anita Ellis	George Greczylo

New Jersey Shakespeare Festival

The Tempest	Paul Barry	David M. Glenn	Dean Reiter	Gary C. Porto
Henry V	Paul Barry	David M. Glenn	Dean Reiter	Gary C. Porto
The Best Man	Paul Barry	David M. Glenn	Dean Reiter	Gary C. Porto
The Devil's Disciple	Paul Barry	David M. Glenn	Dean Reiter	Gary C. Porto
Private Lives	Davey Marlin-Jones	David M. Glenn	Dean Reiter	Gary C. Porto
Stop the World — I Want to Get Off	Paul Barry	David M. Glenn	Jean Steinlein	Gary C. Porto
The Playboy of the Western World	Paul Barry	David M. Glenn	Jean Steinlein	Gary C. Porto
Of Mice and Men	Paul Barry	David M. Glenn	Jean Steinlein	Gary C. Porto
Much Ado About Nothing	Paul Barry	Don C. Coleman	Jeffrey L. Ullman	Gary C. Porto
Titus Andronicus	Paul Barry	Don C. Coleman	Jeffrey L. Ullman	Gary C. Porto
Cyrano de Bergerac	Paul Barry	Don C. Coleman	Jeffrey L. Ullman	Gary C. Porto
An Enemy of the People	Paul Barry	Don C. Coleman	Dean Reiter	Gary C. Porto
The Hot l Baltimore	Davey Marlin-Jones	Don C. Coleman	Dean Reiter	Gary C. Porto
The Glass Menagerie	Paul Barry	Don C. Coleman	Dean Reiter	Gary C. Porto

PRODUCTION	DIRECTOR	SETS	COSTUMES	LIGHTS
The New Playwrights' Theatre of Washington				
Bertie	Paul Hildebrand, Jr.	Carla Messina	Mary Kay McGregor	Robert Graham Small
Mama of the Year	Walter Cedric Harris	Martin Petersilia		Tony Reid
				Robert Graham Small
Sirocco	Ken Bloom		Henry Shaffer	William Turnbull, Jr.
Gymnasium	Kathryn Santaniello	William Turnbull, Jr.	Phillip Wright	William Turnbull, Jr.
Hagar's Children	Robert Graham Small	William Turnbull, Jr.	Carol Ingram	William Turnbull, Jr.
Bride of Sirocco	Ken Bloom	Russell Metheny	Mary Kay McGregor	William Turnbull, Jr.
Fox against the Fence	Paul Hildebrand, Jr.	Robert Graham Small	Carol Ingram	William Turnbull, Jr.
Gus and Company	Robert Graham Small	Robert Graham Small	Carol Ingram	William Turnbull, Jr.
Canticle	Paul Hildebrand, Jr.	Carla Messina	Mary Kay McGregor	Robert Graham Small
New York Shakespeare Festival				
Hamlet	Michael Rudman	Santo Loquasto	Albert Wolsky	Martin Aronstein
The Comedy of Errors	John Pasquin	Santo Loquasto	Santo Loquasto	Martin Aronstein
The Shoeshine Parlor	Marvin Felix Camillo	David Mitchell	Judy Dearing	Spencer Mosse
Jesse and the Bandit Queen	Gordon Stewart	Richard J. Graziano	Hilary M. Rosenfeld	Arden Fingerhut
Rich and Famous	Mel Shapiro	Dan Snyder	Theoni V. Aldredge	Arden Fingerhut
Apple Pie	Joseph Papp	David Mitchell	Timothy Miller	Pat Collins
So Nice, They Named It Twice	Bill Lathan			
Rebel Women	Jack Hofsiss	John Lee Beatty	Carrie F. Robbins	Neil Peter Jampolis
For Colored Girls who have Considered Suicide When The Rainbow is Enuf	Oz Scott	Ming Cho Lee	Judy Dearing	Jennifer Tipton
Trelawny of the "Wells"	A.J. Antoon	David Mitchell	Theoni V. Aldredge	Ian Calderon
Mrs. Warren's Profession	Gerald Freedman	David Mitchell	Theoni V. Aldredge	Martin Aronstein
The Threepenny Opera	Richard Foreman	Douglas W. Schmidt	Theoni V. Aldredge	Pat Collins
The Shortchanged Review	Richard Southern	Marsha L. Eck	Hilary M. Rosenfeld	Cheryl Thacker
Streamers	Mike Nichols	Tony Walton	Bill Walker	Ronald Wallace
The Leaf People	Tom O'Horgan	John Conklin	Randy Barcelo	John McLain
Henry V	Joseph Papp	David Mitchell	Timothy Miller	Martin Aronstein
Measure for Measure	John Pasquin	Santo Loquasto	Santo Loquasto	Martin Aronstein
Mondongo	Dean Irby	David Mitchell	Elsie Rodriguez	Thomas Skelton
Marco Polo Sings a Solo	Mel Shapiro	John Wulp	Theoni V. Aldredge	Jennifer Tipton
Ashes	Lynne Meadow	John Lee Beatty	Jennifer von Mayrhauser	Dennis Parichy
Hagar's Children	Robert Graham Small	Clarke Dunham		Clarke Dunham
Creditors and The Stronger	Rip Torn	John Wright Stevens	Carrie F. Robbins	Ian Calderon
On the Lock-In	Robert Macbeth	Karl Eigsti	Grace Williams	Victor En Yu Tan
The Cherry Orchard	Andrei Serban	Santo Loquasto	Santo Loquasto	Jennifer Tipton
Agamemnon	Andrei Serban	Douglas W. Schmidt	Santo Loquasto	Jennifer Tipton
New York Street Theatre Caravan				
All productions	Marketa Kimbrell			
Odyssey Theatre Ensemble				
The Kid and	Ron Sossi	Chuck Schuman	Carmen Saveiros	Chuck Schuman
Love Scene and Rip Awake		James Ellingwood	Berna Tracht	
		David Hillbrand		
Soap	David Man	Martha Charles	Berna Tracht	
The Adolph Hitler Show	Ron Sossi	Garvin Eddy	Debbie Shore	Bob Sauders
				Ron Schultz
Beauty & the Beast	Michael Wolfe	Norman Jones	Debbie Shore	Daniel Kamesar
Elizabeth One	Ron Sossi	Gary Wissman	Durinda Rice Wood	Fred Plotnick
America Hurrah	Jesse Joe Walsh	Bruce Stevens		Mary Marchette
Noonday Demons	Ron Sossi	Rafigh Ghorbanzadeh	Sherry George	Dawn Chang
A Theological Position	Ron Sossi	Rafigh Ghorbanzadeh	Sherry George	Dawn Chang
Off Center Theatre				
Frankenstein	Tony McGrath	Norman Penn		
Three Little Pigs	Tony McGrath	Diane Van Norman		
Sinbad the Sailor	Tony McGrath	Diane Van Norman		
Beauty and the Beast	Tony McGrath	Mary Frank		
Cinderella	Tony McGrath	Nancy Marshall		
Little Red Riding Hood	Tony McGrath	Nancy Marshall		
Hansel and Gretel	Tony McGrath	Diane Van Norman		
Hope for Life	Tony McGrath	Tony McGrath		
Old Globe Theatre				
The Advocate	Craig Noel	Peggy Kellner	Lissa Skiles	Steph Storer
Our Town	Jack O'Brien	Peggy Kellner	Peggy Kellner	Steph Storer
The Hot l Baltimore	Floyd Gaffney	Peggy Kellner	Peggy Kellner	Steph Storer
			Lissa Skiles	
The Pursuit of Happiness	Bertram Tanswell	Peggy Kellner	Peggy Kellner	Steph Storer
Cat on a Hot Tin Roof	Craig Noel	Peggy Kellner	Peggy Kellner	Steph Storer
U.S.A.	William Roesch	Peggy Kellner	Peggy Kellner	Steph Storer
A Trip to Chinatown	Jack Bender	Peggy Kellner	Peggy Kellner	Steph Storer
Winter Patriot	Craig Noel	Dan Dryden	Lissa Skiles	Steph Storer
The Last Meeting of the Knights of the White Magnolia	Michael Keenan	Peggy Kellner	Lissa Skiles	Steph Storer
The Little Foxes	Asaad Kelada	Peggy Kellner	Donna Couchman	Terry Kempf
Rodgers & Hart: A Musical Celebration	Wayne Bryan	Peggy Kellner	Peggy Kellner	Donald Harris
As You Like It	Jack O'Brien	Peggy Kellner	Steven Rubin	Donald Harris
Troilus and Cressida	Edward Payson Call	Peggy Kellner	Peggy Kellner	Donald Harris
Othello	Daniel Sullivan	Peggy Kellner	Tom Rasmussen	Donald Harris

PRODUCTION	DIRECTOR	SETS	COSTUMES	LIGHTS
The Sea Horse	Robert Bonaventura	John David Peters	Lissa Skiles	Steph Storer
Ring Around the Moon	Craig Noel	Steven Rubin	Steven Rubin	Steven T. Howell
Play Strindberg	Eric Christmas	Steph Storer	Lissa Skiles	Steph Storer
Kennedy's Children	Craig Noel	Steve Lavino	Donna Couchman	Steph Storer
The Queen and the Rebels	Mack Owen	Peggy Kellner	Donna Couchman	Steph Storer
Arms and the Man	Craig Noel	Catherine Hand	Peggy Kellner	Steph Storer
Seascape	Jack Tygett	Robert Zentis	Lissa Skiles	Steph Storer
Tango	Craig Noel	Brigette Sitte	Brigette Sitte	Steph Storer
La Ronde	William Roesch	Peggy Kellner	Peggy Kellner	Steph Storer
The Runner Stumbles	Michael Keenan	John David Peters	Donna Couchman	
Charley's Aunt	Wayne Bryan	Steph Storer	Peggy Kellner	Steph Storer
Timon of Athens	Eric Christmas	Peggy Kellner	Peggy Kellner	John McLain
The Taming of the Shrew	Laird Williamson	Peggy Kellner	Peggy Kellner	John McLain
Hamlet	Jack O'Brien	Peggy Kellner	Robert Morgan	John McLain

O'Neill Theater Center

PRODUCTION	DIRECTOR	SETS	COSTUMES	LIGHTS
G.R. Point	Tony Giordano	1976 Resident Designer: Fred Voelpel		1976 Resident Designers: Arden Fingerhut Spencer Mosse
Benefit of a Doubt	Lynne Meadow			
A History of the American Film	Peter Mark Schifter			
As to the Meaning of Words	John Dillon			
Winds of Change	Tony Giordano			
Pirates	John Dillon			
Secrets of the Rich	Lynne Meadow			
Suckers	Peter Mark Schifter			
Ladyhouse Blues	Tony Giordano			
The Sugar Bowl	Tony Giordano			
Daddy's Duet	Dennis Scott			
The Defense	Dennis Scott			
A Prayer for My Daughter	Robert Ackerman	1977 Resident Designers: Fred Voelpel Bil Mikulewicz		1977 Resident Designers: Ian Calderon Arden Fingerhut
Two Small Bodies	Dennis Scott			
The Last American Dixieland Band	Dennis Scott			
The Elusive Angel	Steven Robman			
Eminent Domain	Lynne Meadow			
Windfall Apples	John Desmond			
Custer	Robert Ackerman			
At the End of Long Island	Sheldon Larry			
Scooter Thomas Makes It to the Top of the World	Dennis Scott			
Terra Nova	John Dillon			
Gazelle Boy	John Dillon			
Uncommon Women and Others	Steven Robman			

Ontological Hysteric

PRODUCTION	DIRECTOR	SETS	COSTUMES	LIGHTS
All productions	directed and designed by Richard Foreman			

Oregon Shakespearean Festival

PRODUCTION	DIRECTOR	SETS	COSTUMES	LIGHTS
The Devil's Disciple	Michael Leibert	Richard L. Hay	Jeannie Davidson	Thomas White
Brand	Jerry Turner	Richard L. Hay	Jeannie Davidson	Thomas White
The Tavern	Pat Patton	Richard L. Hay	Jeannie Davidson	Thomas White
The Comedy of Errors	Will Huddleston	Richard L. Hay	Jeannie Davidson	Thomas White
King Lear	Pat Patton	Richard L. Hay	Jeannie Davidson	Dirk Epperson
Much Ado About Nothing	James Edmondson	Richard L. Hay	Jeannie Davidson	Dirk Epperson
Henry VI, Part II	Jerry Turner	Richard L. Hay	Jeannie Davidson	Dirk Epperson
The Little Foxes	James Moll	Richard L. Hay	Jeannie Davidson	Jerry L. Glenn
The Merchant of Venice	Michael Addison	Richard L. Hay	Jeannie Davidson	Dirk Epperson
Antony and Cleopatra	Robert Loper	Richard L. Hay	Jeannie Davidson	Dirk Epperson
Henry VI, Part III	Pat Patton	Richard L. Hay	Jeannie Davidson	Dirk Epperson
Measure for Measure	Jerry Turner	Richard L. Hay	Jeannie Davidson	Dirk Epperson
The Rivals	William Glover	Richard L. Hay	Jeannie Davidson	Dirk Epperson
A Streetcar Named Desire	Elizabeth Huddle	William Bloodgood	Jeannie Davidson	Dirk Epperson
Angel Street	Pat Patton	Richard L. Hay	Jeannie Davidson	Dirk Epperson
A Taste of Honey	James Edmondson	Richard L. Hay	Jeannie Davidson	Robert Peterson
A Moon for the Misbegotten	Jerry Turner	Richard L. Hay	Jeannie Davidson	Robert Peterson

Organic Theater Company

PRODUCTION	DIRECTOR	SETS	COSTUMES	LIGHTS
The Wonderful Ice Cream Suit	Stuart Gordon	Mary Griswold John Paoletti	Cookie Gluck	Geoffrey Bushor
The Beckoning Fair One	Stuart Gordon	James Maronek		James Maronek
Switch Bitch	Stuart Gordon	Maher Ahmad	Laura Crow	Maher Ahmad
The Adventures of Huckleberry Finn, Parts One and Two	Stuart Gordon	Geoffrey Bushor Mary Griswold John Paoletti	Geoffrey Bushor Mary Griswold John Paoletti	Geoffrey Bushor Mary Griswold John Paoletti
Volpone	Stuart Gordon	Dean Taucher	Maggie Bodwell	Robert Shook
Cops	Stuart Gordon	James Maronek		James Maronek
The Sirens of Titan	Stuart Gordon	James Maronek	Maggie Bodwell	James Maronek
Bleacher Bums	Stuart Gordon			

Otrabanda Company

PRODUCTION	DIRECTOR	SETS	COSTUMES	LIGHTS
The 3rd Annual River Raft Revue			Rachelle Bornstein	
The Doctor in Spite of Himself	Paul Treichler	Susan Horowitz Gregory Frank	Susan Horowitz Gregory Frank Rachelle Bornstein	
The 4th Annual River Raft Revue			Rachelle Bornstein	
Glass	Roger Babb	Roger Babb John Maynard	Margaret Hahn Rachelle Bornstein	John Maynard

PRODUCTION	DIRECTOR	SETS	COSTUMES	LIGHTS
Louisiana Legong	David Dawkins		Rachelle Bornstein	John Maynard

PAF Playhouse

PRODUCTION	DIRECTOR	SETS	COSTUMES	LIGHTS
Same Painted Pony	Fred Chappell	David Chapman Michael Stauffer	David Chapman Michael Stauffer	David Chapman Michael Stauffer
To Kill a Mockingbird	Jay Broad	David Chapman	Randy Barcelo	Michael Stauffer
The Halloween Bandit	J Ranelli	Fred Voelpel	Fred Voelpel	Robert Steinberg
Vanities	Garland Wright	John Arnone	David James	Patrika Brown
The Zinger	Brother Jonathan, O.S.F.	Brother Jonathan, O.S.F.	Jania Szatanski	Bil Mikulewicz
White Pelicans	Jay Broad	David Chapman	Diane DeBaun	Leslie A. DeWeerdt, Jr.
The Signalman's Apprentice	John Stix	Eldon Elder	Catherine Hiller	Leslie A. DeWeerdt, Jr.
How to Rob a Bank	Ernestine Perrie	David Chapman	Diane Finn Chapman	Richard Winkler
In Memory of Long John Silver	Jay Broad	Douglas F. Lebrecht	Jania Szatanski	Edward Effron
Gemini	Peter Mark Schifter	Christopher Nowak	Ernest Allen Smith	Larry Crimmins
Patrick Henry Lake Liquors	Ronald Roston	Ernest Allen Smith	Catherine Hiller	Leslie A. DeWeerdt, Jr.
The Bright and Golden Land	Jonathan Bolt	William Schroder	William Schroder	Marc B. Weiss
The Brixton Recovery	Edward Stern	David Chapman	Carol Oditz	Marc B. Weiss

The Paper Bag Players

PRODUCTION	DIRECTOR	SETS	COSTUMES	LIGHTS
Everybody, Everybody	Judith Martin	Judith Martin	Judith Martin	
Dandelion	Judith Martin	Judith Martin	Judith Martin	
Hot Feet	Judith Martin	Judith Martin	Judith Martin	
Grandpa	Judith Martin	Judith Martin	Judith Martin	Robby Monk

PART (Performing Arts Repertory Theatre)

PRODUCTION	DIRECTOR	SETS	COSTUMES	LIGHTS
The Midnight Ride of Paul Revere	Amy Saltz	Richard B. Williams	Mathew Hoffman	
The Stars & Stripes Forever	Larry Whiteley	Hal Tine	Irving Milton Duke	
Young Abe Lincoln	Jay Harnick	Fred Voelpel	Fred Voelpel	
Aesop and Other Fables	Marshall Izen			
Freedom Train	Gloria Jones Schultz	Hal Tine	Ben Benson	
Young Ben Franklin	John Allen			
Escape to Freedom	Robbie McCauley	Hal Tine	James Corry	
Invasion from the Planet of the Clowns	Sue Lawless			
Young Mark Twain	Jay Harnick			
Dinosaurs, Puppets & Picasso	Marshall Izen			
Young Tom Edison and the Magic Why	William Koch	Richard B. Williams	Joyce Aysta	
The Road to Camelot	Rick Atwell	Richard B. Williams	Joyce Aysta	
Jim Thorpe, All-American	John Henry Davis	Raymond C. Recht	Joyce Aysta	
Give 'Em Hell, Harry!	Sue Lawless	John Fallabella		

The Performance Group

PRODUCTION	DIRECTOR	SETS	COSTUMES	LIGHTS
Sly Mourning	Stephen Borst	Moira Kelly		Don Warsaw
Sakonnet Point	Spalding Gray Elizabeth LeCompte	Elizabeth LeCompte James Clayburgh	Elizabeth LeCompte James Clayburgh	Elizabeth LeCompte James Clayburgh
The Tooth of Crime	Richard Schechner	Jerry Rojo	Franne Lee	Jerry Rojo
The Marilyn Project	Richard Schechner	James Clayburgh	Mary Brecht	James Clayburgh
Mother Courage and Her Children	Richard Schechner	Jerry Rojo James Clayburgh	Theodora Skipitares	Jerry Rojo James Clayburgh
Rumstick Road	Elizabeth LeCompte Spalding Gray	James Clayburgh Elizabeth LeCompte		James Clayburgh Elizabeth LeCompte
Oedipus	Richard Schechner	James Clayburgh	Theodora Skipitares	James Clayburgh

Philadelphia Drama Guild

PRODUCTION	DIRECTOR	SETS	COSTUMES	LIGHTS
The Royal Family	Douglas Seale	John Kasarda	David Charles	Spencer Mosse
The Glass Menagerie	Richard Maltby	John Kasarda	Jane Greenwood	Spencer Mosse
The Birthday Party	Douglas Seale	John Kasarda	David Charles	Spencer Mosse
Hedda Gabler	Brian Murray	John Kasarda	Jane Greenwood	Spencer Mosse
The Miser	Douglas Seale	John Kasarda	Jane Greenwood	Spencer Mosse
Heartbreak House	Douglas Seale	John Kasarda	Dona Granata	Spencer Mosse
Enter a Free Man	Douglas Campbell	John Kasarda	Dona Granata	Spencer Mosse
Five Finger Exercise	Douglas Seale	John Kasarda	Dona Granata	Spencer Mosse
Blithe Spirit	Douglas Seale	John Kasarda	Dona Granata	Spencer Mosse
Hamlet	Douglas Seale	John Kasarda	Dona Granata	Spencer Mosse

Phoenix Theatre

PRODUCTION	DIRECTOR	SETS	COSTUMES	LIGHTS
A Memory of Two Mondays	Arvin Brown	James Tilton	Albert Wolsky	James Tilton
27 Wagons Full of Cotton	Arvin Brown	James Tilton	Albert Wolsky	James Tilton
They Knew What They Wanted	Stephen Porter	James Tilton	Albert Wolsky	James Tilton
Boy Meets Girl	John Lithgow	James Tilton	Clifford Capone	James Tilton
Secret Service	Daniel Freudenberger	James Tilton	Clifford Capone	James Tilton
Ladyhouse Blues	Tony Giordano	James Tilton	Fred Voelpel	James Tilton
Canadian Gothic and American Modern	Daniel Freudenberger	James Tilton		James Tilton
Marco Polo	Lynne Meadow	James Tilton	Carrie F. Robbins	James Tilton
A Sorrow beyond Dreams	Daniel Freudenberger	James Tilton		James Tilton
G.R. Point	Tony Giordano	James Tilton	Frances Ellen Rosenthal	Arden Fingerhut
Scribes	Keith Hack	James Tilton	Frances Ellen Rosenthal	James Tilton

Pittsburgh Public Theater

PRODUCTION	DIRECTOR	SETS	COSTUMES	LIGHTS
The Glass Menagerie	Ben Shaktman	Peter Wexler	Peter Wexler	Peter Wexler
One Flew Over the Cuckoo's Nest	John Going	Peter Wexler	Whitney Blausen	Peter Wexler
Twelfth Night	Ben Shaktman	David Chapman	David Chapman	Bernard J. Brannigan
Uncle Vanya	Ben Shaktman	John Jensen	David Toser	Bennet Averyt

PRODUCTION	DIRECTOR	SETS	COSTUMES	LIGHTS
Sizwe Bansi Is Dead	Woodie King, Jr.	Karl Eigsti	Karl Eigsti	Bennet Averyt
King Henry 5	Ben Shaktman	Peter Wexler	Whitney Blausen	Bennet Averyt

The Play Group

The Piper Man	collaborative			
Cowboys #2	collaborative			
Every Alice	Wanda Cody			
	Katharine Pearson			
The Maids	Katharine Pearson			
200 R.P.M.	Tom Cooke			
Myths 1–10	Katharine Pearson			
Church	Ben Harville			
The T-Rific Two	Ben Harville			
Smoke on the Mountains	Tom Cooke			

Playhouse on the Square

Godspell	Larry D. Riley	Larry D. Riley	Laura Hendrix-Branch	Rubel Burcham
A Shot in the Dark	Stephen Mauer	Stephen Mauer	Laura Hendrix-Branch	Stephen Forsyth
Tobacco Road	Thomas Cooke	Greg Peeples	Laura Hendrix-Branch	Stephen Forsyth
The Fantasticks	Kimberley Dobbs	Jim Lykins	Laura Hendrix-Branch	Stephen Forsyth
Bus Stop	Stephen Mauer	George R. Sprague, Jr.	Laura Hendrix-Branch	Stephen Forsyth
Once upon a Mattress	Kimberley Dobbs	Stephen Mauer	Denise Kaplan Shum Ginger Travis	Stephen Forsyth
Jacques Brel Is Alive and Well and Living in Paris	Phillip Giberson	Stephen Mauer	Ginger Travis	Stephen Forsyth
An Evening of Soul	Erma Clanton	Stephen Mauer	Erma Clanton	Stephen Forsyth
A Streetcar Named Desire	Stephen Mauer	Joe Lowery	Denise Kaplan Shum	Joe Lowery
Happy Birthday, Wanda June	Gene Wilkins	Stephen Mauer	Denise Kaplan Shum	Joe Lowery
Two Gentlemen of Verona	Christopher Cox	Joe Lowery	Robert D. Carver	Joe Lowery
Hay Fever	Gene Wilkins	Joe Lowery	Robert D. Carver	Stephen Forsyth Joe Lowery
A Thurber Carnival	Kenneth L. Miller	Jackie Nichols	Robert D. Carver	Stephen Forsyth
The Misanthrope	Gene Wilkins	Gene Wilkins	Charlotte Cole	Stephen Forsyth
The Threepenny Opera	Gene Wilkins	Jackie Nichols	Charlotte Cole	Stephen Forsyth
Candida	John Irvine	Jackie Nichols	Kris Hanley	Stephen Forsyth
The School for Wives	John Irvine	Jackie Nichols	Kris Hanley	Stephen Forsyth
Of Mice and Men	Gene Wilkins	Jackie Nichols	Kris Hanley	Stephen Forsyth
Fallen Angels	Gene Wilkins	Jackie Nichols	Charlotte Cole	Stephen Forsyth

Playmakers Repertory Company

The Crucible	Arthur L. Housman	David M. Glenn	Nancy Woodfield	David M. Glenn
All's Well That Ends Well	Tom Haas	Rick Pike	Bobbi Owen	David Lochner
A History of the American Film	Bill Ludel	Rick Pike	Polly P. Smith	Larry von Werssowetz
Once in a Lifetime	Tom Haas	Rick Pike	Bobbi Owen	David M. Glenn

Playwrights Horizons/Queens Festival Theater

Clair and the Chair and	Hillary Wyler			Arden Fingerhut
Professor George	Marsha Sheiness			
The Importance of Being Earnest	Paul Cooper	Hope Auerbach	Lorri Schneider	Cheryl Thacker
A Quality of Mercy	Anita Khanzadian	Cliff Simon	Louise Herman	James Chaleff
The Mikado	Barry Keating	Frank Kelly	Bosha Johnson	James Chaleff
The Lymworth Millions	Alfred Gingold	Joe Lazarus	Louise Herman	John Gisondi
Report to the Stockholders	Robert H. Livingston	Clarke Dunham	Allen Munch	Clarke Dunham
Julius Caesar	Paul Schneider	David Sackeroff	Greg Etchison	Paul Kaine
Guy Gauthier's Ego Play	Kent Wood	Minda Chipurnoi	Danny Morgan	Gail Kennison
Misalliance	Robert Moss	Frank Kelly	Susan Sudert	John Gisondi
Vanities	Garland Wright	John Arnone	David James	Tony Santoro
Ocean Walk	Michael Flanagan	John Gisondi	Marya Ursin	Paul Kaine
The Boor and	Philip Himberg	Chris Thomas	Louise Herman	David George
The Marriage and	Jonathan Alper	Chris Thomas	Louise Herman	David George
The Bank Jubilee and	Kent Wood	Chris Thomas	Louise Herman	David George
	Robert Moss			
The Marriage Proposal	Dennis Pearlstein	Chris Thomas	Louise Herman	David George
The Public Good	Leonard Peters	Steve Duffy	Ruth A. Wells	John Gisondi
The Spelling Bee	Harold Scott	John Sheffler	Kenneth M. Yount	Arden Fingerhut
The Boss	Edward Gilbert	Lawrence King	Carrie F. Robbins	William Mintzer
Perched on a Gabardine Cloud	Frank Cento	David George	Greg Etchison	David George
Two for the Seesaw	Michael Heaton	John Gisondi	Louise Klein	William D. Anderson
Magritte Skies	Richard Place	John W. Jacobsen	Greg Etchison	Spencer Mosse
George Washington Slept Here	Paul Cooper		Louise Klein	William J. Plachy
The Caseworker	Leland Moss	Christopher Hacker	Susan Dennison	Jeffrey Schissler
Cakes with the Wine	Edward M. Cohen	Greg Etchison	Louise Herman	Tony Santoro
Dear Ruth	Robert Moss	Greg Etchison	Greg Etchison	Tony Santoro
Paradise	Paul Cooper	Christopher Nowak		Harry Itzkowitz
The Tavern	Ronald Miller	Amanda Klein	Amanda Klein	Tony Santoro
Born Yesterday	Caymichael Patton	Amanda Klein	Amanda Klein	Paul Kaine
Babes in Arms	Peter Mark Schifter	Christopher Hacker	Greg Etchison	William D. Anderson
Boo Hoo	Michael Flanagan	Mark Winkworth	David James	Jeffrey Schissler
The Dybbuk	Philip Himberg	Nancy Winters	Mimi Maxmen	Mary Calhoun
Rio Grande	Leland Moss	Jeffrey Schissler	Michael J. Cesario	Jeffrey Schissler
The Rivals	Robert Moss	John Gisondi	Michael J. Cesario	Patrika Brown
Rebeccah	Tina Shepard	Marcie Begleiter		Beth Helen Glick
Gemini	Peter Mark Schifter	Christopher Nowak	Ernest Allen Smith	Larry Cummings
Hay Fever	Marshall Oglesby	Donato Moreno	Polly P. Smith	William D. Anderson
Stop the Parade	Harold Scott	Paul Eads	Mary Alice Orito	Patrika Brown
The Mousetrap	Larry Carpenter	Miguel Romero	Michael J. Cesario	Frances Aronson

327

PRODUCTION	DIRECTOR	SETS	COSTUMES	LIGHTS
Fair Weather Friends	Richard Place	Christina Weppner	Marcie Begleiter	William D. Anderson
Jacques Brel Is Alive and Well and Living in Paris	Stuart H. Ross	Stephen P. Edelstein	Patricia Adshead	Pat Stern
For the Use of the Hall	Ron Van Lieu	Miguel Romero	David Murin	James Chaleff
Stage Door	Robert Moss	Richard B. Williams	Michael J. Cesario	William D. Anderson
Earthworms	David Schweizer	Christopher Nowak	William Ivey-Long	Ian Calderon
Cracks	Larry Carpenter	Ruth Wells	Jean Steinlein	Frances Aronson
The Gingerbread Lady	Rae Allen	Christina Weppner	Marcie Begleiter	John Gisondi
The Playboy of the Western World	Michael Montel	Bob Phillips	James Edmund Brady	Pat Stern

The Proposition Workshop

The Proposition	Allan Albert			Richard B. Williams
The Boston Tea Party	Allan Albert			Richard B. Williams
The Whale Show	Allan Albert	Allan Albert	Hilary M. Rosenfeld	Richard B. Williams
Corral	Allan Albert	Allan Albert	Hilary M. Rosenfeld	Richard B. Williams
Soap	Allan Albert	Barry & Nancy Bailey	Eloise Lowry	Richard B. Williams
A Fable	Allan Albert	Karen Schulz	Halliday Wallace	Richard B. Williams
The Whale Show	Allan Albert	David Lloyd Gropman	Hilary M. Rosenfeld	Richard B. Williams
The Casino	Allan Albert	Cletus Johnson	Cletus Johnson	Richard B. Williams

Provisional Theatre

All productions	collective direction and	design		

Puerto Rican Traveling Theatre

Windows (Las Ventanas)	Roberto Rodriguez	Robert Strohmeier	Maria Ferreira	Larry Johnson
The Dinner Guest	Alba Oms	Robert Strohmeier	Benito Gutierrez-Soto	Larry Johnson
Everything Not Compulsory Is Strictly Forbidden	Alba Oms	Robert Strohmeier	Benito Gutierrez-Soto	Larry Johnson
				Dan Bartlett
Eleuterio the Coqui	Pablo Cabrera	Robert Strohmeier	Benito Gutierrez-Soto	Dan Bartlett
The Oxcart (La Carreta)	Miriam Colon Edgar	Robert Strohmeier	Benito Gutierrez-Soto	Robert Strohmeier
			Maria Ferreira	Dan Bartlett
I Took Panama	Alba Oms	Carlos Carrasco	Maria Ferreira	David Segal
				Larry Johnson

The Puppet Workshop

All productions	Marc Kohler			

Repertorio Español

Pasos	Francisco Morin	Robert Federico	Robert Federico	Robert Federico
Entremeses	Francisco Morin	Robert Federico	Robert Federico	Robert Federico
La Malquerida	Rene Buch	Robert Federico	Maria Ferreira	Robert Federico
Dona Rosita, La Soltera	Rene Buch	Robert Federico	Maria Ferreira	Robert Federico
Amor de don Perlimplin con Belisa en Su Jardin	Christopher Martin	Robert Federico		Robert Federico
Los Soles Truncos	Rene Buch	Robert Federico		Robert Federico
La Fiaca	Rene Buch	Robert Federico	Robert Federico	Robert Federico
La Celestina	Rene Buch	Robert Federico	Robert Federico	Robert Federico
O.K.	Rene Buch	Mario Arellano	Rene Sanchez	Robert Federico
La Maxima Felicidad	Pablo Cabrera	Robert Federico		Robert Federico
La Dama Duende	Rene Buch	Robert Federico	Robert Federico	Robert Federico
La Pipa Azul	Norberto Kerner	Robert Federico	Maria Ferreira	Robert Federico
El Censo	Delfor Peralta	Robert Federico	Maria Ferreira	Robert Federico
Cien Veces No Debo	Braulio Villar	Robert Federico	Maria Ferreira	Robert Federico
La Decente	Rene Buch	Robert Federico	Rene Sanchez	Robert Federico
Vidas Privadas	Rene Buch	Mario Arellano	Rene Sanchez	Robert Federico
La Valija	Rene Buch	Robert Federico	Robert Federico	Robert Federico
Don Juan Tenorio	Rene Buch	Robert Federico	Maria Ferreira	Robert Federico
Una Mujer Muy...Decente	Antonio Losada	Mario Arellano	Rene Sanchez	Robert Federico
Los Fantastikos	Rene Buch	Mario Arellano	Rene Sanchez	Robert Federico

The Ridiculous Theatrical Company

Caprice	Charles Ludlam	Edward Avidisian	Charles Ludlam	Richard Currie
		Bob Jack Callejo		
Der Ring Gott Farblonget	Charles Ludlam	Charles Ludlam	Charles Ludlam	Richard Currie
Stage Blood	Charles Ludlam	Charles Ludlam	Charles Ludlam	Richard Currie

St. Nicholas Theater Company

American Buffalo	Gregory Mosher	Michael Merritt		Robert Christen
A View from the Bridge	Steven Schachter	David Emmons	David Emmons	David Emmons
Sitcom	Julian Barry	David Emmons	Julie A. Nagel	Robert Shook
The Collected Works of Billy the Kid	Mike Nussbaum	David Emmons	Julie A. Nagel	Robert Christen
Mert & Phil	Steven Schachter	Dean Taucher	Kaye Nottbusch	Robert Shook
Joplin	Steven Schachter	Joseph Nieminski	Julie A. Nagel	Robert Shook
Domino Courts	Gerald Gutierrez	David Emmons	Julie A. Nagel	Rita Pietraszek
A Slight Accident	Gerald Gutierrez	David Emmons	Julie A. Nagel	Rita Pietraszek
The Water Engine	Steven Schachter	David Emmons	Jessica Hahn	Kathleen Daly

Seattle Repertory Theatre

Cyrano de Bergerac	Duncan Ross	Eldon Elder	Lewis D. Rampino	Steven A. Maze
Jumpers	Duncan Ross	John Lee Beatty	Lewis D. Rampino	Steven A. Maze
Seven Keys to Baldpate	Arne Zaslove	Jerry Williams	Lewis D. Rampino	Phil Schermer
The Last Meeting of the Knights of the White Magnolia	Harold Scott	Robert Dahlstrom	Lewis D. Rampino	Richard Devin
The Madwoman of Chaillot	Duncan Ross	Eldon Elder	Lewis D. Rampino	Richard Devin
Private Lives	Duncan Ross	Robert Dahlstrom	Lewis D. Rampino	Richard Devin
Benito Cereno	Arne Zaslove	Michael Mayer	Lewis D. Rampino	Cynthia Hawkins

PRODUCTION	DIRECTOR	SETS	COSTUMES	LIGHTS
Entertaining Mr. Sloane	Clayton Corzatte	Charles Kading	Lewis D. Rampino	Cynthia Hawkins
Made for TV	Arne Zaslove	Charles Kading	Donna Eskew	Jim McKie
Kennedy's Children	Robert Patrick	Michael Mayer	Lewis D. Rampino	Cynthia Hawkins
The Collected Works of Billy the Kid	Arne Zaslove	Phil Schermer	Donna Eskew	Phil Schermer
Music Is	George Abbott	Eldon Elder	Lewis D. Rampino	H.R. Poindexter
Anna Christie	Duncan Ross	Robert Blackman	Lewis D. Rampino	Richard Devin
The Mousetrap	Reginald Denham	Jerry Williams	Lewis D. Rampino	Cynthia Hawkins
Cat on a Hot Tin Roof	Garland Wright	Robert Blackman	Lewis D. Rampino	Cynthia Hawkins
The Show-Off	John Going	Robert Dahlstrom	Lewis D. Rampino	Cynthia Hawkins
Equus	Duncan Ross	Michael Mayer	Lewis D. Rampino	Richard Devin
Bingo	Robert Loper	John Schaffner	Nanrose Buchman	Cynthia Hawkins
Once upon a Time	Gwen Arner	John Schaffner	Lewis D. Rampino	Scott Hawthorn
Suzanna Andler	Duncan Ross	Michael Mayer	Lewis D. Rampino	Cynthia Hawkins
Boesman and Lena	Glenda Dickerson	John Schaffner	Nanrose Buchman	Cynthia Hawkins
Vanities	Larry Carpenter	Michael Mayer	Nanrose Buchman	Cynthia Hawkins

South Coast Repertory

PRODUCTION	DIRECTOR	SETS	COSTUMES	LIGHTS
Jumpers	David Emmes	Charles Tomlinson	Charles Tomlinson	Thomas Michael Ruzika
Scenes from American Life	Asaad Kelada	Susan Tuohy	Rosemary Mallett	Thomas Michael Ruzika
The National Health	Martin Benson	Susan Tuohy	Rosemary Mallett	Susan Tuohy
A Midsummer Night's Dream	Daniel Sullivan	Tom Rasmussen	Tom Rasmussen	Thomas Michael Ruzika
Rubbers and Yanks 3 Detroit 0 Top of the Seventh	Martin Benson	Susan Tuohy	Anni Long	Thomas Michael Ruzika
In Fashion	John-David Keller	Charles Tomlinson	Charles Tomlinson	Thomas Michael Ruzika
The Ruling Class	David Emmes	Susan Tuohy	Sondra Huber	Susan Tuohy
Saturday Sunday Monday	Martin Benson	Susan Tuohy	Sondra Huber	Thomas Michael Ruzika
Old Times	David Emmes	Michael Devine	Jennifer Platt	Thomas Michael Ruzika
Two Gentlemen of Verona	Daniel Sullivan	Michael Devine	Charles Tomlinson	Thomas Michael Ruzika
Equus	Martin Benson	Michael Devine	James Reeves	Brian Gale
Jacques Brel Is Alive and Well and Living in Paris	John-David Keller	Charles Tomlinson	Charles Tomlinson	Thomas Michael Ruzika

Stage South

PRODUCTION	DIRECTOR	SETS	COSTUMES	LIGHTS
Tales of Carolina-South	Gerald Slavet	Vittorio Capecce	Vittorio Capecce	Andrew Bales
U.S.A.	Jon Yates	Hal Tine	Hal Tine	Andrew Bales
Hoptoads, Hardheads and Other Mountain Beasties	Grant Stewart	Vittorio Capecce	Vittorio Capecce	Vittorio Capecce
Green Pond	David Chambers	Marjorie Kellogg	Majorie Kellogg	Arden Fingerhut

StageWest

PRODUCTION	DIRECTOR	SETS	COSTUMES	LIGHTS
Ah, Wilderness!	Rae Allen	Lawrence King	Sigrid Insull	Ronald Wallace
The Tempest	Edward Berkeley	Charles G. Stockton	Sigrid Insull	Judy Rasmuson
The Balcony	Rae Allen	Eugene Warner	Sigrid Insull	Ronald Wallace
The Country Girl	Martin Fried	Marc B. Weiss	Sigrid Insull	Jamie Gallagher
Design for Living	John Milligan	Fredda Slavin	Sigrid Insull	Judy Rasmuson
Serenading Louie	Rae Allen	Fredda Slavin	Sigrid Insull	Jamie Gallagher
Sleuth	Grover Dale	Jerry Rojo	Sigrid Insull	Jamie Gallagher
You Can't Take It with You	Rae Allen	Lawrence King	Sigrid Insull	Ronald Wallace
The Tooth of Crime	Davey Marlin-Jones	Robert Alpers	Carr Garnett	Jamie Gallagher
When We Dead Awaken	Rae Allen	Jerry Rojo	Sigrid Insull	Ronald Wallace
The Hot l Baltimore	Rae Allen	Fredda Slavin	Carr Garnett	Barley Harris
Jacques Brel Is Alive and Well and Living in Paris	Rae Allen	Jerry Rojo	Susan Tucker	Barley Harris

The Street Theater

PRODUCTION	DIRECTOR	SETS	COSTUMES	LIGHTS
The Verdict Is In	George Myles			
The Past Is the Past	George Myles			
Acts of Reality	C. Lester Franklin			
Moments of Loneliness	C. Lester Franklin			
Fish Eyes and Butterflies	Nancy Gabor			
Can't Stop Laughing	George Myles			
The Promise	C. Lester Franklin			
The Corner	Walter Jones			
Sinderella	Walter Jones			
Getting Over	Nancy Gabor / Ralph Lee			
Choices	Nancy Gabor			
Aria Da Capo	C. Lester Franklin			
The Tavern	C. Lester Franklin			
Inside/Outside	C. Lester Franklin / Pat Smith			

Studio Arena Theatre

PRODUCTION	DIRECTOR	SETS	COSTUMES	LIGHTS
Butley	Richard Barr	Frank J. Boros	Frank J. Boros	David Zierk
Scapino	Grover Dale	Frank J. Boros	Frank J. Boros	David Zierk
A Doll's House	Stephen Porter	David F. Segal	Clifford Capone	David F. Segal
Equus	Paul Giovanni	Robert F. Van Nutt	Clifford Capone	Robby Monk
The Magic Show	Jay Fox		Randy Barcelo	Herb Vogler

PRODUCTION	DIRECTOR	SETS	COSTUMES	LIGHTS
A Little Night Music	Tony Tanner	Robert D. Soule	Clifford Capone	Robby Monk
Replika	Jozef Szajna	Jozef Szajna	Jozef Szajna	Jozef Szajna
The Eccentricities of a Nightingale	Edwin Sherin	William Ritman	Theoni V. Aldredge	Marc B. Weiss
Death of a Salesman	Warren Enters	James Tilton	Clifford Capone	David Zierk
Vanities	Larry Carpenter	John Arnone	David James	Patrika Brown
Sizwe Bansi Is Dead	Woodie King, Jr.	Karl Eigsti	Karl Eigsti	Peter Gill
Elizabeth the Queen	Tony Tanner	Scott Johnson	Clifford Capone	Marc B. Weiss
A Very Private Life	Terry Schreiber	Ben Edwards	Jane Greenwood	Ben Edwards

Syracuse Stage

PRODUCTION	DIRECTOR	SETS	COSTUMES	LIGHTS
Morning's at Seven	Arthur Storch	David Chapman	William Schroder	Judy Rasmuson
No Exit	John Dillon	Scott Johnson	Jerry Pannozzo	Lee Watson
The Man with the Flower in His Mouth	John Dillon	Scott Johnson	Jerry Pannozzo	Lee Watson
The Bear and	Gene Lesser	William Schroder	Lowell Detweiler	Jeff Davis
The Harmfulness of Tobacco and				
The Marriage Proposal				
Blithe Spirit	John Going	Eric Head	James Berton Harris	Judy Rasmuson
Dynamo	Arthur Storch	John Doepp	Nanzi Adzima	Judy Rasmuson
A Flea in Her Ear	Philip Minor	Eric Head	James Edmund Brady	James E. Stephens
A Quality of Mercy	Arthur Storch	John Doepp	Lowell Detweiler	Judy Rasmuson
What the Butler Saw	Marshall Oglesby	Virginia Dancy	Patricia McGourty	James E. Stephens
		Elmon Webb		
Twelfth Night	Bill Ludel	Sandro LaFerla	Nanzi Adzima	Lee Watson
The Seagull	Arthur Storch	John Doepp	Lowell Detweiler	Judy Rasmuson
Sleuth	Robert Mandel	Marjorie Kellogg	Jennifer von Mayrhauser	Edward Effron
A Streetcar Named Desire	John Going	Stuart Wurtzel	James Berton Harris	Arden Fingerhut

Theatre Arts Corporation

PRODUCTION	DIRECTOR	SETS	COSTUMES	LIGHTS
The Seagull	Cather MacCallum	Ken Guthrie	Suzanne Jamison	Peter Krebs
The Wax Museum	Martin Weil			Sally Jackson
A Delusion of Grandeur	David Ross	Dean Alatzas		Dean Alatzas
Jesse and the Bandit Queen	Robert Mandel	Kathy Leavelle	Victoria Cross	Peter Krebs
Signals I/II	Carol Ross	Elizabeth Harris	U. Stephen Homsy Suzanne Jamison	Alton Walpole
Seven White and the Snowed Dwarves	Jinx Junkin			
Old Times	Viva Karmati	Viva Karmati		Timothy Thompson
A Slight Ache	Doug Doran	Doug Doran	Candace Burrows	Timothy Thompson
The Stronger	Marianne de Pury Thompson		Suzanne Jamison	Coco de Forrest
After Magritte	Elizabeth Harris	Elizabeth Harris		Coco de Forrest
The Good Doctor	Jinx Junkin	Jinx Junkin	Suzanne Jamison	Coco de Forrest Rick Olszen
You Can't Take It with You	Dale Whitt	P. Alexander Harding	Raye Armour	Rick Olszen Phillip A. Sweeney Bruce MacCallum
The Unseen Hand	Dan Halleck	Richard Lindeborg	Suzanne Jamison	Peter Krebs
Eat Cake and *Almost Like Being*	Charles R. Edwards	Daniel Juckette		Daniel Juckette
Elevators	Diedre Sklar	John Matanock	Sonya Berthrong	Dean Alatzas

Theatre Arts of West Virginia

PRODUCTION	DIRECTOR	SETS	COSTUMES	LIGHTS
Androcles and the Lion	John S. Benjamin			
Angel Street	John S. Benjamin			
The Comedy of Shakespeare	John S. Benjamin			
Honey in the Rock	John S. Benjamin	Thomas P. Struthers	Cynthia T. Crich	Stephen R. Wooding
Hatfields & McCoys	John S. Benjamin	Thomas P. Struthers	Cynthia T. Crich	Stephen R. Wooding
The Emperor's New Clothes	John S. Benjamin	Burt Merriam		
She Stoops to Conquer	John S. Benjamin			
You're a Good Man, Charlie Brown	John S. Benjamin			
Romeo and Juliet	John S. Benjamin			

Theater at Monmouth

PRODUCTION	DIRECTOR	SETS	COSTUMES	LIGHTS
A Midsummer Night's Dream	Earl McCarroll	Karen Schulz	Joyce Aysta	Paul Gallo
The Imaginary Invalid	Robert Johanson	Karen Schulz	Joyce Aysta	Paul Gallo
Antony and Cleopatra	Earl McCarroll	Karen Schulz	Joyce Aysta	Paul Gallo
King Henry IV, Part I	James J. Thesing	Karen Schulz	Joyce Aysta	Paul Gallo
Twelfth Night	Richard Sewell	Stephen R. Woody	Florence L. Rutherford	Stephen R. Woody
Othello	Richard Sewell	Stephen R. Woody	Florence L. Rutherford	Stephen R. Woody
Measure for Measure	Richard Sewell	Stephen R. Woody	Florence L. Rutherford	Stephen R. Woody
She Stoops to Conquer	Tom Markus	Stephen R. Woody	Florence L. Rutherford	Stephen R. Woody

Theatre by the Sea

PRODUCTION	DIRECTOR	SETS	COSTUMES	LIGHTS
Annie Get Your Gun	Russell Treyz	Michael Spellman	Jo Ann Yeoman	Michael Spellman
The Country Girl	Russell Treyz	Michael Spellman	Jo Ann Yeoman	Michael Spellman
Silent Night, Lonely Night	Russell Treyz	Michael Spellman	Jo Ann Yeoman	Michael Spellman
The Owl and the Pussycat	Russell Treyz	Michael Spellman	Jo Ann Yeoman	Michael Spellman
Starshine	Russell Treyz	Michael Spellman	Jo Ann Yeoman	Michael Spellman
Bus Stop	Russell Treyz	Michael Spellman	Jo Ann Yeoman	Michael Spellman
1776	Russell Treyz	Michael Spellman	Jo Ann Yeoman	Michael Spellman
The Music Man	Russell Treyz	Michael Spellman	Donna Meyer	Michael Spellman
The Fantasticks	Russell Treyz	Michael Spellman	Donna Meyer	Michael Spellman
Company	Russell Treyz	Michael Spellman	Kathie Iannicelli	Phil McGuire
Anna Christie	Kent Paul	T. Winberry	T. Winberry	T. Winberry
The Mousetrap	Russell Treyz	Bob Phillips	Anne Sylvester	Bob Phillips
Vanities	Russell Treyz	Bob Phillips	Anne Sylvester	Bob Phillips

PRODUCTION	DIRECTOR	SETS	COSTUMES	LIGHTS
Afternoons in Vegas	Russell Treyz	Bob Phillips	Jo Ann Yeoman	Bob Phillips
Under Milk Wood	Alfred Gingold	Bob Phillips	Anne Sylvester	Bob Phillips
Man with a Load of Mischief	Russell Treyz	Bob Phillips	Anne Sylvester	Bob Phillips
Guys and Dolls	Russell Treyz	Bob Phillips	Varel McComb	Bob Phillips
Carnival	Russell Treyz	Bob Phillips	Varel McComb	Bob Phillips

Theatre Express

PRODUCTION	DIRECTOR	SETS	COSTUMES	LIGHTS
Woyzeck	Rina Yerushalmi	Rina Yerushalmi	Caren Harder	Richard Lenchner
Cat's Cradle	Ken Kuta		Caren Harder	Richard Lenchner / David Loughran
Tuesday	Jewel Walker	Victor McPoland	Heidi Holman Pribram	Ken Kuta
Killing Game	William Turner	William Turner	Caren Harder	William Turner
Mimelite	Randy Kovitz / J. Christopher O'Connor			Richard Lenchner / David Loughran

Theater for the New City

PRODUCTION	DIRECTOR	SETS	COSTUMES	LIGHTS
Feast for Flies	William Perley	Brian Hartigan	Helen Pugatch	
The Cuttlefish	Jaroslaw Strzemien	Margaret Sedgeman	Margaret Sedgeman	Ron Daley
The Tragedy Queen	James Waring	Donald L. Brooks	James Waring	Donald L. Brooks
Memphis Is Gone	Susan Gregg			Marsha Imhof
Jesus Is a Junkie	Ronald Roston	Ernest Allen Smith		
The Only Good Indian....	Crystal Field	Elian Sacker	Robert Strong Miller	Rick Belzer
Baggage	Deborah Fortson	Deborah Fortson	Deborah Fortson	Deborah Fortson
Emma!	Jeff Zinn	Ken Shewer	Susan Hilferty	Rick Belzer
The Warringham Roof	C.W. Sayblack	C.W. Sayblack		Richard Winkler
Day Old Bread	Crystal Field	Donald L. Brooks	Robert Strong Miller	John P. Dodd
Whale Honey	Crystal Field	Donald L. Brooks	Robert Strong Miller	John P. Dodd
The Dinosaur Door	Crystal Field	Donald L. Brooks	Robert Strong Miller	Donald L. Brooks
Cold Cuts	Gregory Gubitosa			
The Colonization of America	Robert Pesola	Tom Durant / David Maurice	Joan Durant	Charles Weiss
Berchtesgaden	Barbara Loden	Donald L. Brooks	Bessie Lou Kazooo	Michael Kushner
Bravo Isabel!	Chuck Roast	Bobby Mazzo / Michael Kushner	Carol Colby	Michael Kushner
Seed from the East	Martin Oltarsh	Donald L. Brooks	Tim Ward	Annie Rech
New York Flesh and Fantasy		Donald L. Brooks		Donald L. Brooks
Winter Sunshine	Robert Dahdah	Donald L. Brooks	Crystal Follett	Donald L. Brooks
Twenty Years after the Man in the Iron Mask	Scott Redman	Bruce Solotoff	Edi Giguere	Gina Minori
High Infidelity	Martin Oltarsh	Jim Fainberg	Varel McCombe	
Seven Days of Shiva	Ronald Roston	Ernest Allen Smith		Virginia Giordano
Carol in Winter Sunlight	Crystal Field / Jacquelynn Colton	Donald L. Brooks	Crystal Follett	John P. Dodd
Clay Campbell's Trip with the Elephant Goddess, Popeye, Eleanor Roosevelt and Others	John Herbert McDowell	Donald L. Brooks	Marty Fuld	Rick Shannin
The Plebeians Rehearse the Uprising	Ruis Woertendyke			Jon D. Andreadakis
Turtles Don't Dream	H.M. Koutoukas	Mario Rivoli	Mario Rivoli	Jim McConnell

Theater of The Open Eye

PRODUCTION	DIRECTOR	SETS	COSTUMES	LIGHTS
Orphee	John FitzGibbon	Michael Massee	Michael Massee	George Gracey
Sun Door	Dan Erkkila / John Genke / Andrea Stark	Dan Erkkila	Carol Oditz	George Gracey
Primordial Voices	Dan Erkkila / Teiji Ito	Dan Erkkila	Carol Oditz	George Gracey
Moon Mysteries	Jean Erdman	Scott Johnson	Ralph Lee / Patricia McGourly	Scott Johnson
Op Odyssey	Valerie Hammer	Doris Chase	Valerie Hammer	George Gracey
Gauguin in Tahiti	Jean Erdman	Frank Marsico	Linda Letta	Frank Marsico
Op Odyssey II	Valerie Hammer	Doris Chase	Valerie Hammer	George Gracey
Fontana	Valerie Hammer	George Gracey	Leslie Green	George Gracey
Raven's Dance	Eric Bass	Eric Bass	Susan Hum Buck	Michael Purri

Theatre of the Riverside Church

PRODUCTION	DIRECTOR	SETS	COSTUMES	LIGHTS
Morning's at Seven	Arthur Bartow	Alan M. Beck	Pat Goldman	Frank Herbert
Old Times, Good Times	Bret Lyon		Pat Goldman	
The Big Reward	Brian O'Connor / Rosemary Foley	Robert Vivona	Roy Finamore	Robert Quaranta
The Cat and the Fiddle	Jack Lee	James Tilton	Peter Joseph	James Tilton
The Garden	Albert Asermely	Thom Edlun		Thom Edlun
Jo Anne!	Carl Weber	Karl Eigsti	Mary Brecht	Spencer Mosse
Bread & Roses	Thom Edlun	David Moore	Molly Maginnis	Thom Edlun
The Double Inconstancy	Albert Asermely	Thom Edlun	Roy Finamore	Al Sayers
Sweet Talk	Jimmy Whitten	Billy Graham	Billy Graham	Harrison Avery
Cocteau	Brian O'Connor / Rosemary Foley	Thom Edlun		Al Sayers
Tuscarora	Michael Holmes	Thom Edlun		Al Sayers

Theatre Project

PRODUCTION	DIRECTOR	SETS	COSTUMES	LIGHTS
Come True!	Ben Carney			
Jenny and the Phoenix	Philip Arnoult			

Theatre X

PRODUCTION	DIRECTOR	SETS	COSTUMES	LIGHTS
Razor Blades	collective			George Keenan

PRODUCTION	DIRECTOR	SETS	COSTUMES	LIGHTS
The Unnamed	collective			George Keenan
The Children's Revolt	Sharon Ott			
Oh Wow! Nancy Drew	collective			
The Wreck	Sharon Ott	John Kishline		George Keenan
		William Dafoe		
Offending the Audience	John Schneider			

Trinity Square Repertory Company

PRODUCTION	DIRECTOR	SETS	COSTUMES	LIGHTS
Cathedral of Ice	Adrian Hall	Eugene Lee	Franne Lee	Mark Rippe
			Betsey Potter	
Another Part of the Forest	Adrian Hall	Robert D. Soule	James Berton Harris	John Custer
The Little Foxes	Adrian Hall	Robert D. Soule	James Berton Harris	John Custer
Two Gentlemen of Verona	Word Baker	Eugene Lee	James Berton Harris	Mark Rippe
Bastard Son	Vincent Dowling	Eugene Lee	James Berton Harris	Mark Rippe
Eustace Chisholm and the Works	Adrian Hall	Eugene Lee	Betsey Potter	Mark Rippe
Seven Keys to Baldpate	Adrian Hall	Robert D. Soule	James Berton Harris	Mark Rippe
			Betsey Potter	Sean Keating
A Flea in Her Ear	George Martin	Robert D. Soule	James Berton Harris	Mark Rippe
			Betsey Potter	Sean Keating
Of Mice and Men	Adrian Hall	Eugene Lee	Betsey Potter	Eugene Lee
Knock Knock	Robert Mandel	Robert D. Soule	Betsey Potter	John Custer
The Boys from Syracuse	Don Price	Robert D. Soule	James Berton Harris	John Custer
Rich and Famous	George Martin	Robert D. Soule	James Berton Harris	John Custer
King Lear	Adrian Hall	Eugene Lee	Franne Lee	Eugene Lee
Bad Habits	Robert Mandel	Robert D. Soule	Betsey Potter	John Custer

Urban Arts Corps Theatre

PRODUCTION	DIRECTOR	SETS	COSTUMES	LIGHTS
I'm Laughin' but I Ain't Tickled	Vinnette Carroll	Marty Kappel	William Schroder	Craig Miller
The Ups and Downs of Theophilus Maitland	Vinnette Carroll	Marty Kappel	Dorothy Weaver	Ken Billington
All the King's Men	Vinnette Carroll	Marty Kappel	Edna Watson	Ken Billington
Play Mas	Vinnette Carroll	Marty Kappel	William Schroder	Ken Billington
The Ups and Downs of Theophilus Maitland	Vinnette Carroll	Marty Kappel	Neil Cooper	Ken Billington
I'm Laughin' but I Ain't Tickled	Vinnette Carroll	Marty Kappel	Neil Cooper	Ken Billington
Alice	Vinnette Carroll	Marty Kappel	Dorothy Weaver	Ken Billington

Victory Gardens Theater

PRODUCTION	DIRECTOR	SETS	COSTUMES	LIGHTS
Endgame	Rick Cluchey			
The Cage	Rick Cluchey			
Strangle Me	Mac McGinnes	Burt Cohen	Burt Cohen	Robert Shook
Dreams	Dennis Zacek	Maher Ahmad	Marsha Kowal	Robert Shook
Three Women	Cecil O'Neal	Cookie Gluck	Cookie Gluck	Robert Shook
The Caretaker	Dennis Zacek	Maher Ahmad	Marsha Kowel	Robert Shook
The Benevolent Devil	June Pyskacek	Rick Paul	Robert Berdell	Robert Shook
			Wendy Khell	
All I Want	Bruce Hickey	Michael Merritt	Shirlie Hickey	Michael Merritt
Volpone	Stuart Gordon	Dean Taucher	Maggie Bodwell	Robert Shook
Jesse and the Bandit Queen	Cecil O'Neal	Mary Griswold	Mary Griswold	Geoffrey Bushor
		Geoffrey Bushor		
The Blood Knot	Dennis Zacek	Maher Ahmad	Marsha Kowal	Robert Shook
Some Kind of Life	Brian & Bruce Hickey	Michael Merritt	Marsha Kowal	Michael Merritt

Virginia Museum Theatre

PRODUCTION	DIRECTOR	SETS	COSTUMES	LIGHTS
Guys and Dolls	Keith Fowler	Richard Norgard	Frederick N. Brown	Michael Orris Watson
Sherlock Holmes in Scandal in Bohemia	Ken Letner	Robert Franklin	Frederick N. Brown	James D. Bloch
The Member of the Wedding	Tom Markus	Richard Norgard	Frederick N. Brown	James D. Bloch
The Crucible	James Kirkland	Richard Norgard	Frederick N. Brown	Michael Orris Watson
Children	Keith Fowler	Tony Straiges	Frederick N. Brown	Michael Orris Watson
The Emperor Jones	Ken Letner	Don Pasco	Don Pasco	Michael Orris Watson
		Richard Norgard	Frederick N. Brown	
The Contrast	James Kirkland	Richard Norgard	Frederick N. Brown	James D. Bloch
The Country Wife	Keith Fowler	Terry A. Bennett	Frederick N. Brown	Michael Orris Watson
The Mousetrap	James Kirkland	Richard Carleton Hankins	Frederick N. Brown	Richard Carleton Hankins
Oh Coward!	Roderick Cook	Richard Bryant	Paige Southard	James D. Bloch
The Caretaker	James Kirkland	Richard Carleton Hankins	Frederick N. Brown	Richard Carleton Hankins
Hamlet	James Kirkland Keith Fowler	Terry A. Bennett	Terry A. Bennett	Michael Orris Watson
Childe Byron	Keith Fowler	Sandro LaFerla	Paige Southard	Michael Orris Watson
A Christmas Carol	Keith Fowler	Robert Franklin	Frederick N. Brown	Michael Orris Watson

Wayside Theatre

PRODUCTION	DIRECTOR	SETS	COSTUMES	LIGHTS
Luv	Norman Gevanthor	Kathleen M. Armstrong	Nancy Thun	Robert Neu
In One Bed and Out the Other	Douglas C. Wager	Kathleen M. Armstrong	Nancy Thun	Robert Neu
In Praise of Love	Douglas C. Wager	Kathleen M. Armstrong	Linda Andrews	Robert Neu
Li'l Abner	David William Kitchen	Kathleen M. Armstrong	Nancy Thun	Robert Neu
In Spite of All	Louis Furman	Kathleen M. Armstrong Janis Kaiser	Nancy Thun	Robert Neu
The Widow's Plight	Louis Furman	Kathleen M. Armstrong Janis Kaiser	Nancy Thun	Robert Neu
Man with a Load of Mischief	Norman Gevanthor	Kathleen M. Armstrong	Nancy Thun	Robert Neu
The Fourposter	William Koch	Richard B. Williams	Karen Kinsella	Allen Hughes
Wait Until Dark	William Koch	Richard B. Williams	Karen Kinsella	Allen Hughes
She Stoops to Conquer	William Koch	Richard B. Williams	Karen Kinsella	Allen Hughes

PRODUCTION	DIRECTOR	SETS	COSTUMES	LIGHTS
Once upon a Mattress	William Koch	Richard B. Williams	Karen Kinsella	Allen Hughes
Bus Stop	Louis Furman	Jan L. Rovins	Linda Andrews	Susan E. Shore
		Richard B. Williams		
Man of La Mancha	William Koch	Richard B. Williams	Karen Kinsella	Allen Hughes

The Whole Theatre Company

More Stately Mansions	Tom Brennen	Paul Dorphley	Nancy Dobrydnio	Marshall Spiller
You Can't Take It with You	Apollo Dukakis	Paul Dorphley	Elizabeth Brikowski	Marshall Spiller
The Price	Stefan Peters	Ernie Schenk	Judith Dorem	Marshall Spiller
Orpheus Descending	Olympia Dukakis	Paul Dorphley	Ruth Brand	Marshall Spiller
The Rose Tattoo	Apollo Dukakis	Ernie Schenk	Ruth Brand	Marshall Spiller
Three Men on a Horse	Larry Spiegel	Susan Hilferty	Susan Hilferty	Marshall Spiller
The Maids	E.H. Cornell	Raymond C. Recht	Julie Schwolow	Marshall Spiller
The Lover	Ernie Schenk	Raymond C. Recht	Julie Schwolow	Marshall Spiller
The School for Wives	Bernard Hiatt	Ernie Schenk	Veronica Deisler	Marshall Spiller
Berlin to Broadway with Kurt Weill	Apollo Dukakis	Paul Dorphley	N. Deborah Hazlett	Marshall Spiller

Williamstown Theatre Festival

Heartbreak House	Nikos Psacharopoulos	Zack Brown	Zack Brown	Roger Meeker
Orpheus Descending	Austin Pendleton	David Chapman	Carol Oditz	Peter Hunt
Born Yesterday	Paul Sparer	Hugh Landwehr	Rita Bottomley	Roger Meeker
Our Town	Tom Moore	Roger Meeker	Rachel Kurland	Roger Meeker
The Three Sisters	Nikos Psacharopoulos	Tony Straiges	Zack Brown	Roger Meeker
A Touch of the Poet	Olympia Dukakis	Hugh Landwehr	Rita B. Watson	Roger Meeker
Sleuth	Michael Montel	Zack Brown	Kristina Watson	Roger Meeker
Misalliance	Nikos Psacharopoulos	Zack Brown	Zack Brown	Roger Meeker
Sherlock Holmes	Peter Hunt	John Lee Beatty	David Murin	Peter Hunt
The Learned Ladies	Norman Ayrton	Hugh Landwehr	Rita B. Watson	Roger Meeker
Equus	Ken Howard	John Kenny	Rita B. Watson	Jonathan Lawson
After the Fall	Austin Pendleton	Hugh Landwehr	Martha Hally	Richard Devin
Platonov	Nikos Psacharopoulos	Steven Rubin	Dunya Ramicova	Roger Meeker

The Wisdom Bridge Theatre

Dignity	David Beaird	Ann Holton		
The Merchant of Venice	David Beaird	Steven E. Burgess		Steven E. Burgess
The Wizard of Id	David Beaird	Eric Fielding	Lisa Lee Melkus	Steven E. Burgess
			Gay Caldwell	
The Threepenny Opera	David Beaird			
The Wager	Mel Shapiro	Bruce Levitt		Bruce Levitt
Oedipus Rex	David Beaird	James Maronek		
Twelfth Night	David Beaird	James Maronek		Michael Handler
Of Mice and Men	Robert Falls	James Maronek		Larry Schoeneman

Worcester Foothills Theatre Company

A Thurber Carnival	Marc P. Smith	Brian Marsh	Anne Fletcher	Robert Ekstrom
The Importance of Being Earnest	Kricker James	Brian Marsh	Anne Fletcher	Robert Ekstrom
The Brewster Papers	S. Harris Ross	Anne Fletcher	Anne Fletcher	Robert Ekstrom
The Comedy of Errors	Kricker James	Brian Marsh	Anne Fletcher	Robert Ekstrom
Dial "M" for Murder	Jack Magune	Brian Marsh	Mary Stark	William B. Lapierre
The Unrest Cure	Dennis Pearlstein	Lindon E. Rankin	Anna Mae Gravel	William B. Lapierre
			Priscilla Eighme	
The Diary of Anne Frank	Rose Dresser	Lindon E. Rankin	Anna Mae Gravel	William B. Lapierre
			Priscilla Eighme	
See How They Run	S. Harris Ross	Lindon E. Rankin	Anna Mae Gravel	Billy Farmer
			Priscilla Eighme	
Dunnigan's Daughter	Douglas R. Capra	Lindon E. Rankin	Priscilla Eighme	Billy Farmer
Ten Nights in a Barroom	S. Harris Ross	Lindon E. Rankin	Anna Mae Gravel	Billy Farmer
		Daniel Walker	Priscilla Eighme	
			Dina Walker	
Send Me No Flowers	Jack Magune	Lindon E. Rankin	Kristine Johnson	Salvatore Gionesi, Jr.
Amphitryon 38	Kricker James	Lindon E. Rankin	Anna Mae Gravel	Salvatore Gionesi, Jr.
Anastasia	S. Harris Ross	Donald Ricklin	Anna Mae Gravel	Salvatore Gionesi, Jr.
Twelfth Night	Rose Dresser	Lindon E. Rankin	Anna Mae Gravel	Salvatore Gionesi, Jr.
My Three Angels	Rose Dresser	Lindon E. Rankin	Linda Kwiatkowski	Salvatore Gionesi, Jr.
The Lion in Winter	Kricker James	Donald Ricklin	Anna Mae Gravel	Salvatore Gionesi, Jr.
Blithe Spirit	S. Harris Ross	Donald Ricklin	Anna Mae Gavel	Salvatore Gionesi, Jr.
Angel Street	George Fleenor	Lindon E. Rankin	Anna Mae Gavel	Salvatore Gionesi, Jr.
The Last Great Nipmuc	S. Harris Ross	Lindon E. Rankin	Anna Mae Gavel	Salvatore Gionesi, Jr.
6 Rms Riv Vu	Paul Mayberry	Donald Ricklin	Anna Mae Gavel	Salvatore Gionesi, Jr.

Yale Repertory Theatre

A Midsummer Night's Dream	Alvin Epstein	Tony Straiges	Zack Brown	William B. Warfel
Don Juan	Robert Brustein	Jeffrey Higginbottom	Jeffrey Higginbottom	Stephen R. Woody
		Michael H. Yeargan	Tony Straiges	
Dynamite Tonite!	Alvin Epstein	Heidi Ettinger	Suzanne Palmer	Lewis A. Folden
	Walt Jones			
Walk the Dog, Willie	Walt Jones	Michael H. Yeargan	Michael H. Yeargan	Donald Bondy Lowy
Bingo	Ron Daniels	David Lloyd Gropman	Annette Beck	Stephen Pollock
General Gorgeous	Lawrence Kornfeld	Ursula Belden	Jeanne Button	Lloyd S. Riford, III
Troilus and Cressida	Alvin Epstein	Tony Straiges	Michael H. Yeargan	Paul Gallo
Julius Caesar	Alvin Epstein	Tony Straiges	Jeanne Button	William B. Warfel
*Suicide in B*b	Walt Jones	Michael H. Yeargan	Jess Goldstein	Paul Gallo
Ivanov	Ron Daniels	Michael H. Yeargan	Jeanne Button	William B. Warfel
The Vietnamization of New Jersey (A American Tragedy)	Walt Jones	Christopher Phelps Clarens	Kathleen M. Armstrong	James H. Gage

PRODUCTION	DIRECTOR	SETS	COSTUMES	LIGHTS
The Durango Flash	Kenneth Frankel	Michael H. Yeargan	Jeanne Button	Thomas Skelton
Mister Puntila and His Chauffeur Matti	Ron Daniels	David Lloyd Gropman	Dunya Ramicova	Thomas Skelton
The Banquet Years	Robert Gainer	Kathleen M. Armstrong	Jeanne Button	Thomas Schraeder
			Lewis Folden	
White Marriage	Andrzej Wajda	Krystyna Zachwatowicz	Krystyna Zachwatowicz	William B. Warfel
				Lewis Folden

Regional Index

TCG Publications

Theatre Profiles/1. The first volume of this reference series, published in 1973, contains 190 pages of pictorial, descriptive and factual information on 89 nonprofit professional theatres in the United States, including production lists for the 1971–72 and 1972–73 seasons. $4.00.

Theatre Profiles/2. The second expanded volume of this series, published in 1975, contains 240 pages of information on 100 nonprofit professional theatres, lists productions for the 1973–74 and 1974–75 season, and includes a name and play title index. $6.00.

Newsletter. This monthly informational digest of theatre activities throughout the country encompasses a variety of topics relating to the nonprofit professional theatre and the arts in general: touring, special events, legislative news, fund-raising, new play production, community services, educational projects, and the media, as well as monthly production schedules for TCG constituent theatres. The *Newsletter* also keeps readers up to date on TCG's programs and services. Regularly published special features include a season schedule listing each October, available touring repertoires every November, biannual new play listings, and an annual bibliography. $15.00 a year.

Theatre Directory. This annual pocket-size address and telephone book includes general performance information and names of directors and managers for more than 150 theatres nationwide, as well as brief descriptions of more than 25 theatre and arts service organizations and associations. Volume 5, 1977–78. $2.00.

TCG Survey. This annual report, generally published in the spring, includes a summary analysis, financial and statistical compilations, and growth patterns for approximately 160 theatres, plus an in-depth study of about 50 large institutions. 1977 edition, $4.00.

Subscribe Now! by Danny Newman. Subtitled "Building Arts Audiences through Dynamic Subscription Promotion," this indispensable reference for audience development directors, managers, fund-raisers and publicists in all the arts contains over 300 pages of text and illustrations. $12.95 ($7.95 in paperback).

Information for Playwrights. This annual compilation of theatres interested in producing new scripts, also describes TCG programs for writers and those of other organizations that assist playwrights. $1.00.

Nonprofit Repertory Theatre in North America, 1958–1975.
Gathered over the past 20 years, TCG's collection of 2,500 programs of nonprofit professional theatres has been microfilmed and is available for $975 from Greenwood Press, 51 Riverside Avenue, Westport, CT 06880. A bound companion index of all plays, authors and directors is also available and costs $39.95.

Photo Credits – **page i:** Hartford Stage Company's production
of *A History of the American Film* (photo: Lanny Nagler);
page ii & iii: Looking Glass Theatre's production of *Earthwatch*
(photo: Johanne Killeen); **page iv & v:** Meredith Monk (photo: Jack Mitchell);
page ix: Honolulu Theatre for Youth's production of *Maui the Trickster*
(photo: Stan Rivera); **page xi:** The Puppet Workshop's production of
Judy's Dream (photo: Terrance Price); **page xiv:** Chelsea Theater Center's
production of *The Crazy Locomotive* (photo: Martha Swope);
page xvii: Folger Theatre Group's production of *A Midsummer
Night's Dream* (photo: JEB).